D1248441

SELECTED WRITINGS OF

Benjamin Nathan Cardozo

Benjamin N Cardozo

SELECTED WRITINGS

of

Benjamin Nathan CARDOZO

The Choice of Tycho Brahe

Including also the Complete Texts of

NATURE OF THE JUDICIAL PROCESS
GROWTH OF THE LAW
PARADOXES OF LEGAL SCIENCE
LAW AND LITERATURE

Edited by

MARGARET E. HALL, B.L.S., LL.B.

Reference Law Librarian, Columbia University Law Library

With a Foreword by

EDWIN W. PATTERSON, S.J.D., LL.D.

Cardozo Professor of Jurisprudence
Columbia University School of Law

FALLON PUBLICATIONS

FALLON LAW BOOK COMPANY
149 BROADWAY
NEW YORK, N. Y.

Memorial by Irving Lehman. Copyright, 1938 by the American Bar Association.

Values. Copyright, 1931 by the Jewish Institute of Religion.

Jurisprudence. Copyright, 1932 by the New York State Bar Association.

Mr. Justice Holmes. Copyright, 1931 by the Harvard Law Review.

Our Lady of the Common Law. Copyright, 1939 by St. John's University Law Review.

Faith and a Doubting World. (Editor's title) Copyright, 1932 by the New York County Lawyers Association.

The Nature of the Judicial Process. Copyright, 1921 by Yale University Press.

The Growth of the Law. Copyright, 1924 by Yale University Press.

The Paradoxes of Legal Science. Copyright, 1928 by Columbia University Press. Reprinted by permission of Columbia University Press.

Law and Literature and Other Essays and Addresses. Copyright, 1931 by Harcourt, Brace and Company, Inc.

Law and Literature. Copyright, 1925 by Yale University Press.

A Ministry of Justice. Copyright, 1921 by Harvard Law Review Association and 1926 by the Association of the Bar of the City of New York.

What Medicine Can Do for Law. Copyright, 1928 New York Academy of Medicine.

The American Law Institute. Copyright, 1925 by American Law Institute.

The Home of the Law. Copyright, 1930 by the New York County Lawyers Association.

The Game of the Law and Its Prizes. Copyright, 1925 by the Albany Law School.

The Comradeship of the Bar. Copyright, 1928 by the New York University Law Quarterly Review.

The Altruist in Politics, Psychology Lectures and the Moral Element in Matthew Arnold are heretofore unpublished and uncopyrighted manuscripts of Benjamin Nathan Cardozo, forming part of the Columbiana Collection of Columbia University and printed herein with the permission of Columbia University, the residuary legatee of the literary estate of Benjamin Nathan Cardozo.

All of the writings of Benjamin Nathan Cardozo contained in this volume are part of the Columbiana Collection and are reprinted herein with the permission of the copyright owners and Columbia University, the residuary legatee of the literary estate of Benjamin Nathan Cardozo.

Printed in U. S. A. Cardozo Selected Writings

FOREWORD

THE publication of Judge Cardozo's collected writings nearly a decade after his untimely death is an appropriate recognition of his enduring contributions to the literature and philosophy of American law. Those contributions are to be found in two distinct sources. One is the body of his judicial opinions as a member of the Court of Appeals of the state of New York (1917–1932) and as a member of the Supreme Court of the United States (1932–1938), which are to be found in official and unofficial reports. The other source is the body of extra-judicial utterances, chiefly addresses and lectures delivered on various occasions, nearly all of which have been brought together in this volume. These two sources are intimately related to each other. Except for the few student essays here reproduced, his unofficial writings were by-products of an exacting judicial career, and most of them reflect in one way or another his work as a judge. One of the chief pleasures of reading his principal contributions, the lectures delivered at Yale and at Columbia, is to come upon his explanation of some freshly decided controversy, used to illustrate some principle of law or ethics or the judicial art which he had just expounded with eloquent but elusive generalities. He often takes the facts and the decision of a case in which he had participated to point a moral which he did not venture to set forth in the official reports. His extra-judicial writings contain his more articulate philosophy of law, and are thus more likely to be enduring than his opinions as a judge.

What are the most significant aspects of Judge Cardozo's contributions to legal literature? One was his rare insight into and eloquent statement of the moral values in the law. This is perhaps the most striking characteristic of his lectures and their most passionate theme. His power to penetrate through a traditional aggregate of legal rules and precedents and to find an ethical justification, or lack of justification for them, was his outstanding virtue as a judge and as a legal philosopher. Scarcely less important though much less obvious was his judicial craftsmanship in either bending the tough legal rule to meet the requirements of ethical principle, or refusing to bend through fear of breaking some paramount value of the legal and political order, such as the limited scope of the judicial function or the need for protecting justifiable expectations. This is the contrapuntal theme of his moral discussions. A third aspect is his aesthetic convictions, his fondness for beauty in literary style and his belief that beauty and morals are closely related. These, the most original and rare of his qualities as a judge and as a philosopher, illuminate nearly every page of this volume.

One test of any man's worth is, how well did he respond to the challenge of a changing social environment? Cardozo's life (1870–1938) spanned a period of profound changes in American culture. He was born at the beginning of postwar industrial expansion and lived to see industry overshadow agriculture. One can find in his writings fleeting or oblique recognitions that this change had affected moral and legal values. The dominant economic and political philosophy of his early years was *laissez-faire*. From it emerged, as the criterion of governmental power over "private" enterprise, the legal conception of "a business affected with a public interest." He lived to see the growth and decline of this concept, and in one of his last public addresses he gently signalized its interment. From his early preceptors (I presume) he learned, perhaps not unwillingly, to express himself in a rather florid Victorian style, as one can see from the two student essays printed in this collection. In his maturity he simplified his sentence structure and enriched the beauty of his metaphors, so that his glowing, sententious prose became characteristic of the man. He could never quite bring himself to call a spade a spade, when his beloved moral or legal values were involved. Yet he was not wholly unaffected by the blunt literary "realism" of the iconoclastic twenties, as is evident in the address delivered before the New York State Bar Association (1932), reprinted in this volume.

In two other respects he responded magnificently to the changing climate of intellectual culture. One was his acceptance and leadership of the movement to bring back moral and ethical values into the making and administration of law. He was born under the star of complacent historicism which, even with men like Holmes, was dominant in the last three decades of the nineteenth century. Appellate judges might have reasons of ethics or policy or convenience for the legal rules they laid down or the decisions in which they concurred, but they thought it somewhat indecent to express these thoughts in their published opinions. When the self-sufficiency of the legal order was challenged during the early decades of the present century, Judge Cardozo became an outstanding American state court judge by making explicit, both in his official and his unofficial writings, the choice of values involved in the judicial process. Closely related to this change was the change in the theory of juridical method, the nature of the judicial process. In *The Growth of the Law* (Chap. III) Cardozo tells us that, as a practitioner at the bar, he shared the belief of his fellow lawyers in the inexorable certainty of the judicial process. He had, he says, a "blind faith" that if he could but find the pertinent authority, "if it fitted well and truly, the court would follow it inexorably to the limit of its logic". By "sad experience" he learned, "that they failed now and again to come out where I expected". When he assumed the judicial role, he became aware of the "creative element" in the judicial process. He responded to this challenge of his preconceptions by creating, with much indebtedness to Roscoe Pound and John Dewey, a conception of the judicial process in which legal stability and certainty became explicit values merely competing with, and not always overriding, the emergent moral and ethical values of the social order, and in which the dangers of individual caprice were minimized by the necessity of giving reasons that were open to public scrutiny. In these two ways Cardozo led the adaptation of law to its changing social environment.

Cardozo's early political and economic philosophy is revealed in his senior oration at Columbia College (1889), reprinted in this collection. "The Altruist in Politics" is a vigorous assault upon Communism. Doubtless some of the youthful hyperboles of this essay he would have rejected or qualified when he became an Associate Justice of the Supreme

Court and concurred in many of the crucial decisions of the Roosevelt New Deal. "In a world where every man is pushing and fighting to outstrip his fellows," he says in the student essay, Communism "would make him toil with like vigor for their common welfare." In the opinion of the Court which upheld the Old Age Benefits of the Social Security Act against the claim that it was unconstitutional (*Helvering* v. *Davis*, 301 U. S. 619 [1937]), he held that Congress might, without arbitrariness, include pensions for the aged within the conception of the "general welfare" (U. S. Constitution, Art. I, sec. 8), for which some taxpayers, presumably, must toil. Yet this youthful essay contains some passages which are fresh and apt today. "Instead of the present world," he says, "where some at least are well-to-do and happy, the Communist holds before us a world where all alike are poor." He also stresses the political and economic serfdom of man under a Communist state. He shows no conception of a *via media* between the *laissez-faire* state of 1889 and the all-dominant Communist state. How he later came to reconcile himself to the New Deal conception of the state, a public welfare state superimposed upon an economic society composed of rival groups, can only be conjectured. From the time when he ascended to the bench in 1917 he refrained from public expression of his political and economic views. One exception to this rule was his repeated avowal of the limited powers of the judiciary. When he took Holmes' place on the Supreme Court, he joined in Holmes' view that the Court is not to declare Acts of Congress unconstitutional merely because the judges deem them economically unwise. That principle, together with his conception of the dependence of law upon the moral and ethical values of society, gave him all the political and economic philosophy that he needed publicly to avow.

The other student essay, "The Moral Element in Matthew Arnold," gives us a clue to the origin of Judge Cardozo's literary craftsmanship. He was deeply impressed by Arnold's exquisite style, by his "intensely moral tone," and by his thesis that "what a remarkable philosopher really does for human thought is to throw into circulation a certain number of new and striking ideas and expressions, and to stimulate with them the thought and imagination of his century or after times." If this was, indeed, an expression of the youth's secret ambition, we can find its fulfillment on many of the pages of this volume. In later years Cardozo avowed his preference for the inspiring generality over the arid though exacter phrase. This choice was, for his unofficial utterances as set forth in this volume, a happy one, since nearly all of them were prepared for oral delivery. Spoken in a tone of modest yet intense conviction, they received the rapt attention of his audience.

If I were asked to name the most original and significant of his works, I should choose *The Nature of the Judicial Process* (1921). Here he poured forth the stuff of his own troubled thoughts and gave them inspiring form with but little aid from the apparatus of professional philosophy. His four methods of the judicial process, the methods of logic, of historical evolution, of custom and tradition and of sociology and justice, were not exactly phrased or clearly delimited; and yet he gave them meaning and emotive power in terms of his own experience. That a judge of a most highly respected and respectable appellate court should thus tear away the veil from the secrets of the consultation room and the judge's study was, even at the beginning of the idol-smashing twenties, a cause of exultant cynicism in some quarters and in others of grave apprehensions that the respect for the judiciary was gone. Neither of these exaggerations was justified because Judge Cardozo never lost his stern sense of duty to observe the limits of his judicial office. In *The Growth of the Law* (1924) he assured his hearers that the creative element in the judicial process was small, indeed, compared with the pressure of the rules and precedents that hem the court in on every side. Nine-tenths of the cases that are brought before an appellate court, he said, are predetermined by "inevitable laws." His fraction seems too high, but it gives us his own estimate of the range of judicial freedom in an appellate court.

For cases in which the highest court was unable to change the law, to abrogate an old rule such as the ones pertaining to sealed instruments, Cardozo advocated, in his essay, *A Ministry of Justice,* the formulation by a board of experts and the enactment by the legislature of statutes changing the traditional rules. This proposal has been adopted in

New York. The Law Revision Commission is a standing committee of experts who continually study the errors and anachronisms of New York law and propose statutory changes, most of which are enacted by the legislature. In this way many of the backward rules of law, especially in such fields as contracts and property, have been abolished or modified.

In *Paradoxes of Legal Science* Judge Cardozo made his most ambitious attempt to state his philosophy of law. He touched here upon the profoundest issues of legal philosophy, and yet I doubt if the reader will find in it as much originality, as much of Cardozo, as in some of his other work. Still, there are passages which illuminate his conceptions of value. One is his discussion of the moral level which the law should strive to maintain. "The law will not hold the crowd to the morality of saints and seers." Another is his recognition that, however much one might wish it in one's dreams of an ideal society, the law does not always and at any cost exact conduct which protects life and limb at the expense of property. The law allows skyscrapers to be built, though it is inevitable that some will be killed or maimed in the process. Here, as at many other points, he touched upon the relations between law and ethics.

This brief sketch of Judge Cardozo's life and work will, I hope, encourage the reader to go on with his own explorations. If he does, he will be amply rewarded. In another place I have given a somewhat more extensive analysis and appraisal of Judge Cardozo's extra-judicial writings.[1] His judicial opinions have been admirably commented upon, in non-technical language, by Dr. Beryl H. Levy,[2] whose volume also reprints a good selection of them.

EDWIN W. PATTERSON,
Cardozo Professor of Jurisprudence,
Columbia Law School.

---

1. Patterson, *Cardozo's Philosophy of Law* (1939), 88 U. of Pa. L. Rev. 71, 156.
2. Levy, *Cardozo and Frontiers of Legal Thinking* (1938).

A MEMORIAL*

by

Irving Lehman

Read at a meeting of the American Bar Association on the Twenty-Fifth of July MCMXXXVIII

1938

Benjamin Nathan Cardozo
1870–1938

BENJAMIN NATHAN CARDOZO was born in New York City on May 24th, 1870. At the age of nineteen, he graduated from Columbia College with high honors. A youth of frail physique, and of reserved manner and spirit, he had little part in the sports or social life of the college; yet, during his whole life, the men who were in college with him gave him their admiring affection. A student of literature and philosophy, a lover of the classics, he showed even in those early days that his deepest interest was in contemporary thought and, especially, in contemporary political and governmental movements and activities. It is significant that for the subject of his commencement oration he chose *The Altruist in Politics,* and for the subject of his bachelor's thesis he chose *Communism.*

The youthful Cardozo studied for two years at the Columbia Law School and then began the practice of law. He tried no sensational cases. He disdained deception and even lack of candor. He would not appeal to the passions or prejudices of a jury. The trickster, rich or poor, could obtain no aid or comfort from him. He was unfitted for any struggle where scrupulous integrity and fine sense of what is right might be a handicap; but judges felt the persuasive force of his legal arguments, and lawyers and laymen sought his counsel and assistance in the solution of intricate legal problems.

---

* *Memorial by Irving Lehman.* Reprinted with the permission of the American Bar Association and Columbia University, the residuary legatee of the literary estate of Benjamin Nathan Cardozo.

In 1913, though he was an independent Democrat who had never been active in politics and was known to few outside of his own profession, he was nominated by a Fusion group and elected a Justice of the Supreme Court of New York. In the campaign he had received the enthusiastic support of the leaders of the bar and, as soon as he was elected, some of them urged Governor Glynn to designate him to serve temporarily as an Associate Judge of the Court of Appeals. In spite of Cardozo's lack of judicial experience, the designation was made and it was received by the bench and bar with general approval. Ten years later Governor Glynn told me that he was prouder of that designation than any other act of his career.

Governor Glynn had good reason for that pride; for he gave to the State of New York, and, indeed, to the English-speaking world, one of the greatest appellate judges of all time. In January 1917, Cardozo was appointed a regular member of the court by Governor Whitman and, in November, he was elected to that position for a term of fourteen years, upon the nomination of both major parties. In 1926, upon similar nomination, he was elected Chief Judge of the court. In 1932 he was appointed by President Hoover Justice of the Supreme Court of the United States. He did not seek the appointment. Those who knew his work demanded it and, when the appointment was made, the whole country acclaimed it. For six years he served in that high position. In no period of its history has that great court been called upon to decide so many cases which were the subject of bitter controversy; in no period have political passions so completely colored appraisal and criticism of its decisions; but when, on July 9th, 1938, Justice Cardozo passed away, the whole country mourned his loss and paid him tribute, not only in admiration for his work and his character, but in affection for his great spirit.

There is little of drama in this brief record of Justice Cardozo's life. It was a life of fruitful thought and study, not of manifold activities. Quiet, gentle and reserved, from boyhood till death he walked steadily along the path of reason, seeking the goal of truth; and none could lure him from that path. I had the privilege of close association with him in the work of the Court of Appeals and at home. I loved him, but so did all who knew him well. I realized that, in truth, he was the Master who was bringing new methods and new ideas into judicial decisions. I felt the influence of his great soul and mind, but so did many others. The significance of the record of his life lies in the fact that in youth at college and in manhood, as a lawyer and as a judge, in work of ever widening importance he gathered an ever widening circle of friends—an ever increasing influence in the development of the law and in the administration of justice.

His work as a judge and legal scholar falls naturally into two periods: while he was in the Court of Appeals and while he was in the Supreme Court of the United States. Cases brought to the Court of Appeals present a wide range of legal problems. Questions of constitutional law and of government engross the attention of the judges less than problems of tort or contract which must be solved by the application of common law principles. In that court, Judge Cardozo developed his method of approach to such problems. In that court, too, he found some associates with spirit and mind akin to his own and there he wielded an influence which made that court great. I became a judge of that court on January 1st, 1924, long after his influence was manifest and the reputation of the court firmly established. I had known Judge Cardozo well for many years. I had often discussed legal problems with him; but in the work of the court I could see more clearly the qualities which made Judge Cardozo a great judge and which contributed to his wide influence.

What were these qualities? I would place first the honesty and integrity of his mind. He was not content to arrive at a conclusion by traditional methods of legal reasoning, nor to justify, by rationalization, a conclusion dictated by impulse or even by social philosophy. He was not content to accept an unjust decision merely because it rested firmly on old precedents nor, on the other hand, was he content to cast aside lighty long accepted rules and precedents merely because they dictated a conclusion which might be unfair to a particular litigant. He sought to know his own mind; to trace the influences which led him to choose one course rather than another; to appraise the value of conflicting considerations of logic and of history, of custom and of morality, of certainty and of flexibility, of form and of substance. "The important thing," he said, "is to rid our prepossessions, so far as may be, of what is merely individual or personal, to detach them in a measure from ourselves, to build them, not upon instinctive or intuitive likes and dislikes, but upon an informed and liberal culture." *

In his lecture on *The Nature of the Judicial Process,* delivered in 1921 before the Law School of Yale University, and in supplementary lectures and addresses, Judge Cardozo set forth his thoughts on these subjects in a manner which constrained other judges to give thought to matters where previously there had been blind acceptance. He knew what students of legal philosophy had written, especially in the universities of continental Europe. He read and he absorbed; he looked to legal scholars for guidance; but the formulation of the problem and the solution which must satisfy him were based almost entirely upon his own experience and his study of the opinions and decisions of the great judges of England and America, and, above all, of Justice Holmes, for whom he had an almost reverential admiration.

The common law rests upon judicial precedents and Judge Cardozo was too wise and too conservative to reject ancient precedents as long as they could serve modern needs. "Certainty and regularity," he said, "have at least a presumption in their favor. They show us the well-worn ways, and as in conduct generally, so in law, what we have done in the past, we are likely to continue to do till the shock of a perturbing force is strong enough to jolt us out of the rut." † And again: "What has once been settled by a precedent will not be unsettled over night, for certainty and uniformity are gains not lightly to be sacrificed. Above all is this true when honest men have shaped their conduct on the faith of the pronouncement." ‡

Nevertheless Judge Cardozo was too sound a realist and too liberal in his social outlook to follow an ancient rule after the reason for the rule had disappeared. He recognized that no judge-made rule, however generally accepted, can long survive after it has become out of harmony with the thoughts and the customs of a democratic people. So a bal-

* *The Paradoxes of Legal Sciences,* p. 127.

† Address before the State Bar Association, 55 Report of the N. Y. State Bar Association, 284.

‡ *The Paradoxes of Legal Science,* pages 29–30.

ance must be found which will permit progress—but progress along a road where the great traditions of the common law can still serve as guide-posts. "You shall not for some slight profit of convenience or utility depart from standards set by history or logic; the loss will be greater than the gain. You shall not drag in the dust the standards set by equity and justice to win some slight conformity to symmetry and order; the gain will be unequal to the loss." *

When an old rule was challenged Judge Cardozo read it over and over again in the light of what students of the law had thought and written about it. "More and more," he said, "we are looking to the scholar in his study, to the jurist rather than to the judge or lawyer, for inspiration and guidance." † Small wonder that when, in the conferences of the court he discussed legal problems with the mental clarity and the great learning which were at his command, his words often swayed the decision of the judges. Small wonder, too, that after his opinions were written, in words perhaps more harmonious and persuasive than any other judicial opinions in the English language, lawyers and laymen were convinced, and accepted the result with acclaim. Small wonder that the students of the law, the specialists in every branch of the law, have hailed Judge Cardozo as a great pathfinder in the progressive development of law.

When Justice Holmes resigned from the Supreme Court of the United States there was a general recognition that Judge Cardozo, beyond all others, was fitted to be his successor. The admiration which Judge Cardozo had for Justice Holmes was returned in full measure by Holmes. Each saw in the other a spiritual brother. Holmes did not regret that age had forced him to lay down the pen which he had used for so many years with trenchant force when he knew that Cardozo would take it up and use it in the same spirit and with equal force. It was a source of abiding satisfaction and pride to Cardozo that Holmes had long hoped that he would succeed him; but Cardozo was so modest that he never ceased to wonder that those who had revered Holmes were sure that as a man, as a scholar, and as a jurist, Cardozo was his worthy successor.

The work of Justice Cardozo upon the Supreme Court is

* *Growth of the Law*, page 88.

† *Growth of the Law*, page 11.

so recent, the decisions in which he took part so momentous, that every lawyer has read, I am sure, each opinion written by him, sometimes for the court, sometimes to give expression to his dissenting views. Some cases called for the appraisal of such conflicting considerations, and the decision might have such important consequences upon the future of the country, that Justice Cardozo arrived at his own conclusions with anguish of soul. Each member of this association has doubtless formed his own judgment as to the soundness of these conclusions, but lawyers and laymen, regardless of their social and political bias, agree that in each opinion certain guiding principles can be traced which dictated the conclusion. Justice Cardozo felt profoundly that America is great not because of its wealth and power but because embodied in its constitution are the ideals of liberty and democracy which have become part of the spirit of America. The constitution, he believed, if properly interpreted, would conserve these ideals without blocking the road of progress. As a justice of the Supreme Court he consecrated himself to the task of finding the right interpretation.

I shall not discuss here Justice Cardozo's views on constitutional law or analyse the decisions in which he had part. In Helvering v. Davis (at 301 U. S. 619), he said: "Needs that were narrow or parochial a century ago may be interwoven in our day with the well-being of the nation. What is critical or urgent changes with the times." Always Justice Cardozo earnestly sought in the language of the constitution a grant of power to the national government sufficient to provide for needs which are critical and urgent and are interwoven with the well-being of the nation.

It is difficult for me, as a friend, to speak publicly of Justice Cardozo as a man rather than as a judge. A man of fastidious reticence, he guarded jealously his personal privacy. He would be distressed if what he disclosed to a friend were exhibited to the world; and yet the life and work of Justice Cardozo can be appraised properly and his influence explained only by those who knew the purity of his soul and the sweetness and strength of his character. Many have found his mental ability remarkable. His friends know that the beauty of his character, his selfless devotion to his work, his firm adherence to principle and, may I add, his love for his friends and his perfect charity to all men were far more remarkable.

His ancestors were driven from the Spanish peninsula more than four hundred years ago because they would not abandon the faith of their fathers. They found a home in New York while it was still a colony of Great Britain. They fought for its independence; they cherished its ideals. The same spirit which impelled Justice Cardozo's ancestors to hold fast to their faith and their principles, though it made them homeless outcasts, animated Justice Cardozo. He could see the force of arguments though he rejected them. He could compromise in matters where there might be difference of opinion among reasonable men, and where no great principle was involved. He could not compromise in a matter of principle; he could not abandon his standards of what is right; he could not reject what he believed to be true. He loved his country with a surpassing love. The honors paid to him gave him added joy because they showed to him, a Jew, and to all the world, that America does not withhold from any of her sons because of creed or race the need of love or praise which he has earned.

In his heart there was love so great that it excluded all other feelings. Shy and retiring though he was, he found his greatest happiness in intercourse with men and women and in the companionship of his friends. The great legal thinker was at all times and under all circumstances the gentle, modest, loving man.

Not long ago he said to a friend that James Russell Lowell's lines on Agassiz were, he thought, the finest compliment that could be paid to any man. Never was there a man whom they fitted better than Justice Cardozo.

His magic was not far to seek,—
He was so human! Whether strong or weak
Far from his kind he neither sank nor soared,
But sate an equal guest at every board.
No beggar ever felt him condescend,
No prince presume; for still himself he bare,
At manhood's simple level, and where'er
He met a stranger, there he left a friend.

EDITOR'S ACKNOWLEDGMENT

The editor wishes to express her sincere appreciation to the following for their kindly and valuable assistance in the preparation of this book:

To my mother, Lizzie Gregg Hall, without whose constant help, this book would have appeared years later.

To Mr. Philip F. Cohen, for suggesting that I edit these writings of Mr. Justice Cardozo, and for his continued counsel and cooperation.

To Professor Edwin W. Patterson, Cardozo Professor of Jurisprudence, Columbia University, for his courteous generosity, in taking time in a particularly busy period, to write the Foreword.

To Mr. Frank Strasser for designing this volume and for his practical advice all along the way.

To Miss Frances Kuchler, Miss Helen Wetzel, Miss Eleanor McClusky and Dr. David Sequeira for their kind assistance in proof-reading and work on the Index.

To Miss Charlotte Holman for assistance in checking references and to Mrs. Margaret Stockfisch for assistance in typing of footnotes.

To the staff of the Columbia University Libraries for their courtesy in making the contents of this volume available for study.

To Mr. Milton Halsey Thomas, Librarian of the Columbiana Collection, for his cooperation in making the manuscript material herein available for my use.

To Columbia University, residuary legatee of the estate of Benjamin Nathan Cardozo, for permission to use all of the material contained, and to Mr. Philip M. Hayden, Secretary of the University, and Mr. Thomas P. Fleming, Assistant Director of Libraries, for their personal attention to this matter.

To the following I am indebted for permission to publish or reprint the various essays, addresses and books in this collection:

To the American Bar Association and American Bar Association Journal for permission to reprint the "Memorial", by Irving Lehman. This appeared originally in book form,

1938, and in the American Bar Association Journal, September, 1938.

To the Jewish Institute of Religion for permission to reprint the address given on May 24, 1931, "Values", and to Miss Gertrude Adelstein for her kindness in making this possible.

To the New York State Bar Association, through the courtesy of its President, Mr. Robert E. Lee, for permission to use the address on "Jurisprudence", given at the Hotel Astor, January 22, 1932.

The Columbia University, residuary legatee of the estate of Benjamin Nathan Cardozo, for permission to publish the "Altruist in Politics", Columbia College essay, 1889; the Psychology Lectures under Nicholas Murray Butler; and the Columbia College essay, "Moral Element in Matthew Arnold".

To the Harvard Law Review and its President, Mr. Elliot L. Richardson, for permission to reprint "Mr. Justice Holmes", which appeared originally in their issue of March, 1931; and "A Ministry of Justice", reprinted from the December, 1921, issue. In regard to the latter I am also indebted to the Association of the Bar of the City of New York, and Mr. Sidney Hill, Librarian, for use of this article which also appeared in Lectures on Legal Topics, 1921–22.

To the St. John's Law Review for permission to reprint "Our Lady of the Common Law", which originally appeared in the April, 1939, issue of that Review.

To the New York County Lawyers Association for permission to reprint, "Faith and a Doubting World", which originally appeared in their Yearbook of 1932; and "The Home of the Law", which originally appeared in their Yearbook of 1930; and to Mr. Lawrence Schmehl, Mr. Charles E. J. Boyd and Mr. Terence J. McManus for their personal attention to this matter.

To Yale University Press for permission to reprint "The Growth of the Law", 1924, and "The Nature of the Judicial Process", 1921, and to Mr. Norman V. Donaldson, personally for his courtesy in this regard.

To Columbia University Press for permission to reprint "Paradoxes of Legal Science", 1928, and to Mr. Raymond J. Dixon for giving this his personal attention.

To Harcourt, Brace and Company, Inc., for permission to

reprint the material in the compilation, "Law and Literature", 1930, and to Miss Catherine McCarthy of that firm, for her courtesy.

To Yale University Press for permission to reprint the essay "Law and Literature", which first appeared in the Yale Review of July, 1925, and to Miss Helen Macafee, Managing Editor, for her response to this request.

To the New York Academy of Medicine for permission to reprint "What Medicine Can Do for Law", the address given before that Academy, November 1, 1928, and to their Director, Howard Reid Craig.

To William Draper Lewis and the American Law Institute for permission to reprint "The American Law Institute", address given on May 1, 1925.

To the Albany Law School for permission to use the Commencement Address of June 10, 1925, "The Game of the Law and Its Prizes".

To the New York University Law Quarterly Review, and to Mr. Julius Marke, Assistant Law Librarian, and to Mr. Francis J. Putman, Faculty Adviser, for their personal attention to the request to reprint "The Comradeship of the Bar", which originally appeared in their January, 1928, issue.

MARGARET E. HALL.

TABLE OF CONTENTS

VALUES: COMMENCEMENT ADDRESS*

or

The Choice of Tycho Brahe

Delivered at the exercises of the
Jewish Institute of Religion
on May 24, 1931

DEFYING an ancient canon of rhetoricians, I begin with an apology. I do not know whether I have the right to talk to you today. I have felt that to earn that right I should be able to say to you that your beliefs are wholly mine, that the devastating years have not obliterated youthful faiths, and that in the darkness of the universe I can see with clearness and certainty a consoling shaft of light. Unable to say this, I have wondered whether my message could be of worth to you—to you who are going forth to spread the teachings of religion—wondered whether with good cause you might not even resent it as an impertinence; at the very least whether fitness and good taste might not exact another spokesman for the lesson of the hour. The great spiritual leader who has given to this Institute the dignity and glory of his leadership has talked with me about these things, and has brought me to believe that my troubles are unreal. He has said that a message would be welcome from any one who has been able, however black the depths of nescience, to hold fast to certain values transcending the physical and temporal. He has assured me that what such a one would say would be listened to without resentment, and even indeed with gladness by those of greater faith, with the gladness born of the perception that what is noble and high and sacred reveals itself in many forms and is discerned in many aspects by the faltering sons of men. Sixty years and more ago Huxley published to the world a memorable volume which is known by the title

* *Values.* Reprinted with the permission of the Jewish Institute of Religion and Columbia University, the residuary legatee of the literary estate of Benjamin Nathan Cardozo.

"Lay Sermons and Addresses." A lay sermon by one whose beliefs are not so very far removed from Huxley's is what you will hear from me today. And to hold fast to what your leader said to me, to shelter myself squarely behind the shield of his authority, I am going to talk to you of "values."

A theme is here, not for a brief fragment of an hour, but for a lecture, a series of lectures, a volume, almost one might say, a library. What values shall we choose—those of today, or of tomorrow, or of a future that is close at hand, or of the unplumbed future, trackless as the sea? Every one of them is a good. Let us not make the blunder of decrying any of them. Asceticism has made that blunder at times, and has suffered for its partial view of the shifting aspects of reality. The values of today are good, and those of tomorrow are good, and those of a future that is not remote, and those of the unplumbed future, trackless as the sea. If we could have them all, it would be well, but seldom can we have them all. There is need to make a choice. How shall it be guided? Not all of us will make the same choice, not all of us ought to make the same. What choice is it worth while to make if one feels the mystery of the universe more deeply than one's fellows? What choice will be made by you? Before that question is answered, let me tell you an anecdote. Let me tell you of the choice that about four centuries ago was made by some one else. Let me tell you of the choice that was made by Tycho Brahe.

Tycho Brahe was born in Denmark of goodly lineage, and educated in youth at the University of Copenhagen. He thought in his boyhood that he would like to study law, but he became diverted from law to the study of astronomy. While yet a young man he discovered a new star, and the discovery brought him fame at home and in many distant lands. Denmark had a king then who was a patron of learning, and the king built an observatory for Tycho at the center of a little island, and Tycho called the place Uraniborg, the City of the Heavens. Here for years and years Tycho worked by day and night, watching the heavens by night, and figuring his observations by day, till star after star with exquisite precision had been set down upon his chart. But Frederick, the King, died, and young Prince Christian came upon the throne with a host of flippant courtiers, who grudged the treasure that had been lavished upon the upkeep of the observatory and this feckless charting of the stars. They could not see the value of it all, and so at last messengers went forward in the name of the new king, who were to visit Tycho Brahe, to learn, if they could, the use of all his labor, to quiz him about it and to pit their values against his.

You will find the tale set forth with moving eloquence and beauty in a poem by Alfred Noyes, the noble and inspiring poem which he calls the "Watchers of the Skies." The messengers asked what Tycho had been doing these five and twenty years. He showed them tables of the stars, seven hundred set down, each in its proper place. "And is this all?" they said. "Not all, I hope," said Tycho, "for I think before I die I shall have marked a thousand." You can almost hear their laughter, can you not? All the prophets and the seers have listened to the like. Einstein has heard it in our day, and every lover of truth and beauty, every man who has seen visions and tried to live them in his life, has heard the same sardonic mirth. "To what end," said the messengers, "to what end the travail and the waste? Show its uses to us now, show them now before we go." Resounding through the centuries I hear familiar echoes. Never a philosopher has lived, nor a saint nor a scientist nor an artist, but has been summoned to a like proof—to show the value for today—not the value for the unplumbed future, but the value for today. I will read you Tycho Brahe's answer as I find it in the poem:

" 'In the time to come,'
" Said Tycho Brahe, 'perhaps a hundred years,
" 'Perhaps a thousand, when our own poor names
" 'Are quite forgotten, and our Kingdom's dust,
" 'On one sure certain day, the torchbearers
" 'Will, at some point of contact, see a light
" 'Moving upon this chaos. Though our eyes
" 'Be shut forever in an iron sleep,
" 'Their eyes shall see the Kingdom of the law,
" 'Our undiscovered cosmos. They shall see it—
" 'A new creation rising from the deep,
" 'Beautiful, whole.
" 'We are like men that hear
" 'Disjointed notes of some supernal choir.

" 'Year after year we patiently record
" 'All we can gather. In that far off time
" 'A people that we have not known shall hear them
" 'Moving like music to a single end.' "

They could not understand—the messengers who had come to appraise the values and report. They went back to the king, their master, and they said that Tycho Brahe's dreams were fruitless, and worse than fruitless, perilous, since "any fruit they bore would fall in distant years to alien hands." Tycho went forth to exile, and Uraniborg, City of the Heavens, went down into the dust.

" 'Yes, I still hope,' he said,
" 'Yes, I still hope in hope in some more generous land
" 'To make my thousand up before I die.
" 'Little enough, I know—a midget's work.
" 'The men that follow me with more delicate art
" 'May add their tens of thousands; yet my sum
" 'Will save them just that five and twenty years
" 'Of patience, bring them sooner to their goal,
" 'That Kingdom of the law I shall not see.
" 'We are on the verge of great discoveries.
" 'I feel them as a dreamer feels the dawn
" 'Before his eyes are opened. Many of you
" 'Will see them. In that day you will recall
" 'This, our last meeting at Uraniborg,
" 'And how I told you that this work of ours
" 'Would lead to victories for the coming age.
" 'The victors may forget us. What of that?
" 'Theirs be the palms, the shouting and the praise,
" 'Ours be the fathers' glory in the sons.' "

That, gentlemen of the Institute, was Tycho Brahe's choice of values. If you are true to your mission as sons of this Institute of Religion, summoned from this day forth to live its deepest verities, your choice will be the same. The submergence of self in the pursuit of an ideal, the readiness to spend oneself without measure, prodigally, almost ecstatically, for something intuitively apprehended as great and noble, spend oneself one knows not why—some of us like to believe that this is what religion means. True, I am sure, it is that values such as these will be found to have survived when creeds are shattered and schisms healed and sects forgotten and the things of brass and stone are one with Nineveh and Tyre.

I have spoken of a man who was one of the famous of the earth, whose name has re-echoed through the corridors of time. Let us not make the blunder of supposing that to live in communion with these ineffable values of the spirit, to spend oneself utterly in sacrifice and devotion, is a lot reserved for a chosen few, for an aristocracy of genius, for those that will be ranked in history among the mighty or the great. Not so, friends and brothers. To the glory of our humanity, the lowly equally with the mighty may be partakers in this bliss. I have seen it in my own life, and so I am sure have many within the compass of my voice. Along the common ways have walked with men and women —you would not know them from the crowd—I have walked with men and women who had made the choice of Tycho Brahe. They had made it in humbler forms, by love, by gentleness, by sweetness, by devotion, by sacrifice of self within the narrow circle of the home; but, be it said to their undying glory, they had made it, none the less. We know it when death takes them if in hours of pride and darkness we have been blind to it before. The life seemed simple while it lasted. We may not always have been conscious of its beauty. The end comes, and behold it is illuminated with the white and piercing light of the divinity within it. We have walked with angels unawares.

This is the summons that I give to you today. These are the values—the values of the spirit—that by your witness shall prevail. I have been reminded by Felix Frankfurter of the noble words of Huxley in celebrating the opening of Johns Hopkins University. "I cannot say" (said Huxley) "that I am in the slightest degree impressed by your bigness (i.e., the bigness of America), or your material resources as such. Size is not grandeur, and territory does not make a nation. The great issue about which hangs a true sublimity, and the terror of overhanging fate, is what are you going to do with all these things? What is to be the end to which these are to be the means?" So it is, my friends, with all the teachings of universities and schools. The learning and the wisdom stored in many books have been taught to the youth, the rabbis of the future, who have come together in these halls. All the study has been wasted except in proportion as it strengthens them to make a choice hereafter between competing and conflicting values. It is wasted unless it strengthens them to the choice of Tycho Brahe.

One life I have singled out as the subject of my parable. I could have chosen many others, the lives of men and women of our race, the lives of prophets and saints and heroes and martyrs, who were kinsmen in spirit of that watcher of the skies. In persecution and contumely they knew that there were values of the spirit greater than any others, values for whose fruits they would have to wait, "perhaps a hundred years, perhaps a thousand," values whose fruits might elude them altogether, yet values to be chosen, unfalteringly, uncomplainingly, with cheer and even joy. What does a ministry of religion mean if it does not mean the preaching and living of that truth? For what have we come together this morning, in the springtime of the year, unless to say to this little band of eager men, still in the springtime of their lives: You are going forth today as preachers of the eternal values. You will find mockery and temptation on the highways, and for the values that you hold to be eternal many a tinsel token will be offered in exchange. Sycophants and time-servers and courtiers and all the lovers of the flesh pots will assail you with warnings that you are squandering the happy days under the sun, and will ask you to tell them to what use, just as in the Danish city of Uraniborg, City of the Heavens, the messengers of the Danish king taunted and challenged and drove at last into exile, that other watcher of the skies. Then will be the time when you will need to gird yourselves with the strength that this Institute of Religion, this Institute of the better life, has striven with all her might to bestow upon her sons. Then will be the time when you will need to bethink yourselves of the values that were chosen by the prophets and saints of Israel, and by the goodly and noble of every race and clime. You will remember in that hour the choice of Tycho Brahe.

When the course is finished, when the task is ended, when the books are closed, may the last appraisal of all values reveal his choice as yours.

JURISPRUDENCE*

Address before the
New York State Bar Association Meeting
Hotel Astor, January 22, 1932

(263) Mr. President, Brethren of the New York State Bar Association, Ladies and Gentlemen:

FOR digests and statutes and text-books the fashion of the hour is the cumulative supplement. Your volume like your overcoat is to be fitted with a capacious pocket (264) into which you can crowd the last quotations of the market, the final output of the legal factory, and study them in motor car or subway like your correspondence or the morning paper. It is time for philosophy to prove to us that she also can be up to date. In years gone by I have afflicted my brethren of the bench and bar with disquisitions on judicial method, on the philosophy of case law, revelations (or shall I say confessions?) of the springs of the judicial process. A decade has gone by since I began these indiscretions. I have thought you might forgive me if I offered you a cumulative supplement that would bring the process down to date.

I read the other day a saying attributed to an Oxford professor that everyone should know enough philosophy to find that he can do without it. I am sure that twenty years ago a thrust of that kind would have aroused the applause and approval of any audience of lawyers, perhaps I may even add, of any audience of teachers unless they happened to be connected with the department of philosophy. I marvel when I observe the change that has come over us in so short a span of years. One of the most significant signs of the times is the ferment of present-day interest

---

* *Jurisprudence.* (Editor's title.) Reprinted with the permission of the New York State Bar Association and Columbia University, the residuary legatee of the literary estate of Benjamin Nathan Cardozo.

New York State Bar Association Report 1932:263.

n.b. Numbers in parenthesis indicate original paging.

in problems that are bound up with the nature and origin of law, problems of judicial method, problems of judicial teleology, problems of legal philosophy, if the word be not anathema. We are talking about ourselves and looking into ourselves, subjecting our minds and our souls to a process of analysis and introspection with a freedom and in a measure that to the thought of our predecessors would have been futile and meaningless or even down-right unbecoming. The lawyers and judges have been talking philosophy or what they thought was philosophy. If they have gone astray at times, there are worthy precedents to comfort them. They may remember that long ago someone said of so respectable an authority as Sir Francis Bacon that he wrote philosophy like a Lord Chancellor, a form of statement which, I think, was not meant to be understood as (265) redounding to the honor of the Chancery. The lawyers, I say, have been talking philosophy or what they thought was philosophy; but then on the other hand the philosophers have been talking law or what they thought was law, and some of them certainly have learned more about the law than the lawyers or the judges have learned about philosophy. So we have today the heartening spectacle of lectures by John Dewey on the place of logic and of ethics in legal science, and lectures by Morris R. Cohen on the meaning of law and the function of the judge, and essays and addresses by others too many to be catalogued—by psychologists on the law of evidence, by moralists on the theory of the state—till indeed it seems at times that the lawyers and the judges are playing a minor role and may soon be elbowed off the stage.

A good many causes have conspired to induce the change of pose. For the lawyer and the judge, a driving force at all times has been the avalanche of precedents. Battered and pelted, we grope for a principle of order that will compose the jarring atoms, or at least permit us to forget them and ignore their oppositions. But there is something more than this. Not even the Phlegethon of precedents will explain of itself the impulse of jurisprudence in these days to fling herself into the arms of philosophy for shelter and consolation. The impulse has its origin in causes more profound and fundamental. It is a response to the agitations and the promptings of a changing civilization demanding outlet and expression in changing forms of law and a jurisprudence and philosophy adequate to justify the changes. The necessity is deeply felt for a rationalizing principle whereby precedents that are outworn may be decently discarded without affront to the sentiment that there shall be no breach of the legal order in the house of its custodians. To gratify this sentiment we are putting the question to ourselves more searchingly than ever, what is the legal order, what are its origins, its implications, its utility, (266) its limits? There came not long ago from the pen of John Dewey a volume with the provocative title, "The Quest for Certainty." Now, the quest for certainty responds to a very deep-seated impulse in the soul of bench and bar. For a long time we sought to satisfy it by turning to the written work, the concrete case, the precedent that was to be adhered to with inflexible devotion. That was very well for a time, but now at last the precedents have turned upon us and are engulfing and annihilating us—engulfing and annihilating the very devotees that worshiped at their shrine. So the air is full of new cults that disavow the ancient faiths. Some of them tell us that instead of seeking certainty in the word, the outward sign, we are to seek for something deeper, a certainty of ends and aims. Some of them tell us that certainty is merely relative and temporary, a writing on the sands to be effaced by the advancing tides. Some of them even go so far as to adjure us to give over the vain quest, to purge ourselves of these yearnings for an unattainable ideal, and to be content with an empiricism that is untroubled by strivings for the absolute. With all their diversities of form and doctrine, they are at one at least in their emphasis upon those aspects of truth that are fundamental and ultimate. They exemplify the method of approach, the attitude and outlook, the concern about the substance of things, which in all its phases and disguises is the essence of philosophy (cf. Wm. Pepperrill Montague, "The Social Sciences and Philosophy" in Ogburn and Goldenweiser, "The Social Sciences"). "The study of philosophy is a voyage toward the larger generalities." (A. N. Whitehead, Process and Reality, p. 14.)

A decade so prolific has a progeny of many strains. Fruitful studies have been made in the relation of law to anthropology and to the social sciences generally (see, e.g., Huntington Cairns, Law and Anthropology, Columbia Law Review, January, 1931, reprinted as part of a collection of essays, "The Making of Man," edited by (267) V. P. Calverton and forming part of "The Modern Library"). There has been reinforcement of the lesson which goes back to Henry Sumner Maine, that the law has different meanings at different stages of its history; that none of the definitions yet framed by historians or jurists is adequate for every stage; that some have been framed in adaptation to advanced cultures, and others in adaptation to rude beginnings; and that there still is need of the generalization that will bridge the culture of the ages. To one who believes, as I do, that many of the most perplexing problems of the judicial process will be solved if once the nature and origin of law shall be better understood, there is a rainbow promise in these gropings toward a definition and a synthesis truer and more comprehensive than any yet attained. But the most distinctive product of the last decade in the field of jurisprudence is not in anthropology. It is not in any social science that is merely historical or descriptive. The most distinctive product of the last decade in the field of jurisprudence is the rise of a group of scholars styling themselves realists, and content with nothing less than revision to its very roots of the method of judicial decision which is part of the classical tradition (see e.g., Oliphant, A Return to Stare Decisis, 14 Am. Bar Assn. Journal, 7, 119; 6 Am. Law School Review, 215; Oliphant and Hewitt, Introduction to Rueff's From the Physical to the Social Sciences; K. N. Llewellyn, The Bramble Bush; K. N. Llewellyn, A Realistic Jurisprudence, 30 Col. L. R. 431; K. N. Llewellyn, Some Realism about Realism, 44 H. L. Rv. 1222; Llewellyn, Legal Thinking and Social Science; Jerome Frank, Law and the Modern Mind; Jerome Frank, Review of Llewellyn's "The Bramble Bush," 40 Yale L. J. 1120; Jerome Frank, Are Judges Human, 80 U. of P. Law Rv. 17; cf. Dickinson, Legal Rules in the Process of Decision, 79 U. of P. Law Rev. 833; Pound, The Call for a Realist Jurisprudence, 44 H. L. R. 697).

I have said that the members of this group style themselves realists,—realists because fidelity to the realities (268) of the judicial process, unclouded by myth or preconception, is supposed to be, in a degree peculiarly their own, the end and aim of their endeavor (Pound, The Call for a Realist Jurisprudence, 44 H. L. R. 697). I shall make bold to vary the description and speak of them hereafter as neo-realists instead. There were brave men before Agamemnon; and before the dawn of the last decade there were those in jurisprudence who strove to see the truth in the workings of the judicial process, to see it steadily and whole, and to report what they had seen with sincerity and candor. In this sense Savigny was a realist, and Jhering, and in our own land Holmes and Pound, and many another too. "Law," says Savigny, "takes actual life as its starting point." "Das Recht geht von der Wirklichkeit des Lebens aus." In so far as the bond of union among the realists of the hour is the will to extend this motto of Savigny's to the workings of the judicial process, to view the process as it is, and not as a facile lip service may at times have represented it to be, there will be few so unregenerate as to remain without the fold. Perhaps the style that the faithful have appropriated to themselves may seem a bit over-pretentious. If so, the pretense may be forgiven as a reflection of a tendency now prevalent in philosophy and art and letters to speak of realism, however and wherever practised, as inherently a good and one of constant value (M. R. Cohen, Reason and Nature, p. 457). On the other hand, when you pass beyond the unifying bond of a spiritual ideal and seek to find among the neo-realists a unifying bond of doctrine, the quest is not so simple. The truth indeed is that the votaries of the new faith do not constitute a school. They are representatives of a movement, an outlook, a tendency, avowing fundamental differences of emphasis and dogma (Llewellyn, Some Realism about Realism, 44 H. L. R. 1222, 1234, 1256). In a critique of the new faith there is thus a constant need to separate the accident from the attribute, the tenet from the gloss. Not a little that has been said (269) by one votary or another must be rejected, at least to my thinking, as ill-advised and exaggerated, though said with incisiveness and force and the arresting charm of novelty. The exaggeration is largely *obiter*. When it shall be excised and pruned away, there will remain a core of truth. Perhaps we may find in the end that here, as so often, the war is chiefly one of words, and that a *rapprochement* between the factions is simpler than we think. Let us not exaggerate unduly the differences that divide the forces of enlightenment and truth when there is need to present a united front to the embattled ranks and outposts of prejudice and error.

Fundamental in the thought of the neo-realists, or of most of them, is the exaltation of what is done by a judge as contrasted with what is said. They cling to the motto that "action speaks louder than words." Indeed they go beyond it, for some of them seem to tell us, not only that conduct is the louder, but that words do not speak at all. In the view of this section of the group—a section growing swiftly in influence and numbers—law is to be found not in anything that a judge says in his opinion, but rather in what he does and only in what he does. Principles and rules and concepts are not law in and of themselves, and have no coercive power to fix the forms of law thereafter. They are nothing but tentative explanations of the implications of an actual holding embodied in a judgment. They are "ballons d'essai," experiments, not finalities. What has been said by a judge in an attempt to rationalize the holding may appear to be inadequate or mischievous if applied to the limit of its logic in novel situations. In that event the principle or rule or concept to the extent that it is found to be an incumbrance is to be jettisoned as useless. I am reminded of Bentham in his Comment on the Commentaries, a treasure only recently unearthed from among his unpublished and neglected manuscripts. "The individual judicial decisions," he says, "are acts of judges; they are acts of authority. But the rules of law are (270) general propositions; these general propositions are conclusions drawn from the above-mentioned individual acts; and these conclusions are formed by any one who happens to bestow his thought upon the subject. If he happens to be a judge, his conclusions will naturally carry more weight with them than those of a common man." But the authority attaching to his conclusions differs in degree and not in kind. Thus the reforming jurist of a century and more ago! The neologisms of the hour—the popular novelties of thought and phrase—are sometimes older than we think.

Now, the thesis of the neo-realists in its beginnings was hardly more than a restatement of the doctrine of *stare decisis* thus formulated by Bentham, a restatement with slightly different emphasis and in modernistic forms and phrases. I do not mean to say that even in its beginnings it was a completely adequate doctrine.[1] Even in its begin-

[1] Some of its weaknesses have been exposed with admirable clarity by Professor Arthur L. Goodhart in his essay, "Determining the Ratio Decidendi of a Case."

nings the doctrine placed the creative potency of the judgment too far into the foreground, and cast too far into the background the significance of words. At the same time I cannot doubt that the teachings of the neo-realists were and still are of great value to jurisprudence in ridding *stare decisis* of something of its petrifying rigidity, in warning us that in many instances the principles and rules and concepts of our own creation are merely *aperçus* and glimpses of reality, and in reminding us of the need of reformulating them or at times abandoning them altogether when they stand condemned as mischievous in the social consciousness of the hour, the social consciousness which it is our business as judges to interpret as best we can. I have preached the same doctrine myself in a modest way (The Paradoxes of Legal Science, pp. 49, 50, 51), and in a still more modest way I have practised what I preached. Nothing that has since happened has brought me a different faith.

Neo-realism in its beginnings, and even now in its essence, is not to be identified with everything put forth under its (271) banner. We are to keep in mind what I have stated, that is the slogan of a movement, not the dogma of a school. One might fancy from enthusiastic phrases here and there that the remedy for our ills is to have the law give over, once and for all, the strivings of the centuries for a rational coherence, and sink back in utter weariness to a justice that is the flickering reflection of the impulse of the moment (see the criticism of this tendency in Dickinson, Legal Rules in the Process of Decision, 79 U. of Pa. Law Rev. 833, 845). I am not wise enough to know whether this or something like it is to be the judicial process of the future. It is not the judicial process yet, and prophecy is not identical with exposition, though very often easier and by far more entertaining. Indeed, I can hardly bring myself to doubt, after reading the most recent and authoritative statements of the creed of the new group, that by none of them is a saving grace attributed to the virtue of mere benevolence, undisciplined by the scrutiny of objective tests and standards. Belief in the efficacy of mere emotion is not essential to the faith whereby a sinful idolizer of precedent may be transported into the beatitude of a regenerate lover of reality (Llewellyn, Some Realism about Realism, 44 H. L. R. 1222; cf. Frank, Are Judges Human? *supra*). I do, indeed, discover here and there an accent of contempt for the old ideals of symmetry and order,—a note of mere derision as if they had been supplanted altogether, made obsolete and futile by a new organon and method; but the accent and the note are not, to my thinking, of the essence of the movement. They are not the leit-motif of the symphony, but mere grace notes, so to speak, mere decorative incidents. It would be strange if they were not heard in these days when the movement is still young. Seldom can one point to stumbling sinners the road to salvation, discerned for the first time, without displaying in so doing some exuberance of manner and hyperbole of phrase. The only sad thing is that so often the road turns out not to be new, and the salvation at the end a distant and receding goal. The neo-realists have suffered at times from this missionary ecstasy. Over-zealous (272) among the faithful,—when I call them over-zealous, I do not mean to disparage their brilliancy and power,—over-zealous ones, have not been satisfied to teach that order and certainty and rational coherence are goods to be subordinated on occasion to others more important. There has been a petulant contempt of them as if to dethrone them from the rank of idols was to prove them evil altogether. Not only are principles and rules and concepts shorn of their ancient tyranny. They are degraded altogether, stripped with contumely of every vestige of their bygone power; indeed, the process of humiliation is carried even farther, and there is taken from them the regenerative capacity to reproduce in their own image. Order in the legal system (so runs the argument) is an illusion, a mirage. The quest for it is a childish dream, the craving of the adolescent for the steadiness that came to him from the guidance of a parent; it is the unwillingness of sheltered youth to face the trials and perils of maturity and manhood. Silver-haired judges in the evenings of their days are as adolescent as the youngest neophyte,—a gospel carrying its solace as well as its reproaches. What began as a doctrine for emergencies —a weapon of peaceful revolution to be kept under lock and key, and employed with circumspection in hours of stress and strain—is turning, it seems, into a tool to be kept at one's elbow in a compartment of the desk, and plied with all the freedom of the screw-driver or the hammer in the grasp of the handy-man at home.

Now, if neo-realism means this or all that this implies, if its gospel is merely one of spasmodic self-expression, it is a false and misleading cult, unless, as I have suggested, its concern is with prophecy only, in which event I stand aloof. But in spite of the fact that at times its votaries have said things from which you might gather that they were professing such a cult or making ready to profess it, I am persuaded that these extravagances are not of the essence of the faith. What they wish to disparage, I believe, or at least to disparage chiefly, is the illusion of order and certainty and coherence which comes from sticking in the bark of congruities that are verbal rather than essential. In saying this I do not mean (273) to acquit them of all fault. Certain it is that jurists of great distinction, critics of their teaching, have understood them to insist on something more (Pound, The Call for a Realist, Jurisprudence, *supra;* Bohlen, Review of Frank's Law and the Modern Mind, 79 U. of Pa. Law Rev. 822; Dickinson, Legal Rules and the Process of Decision, 79 U. of Pa. Law Rev. 833). They can hardly escape the charge of some obscurity of exposition if the tone and temper of their teaching have been misapprehended by readers such as these. When all these allowances are made, I am persuaded, none the less, that there has been no thought to preach a doctrine of undisciplined surrender to the cardiac promptings of the moment, the visceral reactions of one judge or another (Bohlen, *supra).* Such surrender, instead of being vital to the new creed, is in fact essentially opposed to it, opposed to a creed which teaches as a basic article that generalizations of every kind, the subjective creations of the mind, must be constantly checked and restrained and reconsidered in the light of the tests and standards of objective or external verity. I put aside, therefore, as false and unessential the derision and impatience that betray themselves here and there among the priests of the new gospel of juridical salvation. I put aside the outbursts of a solipsism condemned out of their own mouths, since it is at war with other doctrine fundamental to their teaching. One can match these excesses with doctrine more moderate, more in harmony with tradition.[2] The hyperbole and the solipsism

---

[2] A temperate and withal a wise summary of neo-realist tendencies is to be found in the latest exposition of the new creed by one of the most brilliant of its teachers: Llewellyn, Some Realism about Realism, 44 H. L. R. 1222; also the same author's "Legal Thinking and Social Science."

have done damage to the cause of neo-realism by drowning other voices. Let them not deafen us to the message and to the truth that lies within it, if truth can be discerned by a willing and attentive ear.

Not a little confusion of thought has ensued, I am persuaded, from looking at the judicial process as if it had its complete and final summary in the doctrine of the (274) binding force of precedent. Now, *stare decisis* is an important factor in the judicial process, but it is not the entire process by a long shot. The truth is that the problem which the neo-realists have set themselves to solve divides itself into two questions, which are not always kept apart. At the outset is the question whether generative force is to be withdrawn altogether from the principles and rules and concepts which are formulated by judges in the course of their opinions, whether certainty and order and coherence are to have the quality of ends at all. When that question has been answered, another and subsidiary one remains. There is still need to consider to what extent the doctrine of *stare decisis* exacts adherence to a principle, a rule, a concept, an ideal of certainty or order, after the mischiefs attendant upon conformity have made themselves apparent. These two inquiries may run into each other, but they are far from being the same, yet in much juristic writing, whether favorable to neo-realism or opposed to it, there is the assumption that they are, or at least a seeming failure to keep the two apart. It does not at all follow because conformity to a principle or a rule or a concept is a dictate of logic or consistency that therefore we are to insist upon conformity at the cost of every other good. But equally it does not follow because occasions may arise when other goods are greater, that therefore conformity and order are to be spurned by the judge as no longer goods at all. Happily, the bark of philosophers as of canines is often worse than their bite, and the neo-realist is not so indifferent to coherence as his anarchical professions might lead a critic to suppose.

Peril lurks in definitions, so runs an ancient maxim of the law. What is true of definitions is true of universals generally. The snares that are thus set may catch the heedless feet of thinkers who have been loud even as they stumbled in cries of danger unto others. So it is with the subject of our study, the theory of juristic method. Generalizations about the ways in which the judicial process works are quite as likely to be incomplete, and to stand in need of supplement or revision, as the generalizations yielded by the process when in action, the out (275) put of its workings. The fallibility is strikingly exemplified in the dogma that speech is invariably to be held subordinate to acts. Very often it is, but not by any means invariably. Instead of its being true that what was said in an opinion is *always* controlled by what was done, the fact is that what was done is often controlled by what was said. The perception of this at the root of the maxim, *cessante ratione cessat et ipsa lex*. The courts of olden times were rigorous in condemning contracts in general restraint of trade, irrespective of special circumstances. If what was done by the judgments had been sufficient to shape the course of law thereafter, and the reasons held of no account, later developments would have been very different from what they were. Instead of this we find that the reasons were held to be controlling, and the conclusions a mere incident. What has survived is the public policy embodied in the ancient judgments, and not the judgments themselves, which lie buried beneath the lava of the years (Cardozo, the Nature of the Judicial Process, p. 95; Nordenfeldt v. Maxim Co., 1894, A. C. 535, 553; Anchor Electric Co. v. Hawkes, 171 Mass. 101, 104; Diamond Match Co. v. Roeber, 106 N. Y. 473). Other illustrations may be gathered, almost without number. We see a like process in the law of domestice relations with its concession to the wife of privileges that in ancient days belonged solely to the husband (Oppenheim v. Kridel, 236 N. Y. 156; Cardozo, The Growth of the Law, p. 105). We see it in the criminal law, where the ancient rule that a conspiracy or other misdemeanor was merged in a felony has given way with the departure of the reasons that fitted it into a niche of a coherent legal system (People v. Tavormina, 257 N. Y. 84). Wherever we turn, we gather cumulative evidence that it is not merely what was ruled nor merely what was said in explanation of the ruling, but at one time the ruling and at another time the explanation, that has the vitalizing capacity to shape the forms of law thereafter.

Just as confusion is engendered by the failure to keep in mind that *stare decisis* is only a factor in the judicial process, and not the process as a whole, so confusion is engendered by the failure to keep in mind that the word (276) law stands for a good many different notions, and that disproof of a statement that something is or is not law, is often merely proof that it is or is not law in a particular sense. Now, personally I prefer to give the label law to a much larger assembly of social facts than would have that label affixed to them by many of the neo-realists. I find lying around loose, and ready to be embodied into a judgment according to some process of selection to be practiced by a judge, a vast conglomeration of principles and rules and customs and usages and moralities. If these are so established as to justify a prediction with reasonable certainty that they will have the backing of the courts in the event that their authority is challenged, I say that they are law (Cardozo, Growth of Law, p. 52; cf. Huntington Cairns, *op. cit.* p. 337), though I am not disposed to quarrel with others who would call them something else.[3] My main objection to narrowing the definition is that in doing so we come near to squeezing law out of existence. The process of narrowing the definition will drive us to the conclusion that in advance of the adjudication in this or that particular case there is no such thing as law at all, and further that the adjudication when rendered is a law unto itself and not beyond, since the possibility always exists that it will be overruled or disregarded. As I have put it elsewhere, "Law never *is,* but is always about to be. It is realized only when embodied in a judgment, and in being realized expires." (Nature of the Judicial Process, p. 126.) This is analysis carried to such a point as to destroy the very subject that it intended to explain. If these refinements are to be accepted, we may wonder what the law is that every one is expected to obey under grievous pains and penalties if he ventures to transgress, and again what the law is that we have spent our lives in studying and practicing and trying to (277) understand. But the development of this theme will carry me too far afield, and I have tried my hand at it before (The Nature of the Judicial Process, p. 127, *et seq.;* The Growth of the Law, p. 31). The subject matter of a book will not consent to be compressed into a paragraph.

---

[3] "Justinian's Pandects only make precise,
What simply sparkled in men's eyes before,
Twitched in their brow or quivered on their lip,
Waited the speech they called but would not come." (Count Guido Francheschini in Browning's Ring and the Book.)

II

Reason versus Emotion; What Judges Really Do

Let us forget for a moment these niceties of definition, these subtleties of thought and phrase, and ask ourselves what it is that lawyers and judges do in the actual business of making law as it goes on from day to day. Are principles and rules and concepts sterile, or do they exhibit a capacity to reproduce after their kind? The question carries its own answer for any one who has the barest modicum of knowledge as to the shaping of judgments in the daily business of the courts. Indeed, not even the most thorough-going of the realists is prepared to assert the contrary (see Frank, Review of Llewellyn's "The Bramble Bush," 40 Yale L. J. 1120, 1123, May, 1931). The phenomenon of reproduction is conceded, but the concession is coupled with the claim that it is a phenomenon less general and less significant in proportion to the total mass of judgments begotten of the judicial process than is commonly supposed (Frank, *supra*). Even so, the concession goes far in supplying the basis for an *entente* between the neo-realists and others, in smoothing out asperities of difference between factions who are now busily engaged in shaking their fists at one another instead of giving themselves to the task of storming the redoubts in the possession of the common enemy, the redoubts of ignorance and reaction and worship of the written word. There is the beginning I say, of an *entente* when the difference is perceived to reduce itself to one of proportion and degree. The neo-realists are at odds with others in weighing and measuring the ingredients that are thrown into the judicial cauldron. They (278) do not deny that in one measure or another the ingredients are there. It is all a question of more or less.

If I consult my own experience, and ask what judges do in building law from day to day, I find that for the average run of cases what our predecessors have *said* is a generative force quite as much as what they have done. I do not mean what has been said by way of mere dictum, though I have no doubt that even dicta have been propagating forces and have borne a fruitful progeny; I mean what has been said as the professed and declared principle dictating the conclusion. But the average run of cases do not make up the entire body of the law. There are the exceptional cases too, the cases where the creative function is at its highest. These are the cases that have a maximum of interest for the student of legal methods. These are the cases in which neo-realism, as I view it, has its maximum of truth and also its maximum of utility. It is here that mere logic or consistency, though never negligible forces, have a minimum of compulsion. When a conclusion is felt to be unjust or inexpedient, or when the logic or supposed consistency that begat the parent precedent is itself suspect,—when a court is hard put to it, in other words, to find some avenue of escape—the actual thing done in the decision of the earlier case may assume a new importance, and many things professed may be retracted or ignored. This is so though the new case would be held to be fairly within the compass of the earlier one, within the range of its *ratio decidendi,* if the incitement to change were not so violent and compelling. "Every lawyer knows," says Llewellyn (Preface to Cases and Materials on Sales, p. X), "that a prior case may, at the will of the court, 'stand' either for the narrowest point to which its holding may be reduced, or for the widest formulation that its *ratio decidendi* will allow."

(279) The picture of the process will be incomplete and misleading unless other distinctions are placed upon the canvas. We must distinguish between the propagating power of a principle in cases that come within its range and its propagating power in cases where its application is less direct, where it supplies a mere analogy, a signpost, a guide, but not a governing rule, even if its legitimacy in its own domain be conceded to the full. In such cases the analogy will be checked, the seminal principle drained, by many obstacles and outlets, the most important being those of expediency and justice. So also, if the range of the principle is doubtful, if there is a borderland of uncertain application, the extension will be affected by a consideration of the actual necessities of the precedent, words being at times subordinated to acts, and acts, on the other hand, being at times subordinated to words. In brief, just as the law generally is permeated by distinctions of degree, so also is that branch of the law which is concerned with the significance of precedents and the significance of the forms in which precedents

are cast. There is the process of distinction, which may vary from the recognition of differences that are apparent on the surface to the discovery of others that are subtle and obscure; there is the process of limitation, by which the precedent, though not annihilated altogether, is declared to be erroneous in part; and there is the process of annihilation by which it is squarely overruled.

Clarity may be promoted if we descend from the general to the particular. I will take for illustration a subject much discussed in recent cases, the liability for negligent speech. When will mere words, spoken with negligence, but without fraud, impose a liability upon the speaker? Three cases of recent date mark the progress of the law upon the subject in the courts of New York. There was Glanzer v. Shepard, 233 N. Y. 236, decided in 1922; International Products Co. v. Erie R. R. Co., 244 N. Y. 331, in 1927; and Ultramares Corporation v. (280) Touche, 255 N. Y. 170, in 1931. Now, in each of these cases, the author of the opinion essayed the statement of a general principle, though with prudent reservations and qualifications to mark its tentative quality. When the last case in the series was reached, this provisional quality of the earlier principles was clearly recognized. Pronouncements which if applied in their uttermost length and breadth might put the law in shackles to an unworkable doctrine, were confined to the situations of fact that brought them into being. This was made comparatively easy in the particular case in view because of the cautious and tentative terms in which the formulas had been phrased. I conceive, however, that the result would have been the same if the phrases had been somewhat firmer. The court would in all probability have done the same thing, though with the need of more apology. I quote again a dictum of Brandeis, J., to which on more than one occasion I have had recourse in other writings: "It is a peculiar virtue of our system of law that the process of inclusion and exclusion, so often employed in developing a rule, is not allowed to end with its enunciation, and that an expression in an opinion yields later to the impact of facts unforeseen" (Jaybird Mining Co. v. Weir, 271 U. S. 609).

The emergent evolution of a formula into a precept is determined by its dimensions, spatial and temporal. To put the thought in other words: Considerations of space and time affect the capacity of the formula to shape the law thereafter. By considerations of space, I mean the generality or extension of the formula invoked in a particular controversy as establishing the stock of descent from which a conclusion is to be drawn. In the main, we may say, though only as a rough approximation, that obligation will vary inversely with extension. Take some of the principles of constitutional law, such a principle as the one that the due process clause of the constitution forbids a wholly arbitrary interference with liberty or property. Nearly the entire meaning of a (281) principle so general depends upon the application. Much will therefore turn, when a specific act of legislation is in question, upon the social or juridical philosophies of the judges who constitute the court at one time or another (T. R. Powell, State Utilities and the Supreme Court, 29 Mich. L. Rv. 1001, 1028, June, 1931). On the other hand, we must bear in mind that even in this department of the law where the expansive capacity of a principle is greatest, it is an expansive capacity within limits. The principle even here has a coercive force beyond the specific facts of the controversy in which it was announced. We misread history in a most unrealistic fashion if we say that the seeds of generations of later judgments were not in Gibbons v. Ogden and McCulloch v. Maryland.

What is true of constitutional law is true of law in other branches, but in varying degrees. There are many principles or rules or concepts so specific that the play of discretion in applying them is greatly reduced, though seldom absent altogether. Take such a principle as the one that he who seeks equity must do equity, or such a rule as the one that to make rescission effective in an action at law there must be a tender before suit of benefits received, or the concept of a corporation as a distinct juristic person separate from its members—the consequences flowing from these stocks are not invariably certain, yet they have such an element of certainty that in a vast majority of instances prediction ceases to be hazardous for the trained and expert judgment. The body of our case law would be radically different from what it is if these stocks were to be extirpated.

Just as there are distinctions dependent upon extension, distinctions in space, so there are distinctions in time. The principle or the rule or the concept, even though its extension is not great, is pliable in its early stages before the bones have set. This is far from saying that its pliability continues. There comes a time when it has been fitted to a great many combinations of facts, when it has been made to rule them all, and when this (282) has been done so often that at last its application is coincident or nearly so with its maximum extension. At that time pliability ends, and even before that time it is greatly diminished. Hypothesis is now reality. What was once but a hint has been turned into a command. By fitting itself to the instance in multitudinous variations, the formula has won authority when at first it had mere persuasion. It is law now in every sense, law by embodiment in successive judgments through the whole extent of the territory staked out at the beginning as the field of its domain.

Now, the impulse or the energy that thus pushes a formula to mastery is the driving force of order, of certainty, of rational coherence, as a juristic end and aim. The force has capacity to drive because discretion, unmeasured and unregulated, is felt to open the door to tyranny and corruption. So it is that long before a principle or a rule or a concept has become so firmly established that its title to govern is unchallenged by pretenders, long before this, it will still have made its way, slowly and hesitantly, into terrains of the law that are doubtful or disputed, will still have peopled the legal scene with forms in its own mould. Its power is not yet supreme. It must still compete with other analogies, which may be able to show themselves to be more exact, more expedient, more just. If they fail in that showing, it will have the right of way.

I have said that I prefer to give the name of law to formulas that are charged with this procreative power—to give it in advance of the hour of their final triumph—though it may turn out in the end that their lives and the lives of their expected progeny are shorter than was hoped for when the horoscope was cast. If I give them this name, I am merely preserving the analogy between the laws that are the province of jurisprudence and the predictions of orderly succession that are called the laws of nature (cf. The Growth of the Law, p. 34). Lawyers have been quoting these many years the famous saying (283) of Justice Holmes that "a legal duty so-called is nothing but a prediction that if a man does or omits certain things, he will be made to suffer in this or that way by judgment of the court." Now comes Dr. Dewey in his book, "The Quest for Certainty," and shows that the majestic laws of nature are predictions of a like order with not a little of the same chances of fallibility and error. They have lost the quality once ascribed to them of immutable sequences inherent in the constitution of the universe. What is known as the principle of indeterminacy seems to have given the finishing stroke to any such grandiose pretensions (Dewey, The Quest for Certainty, p. 201). They have been pulled down pretty near to the level of the laws declared by judges as approximate hypotheses. "In technical statement," says Dr. Dewey, "laws on the new basis *are formulae for the prediction of the probability of an observable occurrence.* They are designations of a relation sufficiently stable to allow of the occurrence of individualized situations—for every observed phenomenon is individual—within limits of specified probability, not a probability of error, but of probability of actual occurrence" (p. 206) (cf. Prof. Arthur H. Compton, Do We Live in a World of Chance? The Yale Review, p. 86, Sept. 1931). This sounds a good deal like a statement of the kind of law that emanates from the workings of the judicial process. Law as understood and developed by the lawyers may be coming nearer to law as understood and developed by the scientists, but it is also true that the laws of science are coming nearer to the judge-made laws of courts. "Mankind," the words are those of Dr. Whitehead (Alfred N. Whitehead, Process and Reality, p. 21), "never quite knows what it is after. When we survey the history of thought, and likewise the history of practice, we find that one idea after another is tried out, its limitations defined, and its core of truth elicited. * * * The proper test is not that of finality, but of progress."

(284) So it is with law, the law, that is to say, which is the concern of jurisprudence. Its principles or rules or concepts are not always finalities. They may mark what is only a stage of progress, or at times a stage of retrogression. Even so, their implications are something more than vanities. They are to be heeded like the laws of nature till superseded by another formulation more truthful in its expression of the order of the juristic universe. What that order is the judge is to say by his judgments, for he is the appointed searcher of the juristic heavens. The order is made up of

certainty and regularity, but not of these only. It is made up of expediency, too, and justice. Long habitude and a traditional technique must tell which of these component elements is to receive in any given instance the dominating place. Certainty and regularity have at least a presumption in their favor. They show us the well-worn ways, and as in conduct generally, so in law, what we have done in the past, we are likely to continue to do till the shock of a perturbing force is strong enough to jolt us out of the rut.

I know this is all distressingly vague. With the years of crowded thoughts I have given to the subject I cannot make it more precise. The judicial process is one of compromise, a compromise between paradoxes, between certainty and uncertainty, between the literalism that is the exaltation of the written word and the nihilism that is destructive of regularity and order. I ventured to put forward this idea some four or five years ago in a book to which I gave the title "The Paradoxes of Legal Science." Since then, I have won a forceful auxiliary in the philosophy of Prof. Cohen with its insistence upon twilight zones in the world of nature and of ideas, and upon the principle of polarity as the mediating force between them. "To make logic applicable to empirical issues," says Cohen, "we must employ the principle of polarity. By this I mean that the empirical facts are generally resultants of opposing and yet inseparable tendencies like the north and the south poles" (Morris R. Cohen, Concepts and Twilight Zones, vol. 24,—Journal of Philosophy, 673, 678). "From the point of view of the principle of polarity, twilight zones are (285) regions about the point of equilibrium of opposite tendencies" (*ibid.* p. 679). To bring this general notion closer to our theme: "Universality," he says, "and individuality, justice and the law, the ideal and the actual, are inseparable, yet never completely identifiable. Like being and becoming, unity and plurality, rest and motion, they are polar categories. Deny one and the other becomes meaningless. Yet the two must always remain opposed" (Cohen, Reason and Nature, p. 426). Neither the absolutist nor the empiricist is right, yet neither is wrong (*ibid.* pp. 437, 438); neither the lover of stability, of things as they are, nor the zealot who pants for change. Each is a builder of the *Civitas Dei;* and so, let us believe in all humility, is every craftsman in this process of ours; every baffled searcher for the pass-word that will reconcile the irreconcilable, that will bring the poles of these antinomies together, and will give a place, a due place, to movement, and another, and still a due one, to certainty and order too.

In the business of choosing between all these competitive offerings in the legal mart, we hear a good deal now-a-days of the intuitive judgment, more picturesquely styled the hunch, as the real arbiter of values (Hutcheson, The Judgment Intuitive; The Function of the Hunch in Judicial Decisions, 14 Cornell L. Q. 274). I do not seek to minimize its role upon the scene of the judicial process, but I think there is a good deal of misapprehension as to its significance for a philosophy of law. The thought seems to be that to prove the value of the hunch is to establish the empire of mere feeling or emotion, of arbitrary preference, and by the same token to disprove the value of conceptions, rules and principles, the value of all logic, till we are driven, like the sophist in the Greek comedy, to proclaim that Whirl is King (Irwin Edman, The Contemporary and His Soul, p. 4; Lippman, A Preface to Morals, p. 1). I do not mean that there was any such misapprehension in the mind of the distinguished judge and author by whom the hunch may be said to have been given its card of admission into the polite society of juristic methodology. I am fearful, however, that the newcomer's importance, even if justly rated by its sponsor, has been exaggerated by others.

(286) Now, indubitably, the intuitive flash of inspiration is at the root of all science, of all art, and even of all conduct. I have discussed this in my lectures on the Paradoxes of Legal Science (pp. 59, 60, 61), and so have many others. I quoted Graham Wallas. Other testimony may be added, if supplement is needed. "Our fundamental units, light waves, electric current and resistance, rates of metabolism, etc., are never visible except to the eye illumined by all sorts of ideas and rigorous deductions from them. Accidental discoveries of which popular histories of science make mention never happen except to those who have previously devoted a great deal of thought to the matter. Observation unillumined by theoretic reason is sterile. Indeed, without a well reasoned anticipation or hypothesis of what we expect to find there is no definite object to look for, and no test as to what is relevant to our search. Wisdom does not come to

those who gape at nature with an empty head" (M. R. Cohen, Reason and Nature, p. 17; cf. the same author's Vision and Technique in Philosophy, 39 Philosophical Review, p. 127, March, 1930).[4]

(287) The process is not different when we pass from theory to practice, from the sphere of thought to that of conduct. In a paper by Sir Austen Chamberlain, published a few months ago (Bases of British Foreign Policy, vol. 9, Foreign Affairs 535, July, 1931) we learn that the hunch has been for centuries the driving force for British statesmen in international diplomacy. "The Englishman," says Chamberlain, "distrusts logic at all times and most of all in the government of men, for instinct and experience alike teach him that men are not governed by logic, that it is unwise to treat political issues as exercises in logic and that wisdom more often lies in refraining from pressing sound arguments to their logical conclusion and in accepting a workable though illogical compromise. After all, logic lost us the Thirteen Colonies."

The doctrine of the hunch, if viewed as an attempt at psychological analysis, embodies an important truth; it is a

---

[4] A very recent book by Dr. Alfred E. Cohn of the Rockefeller Institute (Medicine, Science and Art, The University of Chicago Press, 1931) develops the same thought. Writing of a process to which he gives the name "intuition," he dwells upon the necessity of enriching it by "experience usually extensive and often profound." This experience is the true root of most of our happy flashes. "Because I have experience of this sort," he writes (p. 49), "though I need not be conscious of its possession, I can in argument or in situation arrive at conclusion far in advance either of one inexperienced or of one not previously interested in a related problem. I arrive at the result I need quickly; I telescope, as I say, with the speed of lightning, the thought perhaps of years which engrosses ponderously the energy and the time of other men. Because I have often reviewed the problem, I do not need now painfully and timeconsumingly to rehearse all the steps in the argument. Intuition in this sense is speed applied to experience—no more." We are to distinguish between "'the clever guessing founded on native shrewdness, often and especially attributed to women,' for which no preparation is required," and "advanced intuition, which denotes the complex process I have been describing in which attention, perception, memory and extra-conscious ratiocination are involved" (p. 51).

The office of mere brooding as a source of illumination is brought out with impressive force by Bertrand Russell (The Conquest of Happiness, p. 76). "I have found," he says, "that if I have to write upon some rather difficult topic, the best plan is to think about it with very great intensity—the greatest intensity of which I am capable—for a few hours or days, and at the end of that time give orders, so to speak, that the work is to proceed underground (i. e., subconsciously). After some months I return consciously to the topic and find that the work has been done. Before I had discovered this technique, I used to spend the intervening months worrying because I was making no progress; I arrived at the solution none the sooner for this worry, and the intervening months were wasted, whereas now I can devote them ot other pursuits."

vivid and arresting description of one of the stages in the art of thought. The hunch is the divination of the scientist, the luminous hypothesis, the apocalyptic insight, that is back of his experiments (The Paradoxes of Legal Science, pp. 59, 60; Graham Wallas, The Art of Thought, pp. 80, 82). If we conceive of it, however, as a summary of the complete judicial process, it is one-sided and misleading. Carried to an extreme, it is merely a transference into the realm of jurisprudence of that gospel of unfettered self-expression which has a passing vogue today in the realm of external conduct. There is nothing new about such systems or lack of systems. The French made the experiment a generation ago. What ensued forms the chapter in the history of their law which is known as "le phénomène Magnaud." The judges were to ask themselves in every instance what in the circumstances before them a good judge would wish to do, and render (288) judgment accordingly. I have considered the episode in other writings (Nature of the Judicial Process, p. 138). Its epitaph has been written by Geny with the authority of a master. We had a similar episode in our own country a decade or more ago when Judge Robinson initiated a like revolt against the existing order of jurisprudence in the State of North Dakota (Nature of the Judicial Process, p. 138). What the Germans call "Die Gefühlsjurisprudencz," the jurisprudence of mere sentiment or feeling (Brütt, Die Kunst der Rechtsanwendung, p. 101; Geny, Méthode d'Intérpretation, p. 307), however notable its merits does not number among them the grace of novelty (cf. The Nature of the Judicial Process, pp. 106, 107).

In condemning or in extolling the ideals of certainty and order and coherence, it is important to fix their meaning. Not a little confusion of thought and speech has grown out of the failure to heed this admonition. There is such a thing as certainty and order and coherence from the standpoint of the lawyer, and such a thing as certainty and order and coherence from the standpoint of the layman. Often we confuse the two. If a choice is necessary between them, we may find it wise to prefer the kind known to the layman, for it is his conduct that is to be regulated, it is from him, not from the lawyer, for the most part, that conformity is due. If the law as declared in a judgment is made to accord with established custom or with the plain and unquestioned dictates of morality it will seldom fail that certainty is promoted, not hindered, though lawyers may espy a flaw in the symmetry of the legal sphere, a break in the *elegantia juris* so precious to their hearts. The layman cares little about *elegantia* and has never had occasion to make a survey of the legal sphere. What is important for him is that the law be made to conform to his reasonable expectations, and this it will seldom do if its precepts are in glaring opposition to the *mores* of the times. Genuine certainty will very often be better attained, the ideal of the legal order more fully realized, by causing these expectations to prevail, than by developing the formula of an ancient dictum to the limit of its logic. Once more it is a (289) question of degree, a matter of more or less, an adjustment of the weights and a reading of the scales.

I have found it interesting to compare this twentieth century analysis of law and scientific method, exhibiting, as it does, the disparagement of general concepts and the exaltation of particulars, with the thought of mediaeval days as recorded for us by Dr. Lynn Thorndike in his book "Science and Thought in the Thirteenth Century." He tells us (pp. 30, 33, 38) of a debate between Coluccio Salutati and Master Bernard, a physician of Florence, upon the theme of the relative superiority of medicine and law. Salutati questions whether medicine is a science at all, since it "keeps growing not merely by the use of man's noble reason, but by magic inventions of remedies and daily experiments." On the other hand, he says that Bernard is wrong in denying that the law is a science "since it proceeds by definitions and divisions and since it has its universals which cannot be otherwise" (cf. Dewey, The Quest for Certainty, pp. 27, 83). The tables have been turned with a vengeance since those days. We tread more familiar ground when we read the discussion of the theme by Nicollo Nicolli of Florence. Upholding the superior virtue of medicine, he argued (p. 47) that there is scarcely a law upon whose interpretation the jurists agree—*tot capita tot sententiae*—and the net results, he says, is chaos and confusion. Here, at least, there is a meeting place between the thought of the Middle Ages and that of our own day. Interesting, too, if not helpful, for our boards of law examiners, is Salutati's announcement, based upon his study of astrology, that children born in the tenth or eleventh month should enter the legal profession (p. 57). If only we could confine the applicants within those limits, some problems that now vex us might have their solution over-night.

Let us come back, however, from the Middle Ages to the problems of the present.

What is useful in neo-realism is its insistence upon the "margin of error," the "increase of entropy," the "principle of indeterminacy," which condition the generalizations of (290) judge-made law just as they do the laws of physics, whose terminology I am borrowing (Jeans, The Mysterious Universe, pp. 28, 54, 154; Eddington, The Nature of the Physical World, p. 73 *et seq.;* Henry Adams, The Degradation of the Democratic Dogma, p. 141). What is wrong in neo-realism is a tendency manifest at times to exaggerate the indeterminacy, the entropy, the margin of error, to treat the random or chance element as a good in itself and a good exceeding in value the elements of certainty and order and rational coherence,—exceeding them in value, not merely at times and in places, but always and everywhere. In emphasizing the danger of extracting principles and formulas from an aggregation of specific cases and adhering to them blindly, we must be on our guard lest we be carried over to the other extreme and left with nothing more coherent than a mass of nebulous particulars (cf. Cohen, Justice Holmes and the Nature of Law, 31 Col. Law Rev. 352, 364). There are times when principles and rules and concepts must be accommodated to ends, yet there must always be remembrance of the truth that of the ends to be achieved definiteness and order are themselves among the greatest and most obvious. Certainly the historic masters of the law have been the boldest in the pursuit of principles, though this is not to say that they have not also been bold in rejecting what had proved itself to be out-worn or untenable. Haldane says in his autobiography that early in his professional career there has come to him the "conviction that not only in philosophy but in science it was true that no systematic knowledge is sufficient in itself unless it leads up and points to first principles. This doctrine later became valuable to me," he says ,"even as a guide in work at the bar. It did not help in the work of cross-examination. I was never good at that, nor in the conduct of *nisi prius* cases. But it was invaluable in the preparation for the presentation of great questions to the Supreme Tribunals, where the judges were keen about first principles and were looking out for help from the advocate." I take it that what is suspect and dangerous is not the search for principles, but the readiness to canonize them too quickly before their saintly character (291) has been attested by the ages. What we need to guard against is the notion that because a principle has been formulated as the *ratio decidendi* of a given problem, it is therefore to be applied as a solvent of other problems, regardless of consequence, regardless of deflecting factors, inflexibly and automatically, in all its pristine generality. On the other hand, a blight would fall upon our law if the opinions of our judges were to be as colorless and concrete as the judgment of a French court in its recitals and conclusions "Those who make no mistakes," we are reminded by Sir Frederick Pollock, "will never make anything, and the judge who is afraid of committing himself may be called sound and safe in his own generation, but will leave no mark on the law." We are not to forget that generalizations have their value, their fructifying virtue, in law as in science generally, though the later years may prune them or even discard them altogether. The judicial method of the future must see to it that judicial inventiveness shall not be desiccated or stunted, that generalization shall be as free and as bold as in the past, perhaps freer and bolder. Unless it can accomplish this, it is headed toward disaster. What is to be changed, if anything, is the capacity of the generalized principle, the *ratio decidendi,* to reproduce in its own image, to reproduce without restraint. Its generative power must depend upon the quality of its progeny. Like the hypotheses of science it is to be judged by its results. There must be a new system of eugenics for the pullulating precedents.

The movement to identify law with the action of the judge to the exclusion of his utterance has not developed without protest. It has found vigorous opposition in an illuminating essay by Prof. Arthur L. Goodhart, "The Ratio Decidendi," first published in the Yale Law Journal, and now reprinted in his collected papers. The opposition has found voice again in an article by Prof. Morris R. Cohen, "Justice Holmes and the Nature of Law" (31 Col. L. Rev. 352). Prof. Cohen, criticizing the tendency, sees in it a reflection of the behavioristic psychology (31 Col. L. Rev. at p. 364). He denies that the reasons put forward in opinions as the professed grounds of a decision are to be laid aside as minor (292) factors in determining the result. In this I quite agree, yet I am wondering whether he does not impute to his opponents a depreciation of the written word more thorough-going than they mean to teach. None of them would be willing to say that the professed reasons are of no importance. What is meant is rather this, that the reasons are to be jettisoned for the safety of the ship when the emergency is adequate, though adequacy remains as in the past a question of degree. One finds it hard to believe that the psychology of behaviorism could lead to any other doctrine. Certainly behaviorism does not depreciate the significance of speech, since one of its central teachings is the doctrine that speech, however dimly unformulated, is an indispensable preliminary to the reality of thought. The thinkers of the new movement have formulated the problem a little more sharply than their predecessors, yet the query propounded is not new. We have to face it, more or less unconsciously, every time that we decide how finely we will draw the line of distinction between one precedent and another. To what extent shall the reasons professed in an opinion be treated by the courts as invested with coercive power, and to what extent with power that is merely persuasive or advisory? In the solution of that problem the behavioristic outlook may at times help us to a clue. I dissent from the neo-realists in their depreciation of order and certainty and rational coherence as merely negligible goods, if depreciation so extreme is of the essence of their teaching. On the other hand, I am wholly one with them in their insistence that the virtues of symmetry and coherence can be purchased at too high a price; that law is a means to an end, and not an end in itself; and that it is more important to make it consistent with what men and women really and truly believe and do than what judges may at times have said in an attempt to explain and rationalize the things they have done themselves. The high priests of the new movement will have to say whether this confession makes me a realist or not. In my case, as in many others, the schism is not wide if lip service to a catechism is less important than the actualities of conduct,—as every genuine realist must concede that it is.

(293) III

The Stare Decisis of the Future

The Philosophy of the Judicial Process at Home and Across the Seas

I have said that *stare decisis* is a factor in the judicial process, but not the process as a whole. The time has come to speak of its present limitations, and of new ones that may be needed. Let me speak of present limitations first. If I may venture my own *credo,* I would say that we must distinguish between the principle that is applied *arguendo,* which will often be susceptible of limitation without affecting the result, and the principle *sine qua non,* which must be accepted as invoked if the result is to stand at all. A principle *sine qua non* may, of course, be abandoned in rare extremities, just as a judgment may be overruled, but only at the price of abandoning or reversing the law previously declared. Holdsworth in a recent book (Some Lessons from Legal History, p. 17) quotes the words of Lord Mansfield, "The law does not consist of particular cases, but of general principles, which are illustrated and explained by those cases." It is easy to press such a dictum too far. It does not mean, as Holdsworth himself reminds us, that "all the words used by the judge, still less all his reasons, are law." This is followed by a pointed quotation from an essay by Sir Frederick Pollock: "Judicial authority belongs not to the exact words used in this or that judgment, nor even to all reasons given, but only to the principle recognized or applied as necessary grounds for the decision." "Every lawyer knows," says Llewellyn,—I have quoted the dictum once before (Preface to his Cases and Materials on Sales, p. X),—"that a prior case may, at the will of the court, 'stand' either for the narrowest point to which its holding may be reduced, or for the widest formulation that its *ratio decidendi* will allow." On the other hand, the principle that is invoked *arguendo* may often be whittled down or even be rejected altogether, and the judgment still stand with all its legitimate implications.

So much for *stare decisis* as I understand it to prevail today. A change I venture to predict, though I may (294) not live to see it. I have little doubt that with the mounting years and the ever mounting mass of precedents there will be need to modify the doctrine by bringing it into harmony with the sounder conception of the meaning of all knowledge. "What is already known," says Dewey in his Experience and Nature (p. 154), "what is accepted as truth, is of immense importance, inquiry could not proceed without it. But it is held subject to use, and is at the mercy of the discoveries which it makes possible. It has to be adjusted to the latter, and not the latter to it. When things are defined as instruments, their value and validity reside in what proceeds from them; consequences, not antecedents, supply meaning and verity. Truths already possessed may have practical or moral certainty, but logically they never lose a hypothetic quality. They are true *if:* if certain other things eventually present themselves; and when these latter things occur they in turn suggest further possibilities; the operation of doubt-inquiry-finding recurs" (cf. C. J. Keyser, Pastures of Wonder, *passim;* also C. J. Keyser, On the Study of Legal Science, 38 Yale L. J. 431).

Jurisprudence must accept something of this provisional quality for the deliverances of her judges, or avow her own failure to establish a due co-ordination between the precepts of the law and those of expediency and justice. No doubt the provisional element will be diminished by the necessity of avoiding retrospective changes that would frustrate the reasonable expectations of well-intentioned men. One of the most obvious exactions of the very expediency and justice which are the final ends of law is that expectations so conceived shall not be thwarted and disappointed with hardship to the innocent. The necessity for such adjustments will sometimes call for the continuance of an existing rule of law after its intrinsic error or inconvenience has declared itself in practice. Even so, the times are many when the declaration of a new rule, the announcement of a new doctrine, will work no disappointment to any one who has shaped his conduct by (295) it, or if disappointment, perhaps, to some, yet only to those who are using it as a weapon of deceit or malice. In such conditions, we need not trouble ourselves if the retroactive declaration makes the weapon ineffective.

My impression is that the instances of honest reliance and

genuine disappointment are rarer than they are commonly supposed to be by those who exalt the virtues of stability and certainty. For such cases and others where a retroactive declaration is for any reason inexpedient, I find myself driven more and more to the belief that courts should be competent to follow the practice proposed by Mr. Wigmore in his suggestive little book "The Problems of Law" and since espoused by others; they should apply the outworn rule to the case that is then at hand, and couple their judgment with the declaration that they will feel free to apply another rule to transactions consummated in the future.

Let me show by a recent group of decisions in this state the need of such a jurisdiction, and how it would be made to work. We had before us not long ago the question whether gas ranges in an apartment house were to be classified as fixtures (Cohen v. 1165 Fulton Corp., 251 N. Y. 24 [1929]; Madfes v. Beverly Development Corp., 251 N. Y. 12 [1929]; Alf Holding Corp. v. American Stove Co., 253 N. Y. 450 [1930]). If the intention to be imputed to the owner of the building in annexing such appliances was to be tested by the probabilities as they might have manifested themselves a hundred years ago when men lived for the most part in separate dwellings and the modern apartment was unknown, much could be said for maintaining that the ranges were mere personalty, not permanent accessions to the building or the land. Such a conclusion, however, has an aspect unreal and almost farcial when applied to apartment life today. But what did *stare decisis* have to say upon the subject? Why, as late as 1913, in days when the apartment house had been fully developed, the Court of Appeals held in a carefully considered case that ranges were not fixtures, and this in the face of an opinion at (296) the Appellate Division which had maintained that they were and had emphasized the new conditions of apartment life as justifying a departure from ancient precedents (Central Union Gas Co. v. Brown, 210 N. Y. 10, reversing 146 App. Div. 783). Now what was a court to do in 1929 when the same court in 1913 had considered the same argument and found it insufficient? What was it to do, bearing in mind the fact that sellers of the ranges under contracts of conditional sale had made their sales in the faith that the ranges were personalty merely, and had refrained from taking measures to protect themselves by recording their bills of sale in ways that would have been appropriate if they had supposed that the ranges were annexations to the land? Well, a majority of the court believed that in view of the probable reliance by innocent parties upon a decision which the same majority would have refused to make if the question had been a new one, there was nothing to do except to adhere to what its predecessors had done, and let *stare decisis* control the judgment. That is what we did, though there was a dissenting vote at that. But was there not a third thing that might better have been done, better than what the majority or the dissenting judge approved? Would it not have been the sensible thing to say, this judgment will be affirmed because injustice would otherwise be done to the seller of the ranges who relied upon a declaration of the law now believed to have been wrong, but as to all who propose to have like transactions in the future, we give notice here and now that they are not to trust to the mistaken declaration to guide their course hereafter?

The objection will be made that courts are without power to tie the hands of their successors by a declaration of purpose not wrought into a judgment. If I conceive the situation justly, they are not attempting to tie the hands of any one. They are untying and releasing. A fair paraphrase of what they say is this: "The rule that we are asked to apply is out of tune with the life (297) about us. It has been made discordant by the forces that generate a living law. We apply it to this case because the repeal might work hardship to those who have trusted to its existence. We give notice, however, that any one trusting to it hereafter will do so at his peril." The effect of such a declaration would be to leave the law uncertain in respect of new transactions until the court could speak again, though the uncertainty would not be grievous, for litigants could assume with little likelihood of disappointment that the dictum would be followed when the opportunity arrived to turn it into a decision. Whatever evil might inhere in the small margin of uncertainty would be something hardly to be complained of in a system of case law which by the very nature of its existence leaves so many other things unsettled. I am not persuaded altogether that competence to proceed along these lines does not belong to the judges even now without the aid of statute. If the competence does not exist, it should be conferred by legislation, reinforced, if need be, by constitutional amendment. The statute should be declared to apply whenever the situation is one in which a court would be justified in overruling its previous decision if vested rights or interests did not stand in the way. The draft of such a law, conferring the requisite power in half a dozen simple sentences, has been prepared by Albert Kocourek, Professor of Law in Northwestern University. You will find it in a recent number of the American Bar Association Journal (Kocourek, Retrospective Decision and Stare Decisis, vol. 17, Am. Bar Assn. Journal, p. 180, March, 1931). Some of its terms may call for fuller definition, but the framework, the skeleton, is there. Much of the evasion, the pretense, the shallow and disingenuous distinctions too often manifest in opinions—distinctions made in the laudable endeavor to attain a just result while preserving a semblance of consistency—would disappear from our law forever if there were such a statute on the books. Thus would *stare decisis* re (298) tain what it has of value, retain its stabilizing virtue, and be purged of its congealing humors.

A good deal of what has been written of recent years by neo-realists and others may seem to break with all tradition and to presage far reaching change. It is easy, in thus estimating their labors, to be misled by forms and phrases. What is new in juristic thought today is chiefly the candor of its processes. Much that was once unavowed and kept beneath the surface is now avowed and open. From time immemorial lawyers have felt the impulse to pare down the old rules when in conflict with the present needs. The difference is that even when they yielded to the impulse, it was their habit in greater measure than today to disguise what they were doing, to disguise the innovation even from themselves, and to announce in all sincerity that it was all as it had been before. "Under our common law system," said deTocqueville, "laws are esteemed not so much because they are good as because they are old, and if it be necessary to modify them in any respect, to adapt them to the changes which time operates in society, recourse is had to the most inconceivable subtleties in order to uphold the traditionary fabric and to maintain that nothing has been done which does not square with the intentions and complete the labors of a former generation."

Then, as now, the method of free research did not escape the lash of criticism by cloaking itself in the garb of orthodox conformity. Bentham in his Comment on the Commentaries emits a blast of rage against Blackstone for preaching the right of judges, when interpreting a statute, to wander from the letter. "He teaches them, the judges, the most ingenious method of supporting themselves in an usurped supremacy, and shows them how to save themselves from the reproach of disobedience they may call in fraud to cover it." In support of this indictment, he quotes the following from the Commentaries: "Where some collateral matter," said the Commentator, "arises out of the general (299) words and happens to be unreasonable, then the judges are *in decency* to conclude that this consequence was not foreseen by the Parliament, and therefore they are at liberty to expound the statute by equity, and only *quoad hoc* to disregard it." At this Bentham explodes in a paroxysm of fury. "To conclude," he says, "when it is thought convenient to conclude that the legislators did not see a thing, not because the truth is so, but out of decency, rather than set your will openly against theirs, to pick and choose, to obey *quoad hoc,* to disobey *quoad illuc,* to let this be 'valid', and that be 'void', such is the advice our author gives you if you are a judge. This is his notion of what is 'decent'; for my part I should talk no more of decency, if I taught men to disregard the law that governs them, a statute *quoad* anything."

Thus they were flinging reproaches at one another a century and a third ago. Indeed the plaint is a much older one than that. Bentham could have found ammunition for his batteries if he had gone across the Channel, and studied the legal history of France. He would have sympathized with the framer of the "Ordonnance de Blois," promulgated by royal decree in 1579. The Ordonnance de Blois enjoins on everyone—judges, magistrates and officers, both ecclesiastical and secular—to observe the statutes and cause them to be observed both in decisions and otherwise without contravening them or dispensing with them for any reason or under any pretext, whether that of equity or any other, and couples with the command a declaration that all judgments, sentences and decrees which shall be given contrary to the form and tenor of such command shall be null and void and of no effect (Marty, La Distinction du fait et du droit, p. 42). Equally emphatic in its prohibitions is the Ordonnance of 1667: "If in litigations which shall hereafter be pending in our courts of parliament or in other courts, there shall be any doubt or difficulty as to the application of any articles of our statutes, edicts, declarations or letters (300) patents, we forbid the judges from attempting to construe them, and it is our will that in such event the judges shall come to us, and ascertain what our intention was or shall thereupon be declared to be" (Marty, *supra,* p. 52; cf. pp. 61, 70).

One seems to hear in all this the premonitory rumblings of recriminations and rivalries that echo to this day. A change there has been since the present century was born, a change tending towards the concession of a larger freedom of development, yet a change not unopposed, and one mainly of degree. The controversy is as old as the feud between the Sabinians and Proculians in the days of ancient Rome. Even so, the new emphasis has been strong enough to awaken a new life, to impart a new impetus. We are in need more than ever of a theory of legal apologetics. We must have a system of philosophy that will justify and rationalize what might otherwise be lawless, that will save us from the reproach of a usurped and impudent supremacy.

I have spoken of a mounting interest in theories of judicial method. Recent studies have impressed me with the growth of a like interest among lawyers and judges across the seas, trained often in a legal system other than our own. The signs of change can be read in many quarters of the firmament. In England the tendency is perhaps less manifest than elsewhere. You will find, however, in a recent number of the Law Quarterly Review a delightful little lecture by Sir Frederick Pollock which bears the suggestive title, "Judicial Caution and Valour." What is to guide the court, he asks, in the constructive process imposed upon it of finding a rule for the case in hand when none has heretofore been stated? "The usual and accepted answer is that it must find and apply the rule which in all the circumstances appears most reasonable, and I do not know (he says) that any plausible improvement on this has been suggested." I should be sorry if he had left the answer there, for this by itself would amount to little more than a statement (301) of the problem. Luckily the modest disclaimer of plausible improvements is coupled with a penetrating analysis of the methods appropriate and reasonable in varying situations. "The problem of judicial interpretation," we are told, "is to hold a just middle way between excess of valour and excess of caution." This is followed by wise hints that may help us to a choice between valorous impatience and "pedestrian timidity." So in a recent book by an English barrister, "Justice and Administrative Law," the work of Dr. Robson, lecturer in law at the London School of Economics and Political Science, you will find the judicial mind and temper subjected to a process of dissection which marks a spreading interest in the problems of judicial method.

Even in England, therefore, the new spirit, if less insistent, is still declaring itself audibly and giving evidence of its power. But more striking perhaps is the stirring of the same spirit in the countries of Continental Europe, where the freedom of the judicial function has been restrained to a greater degree by the forms of legislation, the shackles of a code. I will take one illustration only among many that are available. There was published in 1928 a draft of a new civil code for the Republic of Poland, or of part of such a code, as well as a statement of the principles that had guided the labors of the draftsmen. One will find there an emancipation of the judge from hampering restraints and a license of recourse to things *dehors* the statute, to the realities of life, to the standards of morals, of business, of economic or social welfare, that mark a close approach to a system of judge-made law and justice. "The precepts of the statute," says the proposed code, "are the source of rules of conduct which have obligation for individuals in so far as the social and economic ends established by the statute can be objectively realized thereby." "The statute must be interpreted with reference to contemporary relations, social and economic, according to the contemporary meaning of its terms and in conformity with its purpose, taking account in so doing of the whole body of existing (302) law." "In any case in which it becomes impossible to ascertain the precise meaning of a statute, as well as in one in which a statute is lacking altogether, the question must be decided according to the fundamental principles of the juridical order of the Polish

State, seeing to it that no one shall ever without requital be the victim of a wrong." "If the circumstances which have inspired a statute shall finally disappear, or if there are new statutes whose purpose is contrary to that of earlier ones, all the earlier ones are to be deemed abrogated, even if they can be reconciled with the letter of the new ones."

The commentary by Prof. Lyskowski is as interesting as the text, but time does not permit that I should give more than an imperfect extract. "I have adopted," he says, "as the guiding conception of my project the conception that the legal order and jurisprudence must have an objective basis." "A judge adopting the objective basis will take as his point of departure the economic or social end and aim of a juridical relation." "I am of the opinion that the duty of appreciating the social and economic end of a juridical relation existing between the parties will be a surer guide to the judge than particular precepts enunciated by a statute." "Certainly," he adds, "one must act with moderation. Great reforms cannot succeed unless they are carried out temperately. I believe, nevertheless, that we are right in wishing to confer on a judge large powers of interpretation, even if they are not as large as those of the judges of England or of the United States." One will find much the same doctrine in a book, "La Valeur de la Loi," by Prof. G. Renard of the University of Nancy (cf. Aus dem Amerikanischen Rechtsleben by Dr. Robert Fritz, Berlin, 1930). I am not sure that they have not gone ahead of their Anglo-American brethren in the freedom of interpretation they have allowed themselves, though professing to lag behind us. True, indeed, it is that there have (303) been also prophecies of ruin if the movement be not checked. What has happened in the United States has been held up to his countrymen for warning and example by Prof. Lambert of the University of Lyons in his notable book, "The Government of Judges." He has been unable for all his diatribe to stem the swelling tide. Let him look to his dykes and dams, or the waters will descend upon the codified expanses of the statutory law.

The judicial process comes in for a good deal of criticism in these days, and I am far from complaining of this or from denying that some of it is just. On the other hand, a sense of loyalty to my guild prompts me to insist that the judges are often the scape-goats of others, bearing a weight of odium heavier than any they have earned. In a suggestive series of lectures, "Some Modern Tendencies in the Law," given on the White Foundation at the University of Virginia, Professor Williston observes (p. 24): "It is probable that much of the popular dislike of the law and disbelief in its justice is due to observation and dissatisfaction with the results in particular instances." Now, the results in particular instances are nearly always the work of the judges, and so the odium is theirs, no matter though the result was the predestined development of a rule imposed upon them from above by the representatives of the People or even by the People itself. There seems to be a general notion that statutes or constitutions are never harsh or technical, and that if they seem so in any particular case, the fault is with the judges who apply or construe them. Indeed, it is extraordinary with what readiness Demos will impose fetters upon the action of its representatives in the legislature by constitutional amendments, and equally extraordinary with what impatience the same Demos will view the action of a court in paying any attention to the amendments when they stand in the way of some results that in the particular instance would be convenient or desirable. The truth, of course, is that a statute or a constitution may lead to consequences just as harsh and just as technical as any that could ensue from the undirected action of the courts in the development of the (304) judicial process. Take the statute regulating the enforcement of mechanical liens. The lienor must file a notice which shall state enumerated particulars; there must be a description of the property, a statement of the nature of the work, and so on. An honest mechanic files a notice which fails to comply with the statutory requirements. There is wailing and gnashing of teeth when the courts reject the lien. The odium is visited on the cruel judges. We never hear of the cruel legislature that imposed a rigid rule, when very likely one more pliable would have comported as well, if not better, with expediency and justice. So it is also with constitutional amendments. A home-rule article is embodied in the constitution with a great flourish of trumpets. Home-rule is a slogan that has captivated the popular fancy, like arbitration and some others. For a thousand that cry hosanna when they hear the taking words, there is hardly one who has thought out the consequences of the policy so airily espoused. The legislature passes a statute which trenches on the exclusive powers of a city, or the city passes a local law which trenches on the reserved powers of the legislature. Hardly any one is interested in the question whether the zone of legitimate power has been overstepped or not. The only question that is asked, is something very different: is the particular measure a good one or bad one considered by itself? If it is good, a plague upon the judges who annul it; if it is bad, a plague upon them if they sustain it. Take the amendments to the Tenement House Law which were recently assailed in New York as involving a violation of the article of the the constitution conferring upon municipalities the power of Home Rule as to some subjects and some only (Adler v. Deegan, 251 N. Y. 467). The comments on our decision in the public press and by citizens and public bodies would make one suppose that the only question we had considered was whether in its practical application the new statute, assailed as void, would be an improvement on the old one. Hardly any one troubled himself with the one question that had troubled us, the power to enact the statute, whether its effect was good or vicious. The result of this myopia is that the (305) judges are often blamed for evils that are in truth the work of others. This does not mean, of necessity, that the balance of blame and praise is grievously upset. There are times, though perhaps less frequent, when blessings due to others are in praise ascribed to them. The wise judge, in either event, will try to look upon the blame, as upon the praise, with serenity and calmness, if not with indifference and contempt. He will know himself to be a worker in a movement too deep to be stirred by these little eddies on the surface.

Was there ever such a profession as ours, anyhow? We speak of ourselves as practicing law, as teaching it, as deciding it; and not one of us can say what law means. Start a discussion as to its meaning, try to tell how it is born, whence it comes, out of what we manufacture it, and before the dispute is fairly under way, the vociferous disputants will be springing at each other's throats. Their inability to agree about the basic implications of their calling has in it elements of comedy when at the end of the dispute they are seen to be peacefully engaged in the manufacture of the finished products—out of what, they cannot tell you, and by a formula they cannot state.

How much of the process is to be classified as reasoning and how much as mere emotion, the students of juristic method are unable to agree. That is disconcerting enough, but even more disconcerting it is to learn that neither jurists nor philosophers can explain the rationality of reasoning, can set the process on its feet, and justify our faith in it. In the days of my youth the situation was not so hopeless. We were taught in a consoling way that back in the dark or middle ages there were thinkers who were known as the schoolmen; that they had no understanding of reasoning as a tool for the discovery of truth; and that with extraordinary imbecility they spent their days and nights in spinning mental cobwebs, in arguing deductively from premises which they never tried to verify. The consoling tale assured us, however, that in the sixteenth century, Francis Bacon came along and taught men to reverse the process, taught them to begin with particulars and ascend to universals, instead of beginning (306) where they ought to end, and that as a result of this teaching there came into being the inductive method, and thereafter we were wise and happy.

But the trouble is we did not stay so. The philosophers are after us again and are making fun of induction just as much as they did of the method that it ousted. What induction does, they say, is to gather together a lot of instances and then leap to the the conclusion that because A, B, C and D have behaved in a certain way, therefore all other men or things of the same class will behave in the same way, which is the very thing to be proved, and is only an assumption, just like the premises of the schoolmen. Not only that, but the old process of deduction, the grouping of these instances into universals, and then splitting them up into particulars again, is found to reveal all sorts of new truths and new harmonies and the stuff for new hypotheses that were never thought of till the inductive process was reversed, and the universals were redistributed.

So today we find Bertrand Russell saying of the vaunted method of induction, that it "is as indefensible intellectually as the purely deductive method of the Middle Ages" (Bertrand Russell, article "Science" in "Whither Mankind,"

p. 65; cf. Cairns, article "Law and Anthropology" in "The Making of Man," p. 331; Bertrand Russell, Philosophy, chap. XXI; Bertrand Russell, Heads or Tails, The Doctrine of Chance, Atlantic Monthly, August, 1930, p. 167), and in the same vein we hear from Dr. Whitehead that "the theory of induction is the despair of philosophy—and yet all our activities are based upon it" (Whitehead, Science and the Modern World, p. 34); and then from another quarter come voices reminding us that the difference between the two methods is one of degree only, and that for the discovery of new truth, as distinguished from the exposition of what is old, no monopoly of merit is to be assigned to either (cf. Cohen, Reason and Nature, p. 119, *et seq.* Alf Ross, Theorie der Rechtsquellen, 198).

I do not know how it will all end. I know that it has been an interesting time to live in, an interesting time in which (307) to do my little share in translating into law the social and economic forces that throb and clamor for expression. Like any other era of unrest, it has had its pangs of uncertainty, its doubts and hesitations. "The secret desire of our hearts," says Croce, speaking of writers of history, "is that things should remain as they are, and we do not consider that if they did so, there would be no history to write, or at least none of the kind which we are accustomed to write" (B. Croce, A History of Italy). Judges, if they search their hearts, may have to make the same confession. In the silences of meditation, they sigh for the good old days when lives were simple and sociologists unknown. They forget now and again that if such eras were unbroken, their calling would be shorn of a large, perhaps the greater, part of its significance and power. I picked up the other day a copy of one of Bacon's books, not so often read as others, his life of Henry VII. In the preface I found this: "It is with Times as it is with Wayes. Some are more uphill and downhill, and some are more flat and plane." The flat time, he adds, is better for the man who lives in it, but the other is better for the author who is writing of it.

The aphorism, true for authors, will hold as well for judges. The "wayes" we have to travel nowadays are not flat and plane, if indeed they ever were. They are uphill and downhill with many a signpost that is false and many another that has fallen. Even so, there is the joy of an adventure interesting in itself, and perhaps not wholly without its bearing upon the welfare of the humanity. If I have not lost the road altogether, if my feet have not sunk in a quagmire of uncoordinated precedents, I owe it not a little to the signposts and the warnings, the barriers and the bridges, which my study of the judicial process has built along the way.

THE ALTRUIST IN POLITICS*

Commencement Oration
From the Columbia College
Class Book, 1889

THERE comes not seldom a crisis in the life of men, of nations, and of worlds, when the old forms seem ready to decay, and the old rules of action have lost their binding force. The evils of existing systems obscure the blessings that attend them; and, where reform is needed, the cry is raised for subversion. The cause of such phenomena is not far to seek. "It used to appear to me," writes Count Tolstoi, in a significant passage, "it used to appear to me that the small number of cultivated, rich and idle men, of whom I was one, composed the whole of humanity, and that the millions and millions of other men who had lived and are still living were not in reality men at all." It is this spirit—the spirit that sees the whole of humanity in the few, and throws into the background the millions and millions of other men—it is this spirit that has aroused the antagonism of reformers, and made the decay of the old forms, the rupture of the old restrictions, the ideal of them and of their followers. When wealth and poverty meet each other face to face, the one the master and the other the dependent, the one exalted and the other debased, it is perhaps hardly matter for surprise that the dependent and debased and powerless faction, in envy of their opponents' supremacy, should demand, not simple reform, but absolute community and equality of wealth. That cry for communism is no new one in the history of mankind. Thousands of years ago it was heard and acted on; and, in the lapse of centuries, its reverberations have but swelled in volume. Again and again, the altruist has arisen in politics, has bidden us share with others the product of our toil, and has proclaimed the communistic dogma as the panacea for our social ills. So

* *The Altruist in Politics.* Reprinted with the permission of Columbia University, the residuary legatee of the literary estate of Benjamin Nathan Cardozo.

today, amid the buried hopes and buried projects of the past, the doctrine of communism still lives in the minds of men. Under stress of misfortune, or in dread of tyranny, it still is preached in modern times as Plato preached it in the world of the Greeks.

Yet it is indeed doubtful whether, in the history of mankind, a doctrine was ever taught more impracticable or more false to the principles it professes than this very doctrine of communism. In a world where self-interest is avowedly the ruling motive, it seeks to establish at once an all-reaching and all-controlling altruism. In a world where every man is pushing and fighting to outstrip his fellows, it would make him toil with like vigor for their common welfare. In a world where a man's activity is measured by the nearness of reward, it would hold up a prospective recompense as an equal stimulant to labor. "The more bitterly we feel," writes George Eliot, "the more bitterly we feel the folly, ignorance, neglect, or self-seeking of those who at different times have wielded power, the stronger is the obligation we lay on ourselves to beware lest we also, by a too hasty wresting of measures which seem to promise immediate relief, make a worse time of it for our own generation, and leave a bad inheritance for our children." In the future, when the remoteness of his reward shall have weakened the laborer's zeal, we shall be able to judge more fairly of the blessings that the communist offers. Instead of the present world, where some at least are well-to-do and happy, the communist holds before us a world where all alike are poor. For the activity, the push, the vigor of our modern life, his substitute is a life aimless and unbroken. And so we have to say to communists what George Eliot might have said: Be not blinded by the passions of the moment, but when you prate about your own wrongs and the sufferings of your offspring, take heed lest in the long run you make a worse time of it for your own generation, and leave a bad inheritance for your children.

Little thought has been taken by these altruistic reformers for the application of the doctrines they uphold. To the question how one kind of labor can be measured against another, how the labor of the artisan can be measured against the labor of the artist, how the labor of the strong can be measured against the labor of the weak, the communists can give no answer. Absorbed, as they are, in the principle of equality, they have still forgotten the equality of work in the equality of pay; they have forgotten that reward, to be really equal, must be proportionate to effort; and they and *all* socialists have forgotten that we cannot make an arithmetic of human thought and feeling; and that for all our crude attempts to balance recompense against toil, for all our crude attempts to determine the relative severity of different kinds of toil, for all our crude attempts to determine the relative strain on different persons of the same kind of toil, yet not only will the ratio, dealing, as it does, with our subjective feelings, be a blundering one, but a system based upon it will involve inequalities greater, because more insidious, than those of the present system that it would discard.

Instances, indeed, are not wanting to substantiate the claim that communism, by unduly exalting our altruistic impulses, proceeds upon a false psychological basis. Yet if an instance is to be chosen, it would be hard to find one more suggestive than that afforded by the efforts of Robert Owen. The year 1824 saw the rise of Owen's little community of New Harmony, and the year 1828 saw the community's final disruption. Individuals had appropriated to themselves the property designed for all; and even Owen, who had given to the enterprise his money and his life, was obliged to admit that men were not yet fitted for the communistic stage, and that the moment of transition from individualism to communism had not yet arrived. Men trained under the old system, with its eager rivalry, its selfish interests, could not quite yet enter into the spirit of self-renunciation that communism demands. And Owen, therefore, was led to put his trust in education as the great moulder of the minds of men. Through this agency, he hoped, the eager rivalry, the selfish interests, the sordid love of gain, might be lost in higher, purer, more disinterested ends; and, animated by that hope—the hope that in the fullness of time another New Harmony, free from the contention and the disappointments of the old one, might serve to immortalize his name—animated by that hope, Owen passed the last thirty years of his life; and with that hope still before his eyes he died.

But years now have passed since Owen lived; the second New Harmony has not yet been seen; the so-called rational system of education has not yet transformed the impulses or the aims of men; and the communist of today, with a history of two thousand years of failure behind him, in the same pathetic confidence still looks for the realization of his dreams to the communism of the future.

And yet, granting that communism were practicable, granting that Owen's hopes had some prospect of fulfillment, the doctrine still embodies evils that must make it forever inexpedient. The readers of Mr. Matthew Arnold's works must have noticed the emphasis with which he dwells on the instinct of expansion as a factor in human progress. It is the refutation alike of communism and of socialism that they thwart the instinct of expansion; that they substitute for individual energy the energy of government; that they substitute for human personality the blind, mechanical power of the State. The one system, as the other marks the end of individualism. The one system, as the other, would make each man the image of his neighbor. The one system, as the other, would hold back the progressive, and, by uniformity of reward, gain uniformity of type.

I can look forward to no blissful prospect for a race of men that, under the dominion of the State, at the cost of all freedom of action, at the cost, indeed, of their own true selves, shall enjoy, if one will, a fair abundance of the material blessings of life. Some Matthew Arnold of the future would inevitably say of them in phase like that applied to the Puritans of old: "They entered the prison of socialism and had the key turned upon their spirit there for hundreds of years." Into that prison of socialism, with broken enterprise and broken energy, as serfs under the mastery of the State, while human personality is preferred to unreasoning mechanism, mankind must hesitate to step. When they shall once have entered within it, when the key shall have been turned upon their spirit and have confined them in narrower straits than even Puritanism could have done, it will be left for them to find, in their blind obedience and passive submission, the recompense for the singleness of character, the foresight, and the energy, that they have left behind them.

In almost every phase of life, this doctrine of political altruists is equally impracticable and pernicious. In its social results, it involves the substitution of the community in the family's present position. In its political aspects, it involves the absolute dominion of the State over the actions and the property of its subjects. Thus, though claiming to be an exaltation of the so-called natural rights of liberty and equality, it is in reality their emphatic debasement. It teaches that thoughtless docility is a recompense for stunted enterprise. It magnifies material good at the cost of every rational endowment. It inculcates a self-denial that must result in dwarfing the individual to a mere instrument in the hands of the State for the benefit of his fellows. No such organization of society—no organizaiton that fails to take note of the fact that man must have scope for the exercise and development of his faculties—no such organization of society can ever reach a permanent success. However beneficent its motives, the hypothesis with which it starts can never be realized. The aphorism of Emerson, "Churches have been built, not upon principles, but upon tropes," is as true in the field of politics as it is in the field of religion. In a like figurative spirit, the followers of communism have reared their edifice; and, looking back upon the finished structure, seeking to discern the base on which it rests, the critic finds, not principles, but tropes. The builders have appealed to laws whose truth they took for granted; they have appealed to a future that has no warrant in the past; and fixing their gaze upon the distant dreamland, captivated by the vision there beheld, entranced by its ideal effulgence, their eyes were blinded to the real conditions of the human problem they had set before them. Their enemies have not been slow to note such weakness and mistake; and perhaps it may serve to clear up misconceptions, perhaps it may serve to lessen cant and open the way for fresh and vigorous thought, if we shall once convince ourselves that altruism *cannot* be the rule of life; that its logical result is the dwarfing of the individual man; and that not by the death of human personality can we hope to banish the evils of our day, and to realize the ideal of all existence, a nobler or a purer life.

PSYCHOLOGY LECTURES*

Selected notes from
Benjamin Nathan Cardozo's undergraduate classbook in the course in Psychology given by Nicholas Murray Butler

(Original is in the *Columbiana Collection* of the Columbia University Library)

LECTURE ON ATTENTION

IN the times of Plato and Aristotle consciousness was regarded as a faculty, and only in later times has it come to be regarded as a state. It can only be described, not defined. To define an object, its proximate genus and its difference must be stated. Any statement, however, that can be made of consciousness implies consciousness. It can therefore be simply described. We may say, for example, that it involves immediate knowledge, and that it implies judgment. Closely connected with the subject of consciousness is the subject of attention which constitutes one of the most important and newest questions in psychology today.

If, fixing your eye upon a distant object, you endeavor to focus your attention, say on a particular brick, and there analyze the resulting state of mind, you will find this particular object clearly before your mind, and you will have also a picture fading off into indistinctness on either side. Only one object, however, occupies the attention. The others do not occupy attention, though they are before consciousness. Attention, then, is simply focalized consciousness—consciousness focused upon one particular object or group of objects. It is a subdivision of consciousness.

The first question to be asked with regard to attention is: "to what may attention be paid? What are its objects?" The answer is, Any mental state whatsoever. Attention may

* *Psychology Lectures.* Reprinted with the permission of Columbia University, the residuary legatee of the literary estate of Benjamin Nathan Cardozo.

be paid to a sensation, emotion, act of will, and so on. When it is so made the subject of attention, it increases not only in its relative, but also in its absolute importance. In connection with attention, there are two sets of accompanying series of phenomena. The first is the physical concomitant of attention. If we endeavor to fix our attention through sight on an object, we are conscious of a strain on the eye; if we endeavor to fix our attention through hearing, the physical concomitant consists often in turning the head in the direction from which the sound is coming The physical concomitant has a curious analogy in the attention paid to some mental fact, not external. In the effort to recall a person's name, we are conscious of a sort of pressure within the head. The reason of this feeling of tension is that the fixing of attention stimulates the brain and increases the amount of blood supplied through it.

The second concomitant of attention is the physiological concomitant. When attention is focused upon a particular act, there is set free from certain motor centres in the brain a nervous disturbance: there is, in other words, a discharge of nerve force by the mind itself in the act of attention.

The amount of attention depends upon two factors. The first is the amount of dispensable energy which we have at our command. If we are in good health, the amount is large; if we are suffering from nervous exhaustion or from pain, it is small. In the second place, the amount of attention varies as the stimulus. If two persons have the same amount of disposable energy, and stimulus A is twice as powerful as stimulus B, A will attract twice as much attention as B.

The earlier stage of attention is non-voluntary. There is no intervention of the will. Non-voluntary attention is paid by young children. If a child has put before it a grey and a red ball of worsted, it will pay attention to the red because the stimulus is greater. In non-voluntary attention, all the stimuli are external, and one object of education is to replace non-voluntary attention by voluntary attention. If attention were altogether non-voluntary, the mind would always turn to the greatest stimulus. Even as matters stand, it is difficult enough to control the attention. Kant, for example, used to fix his eyes on the weather vane of a neighboring church; for the stimulus being small, did not divert his attention; and his mind was left free to carry on abstract thought. When, however, the attention has been controlled, we have the highest accomplishment that education can give.

In training the attention, two things must be borne in mind as desirable. The first is grasp of attention—the power to seize the salient points of a subject and to hold them. It is characteristic of the executive mind. The second requisite is flexibility of attention—an attention which sweeps rapidly from one subject to another. This is, indeed, characteristic of the superficial mind; nevertheless, flexibility should be joined with grasp of mind, to produce the highest type. Otherwise, one's work will lie always along a narrow groove.

There is a further question in connection with our subject: How many things can we attend to at one time? The natural answer would be, one. Sir Wm. Hamilton, however, says that the human mind can grasp six things at one time. Get before your attention a name: keep that before your attention and also put there an act; then recall some memory; add some act of imagination; and so on till you get six in all. Hamilton says that as you add a seventh, the first drops off, and so forth. Probably in point of fact, instead of all being before your mind at once, you have a rapid transition from one to six. This would accord with the principle of natural science, the impenetrability of matter —only one thing can occupy one place at one time. There is one difficulty, however, about this view. Where you make a proposition or statement or judgment, you compare two objects. How can you make the comparison unless both things are before your attention? Memory, it is sometimes said, furnishes one member of the equation. This, however, is only begging the question, because memory brings it at all events before the attention. As long as it comes before the attention, it is indifferent how it gets there. The problem must as yet be regarded as unsettled.

LECTURE ON MENTAL DEVELOPMENT

An interesting subject in psychology is the subject of mental development, the conditions which operate in mental development, and the factors which tend to produce it. At the outset, we must distinguish between growth and development first in the abstract, and then between mental growth and mental development. Growth is increase in size or bulk. Development is increase in complexity or function. The brain grows only up to the seventh or eight year. It develops from birth to death. So with mental phenomena. When the mind grows, it acquires a fact. When it develops, it coordinates that fact with other facts. Four factors operate in constituting mental development. They may be represented by the following diagram:

Mental Development	
Internal Factor	External Factor
1. Fundamental Capacities	1. Social Environment
2. Inherited Tendencies	2. Physical Environment

These four factors operate in every mind. By fundamental capacities are meant our mental powers—the ability to see, hear, move, and so on. This is the least important difference of the four, because it least seldom operates. More important are inherited tendencies. Heredity, indeed, is one of the great facts of the nineteenth century. Physiological heredity, it is true, has long been commonly recognized; psychological heredity is a more complex thing. Heredity simply means that like tends to produce like. It is a biological law coextensive with living beings. It was formerly formulated thus: like produces like; but as thus expressed, it is incorrect. The factors which operate—to prevent like from producing like are the external factors. Like may be seen to tend to produce like in instincts, for example. The power of walking will serve as an instance. This, which is an instinct with some of the lower animals is as perfect with them at birth as in later days. An instinct is sometimes known as an organized intelligence, sometimes as the adaptation of means to end without knowledge of the end. The sensorial qualities apparently are also hereditary. Darwin shows that the Fuegian Indians have extraordinary acute sight. Color blindness is inherited. Heredity would seem to extend also to memory. The Seneca family in Rome, for instance, were noted for their memory; so also in England the family of Richard Porson. The imaginative power is plainly hereditary, as seen, for example, in the Coleridge family. As instances of heredity in executive ability and will power, we have the Adams family in America and the Wordsworth family in England. There are, in all, three forms of heredity: direct heredity, which goes from father to son; atavism or reversional heredity, which skips one generation; and indirect heredity, as in the Coleridge family.

Heredity has been called the conservative force in human progress. Were it not for this force, every generation would have to repeat the process of the preceding. Heredity tends to fix in the race useful adaptations. The radical factor, of course, is Individualism. In illustration of this, Galton points out the difference in character of twins who, of course, are subject to the same internal influence.

In addition to the internal factors, we have the external factors. The effect of physical environment is well known. A nation's character is materially affected by its climate. A prohibition on the eating of animal food, such as is common among Eastern peoples, would be impossible in the religion of a Laplander.

By the fourth factor, social environment, we mean the influences of the society by which the developing mind is surrounded. The importance of this factor is every day becoming more apparent. The result may be seen in the present tenement house movement.

LECTURE ON THE PROCESS OF THE ACQUISITION OF KNOWLEDGE

All the raw materials of knowledge, all facts, all experience, are derived from the senses. We shall now examine sensation with reference to the process of mental development; and before doing this a definition of sensation is desirable. In sensation, there are two mysteries. Take, for example, a sensation of light. We know from physical science that light consists of vibrations of luminiferous ether. Let a series of vibrations fall on the eye; nerve stimulation follows; and the optic nerve sets up a corresponding motion. Now, it is beyond our power to tell why nervous vibrations should result, and in the second place, why this should appear in a sensation of light. In attempting, however, to define sensation, we have to take notice of two schools. One school makes nervous excitation sensation, and make perception consist in change in consciousness and recognition. The other school makes nervous excitation and change in consciousness constitute sensation, and makes perception consist in recognition. . . . The opposing views may be represented by a diagram:

Sensation	Perception	
nervous excitation	*change in consciousness*	*recognition*
Sensation		Perception

The trouble about the first view is this: suppose you strike a note yielding only ten vibrations a second. You will hear nothing. Yet the air will have been agitated, and the vibrations, striking the drum, will have produced a nervous shock. Hence, according to this theory, there must be thousands of sensations which we have never felt. The second doctrine is the more scientific; and hence we may define sensation as that process in the acquisition of knowledge which requires the smallest amount of mental cooperation. By this, we mean simple receptivity. The moment you recognize, the moment you objectify a sensation or refer it to its external cause, you perceive; and in the adult mind, indeed, there is no such thing as sensation without perception.

Sensations differ in degree, quantity, and number; and the question arises, what is the difference between the various mental effects and changes in the external world? That part of psychology which discusses the question of the relation between physical and psychical phenomena, between phenomena of matter and those of mind, is called psychophysics. Certain physical changes, it is observed, will not produce any mental effect, though if increased in number they will produce a mental effect. The limit at which they begin to produce mental effects is not the same for every person, although it is approximately so. This is called the liminal intensity of a sensation; and experiments have been made in order to show what this liminal intensity is. For example, to test the smallest possible sound the ear could hear, a person was blindfolded, a velvet cushion held a short distance from the ear, and a soft object was dropped from a certain height. The average of the results represented the unit for the sensation of sound. Similar experiments have been made in the case of the other senses.

The next question is this: If you increase the physical change, do you correspondingly increase the mental change? In answer, there has been formulated the psychophysical law, known also as Weber's Law or Fechner's Law. The law is as follows: In order that sensation may increase in arithmetical ratio, the physical stimulus must increase in geometrical ratio. . . .

The division into three phases of mental phenomena, knowledge, feeling, and will, is called the tripartite or threefold division, and was introduced into philosophy about 120 years ago by the Germans, Moses Mendelssohn and Tetus, and was taken up by Kant and through him made the generally accepted division. The old division was that of Aristotle, who divided the mental phenomena into the knowing and the acting, the latter including feeling and will. The division of Aristotle is known as the bipartite division, and it is represented in our time by the Scottish school of psychology. Reid, for example, speaks of the intellectual and active powers; Dr. McCosh, of the cognitive and motive powers. The first division, however, is the more usual at the present time. There have, moreover, been two or three schools of thought which have attempted to reduce feeling and will to one. Bain reduces will to feeling, and some German psychologists reduce feeling to will.

In every stimulus, in every sensation, some trace of each of these three elements, knowledge, feeling and will, is present. There is no sensation that does not contribute something, however small, to our knowledge, to our pleasure and pain, and to our future action. An act is distinguished as an act of knowledge, feeling, or will, according to that feature of it which is predominant at the moment.

THE MORAL ELEMENT IN MATTHEW ARNOLD*

A Columbia College essay in manuscript form in the Columbiana Collection of the Columbia University Library

IT will be found true, I think, of the works of every master mind that there is in them some recurring note, some theme, some refrain, that stamps the author's personality upon them, and forms a principle of unity throughout them all. The works of any man must always partake, in large degree, of the spirit of the man himself; and the more pronounced and earnest his views may be, the more the truths he has discerned burden him and press for utterance, the more constantly will they dominate his writings, and the more clearly will his writings reflect the workings of his spirit. And so it seems to me that, in many cases at least, a tendency toward repetition in an author is a token, not of sterility, but of strength. It marks the sincerity, the truth, of his convictions, it shows that his writings stand for thoughts that have become imbedded in his being; and after all only such thoughts that grow and prevail and survive us; and thus we can judge him, if not more favorably, at least with a keener sympathy. It is given, indeed, to but few men to have in reality more than one or two thoughts: the rest that receive the name are in fact mere outgrowths of these central ideas of their being: and we ought hardly to quarrel with those who have the frankness to *show* us these ideas, running through all their works, coloring all their conceptions, and yielding them an infallible test of truth and beauty. That he possessed this degree of frankness is not the least among the merits that an admirer may justly claim for Matthew Arnold. Melodious, clear, often sad, always judicial and calm, his voice was the voice of one who, grasping a few truths of

* *The Moral Element in Matthew Arnold.* Reprinted with the permission of Columbia University, the residuary legatee of the literary estate of Benjamin Nathan Cardozo.

primary importance, held to them steadfastly, and preached and taught and applied them in every walk of life. This feeling of moral weight and earnestness that he inevitably arouses, renders Arnold, to my mind, one of the most suggestive, the most inspiring, the most enlightening, of authors; and these qualities, coupled with a marvellous style, have made of him a power.

The most striking trait, it seems to me, exhibited in Mr. Arnold's works is their intensely moral tone. He was deeply impressed with the need for men of that spirit of piety and justice, without which, as Plato tells us, states cannot endure. He was primarily an ethical writer; and his conception of the importance of conduct—of conduct which, as he himself says, is three-fourths of human life—asserts itself even in his criticisms of poetry and prose. It is very interesting, I think, to observe how in that chaste and suggestive essay of his on the Study of Poetry there is dominant the same high moral note as pervades a work like "Literature and Dogma." "The noble and profound application of ideas to life is," he tells us, "the most essential part of poetic greatness." Poetry is "a criticism of life, a criticism under the conditions fixed by the laws of poetic truth and beauty," and poetry has its value for us because in poetry "the spirit of our race will find, as time goes on and as other helps fail, its consolation and stay." And further in the criticism of life of the very greatest poets, he discerns an element of high truth and seriousness, in which he sees the crowning achievement of the art and the surest test of genius.

Now, the entire conception of poetry, with its emphasis on the ethical side of life, is preeminently a moralist's conception. It may be that it fails to present the whole truth as to what poetry is, but it certainly presents a part of the truth and a very important part. We know indeed, how it has excited Mr. Swinburne's disapprobation; but I venture for my part to think that the substitute Mr. Swinburne offers is at once less complete and less suggestive. Poetry, according to Swinburne if I correctly understand him,—poetry must, above all else, possess imagination and harmony. "Where these qualities," he writes, "are wanting, there can be no poetry properly so-called; and where these qualities are perceptible in the highest degree, there, even though they should be unaccompanied and unsupported by any other great quality whatever—though the ethical or critical faculty should be conspicuous by its absence—there, and there only, is the best and highest poetry."

Now, that imagination, at all events, is an important element in poetic composition, no student of poetry will deny, least of all, I conceive, would Mr. Arnold have denied it. The qualities of intelligence, he has somewhere said, are the distinctive support of prose; the qualities of genius and imagination are the distinctive support of poetry. Imagination is, indeed, a requisite for what Mr. Arnold himself has called the inestimable virtue of concreteness. It is one of those "conditions fixed for the criticism of life by the laws of poetic truth and beauty"; and this is a clause in Mr. Arnold's definition that I fancy, Mr. Swinburne dwelt upon too lightly. But to represent imagination as itself the all sufficient condition, the essence of poetry seems to me emphatically one-sided. Mere imagination is the sport, the revelry, the madness of the brain; it gives us dreams, pictures, phantasms; but it does not give us poetry. Not till the criticism of life has lent meaning, soberness, coherence to the play of the imagination, has toned and subdued it, not till then have we a really poetic creation. In like manner, the importance within just limits of Mr. Swinburne's second principle—the principle of harmony—few critics, it is probable, will dispute; though to many, the stress that Mr. Swinburne lays upon this quality may seem a somewhat undue exaltation of the sensuous, at the expense of the emotional and intellectual qualities of style. Such a conception, moreover, would apparently confine poetry to the verse form; and in so doing, would set up a purely formal rather than an organic criterion. In short, Mr. Swinburne's definition with the added words that I have quoted amounts to little more than a statement that sound is more important than sense, fancy than reason, manner than substance. It is hardly strange that the author of "Chastebard" and of a "Century of Roundels" should have dwelt upon the value of imagination and music; but, it surely is strange that he should have professed his devotion to these qualities to the avowed exclusion of all others. And so I repeat that to me Swinburne's definition seems the more one-sided of the two; and when we say with Arnold that poetry is a criticism of life under the conditions fixed by the laws of poetic truth and beauty—remembering that of these conditions the presence of an imaginative element is one of the chief—when we speak thus, we give, I think, a fairly satisfactory expression of what poetry really is—an expression which, doubtless, each man will amplify to suit himself, but which cannot be made much more definite without losing its breadth of application.

I have said that Mr. Arnold was preeminently an ethical writer; and it becomes of interest to trace the lines of his moral theory. A study of his works is the best possible antidote at once to the prevailing Hedonism of Bentham, Mill and Spencer, and to the opposite extremes of intuitional moralists. Arnold is the philosopher of "perfection," and he allies himself most closely, I think, with Plato among ancient, and with Leibnitz among modern thinkers. Perfection, that is, the full and free development of man's being,—this, if I correctly follow Arnold, is in his eyes the supreme good. "Civilization," he tells us, "is but the humanization of man in society" and man is humanized only when he lives a life in harmony with "his true aspirations and powers." Now, in order to attain this full and free development, we must know the elements of which human life is composed; and Arnold accordingly begins with an analysis of human nature. "I put first," he says, "among the elements in human civilization the instinct of expansion, because it is the basis which man's whole effort to civilize himself presupposes. General civilization presupposes this instinct which is inseparable from human nature; presupposes its being satisfied, not defeated. The basis being given, we may rapidly enumerate the powers which, upon this basis, contribute to build up human civilization. They are the power of conduct, the power of intellect and knowledge, the power of beauty, the power of social life and manners. Expansion, conduct, science, beauty, manners,—here are the conditions of civilization, the claimants which man must satisfy before he can be humanized."

Such, then, are the categories under some one of which Arnold classes every virtue and every aspiration of man. They are to Arnold's philosophy as vital as the Aristotelian categories are to the Organon or the Kantian categories to the Kritik der Reinen Vernunft. And just in proportion as man fails to develop some one of these primary powers of his nature—as his instinct for beauty is stunted, or his craving for knowledge unfed, or his power for conduct unexercised,—by just so much will his humanity be atrophied and dwarfed. In the preface to his Mixed Essays, Mr. Arnold says: "That the requisites for civilization are substantially what have been enumerated, that they all of them hang together, that they must all have their development, that the development of one does not compensate for the failure of others, that one nation suffers by failing in this requisite and another by failing in that; such is the line of thought which the essays in the present volume follow and represent." Looking back through the history of the world and watching the play of forces that have worked out the civilization of today, two forces he discerns of transcendant scope and power, Hellenism and Hebraism, the power of beauty and intelligence and the power of right conduct,—these forces are pulsing and throbbing today, and their symmetrical union means the order of the world.

Of the correctness—substantial at least—of his classification of our powers, Arnold seems never to have entertained even a passing doubt. He followed the lines of his analysis to their furthermost conclusions, and applied his primary categories to fields of thought where they might at first sight have seemed irrelevant. Is it the question of the comparative advantages of monarchy and democracy? He answers that democracy must be preferred, because it gratifies the instinct of expansion. Is it the question of the relative merits of equality and inequality? He answers that inequality must be condemned, because it perverts the popular ideal of social life and manners. Is it again the well-worn question of the relative importance of literature and science? He answers that letters can never lose their place because they gratify an undying need of man, the need in him for beauty. It is this constant dwelling upon an ideal humanity, this constant testing of things by their tendency to promote men's ultimate perfection, that gives so high a moral tone to Arnold's speculations in letters and aesthetics. That culture which he so praises and to gain which is the final aim of education is with him substantially an ethical end. "Culture," he writes, "is a pursuit of our total perfection of getting to know, on all the matters which most concerns us, the best which has been thought and said in the world, and through this turning a stream of fresh and free thoughts upon our stock notions and habits, which we now follow staunchly, but mechanically, vainly imagining that there is a virtue in following them staunchly which makes up for the mischief of following.

The more I read, the more I feel that few things can so democraticize as can literature. To the student of literary history, new kinships are ever revealing themselves: and the genealogies of relatives in thought and spirit follow very different lines from the genealogies of relatives in blood. We are only half awake as yet to the truth that the latter kind of kinship is often well nigh meaningless; and that to the former it is left either to debase or to ennoble. Akin, as they are, in their love of beauty, akin in their reverence for truth, perhaps a sounder heraldry than ours would award a common emblem to Keats, the son of the stable-keeper, and Arnold, the son of the scholar. Certain it is that since Keats announced the gospel of beauty as the end of action, few equally with Arnold, have discerned in the loveliness of things an ethical significance. He never felt a truth, he never reached a doctrine, but he saw in it—to him distinct—the germ of a principle of conduct. One-sided in his view of things he may have been; but on the side he saw, he cast a flood of light that revealed a beauty and a meaning yet unknown.

Now, from the common weakness that seems to pervade every moral system other than the purely intuitional, Arnold's system, doubtless, is not free. It fails to supply any adequate ground for obligation; or, in philosophical language, it fails to identify the "that" of moral duty with the "what". Perhaps the weakness is an organic one to any scientific theory of morality; certainly no empirical theory has ever yet escaped it. But this much may be said for Arnold's system. It is based at least upon an analysis of human nature. It simply seeks to develop what already in latent form exists. And as to no one but the pessimist atrophy can seem to be the rule of life, as the presence of powers implies the duty of their exercise, Arnold perhaps has come nearer than have most thinkers toward bridging the gulf between the knowledge that there is a right and the knowledge of what that right may be. Gaps in his theory there indisputably are. Problems of the deepest moment are left unsolved, indeed untouched: but none the less his works are full of inspiration. "Schools of philosophy," he has himself said, "arise and fall: their bands of adherents inevitably dwindle; no master can long persuade a large body of disciples that they give to themselves just the same account of the world as he does: it is only the very young and the very enthusiastic who can think themselves sure that they possess the whole mind of Plato, or Spinoza, or Hegel, at all. The very mature and the very sober can even hardly believe that these philosophers possessed it themselves enough to put it all into their works, and to let us know entirely how the world seemed to them. What a remarkable philosopher really does for human thought is to throw into circulation a certain number of new and striking ideas and expressions, and to stimulate with them the thought and imagination of his century or of after-times."

Tried by this test, Arnold need hardly have feared for himself the judgment of posterity. Few writers have thrown into circulation a greater number of new and striking ideas and expression,—which have become part and parcel of the vocabulary of the age.

He did not, indeed formulate a definite system of philosophy; and, in fact, he often disclaimed any title to philosophic completeness and consistency. He admitted himself "to be sadly to seek," as one of his critics had said, "in a philosophy with coherent, interdependent, subordinate, and derivative principles." But these systems of philosophy are slow developments. Their roots often reach back to the works of poets, psalmists, dreamers; nor does the influence of schools of thought increase directly with the subtlety of their metaphysics. Most readers will find the Bible a nobler work than the discussions of the schoolmen; and many will see in Arnold a surer guide than in thinkers more exact and more coherent.

The theory of ethics that I conceive Mr. Arnold to have held bears, it will be seen, a superficial resemblance to the well-known theory of Mr. Spencer; but the resemblance is, I think, only superficial. Basing itself on the principle that normal development brings pleasure and abnormal development, pain, Mr. Spencer's philosophy is equivalent really to an identification of perfection and pleasure. To the inadequacy of such a system the entire history of morality is the best witness. There are undoubtedly manifold cases where men are conscious that they are acting abnormally and yet find in this abnormal action the keenest kind of enjoyment—Mr. Spencer seems to have confused the proposition that normal development gives pleasure with the proposition that it gives the highest or the only kind of pleasure. The difficulty springs from an attempt to make pleasure, which is essentially subjective and variable, play the part of an ideal of conduct, which should be essentially, objective and constant. Mr. Spencer's system in last analysis is a pure system of Hedonism.

Now, Mr. Arnold's view of ethics is very different. His ideal, much as Mr. Spencer's, is normal development; but he says nothing, it will be observed, about pleasure or pain. He simply starts with the proposition that it is the duty of men to develop their faculties, avoiding atrophy on the one side and hypertrophy on the other. He does not prove this proposition, he simply assumes it, takes it for granted, makes it his starting point; and having assumed it, he holds that its binding force is quite independent of the degree of pleasure or pain that may accompany its observance. His fundamental proposition is, I take it, substantially identical with that laid down in M. Paul Janett's Theory of Morals—the proposition that every being owes it to himself to attain the highest degree of perfection and excellence of which his nature is capable. Given this proposition, the business of the moralist from that point on is simply to trace the lines along which normal development must proceed, and here Mr. Arnold adopts the five fold categories to which reference already has been made.

It is possibly as a critic that Mr. Arnold is best known; but his criticism, like his culture, took an ethical turn. To know the best that has been thought and said in the world as a means to the expansion of all our powers,—this is culture; but it is criticism's part to distinguish and separate in the first instance what has been *well* from what has been badly said. And thus since criticism is a means to culture, and culture a means to perfection, the critic too may rank among those workers whose efforts are making for the happiness and order of the world.

Such was the conception of the critic's function with which Arnold turned himself to his scrutiny of men and things.

With what rich results he prosecuted his labors, lovers of letters everywhere will tell. It has always seemed to me that the study of the Greeks, of Grecian art and letters, of Grecian life and manners, has been invested with a new poetry and dignity—since Arnold wrote and taught. He stripped from the study that character of a pretty but vain accomplishment which popular estimation had attached to it; he showed that the need and the love for beauty are implanted in the very nature of man; and he brought into clear relief, the spiritual power of that Grecian people to whose ideals of literature and art the world still turns for guidance. "The garners of Sicily," says Mr. Lowell in his eloquent way, "the garners of Sicily are empty now, but the bees from all climes still fetch honey from the tiny garden plot of Theocritus." And Arnold saw and felt this truth. He saw and felt that the humanities gratify something more than the demands of an idle social convention; and that whatever the apostles of positivism and of material progress may declare, there is in spiritual things a virtue that lapse of time cannot efface.

Against the caprices of popular fancy, against the love of glitter and of novelty, he saw the surest safeguard in that old Hellenic ideal of "fit details strictly combined in view of a large general result nobly conceived." That a work of merit of art is a unit, not a conglomerate of epigrams, this was the principle for which he fought; and in proof of it he pointed to the poetry and dramas of the Greeks. For poetry with them was a serious art. It called for a certain forbearance in him who was blessed with a knowledge of its mysteries; and a sort of code of ethics forbade the poet to squander the thoughts that were inspired in him, or to deal with his subject in any other fashion than befitted his divine calling. No ornament for the sake of ornament, no yielding to personal whims and fancies; but a stern, severe remorseless progress onward toward the ideal that lay before him! And Arnold with his intense moral sense, with that feeling of the importance of conduct which transfigured and colored for him every subject to which he turned his mind, caught hold with eagerness of this old Hellenic thought; and viewing poetry as a criticism of life, he sought to make it as stern and severe and remorseless, as free from caprice and as true to law, as human as life itself.

All this he taught with a grace and a vigor that are at once delightful and persuasive. It would be, indeed, an inadequate estimate of Arnold's genius that would fail to take notice of the power of his style. "Style," it has been said by Mr. Motley, "style above all other qualities seems to embalm for posterity." Nothing could be better put than this, and nothing could hit off more precisely just what style really effects. Men care a great deal more about the outward forms of things than they let themselves believe. Most of our so-called noble thoughts have been at bottom pretty prosy and commonplace sentiments. It is the vitalizing power of style that lends them force and loftiness, and imparts a semblance of novelty to notions as old as man himself. Now, a sounder, surer, more even, more placid style than Arnold's there never has been. He handled his sentences tenderly, lovingly, and one almost hears at times a half-suppressed ring of exaltation at the dexterous turning of some balanced period. He had a habit of iteration that, as Mr. Henry James observes, almost degenerated into a mannerism; and he had a curious way, which I can only liken to the form of argument known in logic as a sorites, of catching up the closing words of one sentence and incorporating them into the beginning of the sentence following. He has himself said that the primary requisites of a fit prose are regularity, uniformity, precision, balance; and all these, his own prose possessed in an eminent degree. The keenness of his irony and his wit has been attested in many a controversy; but their thrusts were so delicate and covert that their author never seemed other than bland and unruffled. In short, Arnold's style is such that, as Mr. James happily observes, lovers of literature never tire of him—they read him again and again. I know that as regards myself at least the words of Mr. James are true. I never tire of Arnold, and I read him again and again. I admire him, indeed, so much that I feel the danger of falling into that "personal estimate" of his worth against which he himself warned the critic. His, truly, is the "embalming style," the style that heightens, transforms, illumines, idealizes all it touches, a style that is as rare and unmistakable as it is precious and inspiring.

"The perfect sureness of touch which marks the artist's work was the birthright of his genius. One can fancy him assenting to those words of M. de Maupassant quoted in Mr. Thompson's Philosophy of Fiction: 'Whatever be the thing one wishes to say, there is only one noun to express it, only one verb to give it life, only one adjective to qualify it. Search, then, till that noun, that verb, that adjective, are discovered.' "

But Arnold's prose is not only clear and calm and finished and precise; he can be eloquent too at times with an eloquence that stirs the reader's soul. The closing words of the Essay on Emerson, in which the author calls up before our view the image of the dead sage, have in their simple grandeur seldom been surpassed—"I figure him to my mind," says Arnold, "as visible upon earth still, as still standing here by Boston Bay or at his own Concord in his habit as he lived, but of heightened stature and shining feature, with one hand stretched out toward the East to our laden and labouring England, the other toward the ever growing West to his own dearly loved America, great, intelligent, sensual, avaricious America. To me he shows for guidance his lucid freedom, his cheerfulness and hope, to you his dignity, delicacy, serenity, elevation."

It is to be said, and said to Mr. Arnold's honor, that he never stooped to flattery of his audience. Reversing the phrase that he was fond of applying to Gray, we may say of him that he "always spoke out." His famous arraignment of the English as a nation whose upper class is materialized, whose middle class is vulgarized, whose lower class is brutalized, has passed into the vocabulary of stock quotations. Barbarians, Philistines, Populace are the names with which he christened the luxurious upper class, the narrow middle class, the coarse and animal lower class of English civilization; but the terms stand, indeed, for more than this; they stand for enduring types of human character, for a spirit and a temperament not confined within the limits of the British Isles, and hence they will have meaning and currency forever. Arnold seldom deigned to defend or palliate his frankness; and indeed to a writer of his life and serious nature, such a bent of mind was both natural and necessary. Nations, he held, could gain nothing in dignity by any praise he could bestow; but the faults that he discerned and the remedies that occurred to him, a social duty bound him to divulge. In the preface to his Discourses in America, he says: "I am glad of every opportunity of thanking my American audiences for the unfailing attention and kindness with which they listened to a speaker who did not flatter them, who would have flattered them ill, but who yet felt and in fact expressed more esteem and admiration than his words were sometimes at a hasty first hearing supposed to convey."

And yet, in the main, Arnold suffered less, I think, in popularity from his freedom of expression than might at first have been expected. It is a somewhat curious characteristic of men that often it pleases them to be chided as much as to be praised. One marks the trait less clearly in connection with one's personal, one's individual affairs; but in the broader fields of national policy, of social foibles, of public life, reproof is so vastly more exhilarating than commendation; it is such a spur to controversy and such a stimulant to thought it gives to one class of readers a new sense of the discernment of an author who has detected just those flaws they were themselves preparing to unearth; it fills another class with condescending compassion for one whose arguments they have felt themselves in duty bound to demolish; and thus—such are the ways of this paradoxical world—by scolding, it pleases all. Whether or not Mr. Arnold had taken this principle to heart, it is certain, as I have said, that he was never niggardly in his reproof; and perhaps at times he even pressed his criticisms with a trifle too much keenness and persistence, one might almost say, a trifle too much malice. There was sometimes a tinge of personal invective in his criticisms; and sometimes he assailed the special objects of national pride too directly and too fiercely to escape unscathed by popular indignation. We know what a storm of controversy was aroused by his last essay on Civilization in the United States; and if the truth must be told, this essay is to my mind one of the least satisfactory of Arnold's writings. It is unsatisfactory to my mind, not because its criticisms are unjust, but because its praises, I think, are trivial. It strikes one as a somewhat petty estimate of a great and powerful nation that would apparently single out as the chief national virtue the use of the word Mr. rather than Esquire; and one is tempted to say that Mr. Arnold has shown here too little of that "largeness, freedom, shrewdness, and benignity" which he has himself so admirably extolled.

I have spoken of Mr. Arnold's habit of iteration. It

extended at once to language and to ideas. Few writers have indulged so often in quotations from their own works. Once having said a thing and said it as well as he knew how, he seldom saw fit in his later writings to change the earlier phraseology. His purpose was primarily a serious one; it was, above all else, to stimulate his readers, to instruct them; and, to that end, a certain tendency toward repetition was, doubtless, not without its benefits. "This habit," as an anonymous writer observes, "had at least the effect of fixing in the mind his phrases, and therefore the thoughts or ideas which the phrases conveyed, and with which for the moment he was concerned." He had his hobbies, as indeed most authors have, which he was perpetually bringing to the front. Among these was the reforming of the English public schools—an operation in which he appeared to see a cure for nearly every distemper of the social body. But, notwithstanding this tendency to repetition, his ideas are usually so sound and fresh and suggestive, and his language so clear and strong, that the admiring reader can only say in the words of one of his own quotations from the Greek: "Let us have fine things two and three times over."

And yet in spite of the preciousness of Arnold's teachings, in spite of what we must all recognize as his title to an imperishable fame, we are left, I think, filled with a vague conviction that the man himself was not all that we might have wished. There was in him at times a lack of the sternness, the vigorous, the manly, a lack of sympathy with energy as energy, a certain primness and precision and daintiness that almost reached the point of affectation. Arnold spent his life in decrying the Puritans; but there was more of the Puritan in him than he knew. He had the Puritan stiffness, the Puritan insistence on form and he walked through life with a supercilious condescension. His admirers will prefer, I think, to remember him by his books alone without tracing in them the lines of their author's character. No one will think of Arnold as Emerson is thought of, or Newman, or even Carlyle with his strong and rugged manliness. Arnold's personality is a forcible reminder of how narrow is the line between culture and foppishness, between a "sweet mild reasonableness" and a sort of effeminate sentimentalism.

But I cannot let this essay close with words other than praise. The world, his own monstrous, dead, unprofitable world, ignores his voice, as it has ignored many of the strongest and sweetest voices that ever sounded in men's ears. Perhaps the time has not yet come when the average mind can compass its full melody, or grasp to the full the meaning it conveyed. Arnold had himself perceived that his doctrines were not for today and that he and such as he must look to the future for their time of triumph. "Docile echoes of the eternal voice, pliant organs of the infinite will, such men," in his own words, "are working along with the essential movement of the world, and this is their strength and their happy and divine fortune." We ought all to love and admire Arnold for his sincerity, for his earnestness, for his scorn of low ideals, for his love of a life in the spirit. In the stress and hurry of our business life, I can fancy no more ennobling and inspiring image than he has held before us. All the petty animosities, all the mean struggles, all the shams and affectations and trivialities of life—all these he ridiculed and scorned; but a concord of mind and body, a happy coordination of all the elements of our nature, a culture that like the Platonic virtue is the peace and harmony of the soul, such are the ends—the all-absorbing ends—for which alone the wise man is to labor, to contend, and to achieve." We all remember the Miltonic prayer: "What is dark in me illumine, what is low raise and support." I find in these words the tone and the drift of Arnold's whole philosophy, light and elevation,—they are Arnold's own favorite terms, and they represent to him the all engrossing needs of men. With the mass of his compatriots in England pointing to very different ideals, with Huxley and Spencer and Frederic Harrison and John Bright extolling the practical and measuring nations by their crops, Arnold never faltered in his convictions that, as moral causes govern the standing and the falling of states, man needs, if he would run, a clear vision and a lofty soul. With a curious persistence Arnold presses that point in every volume of his writings; it is as clear in the essay upon Emerson as it is in the essay upon Numbers, in season and out of season, he recurs to it, unexpectedly at times, as if fearful of his doctrines being forgotten or their importance underrated. He spoke, it has been said, as a preacher speaks, and perhaps, one may add, with a trifle of priestly dogmatism and self-confidence. He felt that he had grasped an imperishable truth, and he let it color all his speculations, whether in philosophy, in politics, or in letters.

More and more as man is humanized, more and more in the fulness of time, will that truth which Arnold so clearly saw and to which he so firmly held, grow and advance and triumph. I cannot doubt that criticism will show, if it has not already shown, much of his philosophy to be false and much of his theology fantastic. I hope at least that from many of the faults that in his lifetime he denounced, later generations will be free. But, I am sure that it will be many a day before we shall cease to need his lesson of a clear vision and a lofty soul, and many will be the day before we shall find a teacher so just and wise and truthful to install it. (I cannot but believe that he chose the noble part when, scorning to flatter or to please, he stood forward with warning finger, with prophetic voice, serene, undaunted, resolute, to preach the truth as he discerned it.) I for one, am impatient when I hear it urged against him that his message was not new. It is a shallow estimate that would guage the greatness of men solely by the novelty of the truths they may proclaim. The world owes its homage, not only to those upon whom dawns the vision of a new truth, but also, to those more silent workers that bringing forward an old timeworn principle, long lazily and carelessly acknowledged by the multitude, breathe into it a new life and a power, for the future, to warn, to arouse, and to inspire. That, indeed, is the prerogative of genius; that is its magic and its spell—to make the old new, and the new old, and to lead us where it will, and never to reveal to us that the divine path we are treading is the path we had been following before. Like some devotee of old, we find, when the dream is over, that the glory which filled the temple, though real enough to our own mind, is called by the world illusion. And Arnold saw and felt this truth; if genius and all else that we have been taught to honor are but the shows and fantasies of things, he saw and felt, that, as Mr. Mallock has said: "The dream will continue when the reality has passed away. It is a hard truth to many of us, that the realities are often the illusions, and the illusions are in fact the realities. What wonder then that bearing such a message, Arnold exerted but little present influence on the England of his day! What wonder then that the world, his own monstrous, dead, unprofitable world, ignores his voice, as it has ignored many of the strongest and sweetest voices that ever sounded in men's ears. Arnold had himself perceived that his doctrines were not for today, and that he and such as he must look to the future for their time of triumph." "Docile echoes of the eternal voice, pliant organs of infinite will, such men," in his own words, "are working along with the essential movement of the world and this is their strength and their happy and divine fortune."

BENJAMIN NATHAN CARDOZO

MR. JUSTICE HOLMES*

How can I praise thee, and not overpraise,
And yet not mar the grace by stint thereof?

(Euripides, "Iphigenia at Aulis,"
translated by Arthur S. Way)

TO the lips of eager youth comes at times the halting doubt whether law in its study and its profession can fill the need for what is highest in the yearnings of the human spirit. Thus challenged, I do not argue. I point the challenger to Holmes. In those hours of discouragement to which not even experience is a stranger, I feel at moments the same doubt, paralyzing effort with its whispers of futility. The distrust is shamed and silenced by the vision of a great example.

Historian he is and scholar, a master of the learning of the law and of its traditional technique. High praise this would be for many. One almost feels the need of an apology in saying it of him, in saying it of one who is famed for so much else. There are things one takes for granted in those who stand upon the heights. The learning proper to his calling is visible at every turn, in his slightest work as in his greatest, yet a learning that knows its place, a learning subdued and harnessed to the service of philosophy. He may be groping for things vanished. He gives us glimpses of the things eternal. There are rifts in the common air that reveal an æther more luminous in the unmeasured depths beyond. Little side-remarks and comments, falling from his lips incidentally and casually, thrown off by the way in the discussion of a larger theme, have in them stuff sufficient for a treatise or a library. Who else has been able to pack a whole philosophy of legal method into a fragment of a paragraph, as in those reverberating sentences on the opening page of his lectures on the Common Law, written in comparative youth a half century ago? One cannot renounce the joy of

* *Mr. Justice Holmes.* Reprinted with the permission of the Harvard Law Review and Columbia University, the residuary legatee of the literary estate of Benjamin Nathan Cardozo.
Harvard Law Review 44:682–92 (1931).

quoting them, familiar though they are. "The life of the law has not been logic; it has been experience. The felt necessities of the time, the prevalent moral and political theories, intuitions of public policy avowed or unconscious, even the prejudices which judges share with their fellow-men, have had a good deal more to do than the syllogism in determining the rules by which men should be governed. The law embodies the story of a nation's development through many centuries, and it cannot be dealt with as if it contained only the axioms and corollaries of a book of mathematics." The student of juristic method, bewildered in a maze of precedents, feels the thrill of a new apocalypse in the flash of this revealing insight. Here is the text to be unfolded. All that is to come will be development and commentary.

Flashes there are like this in his earlier manner as in his latest, yet the flashes grow more frequent, the thunder peals more resonant, with the movement of the years. At the outset he was more preoccupied with learning as a present end. One sees the marks of the preoccupation in the lectures on the Common Law; one sees it in other essays, the studies of early English equity, and of the law of executors and agents, and in many of the opinions written while he was still a judge in Massachusetts. This does not mean, indeed, that in seeking the present end he was forgetful, even at the beginning, of the relation of that end to others more nearly ultimate in value. History for him at all times has been something more than archæology. He has relished the study of the past for its own interest and savor, but even more for its capacity to give coherence and significance to the study of the present. He has gone down into the depths, but he has remembered that the depths are the foundations of the heights. Yet withal, a change of emphasis has declared itself with the passing of the years. As time goes on, he is less content than of old with adherence to a method whereby research into the recesses of the past holds the centre of the stage in the unfolding through the ages of the endless drama of the law. Perhaps this is merely because he has explored the depths already and wrung from their recesses whatever secrets they can tell. One seems to read in him at all events the tokens of a growing sympathy with the present and the future when their voices are heard decrying all this deference for things departed, are heard pleading with some petulance their own capacity and privilege to hold the centre of the stage themselves. "It is revolting," he responds, "to have no better reason for a rule of law than that it was laid down in the time of Henry IV. It is still more revolting if the grounds upon which it was laid down have vanished long since, and the rule simply persists from blind imitation of the past." "For the rational study of the law the black-letter man may be the man of the present, but the man of the future is the man of statistics and the master of economics." This in 1897, eleven years before the coming of Muller v. Oregon. In professing the new ardor, he can still be loyal to the old love. "I have done some black-letter reading of my own," he tells us in one of his addresses, though I quote him from uncertain and perhaps imperfect recollection. One detects a lingering note of tenderness, a note half-way between pride and elegiac reminiscence.

As historian and mere technician his place would be secure in any survey of the legal scene. But he has come in these later years to fill another place also, and that still more august. He is today for all students of the law and for all students of human society the philosopher and the seer, the greatest of our age in the domain of jurisprudence, and one of the greatest of the ages. So deeply infused is his philosophy into the texture of his creative work that to separate it from its setting, to make explicit what is implicit everywhere, is not an easy task, not easy because the light seems to lose a little of its mellow radiance when extracted and diverted into a concentrated ray. What is law? What is its origin? What are its capacities and its limits? What its ends and aims, the purpose of its being? In this complex modern world of ours, questions such as these are at the root of many a legal problem which to the thought of a simpler age could have been solved by a mere comparison of precedents without summoning divine philosophy. Our philosopher has known better. Zones, of course, there are where precedents are so controlling that choice is predetermined. These are the trodden highways, builded by the centuries, builded as long ago at times as the roads of ancient Rome. But highways are not everywhere. Once turn into the fields and you will hardly stir a step in the solution of a novel problem, in particular a problem in the domain of public law, without finding yourself face to face with queries that are ultimate.

Is a legal concept a finality, or only a pragmatic tool? Shall we think of liberty as a constant, or, better, as a variable that may shift from age to age? Is its content given us by deduction from unalterable premises, or by a toilsome process of induction from circumstances of time and place? Shall we say that restraints and experiments will be permitted if all that is affected is the liberty to act, when experiment or restraint will be forbidden if the result is an encroachment upon liberty of thought or speech? In the development of a system of case-law is logic one organon among many, or an umpire that displaces rivals? Are the origins of a precept subordinate to its ends, or are ends to be sacrificed if to adhere to them is to be unfaithful to beginnings?

I do not dare to say how Holmes would make answer to these queries or others like to them in spirit. All that I can say with certitude is that such queries are slumbering within many a common law-suit, which can be lifted from meanness up to dignity if the great judge is by to see what is within. I may think that I am able, however dumbly or intuitively, to divine the tenor of his answers, but safer it will be by the touchstones of a few examples to let him answer for himself. The examples that I choose are part of the common coinage of juristic thought, a little worn, some of them, in passing constantly from hand to hand, but recognized as legal tender wherever truth is sovereign.

"The Fourteenth Amendment does not enact Mr. Herbert Spencer's Social Statics." "While the courts must exercise a judgment of their own, it by no means is true that every law is void which may seem to the judges who pass upon it, excessive, unsuited to its ostensible end, or based upon conceptions of morality with which they disagree. Considerable latitude must be allowed for difference of view as well as for possible peculiar conditions which this court can know but imperfectly, if at all. Otherwise a constitution, instead of embodying only relatively fundamental rules of right, as generally understood by all English-speaking communities, would become the partisan of a particular set of ethical or economical opinions, which by no means are held *semper ubique et ab omnibus*." "When men have realized that time has upset many fighting faiths, they may come to believe even more than they believe the very foundations of their own conduct that the ultimate good desired is better reached by free trade in ideas—that the best test of truth is the power of the thought to get itself accepted in the competition of the market, and that truth is the only ground upon which their wishes safely can be carried out. That at any rate is the theory of our Constitution. It is an experiment as all life is an experiment." "When a legal distinction is determined, as no one doubts that it may be, between night and day, childhood and maturity, or any other extremes, a point has to be fixed or a line has to be drawn, or gradually picked out by successive decisions, to mark where the change takes place. Looked at by itself without regard to the necessity behind it, the line or point seems arbitrary. It might as well or might nearly as well be a little more to the one side or the other. But when it is seen that a line or point there must be, and that there is no mathematical or logical way of fixing it precisely, the decision of the legislature must be accepted unless we can say that it is very wide of any reasonable mark." "In the organic relations of modern society it may sometimes be hard to draw the line that is supposed to limit the authority of the legislature to exercise or delegate the power of eminent domain. But to gather the streams from waste and to draw from them energy, labor without brains, and so to save mankind from toil that it can be spared, is to supply what, next to intellect, is the very foundation of all our achievements and all our welfare. If that purpose be not public, we should be at a loss to say what is."

There is a famous passage in the essay on the Study of Poetry where Matthew Arnold tells us how to separate the gold from the alloy in the coinage of the poets by the test of a few lines which we are to carry in our thoughts. The lines that I have quoted from a few opinions among many may do the like for those who would know the philosophic mind in law. How he views as from a peak the horizon of the lives of men, the whole scene of their activities with all its regions and its divisions, whether of nature or of art! There is the keenness of perception that marks the little barriers between one region and another, but along with this there is the humor, the charity, the sense of historic values, that recalls with plangent iteration how many another barrier, as lofty and intimidating, has been leveled to the dust. "I have labored carefully," says Spinoza in that famous statement of his outlook upon life which time and repetition are without capacity to mar, "I have labored carefully not to mock, lament and execrate the actions of men; I have labored to understand them." An echo of that cadence is sounding in our day and land.

Men speak of him as a great Liberal, a lover of Freedom and its apostle. All this in truth he is, yet in his devotion to Freedom he has not been willing to make himself the slave of a mere slogan. No one has labored more incessantly to demonstrate the truth that rights are never absolute, though they are ever struggling and tending to declare themselves as such. "There is nothing that I more deprecate than the use of the Fourteenth Amendment beyond the absolute compulsion of its words to prevent the making of social experiments that an important part of the community desires, in the insulated chambers afforded by the several states, even though the experiment may seem futile or even noxious to me and to those whose judgment I most respect." He has known how to distinguish between one freedom and another. He has vividly perceived what was pointed out by de Tocqueville a century ago that one kind of liberty may cancel and destroy another, and that stronger even that the love of liberty is the passion for something different, different in name and yet at its core the same, the passion for equality. Restrictions, vexatious if viewed alone, may "be seen to be necessary in the long run to establish the equality of position" in which true liberty begins. Many an appeal to freedom is the masquerade of privilege or inequality seeking to intrench itself behind the catchword of a principle. There must be give and take at many points, allowance must be made for the play of the machine, or in the clash of jarring rivalries the pretending absolutes will destroy themselves and ordered freedom too. Only in one field is compromise to be excluded, or kept within the narrowest limits. There shall be no compromise of the freedom to think one's thoughts and speak them, except at those extreme borders where thought merges into action. There is to be no compromise here, for thought freely communicated, if I may borrow my own words, is the indispensable condition of intelligent experimentation, the one test of its validity. There is no freedom without choice, and there is no choice without knowledge—or none that is not illusory. Here are goods to be conserved, however great the seeming sacrifice. We may not squander the thought that will be the inheritance of the ages.

No one has been able to combat more effectively than he the repression of a formula, the tyranny of tags and tickets. Is it a question of the competence of a legislature to respond by novel legislation to the call of an emergent need? Fettered by the word, we are too often satisfied to say that competence exists if it can be brought within a cliché, "the police power" of the state; and at home in the protective phrase, we settle back at peace. Is it a question of the quality of the need, the pressure of the emergency, that will bring the power into play? We say the need must have relation to an activity "affected with a public interest"; and again at home in the protective phrase, we are happy in the thought that while we keep within that shelter there can come no damage to the state. The familiar form beguiles into an assurance of security. Danger as well as deception may indeed be lurking ill-concealed, danger as well as deception in a false appearance of exactitude. The threat is too remote to jolt us out of the deeply-cloven ruts. In the end we may find we have been sinking a little deeper than we willed. For a cliché is not a barrier to power intent upon its aims, though sluggishness of thought may lead us for a season to act as if it were. A label is not a dyke or dam that will repel the onset of the flood—the rush of an emergent need—though it may breed a sense of safety till the flood has swept beyond. All this the great master has been quick to see. He has seen it when, paternally indulgent, he has been willing for the hour to let the cramping phrases pass, to let them pass with a word of warning that the need may yet arrive to throw them over or expand them, to pull out of the rut at whatever cost of pain and effort. The repetition of a catchword can hold analysis in fetters for fifty years or more.

There are other marks of greatness that even the briefest survey will be reluctant to ignore. In our homage to the philosopher we must pause to pay homage to the literary craftsman. "I am studying law," writes the youthful James Russell Lowell in a letter to a comrade, "and shall probably become Chief Justice of the United States." Unfortunately for the law, and perhaps also for the Chief Justiceship, he was enticed into the paths of literature, though every now and then one will find in his essays the phrases and allusions that bespeak the training of the lawyer. The professions look with jealous eyes upon genius and scholarship kidnapped and converted. "I wish," says Leslie Stephen, "that Disraeli could have stuck to his novels instead of rising to be Prime Minister of England." One does not need, when one thinks of Holmes, to lament the decline or the rise—according to one's point of view—of a great writer into a jurist. One does not need to lament, for here is one who has known how to combine the two callings, and to combine them to the glory of each. Law in his hands has been philosophy, but it has been literature too. If any one has ever been sceptical of the transfiguring power of style, let him look to these opinions. They will put scepticism to flight. How compact they are, a sentence where most of us would use a paragraph, a paragraph for a page! What a tang in their pointed phrases; what serenity in their placid depths; what a glow and a gleam when they become radiant with heat! One almost writhes in despair at the futility, too painfully apparent, of imitation or approach. These qualities of style are visible, of course, when he has spoken in great causes. What interests me as much is to find them as clearly visible in causes less pretentious, causes that to an art less consistent or fastidious might have seemed trivial and humble. He has known that greatness in such matters can be independent of the stakes. "Great cases," he tells us, "are called great not by reason of their real importance in shaping the law of the future, but because of some accident of immediate overwhelming interest which appeals to the feelings and distorts the judgment." Many a time, in turning the pages of an opinion devoted to a humdrum theme, some problem perhaps of contract or of negligence, I have come across a winged sentence that seemed with its wings to chase obscurity away. Curious, I have gone back to the beginning, to find the name of Holmes.

There is a fine conscience in such matters, a conscience that is scornful, even in trifles, of work lower than one's best. Not even the draftsman of an ordinary lease, we are reminded by Sir Frederick Pollock, can produce really good work "unless he has a share of artistic feeling in the eminent sense, and takes a certain artistic pride in the quality of his workmanship, apart from the reward he will get for it." More recently Dr. Whitehead has been preaching the same lesson. "Style," he says, "is the ultimate morality of mind." "The administrator with a sense of style hates waste; the engineer with a sense of style economizes his material; the artisan with a sense of style prefers good work"; to which we may add that the judge with a sense of style will balk at inaccurate and slipshod thought. Style is thus a form of honor and courage, just as, Santayana tells us, is the pursuit of truth always. One cannot read these opinions without seeing honor and courage written down on every page.

The calendar tells us he is old as longevity is reckoned by the generations that wither like the grass. So, I suppose, he is, for the volume following this introduction has been planned to be a tribute of devotion at the end of ninety years. One speaks a commonplace, however, when one says that his spirit is still young. Perhaps we may find in his own words the key to the mystery, or at least the keynote of his thought. "One of my favorite paradoxes," he writes in a letter to a friend, "is that everything is dead in twenty-five (or fifty) years. The author no longer says to you what he meant to say. If he is original, his new truths have been developed and become familiar in improved form—his errors exploded. If he is not a philosopher but an artist, the emotional emphasis has changed." There is little danger that a mind impressed so deeply with a sense of the transient and ephemeral in the achievements of the human spirit, will lose the spring of its fine coils with the rust of the corroding years.

Reading these pages over, I am haunted by the fear that I may have given an impression of aloofness, of a being less or more than human. Those of us who know him can bear devoted witness that the impression, if given, would be woefully at odds with truth. A majestic intellect is there, as any one would know after the privilege of the barest glimpse. Wit there is too, and eager interest, and nimbleness of thought and fancy. But there are many things besides. Serenity is there, and gentleness, and most of all benignancy —the benignancy of a soul that has fashioned its own scale of values, and in those deeply-graven markings has found the quietude of peace. Not even benignancy, however, sums up the tale of the impression. A pervasive sense one has of something not to be defined, a quality which, for lack of a better term, one may speak of as simplicity. I do not mean that he is without the pride of mind inseparable from gifts so rare. No one favored so superbly by the gods and the muses could be lacking altogether in a sense of his own powers. The knowledge has not saved him from something like a shy distrust, a questioning and a doubting, as if he felt the need to reassure himself that in looking into his own soul he was viewing something more than the gleam of a mirage. Sceptic of many things, of many boasted certainties, he is sceptic even of himself.

Among my hoarded treasures is a letter from his hand. He has given me his consent to quote from it. "I always have thought," he writes, "that not place or power or popularity makes the success that one desires, but the trembling hope that one has come near to an ideal. The only ground that warrants a man for thinking that he is not living the fool's paradise if he ventures such a hope is the voice of a few masters. . . . I feel it so much that I don't want to talk about it." This from the great overlord of the law and its philosophy.

One does not know where to match the thought in its perfection and engaging modesty unless in the "trembling hope" of another worshipper of truth and beauty. The wistful words of Keats re-echo through the spaces of a century. "I think I shall be among the English poets after my death."

There was no "fool's paradise" for Keats, nor will there be for Holmes.

OUR LADY OF THE COMMON LAW*

In respectful memory of Justice Benjamin N. Cardozo, jurist, philosopher, humanitarian and man of letters, we republish his inspiring address to our first graduating class in 1928. No words can honor him so adequately as his own. No eulogy can proclaim his position among the immortals so eloquently and so convincingly as his tribute to our Lady of the Common Law. As words of wisdom are eternal so in like manner is the memory of their gifted author.

OUR Lady of the Common Law has indeed no lack of wooers.

Three years ago the word went forth that there was to be opened a new shrine to be devoted to her cult. She would not show her face to any who failed to prove their worth. She would not be won by amorous glances or soulful prayers or threats or sighs or groans. Comely looks would be lost upon her, and so would riches and birth and all the accidents of fortune. Nothing would avail except service in her cause, service not for a day or a month, but for three long years of vigil and devotion. Behold a marvel happened! Hardly had the word gone forth before a band of worshippers had gathered. They were eight hundred strong the first year. With each succeeding year, the volume swelled. Now the triennial term has ended; and here in this hall, the faithful have been brought together to claim the guerdon of their toil, the privilege of enrollment among our Lady's well beloved, the servants of her law.

I speak of it as a service not ended, but persisting. If you have fancied it was ended, you have been a victim of the Lady's wiles. Like other flirts and beauties, she can speak with a double meaning, and is not above playing a sly trick on those whose sighs and service are offered at her feet. I

---

* *Our Lady of the Common Law.* Reprinted with the permission of St. John's University Law Review and Columbia University, the residuary legatee of the literary estate of Benjamin Nathan Cardozo.
St. John's Law Review 13:231-241 (1939).

give you warning now lest you become dupes of her caprice. Do not think for a moment that the three years of devotion that have been given for the bare and meagre privilege of being numbered on her roll,—do not think that these exhaust the measure of your sacrifice. What has been endured is merely a novitiate, a term of test and trial, a period of probation in which slackers may fall aside, and the strong and brave and earnest be left within the ranks. The truth is that our Lady is growing more exacting with the years. When I was placed upon her roll these many years ago, she was content with very little. The barest rudiments of law sufficed to give to the acolyte of those days the privilege to kiss the hem of her flowing and unspotted robe. But it is otherwise in this year of grace. Our Lady of the Common Law—I say it with the humility that is due from an old and faithful servant—our Lady in these days is no longer an easy one to please. She has become insatiate in her demands. Not law alone, but almost every branch of human knowledge, has been brought within her ken, and so within the range of sacrifice exacted of her votaries. Those who would earn her best rewards must make their knowledge as deep as the science and as broad and universal as the culture of their day. She will not be satisfied with less.

I was reading the other day a very interesting document, the report for the academic year of 1926–27 made to the Overseers of Harvard University by the President of the University, Dr. A. Lawrence Lowell. He speaks of a new educational concept, the concept, as he calls it, of the continuity of knowledge. The idea is taking root that the subdivisions of education like those of time itself have been treated too often as absolute and genuine,—that there is need to recognize them more fully as mere figments of the brain, mere labor-saving devices, helps to thinking, but, like other helps to thinking, misleading if their origin is neglected or forgotten. Thus it is that the physicist is learning from the chemist, the zoologist from the botanist, the economist from the statesman and the student of social science, the physician from the psychologist, and so on interchangeably and indefinitely. "The sharp severance," we are told, "is giving way, and we perceive that all subjects pass imperceptibly into others previously distinct." Something of this same concept of the continuity of knowledge is making its way into the law. In my own court at a recent session, we had one case where a wise decision called for the wisdom of a chemist; another for that of one skilled in the science of mechanics; another for that of the student of biology and medicine, and so on through the list. I do not say we were able to supply this fund of wisdom out of the resources of our knowledge, yet, in theory at least, the litigants before us were entitled to expect it, and our efficiency as judges would be so much the greater, the quality of the output so much the sounder and richer, in proportion to our ability to make the theory one with fact. Of course, complete knowledge of the body of organized learning is an unrealized achievement. So vain an aspiration is not to fret our waking hours. We cannot sound the depths; there will be strain enough upon our energies if we do so much as skim the surface. Even to do this, however, there is need for an equipment of learning fuller by far and richer than any that was exacted of the bar of simpler days. Few of us can hope to solve for ourselves the problems that perplex the historian or the economist or the physician or the chemist. We shall have to look to the expert for a definitive answer to the queries that are proper to his chosen field. The point is, however, that without a full and rich background of knowledge and culture in fields foreign to the law itself, we shall never reach the perception of the problems to be solved. We shall never see it in its true relation to the lives of those about us, and missing its relation to life, we shall miss its relation to the law, which is to give the rule of life. One must know the method of approach if one would hope to gain the goal. The concept of the continuity of knowledge is teaching us day by day the need for an enriched equipment, and is pointing the path to be followed by the lawyer of tomorrow.

Let me not seem to stress the element of knowledge to the exclusion of all else. Knowledge is indeed an important part of our equipment, yet knowledge is not the whole. At an hour like this, the fitting thing perhaps is to lay the weight of emphasis on other strains and elements that unite to form the blend. I was told when I was asked to talk to you today that this was to be a sort of uplift meeting to bring home to us all, and, in particular to the fledglings of the bar,—to bring home in a vivid way the dignity and glory of the profession of the law, its capacities realized and unrealized for service to mankind. I gathered that somehow or other it was my duty to talk at such a time, however great my dread of speeches, and my resistance was broken down by the covert suggestion that if I failed to talk today—however silent I might be through the other days of the year—if I failed to talk today, I should be recusant to the great trust that has been laid upon me as the titular chief—though chief in no other way—of the judicial system of the state.

So I come before you here charged with a duty to rehearse the ancient platitudes. I do not mean by that epithet to cheapen or deride them. We are wont to call things platitudes when we know them to be truths, but have a disagreeable sense that we have failed to live up to them altogether in the conduct of our lives. Perhaps it will be easier, if only we call them platitudes, to silence or forget them. We have a nameless feeling of irritation and discomfort, as if there were a challenge to our virtue, when they are ding-donged in our ears with provocative iteration. Not for me today are these hesitations and misgivings. Today I am commissioned to be as stale and unoriginal as I please, and to count the yawns of my audience as proof of duty done.

So, of course, they often are. The bores of the hour have often been the heroes of the future. Socrates was voted by the Athenians to be a horrid old bore who deserved nothing better than his hemlock. He has been rewarded for his boredom by an immortality which even we may miss. Boswell was a bore who was snubbed for his pains by the man he was exalting. He has had his reward in winning immortality for himself and incidentally perhaps for the snubber too. I suppose judges, or nearly all of them, are bores. Outside of the pages of Judge Holmes, who is in a class by himself, I am not aware that men resort to the opinions of the courts as a spiritual elixir in hours of depression. So I console myself with the thought that if I preach sterile truths, I shall be playing true to form.

I suppose the traditional thing to say to the young men of the bar with the future yet before them is that what counts above all else is character. That is a tiresome thing to say because it has been said so often, and I wouldn't say it now if I hadn't received a license to make myself a bore. With this license afforded to me, I feel I must say it because it happens to be true. Character includes many things, industry and fidelity as well as conscience and honor. At the one end of the scale are the Poor Richard maxims of frugality and diligence and at the other the sacrifice and devotion and idealism of saints and heroes. Those who fancy that success comes by chance might learn something from the life of Lord Cairns, who became Lord Chancellor of England, and one of the most famous of English judges. His biographer records the fact that when Cairns was called to the bar, he set himself to practice with all his solemn earnestness. "No reason or excuse did he allow himself to leave the precincts of the law while a barrister might be expected to remain there." It was this circumstance, we are told, that gave him an early start. Let the week-end golfers of our day take heed! "He had declined an invitation for a Saturday, though he had no work to do, and was sitting in his chambers close on four in the afternoon when the unexpected happened. An eminent advocate, Mr. Gregory of Bedford Row, had a sudden occasion to consult counsel. He tried many chambers only to find them closed. "At last," says the biographer, "he came to the address where Cairns was keeping his lonely vigil and found, not merely a barrister, but the barrister for whom solicitors are looking—a young man of ripe learning and sound judgment. From that day Mr. Gregory's firm were constant clients." Here is a good instance of the rewards that come to the faithful and steady practice of those qualities of sobriety and diligence which I placed at the lower end of the scale of virtues appropriate to beginners at the bar. But there are shining instances too of rewards, more splendid even and enduring, that attend the practice of other virtues, the virtues at the upper end of this great chromatic scale. Think of the glory that is still shed upon our judicial history by the example of Lord Mansfield, and the fame of his unyielding honor. I like to retell the tale, so often told before, of his conduct during the anti-papist riots of 1780. The mob, instigated by Lord George Gordon, destroyed his house, looted its contents, and ruined his law library, the law books which he had annotated with jealous care. Such was his reputation for judicial impartiality that the leader of the mob elected to be tried before him, and not before some other judge. When it was over, there was no challenge, even from the prisoner, of the fairness of the trial. Character had triumphed over prejudice and passion.

I take comfort in memories like these when I am told, as I often am, that lawyers and judges are brakes, and old-fashioned ones at that upon the forward movement of the race. I was reading not long ago,—it happened to be New Year's Eve, when I was preparing the usual stock of resolutions for the future—I was reading an indictment of the legal mind in the days of Voltaire, which expanded itself into one of the legal mind generally. "Reverence," said the author, "for precedent, attachment to the letter of the law, the effort to bend changed ways of life to obsolete statutes, habits of chop-logic, pedantry and cynicism masquerading as austerity, habitual distrust of human nature and of generous impulses, professional vanity, all these render members of the legal profession liable to fanatical reaction, to frigid cruelty, to oppressive injustice in an often honest passion for social order."

This was salutary reading for New Year's Eve, if a penitential state of mind might be expected to yield a fair crop of goodly resolutions for the year about to start. Sobering as the indictment was, I found another book more chastening, more provocative of thought and introspection and humility. You will find a series of essays, gathered together under the title Historical Trials, the work of the late Sir John MacDonnell, who in his life was King's Remembrancer and senior Master of the Supreme Court of Judicature. His theme is one that is never stale, the correspondence between law and justice, the extent to which courts do in very truth fulfill the function of their being, and this not in fair weather, but in foul, in times of stress and strain, when the legal mechanism should hold good against passion and prejudice and cruelty, and show what it can do. I admit that the record is not a soil for smooth and joyous gratulation. It is a challenge to one and all of us. Remember, if you please, that the author is no muckraker, but a skilled and scholarly lawyer, and himself a cog in the law machine of a progressive and enlightened country. Here gathered together in a slender volume are the trials of Socrates, the Knights Templars, Jeanne d'Arc, Giordano Bruno, Mary Queen of Scots, Galileo, Servetus, Katharine of Aragon, Sir Walter Raleigh, the witchcraft trials and others. "A trial," says our author, "a trial is in substance a struggle, a battle in a closed arena. It is a shock of contending forces, a contest which may arouse the fiercest passions. The issues involved in the trial, say of Socrates, of Jeanne d'Arc, of Bruno, or Calas, or Dreyfus, are among the deepest and greatest known to humanity. I would not, even if I could, deal with them. They are above my task. They are for the philosopher, the historian, the moralist. I approach these trials," he continues, "solely as a lawyer examining the documents as a lawyer; trying to find answers to questions which a lawyer must put, necessarily passing over many of the greatest aspects of such trials, but also perhaps adverting to some apt to be ignored. I want to look at these cases just as if they were about to come into court, or had just been decided; to view them as legal phenomena, part of the legal history of men, not the least part of the long story of the evolution of the human conscience."

Take the first trial that he gives us, the trial of Socrates; will its lessons ever fade?

"I come to the questions," says Sir John, "which twenty centuries have reiterated and which are still fresh. Was it a fair trial? Was Socrates guilty? Was the defense a long sophism? Did he corrupt the youth? Was the result a judicial error or a judicial murder? I do not believe that to these questions there ever will be one answer. There will always be those who prize order, the interests of the community, above all else; who make the safety of the State the supreme law; and they will answer, as did Hegel, as many others have done since, 'It was a good deed' a necessary deed; 'Socrates must die that the people might live and be strong.' That was the opinion of the majority of his fellow citizens; and there is no reason to believe that they repented, at all events until long afterwards. * * * If the prosecution and condemnation of Socrates were acts of State, they were at least done decently and in order, and with no desire to stifle the voice of the victim, and there are none of the circumstances of brutality which I shall often have to note in medieval and modern trials. That is one view of the trial still often expressed. But there will always be others who prizing individual freedom and the inner life above all things, thinking much of the invisible and imponderable things about us, will regard the result as a crime, the victim as the first and greatest martyr for true freedom and true progress. In the presence of these antinomics among the irreconcilable things of life, the mere lawyer cannot give much assistance. But he will try to put himself in the position of the judges, and seek to understand the law which they administered; he will apply to their conduct the tests, not of our time, but of their own. And he will also put to himself the question: would the results have differed if Socrates had been tried elsewhere and at some other time?"

Sir John's answer to the question is not one to kindle the pride of our profession. Socrates put on trial elsewhere and at some other time might have fared, in Sir John's judgment, no better, perhaps worse. Later days would have brought torture, and still later days contempt and ostracism and misunderstanding and belittlement. The indictment would have been cast in other moulds and the penalty would have been less than death; but law would still have been used to sanctify the prejudices and hatreds of the hour, and to crush the weakling who resists them. With impressive force our author sums up the lesson to be drawn from his studies; and the lesson is one of the corroding power of fear—fear of the unknown and the strange and the prejudice that goes with fear. "Fear," he says, "brings back the primitive conception of the function of courts; not necessarily, or indeed often, personal fear, but fear of changes; fear on the part of the upholders of the old order; fear of the effects of the discoveries of new truths; fear of emerging into the full light. Where such fear is, justice cannot be; a court becomes an instrument of power; judges are soldiers putting down rebellion; a so-called trial is a punitive expedition or a ceremonial execution—its victim a Bruno, a Galileo, or a Dreyfus."

I do not know whether it can ever be different, or so at least I say in hours of depression. Perhaps this is what law means. It is the medium, the instrument, by which society represses conduct which awakens fear of such intensity as to make tolerance impossible. We shall rationalize law only when we rationalize our fears—our fears and our wishes, the counterpart of our fears. I heard a distinguished physician say the other day that psychologists were coming over to the view that the fruitful method of education is not so much to control the behavior of men as to direct their desires—their impulses and desires. He put it in such a way as to challenge my interest and attention, but the thought is now becoming a commonplace of the schools. There is a lesson in all this for the law and for those who follow the law as judges and as advocates. In directing desires—in rationalizing hopes and fears—in shaping and guiding character, we shall be doing something more, we shall be rationalizing law.

So the problem, as I said at the beginning, is one of character, which turns out in the end to be the key to behavior and so to social order. How does it stand with us today, with us of the legal profession, with us whose business it is to see that law is rational? How have we fulfilled our task? Has fear, unworthy fear, been cast out of our juristic methods? Is law the instrument of the passion or the guile or the craftiness of the hour, or of its serenity and peace and order? Has it been purged and sanctified and dignified so that Socrates and Raleigh and the witches—the ugly, the alien, the unpopular, the bothersome—would fare better at its hands today? It is what you and I are making it. That is the heavy burden of our calling, but that is also its unfading glory. That is the strain and the woe of it, leaving creases and scars in the faces of the veterans, but that is also the heartening appeal of it, reflecting light and joy and hope in the faces of the new recruits, eager to join the fray and fill the thinning ranks. Here is the age-long battle, worthy of the best that we or they can offer. Here is the combat and the travail, but beyond are the sunlit hills to be gained at any cost of blood and sweat and agony. For "the path of the just is as the shining light, that shineth more and more unto the perfect day."

Sometimes secreted in ancient forms and ceremonies one finds the inner life and meaning of an institution revealed in all its essence. I felt this not long ago while reading the form of oath administered even now in all its ancient beauty to the grand jurors of the county. You will find it in the Code of Criminal Procedure; but one not greatly different is in use by our English brethren in their home across the seas, and Sir Frederick Pollock has traced it back, in germ at least, to the days of the Saxon kings. In fitness and beauty and impressiveness it rivals the famous Hippocratic oath, the glory and the pride of our brethren, the physicians. Here is its form as it has endured through all the changing centuries:

> "You shall diligently inquire and true presentment make, of all such matters and things as shall be given you in charge; the counsel of the people of this state,

your fellows' and your own, you shall keep secret; you shall present no person from envy, hatred or malice; nor shall you leave any one unpresented through fear, favor, affection, or reward, or hope thereof; but you shall present all things truly as they come to your knowledge, according to the best of your understanding. So help you God!"

Like the tones of a mighty bell, these echoing notes of adjuration bring back our straying thoughts to sanctity and service. I cannot listen to them without a thrill. Here, I say to myself, here indeed, secreted in this solemn formula, is the true spirit of the law, which knows no fear nor favor. Not all her ministers have been true to the ideal which she has held aloft for them to follow. But here, imperishably preserved amid the grime and dust of centuries, the word has been proclaimed, to steady us when we seem to falter, to strengthen us when we seem to weaken, to tell us that with all the failings and backslidings, with all the fears and all the prejudice, the spirit is still pure.

So today, as preacher of the ancient platitudes, I summon you, the new recruits, to do your part in this unending struggle, the charge on the redoubts of fear and hatred and prejudice and passion, and the injustice that is born of them. You will need to know much more than the piffle-paffle of procedure. You will need to know much more than law, or rather till you know many other things not often ranked as law, you will find that law itself is in reality unknown. As in any other fight, you will hear the call for patience and skill and courage and firmness and endurance. I have faith you will not fail us. As I look into your faces, I figure to myself what it will mean, in days to come, to the profession of the law if you and those to follow you out of this school will think worthily and highly of this great vocation of your choice. What a spiritual power you will then be in the age-old fellowship into which you are to enter! What a leavening force you will become in this great conglomerate bar of ours, moved as it is, at times, by the ferment of high thoughts and fine ideals, and yet at times in danger of becoming sodden and inert by reason of that very mass which might make it so irresistible a power for good! How it lies with you to uplift what is low, to erase what is false, to redeem what has been lost, till all the world shall see, and seeing shall understand, that union of the scholar's thought, the mystic's yearning, the knight's ardor, and the hero's passion, which is still, in truest moments of self-expression, the spirit of the bar! You will not fail us, I am sure. After all, the main thing is to dare. "As at the Olympic games," says Aristotle, "as at the Olympic games, it is not the finest and strongest men who are crowned, but they who enter the lists, for out of these the prisemen are selected; so, too, in life, of the honorable and the good, it is they who act who rightly win the prizes." The bugle call is heard, and its echoes wake the hills.

Like Socrates and other bores, I have earned the draft of hemlock if you choose to pass the cup.

FAITH AND A DOUBTING WORLD*

Address by the Honorable Benjamin Nathan Cardozo at the annual dinner of the New York County Lawyers Association given in his honor, December 17, 1931.

Mr. President, friends and brethren:

ONLY great luck or great merit could give a man such a greeting as has come to me tonight. If I know in my heart of hearts that luck is the efficient cause, I prize the greeting none the less.

I have been a good deal puzzled to understand why at this particular stage in the journey of my life there should be a dinner in my honor. When Lord Salisbury, then the English Premier, was asked for what sort of a reason he had appointed Mr. Alfred Austin poet laureate in the place of Lord Tennyson, he is reported to have said, "I don't think anybody else applied for the post." Now, I like a crown of laurels just as Mr. Austin, it seems, liked one, and yet I beg you to believe that though I resemble him in not being as worthy of the crown as others who have been crowned before me, I differ from him in this, that I was lucky enough to win the prize without incurring the reproach of being the only one to ask for it. My independence was greater than that statement would imply. My independence went so far as to embolden me to affix a condition to my acceptance of the crown. It was understood, or so I thought, that I was to be a figurehead and nothing more; that the guests were to look at the figurehead but were to be told nothing about him; and that the speakers would refrain from eulogy upon the one hand, although it was humbly petitioned that they would equally refrain from detraction upon the other. Well, the conditions that I imposed have been only half fulfilled. The

* *Faith and a Doubting World.* (Editor's title.) Reprinted with the permission of the New York County Lawyers Association and Columbia University, the residuary legatee of the literary estate of Benjamin Nathan Cardozo.

New York County Lawyers Yearbook 1932:369.

speakers have held aloof from detraction. They have ventured, however, into the field of eulogy. I liked it ever so much better than I expected. Years ago, as Dr. Butler told you, I discovered altruism in politics, a place where nobody ever looked for it before. Today, after a lapse of forty years and more, I have discovered generosity—generosity undeserved and overflowing—in my brethren of the bench and bar and in the spokesmen of the light and culture of the city of my home.

I am often at my wits' end to satisfy myself—let alone to satisfy others—as to the qualities that go to the making of a wise and useful judge. It is pretty hard to say. When one looks back at one's work and tries to estimate it impartially, one has hours of disillusionment, hours filled with wonder whether one has been travelling on the right track or the wrong one or on any track at all. Should one have been more liberal or more conservative or should one have tried more consistently to follow a line along the middle of the road? The very work that one thought was one's best and wisest when one did it, may seem to a good many others, quite as sincere and able, to be a pattern of egregious error, and the work that one most distrusted may win the approval of the years, the wise and discerning years, so much juster than the passing hour. Some of you may have read an interesting and original little book, "The Letters of John Marin," the modernist painter, who delights some of us and repulses others, and puzzles and baffles all. "There is always," (he writes) "a loophole for the poor human. He can never do a perfect thing, thank the Lord. There's the feeling that some day he will create a masterpiece, and—there are no masterpieces." Meanwhile a divine unrest pricks us to act as if there were and as if it were given unto us to shape them. The disillusionment is not likely to be long postponed if one happens to be a judge. I have thought in certain moods that there is only one test of merit for a decision, and that is whether it was in favor of the critic or against him. In the old fable of the Greeks, Midas, King of Phrygia, was chosen to decide between Pan and Apollo when they engaged in a musical contest on the flute and lyre. Midas gave his vote to Pan, whereupon Apollo turned his ears into those of an ass. There are times in reading the comments in the law reviews when I wonder whether Phoebus Apollo is at his elfish tricks again.

A heart-breaking sort of a game it is that we play from day to day, heart-breaking for litigants, we may be sure, and yet for lawyers and judges also, but no game that is quite without heart-break was ever worth the playing. I have tried hard to learn it, but then I have tried also to learn golf, and sometimes I wonder whether I know much more about the one than I know about the other, which is saying a good deal, as credible witnesses present in this room would be able to testify if they were mean enough to do it. Heaven knows I have done my best to find out what the business of judging really is, going so far as to lay bare my own soul and the souls of my associates and tell you what was going on inside. Indeed, I find there is a fairly general notion among my brethren at the Bar, that in some occult way I invented the judicial process and am responsible for its existence. Before my malign influence began, the process was like our first parents before the fall. It was simple, natural, spontaneous, knowing not the difference between good and evil, but now it is conscious of itself, crafty like the serpent, and its serpentine spirit is reflected in the judgments that it spawns.

All this, however, as most of you must know, is calumny and fable. If my brethren of the Bar have been banished from the Eden in which they roamed once upon a time carefree and unafraid, it is not the sword of jurisprudence that has driven them afar. The sword that has disturbed their idyllic ease is a changing civilization with accumulating precedents and the call for a new philosophy of law, a new juristic method, to bring order out of chaos. I was reading the other day a book by Claud Mullins, an English barrister, a book with the provocative title, "In Quest of Justice." It seems that the notion that there is a judicial process which is in need of some repair has even traveled across the seas. Yet the truth, of course, is—a truth very obvious when we follow the history of our law--that the recognition of this need is not a novel one at all. Down through the centuries we are given glimpses of an endeavor—intermittent, but persistent—to make the processes of justice more faithful in their response to the cause which they are meant to further. Progress goes by fits and starts; seasons and decades of improvement being followed at times by others of self-satisfied inaction. Even so, when lethargy is put aside and the hour of awakening arrives, there is no lack of watchwords to kindle the leaders of the march. Where shall we find a more stirring one than the great speech delivered by Lord Brougham a century ago in the English House of Commons? He spoke in support of a motion that an address be presented to the King petitioning that "a commission be established to inquire into the defects, occasioned by time and otherwise in the laws of this realm of England as administered in the courts of common law, and the remedies which may be expedient for the same." You will find it in the book by Mullins, which I commend to your attention. "It was the boast of Augustus (I quote the closing words) that he found Rome of brick and left it of marble. But how much nobler will be our sovereign's boast, when he shall have it to say that he found law dear and left it cheap; found it a sealed book, left it a living letter; found it the patrimony of the rich, left it the inheritance of the poor; found it the two-edged sword of craft and oppression, left it the staff of honesty and the shield of innocence." Here is a kindling oriflamme for all of us, a little gaudy and extravagant perhaps, but moving all the same. Are there knights among our number that will put it within the power of our sovereign lords, the People, to utter a like boast?

I have said that a spirit of unrest is manifest in these days among our brethren across the seas, among brethren more habituated than ourselves to acquiescence in the established order. I would not have you think, however, that our function in the new ferment, our part in the new movement, has been one of slavish imitation. On the contrary, I have been interested, and perhaps my hearers will be too, in observing the mounting evidences of the truth that we are developing a juristic method and philosophy of our own, differing a good deal from the philosophy and method of the country where the common law was born. Curiously enough I found two significant bits of evidence in the little essay that Sir Frederick Pollock contributed to the Holmes memorial number of the Harvard Law Review. He singled out for special admiration and approval the decision of the great master in United Zinc Co. v. Brett (258 U. S. 268), where the holding was that the possessor of land is never liable to a child trespasser unless the trespass was induced by the allurement of a dangerous condition known to the child in advance of the unlawful entry, and the decision in B. & O. R. R. v. Goodman (275 U. S. 66), where the holding was that a motorist meeting a dangerous railroad crossing is under a duty to get out of his car and look up and down, though unfortunately the decision does not tell us how this act is to give protection against the train that may bear down upon the victim in a moment as he clambers back into the vehicle. Now, my admiration for Holmes goes almost to the point of worship. I do not presume to say that his opinions in those two cases were wrong, though I feel pretty sure that one or both would have been decided differently in a great many courts and perhaps in the Court of Appeals of New York. Accepting, however, the not improbable asssumption that he is right and I am wrong, I think it is still a strange and significant fact that these two cases should have been singled out by Sir Frederick as specially worthy of approval and applause. I strongly suspect that if those two cases were to be put to the assembled lawyers at a meeting of this association or of the association of American Law Schools, the vote would be quite different. I do not say they would be voted to be wrong. I feel very certain that at least they would be voted to be doubtful. I can hardly imagine that they would be singled out as triumphant exhibitions of the master's power. One can find many other instances. To descend from great men to small, let me take my own opinion in MacPherson v. Buick Manufacturing Co. (217 N. Y. 382), where the manufacturer of a car was held liable to some one other than the buyer for the negligent construction of the wheels resulting in damage to the person. Only a year or two ago Sir Frederick waved that doctrine aside with what was almost a gesture of impatience. I might feel that the impatience was justified if the doctrine had no better support than my own opinion of its merits. When I remember, however, that it has won approval in a number of other states and has now been adopted by the American Law Institute in the restatement of the law of torts, I see that we have come to a fork in the road; that the branch we have laid out is something more than a blind alley; that we are developing a technique of our own, and are shaping the law of today in response to a philosophy which is indigenous, which is something more than a mechanical reproduction of philosophy abroad. If one wishes other illustrations, one will find them in a paper by an American scholar, a member of our Bar, who to the delight and honor of us all has recently been chosen for the chair of jurisprudence in the University of Oxford. In this paper by Prof. Goodhart, now included in his collected essays, you will see the points of difference as they have been perceived by an observer with peculiar opportunities for following the lines of juridical development both here and across the seas. What is certain in any event is that here in our own land there has been a notable accession of interest in the problems of juristic method. Out of the new ferment there will come a new philosophy that will guide the thought of our successors when those of us in place today shall have vanished from the scene.

One other thought I should like to leave with you tonight. I should like you to feel as I do the power and significance of myths. It is not about the myths that gather around men that I wish to say a word. It is about the myths that gather around institutions and events. You will find every now and again that the myths are really the main thing, and that the events and institutions to which they are supposed to be secondary would have little meaning today, and little value—whatever meaning and value they may have had once upon a time—if it were not for the incrustations of myth and fable.

Take Magna Charta for example. Today it is not what is written in the charter—if the words are read in the sense in which they were understood by those who wrote them—that has any commanding interest, any throbbing and vital meaning, for those who walk the earth. What lives in the charter today is the myth that has gathered around it—the things that it has come to stand for in the thought of successive generations—not the pristine core within, but the incrustations that have formed without.

The thought is tellingly expressed by Plucknett in his short history of the common law. "The charter," he writes, "gradually grew bigger than the mere feudal details which it contained and came to be a symbol of successful opposition to the Crown which resulted in a negotiated peace representing a reasonable compromise. As time goes on, therefore, the Charter becomes more and more a myth, but nevertheless a very powerful one, and in the seventeenth century all the forces of liberalism rallied around it. . . . To explode the 'myth' of the great Charter is indeed to get back to its original historical meaning, but for all that, the myth has been much more important than the reality, and there is still something to be said for the statement that 'the whole of English constitutional history is a commentary upon the great Charter.'"

Now, what is true of Magna Charta is true, I think of our own constitution in many of its provisions; true, for example, of the bill of rights, which is much more important for the spirit it enshrines than for this or the other privilege or immunity which it professes to secure. Some of them have a vital meaning even to this day, others are reminiscent of battles long ago. The myth that has enveloped them has become greater than the reality, or rather in a sense the genuine reality. But the lesson does not end there, the parable goes deeper. What is true of events and documents is true also of institutions, and, in particular of the institution that is of chief concern to you and me, the profession of the law.

A myth has grown up about the profession of the law, a fable, a tradition, not always the truth as seen and realized in conduct, but none the less the chief thing about the profession, the thing that makes it worth while, the thing that ennobles it, the thing that it really is in its best and truest moments, the thing without which, we may be sure, it would wither and die. The tradition, the ennobling tradition, though it be myth as well as verity, that surrounds as with an aura the profession of the law, is the bond between its members and one of the great concerns of man, the cause of justice upon earth. Like the old charter extorted by the barons, the body of our law when we read it line upon line may smack of mere antiquities, the customs of a vanished past. The myth, however, is still there, the myth of a great bible, the myth of mighty tablets hewn and hammered out by successive generations of advocates and judges under the imperious drive of a passion to shape the forms of justice.

Here, indeed, is the explanation of the place and potency of the moralities in levelling the walls of precedents and raising others up that leave the path of progress free. We may tell judges till doomsday that they are to love logic more than justice: as in affairs of the heart generally it is easier to give the command than to cause it to be heeded. A suggestive little book was published not long ago with the mystifying title, "The Endless Adventure," which turns out to be the government of men. The author reminds us that the art of politics like everything else, is mixed up with morals. We are told, he says, that there is water in all our food, even in a cracknel biscuit, and that in most of our food there is more water than anything else. It is much the same, he insists, with morals as with water. The metaphor may be carried over with profit into the field of my labors and of yours. I know the stock distinctions between morals and law. I know that oftentimes the distinction is genuine. I have had occasion not infrequently to deplore the fact. But with it all I like to believe that law has the qualities of a cracknel biscuit, and that however solid and dry it seems when we bite into its crust, there is a fluid mixed with the solid and forming the better part.

We are fallen upon days that are spoken of by many as cynical and sordid. The profession is given over, we are told, to the pursuit of power and pelf. Let us beware of underrating the springs of altruism and energy that lie ready to be released at the call of a great example, the summons of an urgent need. With all our cynicism and sordidness, how our pulses quicken even now at the tale of those of our comrades—our comrades dead and living—who have felt the magic of the ancient myth and, yielding to its glamor, have flung baser things away.

It has been given to you and me to be partakers of these blessed memories. It has been given to you and me to prove in our own lives that the truth is in the myth and not in the sordid appearances, at times misnamed reality, which hide what is within.

I shall treasure it as a proud memory if I may carry away with me tonight the thought that in the deliberate judgment of my dear brethren of the Bench and Bar, I have been able to do something to make this faith incarnate and to display it to a doubting world. To carry that memory away is enough to make it worth while to have posed as a figurehead at a dinner in one's honor.

I must close as I began with words of grateful appreciation. Only the other day I was reading a new volume of the letters of Henry James, the letters to Edward Benson. He starts them by saying, "I am singularly accessible to demonstrations of regard." Perhaps that is a confession. Perhaps it is an avowal of weakness. I make it without shame.

Complete Text

of

THE NATURE OF THE JUDICIAL PROCESS*

Before the lectures embraced in "The Nature of the Judicial Process" were given at Yale, Justice Cardozo said that he did not believe anybody would be greatly interested in them. The Yale Law School arranged for him to appear in a comparatively small auditorium on the theory that the lectures would be technical and not attract a great many. Contrary to expectations the crowds increased until they finally ended in the largest auditorium available.

(5)

IN MEMORIAM

THIS VOLUME IS PUBLISHED IN MEMORY OF

ARTHUR P. MCKINSTRY

Died, New York City, July 21, 1921

BORN in Winnebago City, Minnesota, on December 22, 1881, he was graduated from Yale College in 1905, and in 1907 received the degree of LL.B. *magna cum laude* from the Yale Law School, graduating at the head of his class. Throughout his career at Yale he was noted both for his scholarship and for his active interest in debating, which won for him first the presidency of the Freshman Union and subsequently the presidency of the Yale Union. He was also Class Orator in 1905, and vice-president of the Yale Chapter of Phi Beta Kappa.

Following his graduation from the School of Law he entered upon the practice of his profession in New York City and early met with the success anticipated for him by his friends,—his firm, of which he was the senior member, being recognized at the

* *The Nature of the Judicial Process.* Copyrighted 1921 by Yale University Press. Reprinted with the permission of the Yale University Press and Columbia University, the residuary legatee of the literary estate of Benjamin Nathan Cardozo.

n.b. Numbers in parenthesis indicate original paging.

time of his death as among the most prominent of the younger firms in the city. He was counsel for the Post-Graduate Hospital of New York, the Heckscher Founda (6) tion for Children, of which he was also a trustee, and from 1912 to 1914 served as associate counsel to the Agency of the United States in the American and British Claims Arbitration. By his untimely death the bar of the City of New York lost a lawyer outstanding for his ability, common sense, conscientiousness, and high sense of justice; and Yale University lost an alumnus of whom she was proud, who gave freely of his time and thought to his class of 1905, to the development of the Yale School of Law, and to the upbuilding of the Yale University Press, which he served as counsel.

(9)

Lecture I. Introduction. The Method of Philosophy.

THE work of deciding cases goes on every day in hundreds of courts throughout the land. Any judge, one might suppose, would find it easy to describe the process which he had followed a thousand times and more. Nothing could be farther from the truth. Let some intelligent layman ask him to explain: he will not go very far before taking refuge in the excuse that the language of craftsmen is unintelligible to those untutored in the craft. Such an excuse may cover with a semblance of respectability an otherwise ignominious retreat. It will hardly serve to still the pricks of curiosity and conscience. In moments of introspection, when there (10) is no longer a necessity of putting off with a show of wisdom the uninitiated interlocutor, the troublesome problem will recur, and press for a solution. What is it that I do when I decide a case? To what sources of information do I appeal for guidance? In what proportions do I permit them to contribute to the result? In what proportions ought they to contribute? If a precedent is applicable, when do I refuse to follow it? If no precedent is applicable, how do I reach the rule that will make a precedent for the future? If I am seeking logical consistency, the symmetry of the legal structure, how far shall I seek it? At what point shall the quest be halted by some discrepant custom, by some consideration of the social welfare, by my own or the common standards of justice and morals? Into that strange compound which is brewed daily in the caldron of the courts, all these ingredients enter in varying proportions. I am not concerned to inquire whether judges ought to be allowed to brew such a compound at all. I take judge-made law as one of the existing realities of life. There, before us, (11) is the brew. Not a judge on the bench but has had a hand in the making. The elements have not come together by chance. *Some* principle, however unavowed and inarticulate and subconscious, has regulated the infusion. It may not have been the same principle for all judges at any time, nor the same principle for any judge at all times. But a choice there has been, not a submission to the decree of Fate; and the considerations and motives determining the choice, even if often obscure, do not utterly resist analysis. In such attempt at analysis as I shall make, there will be need to distinguish between the conscious and the subconscious. I do not mean that even those considerations and motives which I shall class under the first head are always in consciousness distinctly, so that they will be recognized and named at sight. Not infrequently they hover near the surface. They may, however, with comparative readiness be isolated and tagged, and when thus labeled, are quickly acknowledged as guiding principles of conduct. More subtle are the forces so far beneath the (12) surface that they cannot reasonably be classified as other than subconscious. It is often through these subconscious forces that judges are kept consistent with themselves, and inconsistent with one another. We are reminded by William James in a telling page of his lectures on Pragmatism that every one of us has in truth an underlying philosophy of life, even those of us to whom the names and the notions of philosophy are unknown or anathema. There is in each of us a stream of tendency, whether you choose to call it philosophy or not,[1] which gives coherence and direction to thought and action. Judges cannot escape that current any more than other mortals. All their lives, forces which they do not recognize and cannot name, have been tugging at them—inherited instincts, traditional beliefs, acquired convictions; and the resultant is an outlook on life, a conception of social needs, a sense in James's phrase of "the total push and pressure of the cosmos," which, when reasons are nicely balanced, must determine where choice shall fall. (13) In this mental background every problem finds its setting. We may try to see things as objectively as we please. None the less, we can never see them with any eyes except our own. To that test they are all brought—a form of pleading or an act of parliament, the wrongs of paupers or the rights of princes, a village ordinance or a nation's charter.

I have little hope that I shall be able to state the formula which will rationalize this process for myself, much less for others. We must apply to the study of judge-made law that method of quantitative analysis which Mr. Wallas has applied with such fine results to the study of politics.[2] A richer scholarship than mine is requisite to do the work aright. But until that scholarship is found and enlists itself in the task, there may be a passing interest in an attempt to uncover the nature of the process by one who is himself an active agent, day by day, in keeping the process alive. That must be my apology for these introspective searchings of the spirit.

(14) Before we can determine the proportions of a blend, we must know the ingredients to be blended. Our first inquiry should therefore be: Where does the judge find the law which he embodies in his judgment? There are times when the source is obvious. The rule that fits the case may be supplied by the constitution or by statute. If that is so, the judge looks no farther. The correspondence ascertained, his duty is to obey. The constitution overrides a statute, but a statute, if consistent with the constitution, overrides the law of judges. In this sense, judge-made law is secondary and subordinate to the law that is made by legislators. It is true that codes and statutes do not render the judge superfluous, nor his work perfunctory and mechanical. There are gaps to be filled. There are doubts and ambiguities to be cleared. There are hardships and wrongs to be mitigated if not avoided. Interpretation is often spoken of as if it were nothing but the search and the discovery of a meaning which, however obscure and latent, had none the less a real and ascertainable pre-existence in (15) the legislator's mind. The process is, indeed, that at times, but it is often some-

thing more. The ascertainment of intention may be the least of a judge's troubles in ascribing meaning to a statute. "The fact is," says Gray in his lectures on the "Nature and Sources of the Law," [3] "that the difficulties of so-called interpretation arise when the legislature has had no meaning at all; when the question which is raised on the statute never occurred to it; when what the judges have to do is, not to determine what the legislature did mean on a point which was present to its mind, but to guess what it would have intended on a point not present to its mind, if the point had been present."[4] So Brütt: [5] "One weighty task of the system of the application of law consists then in this, to make more profound the discovery of the latent meaning of positive law. Much more important, however, is the second task which the system serves, namely (16) the filling of the gaps which are found in every positive law in greater or less measure." You may call this process legislation, if you will. In any event, no system of *jus scriptum* has been able to escape the need of it. Today a great school of continental jurists is pleading for a still wider freedom of adaptation and construction. The statute, they say, is often fragmentary and ill-considered and unjust. The judge as the interpreter for the community of its sense of law and order must supply omissions, correct uncertainties and harmonize results with justice through a method of free decision—"libre recherche scientifique." That is the view of Gény and Ehrlich and Gmelin and others.[6] Courts are to "search for light among the social elements of every kind that are the living force behind the facts they deal with." [7] The power thus put in their hands is great, and subject, like all power, to abuse; but we are not to flinch from granting it. In the long run "there is no guaranty of (17) justice," says Ehrlich,[8] "except the personality of the judge." [9] The same problems of method, the same contrasts between the letter and the spirit, are living problems in our own land and law. Above all in the field of constitutional law, the method of free decision has become, I think, the dominant one today. The great generalities of the constitution have a content and a significance that vary from age to age. The method of free decision sees through the transitory particulars and reaches what is permanent behind them. Interpretation, thus enlarged, becomes more than the ascertainment of the meaning and intent of lawmakers whose collective will has been declared. It supplements the declaration, and fills the vacant spaces, by the same processes and methods that have built up the customary law. Codes and other statutes may (18) threaten the judicial function with repression and disuse and atrophy. The function flourishes and persists by virtue of the human need to which it steadfastly responds. Justinian's prohibition of any commentary on the product of his codifiers is remembered only for its futility.[10]

I will dwell no further for the moment upon the significance of constitution and statute as sources of the law. The work of a judge in interpreting and developing them has indeed its problems and its difficulties, but they are problems and difficulties not different in kind or measure from those besetting him in other fields. I think they can be better studied when those fields have been explored. Sometimes the rule of constitution or of statute is clear, and then the difficulties vanish. Even when they are present, they lack at times some of that element of mystery which accompanies creative energy. We reach the land of mystery when constitution and statute are silent, and the judge must look to (19) the common law for the rule that fits the case. He is the "living oracle of the law" in Blackstone's vivid phrase. Looking at Sir Oracle in action, viewing his work in the dry light of realism, how does he set about his task?

The first thing he does is to compare the case before him with the precedents, whether stored in his mind or hidden in the books. I do not mean that precedents are ultimate sources of the law, supplying the sole equipment that is needed for the legal armory, the sole tools, to borrow Maitland's phrase,[11] "in the legal smithy." Back of precedents are the basic juridical conceptions which are the postulates of judicial reasoning, and farther back are the habits of life, the institutions of society, in which those conceptions had their origin, and which, by a process of interaction, they have modified in turn.[12] None the less, in a system so highly developed as our (20) own, precedents have so covered the ground that they fix the point of departure from which the labor of the judge begins. Almost invariably, his first step is to examine and compare them. If they are plain and to the point, there may be need of nothing more. *Stare decisis* is at least the everyday working rule of our law. I shall have something to say later about the propriety of relaxing the rule in exceptional conditions. But unless those conditions are present, the work of deciding cases in accordance with precedents that plainly fit them is a process similar in its nature to that of deciding cases in accordance with a statute. It is a process of search, comparison, and little more. Some judges seldom get beyond that process in any case. Their notion of their duty is to match the colors of the case at hand against the colors of many sample cases spread out upon their desk. The sample nearest in shade supplies the applicable rule. But, of course, no system of living law can be evolved by such a process, and no judge of a high court, worthy of his office, views the function of his place so narrowly. If (21) that were all there was to our calling, there would be little of intellectual interest about it. The man who had the best card index of the cases would also be the wisest judge. It is when the colors do not match, when the references in the index fail, when there is no decisive precedent, that the serious business of the judge begins. He must then fashion law for the litigants before him. In fashioning it for them, he will be fashioning it for others. The classic statement is Bacon's: "For many times, the things deduced to judgment may be meum and tuum, when the reason and consequence thereof may trench to point of estate."[13] The sentence of today will make the right and wrong of tomorrow. If the judge is to pronounce it wisely, some principles of selection there must be to guide him among all the potential judgments that compete for recognition.

In the life of the mind as in life elsewhere, there is a tendency toward the reproduction of kind. Every judgment has a generative power. It begets in its own image. Every precedent, in (22) the words of Redlich, has a "directive force for future cases of the same or similar nature."[14] Until the sentence was pronounced, it was as yet in equilibrium. Its form and content were uncertain. Any one of many principles might lay hold of it and shape it. Once declared, it is a new stock of descent. It is charged with vital power. It is the source from which new principles or norms may spring to shape sentences thereafter. If we seek the psychological basis of this tendency, we shall find it, I suppose, in habit.[15] Whatever its psychological basis it is one of the living forces of our law. Not all the progeny of principles begotten of a judgment survive, however, to maturity. Those that cannot prove their worth and strength by the test of experience, are sacrificed mercilessly and thrown into the void. The common law does not work from pre-established truths of universal and inflexible validity to conclusions derived from them (23) deductively. Its method is inductive, and it draws its generalizations from particulars. The process has been admirably stated by Munroe Smith: "In their effort to give to the social sense of justice articulate expression in rules and in principles, the method of the lawfinding experts has always been experimental. The rules and principles of case law have never been treated as final truths, but as working hypotheses, continually retested in those great laboratories of the law, the courts of justice. Every new case is an experiment; and if the accepted rule which seems applicable yields a result which is felt to be unjust, the rule is reconsidered. It may not be modified at once, for the attempt to do absolute justice in every single case would make the development and maintenance of general rules impossible; but if a rule continues to work injustice, it will eventually be reformulated. The principles themselves are continually retested; for if the rules derived from a principle do not work well, the principle itself must ultimately be re-examined." [16]

(24)The way in which this process of retesting and reformulating works, may be followed in an example. Fifty years ago, I think it would have been stated as a general principle that A may conduct his business as he pleases, even though the purpose is to cause loss to B, unless the act involves the creation of a nuisance.[17] Spite fences were the stock illustration, and the exemption from liability in such circumstances was supposed to illustrate not the exception, but the rule.[18] Such a rule may have been an adequate working principle to regulate the relations between individuals or classes in a simple or homogeneous community. With the growing complexity of social relations, its inadequacy was revealed. As particular controversies multiplied and the attempt was made to test them by the (25) old principle it was found that there was something wrong in the results, and this led to a reformulation of the principle itself. Today, most judges are inclined to say that what was once thought to be the exception is the rule, and what was the rule is the exception. A may never do anything in his business for the purpose of injuring another without reasonable and just excuse.[19] There has been a new generalization which, applied to new particulars, yields results more in harmony with past particulars, and, what is still more important, more consistent with the social welfare. This work of modification is gradual. It goes on inch by inch. Its effects must be measured by decades and even centuries. Thus measured, they are seen to have behind them the power and the pressure of the moving glacier.

We are not likely to underrate the force that has been exerted if we look back upon its work. "There is not a creed which is not shaken, not an accredited dogma which is not shown to be (26) questionable, not a received tradition which does not threaten to dissolve." [20] Those are the words of a critic of life and letters writing forty years ago, and watching the growing scepticism of his day. I am tempted to apply his words to the history of the law. Hardly a rule of today but may be matched by its opposite of yesterday. Absolute liability for one's acts is today the exception; there must commonly be some tinge of fault, whether willful or negligent. Time was, however, when absolute liability was the rule.[21] Occasional reversions to the earlier type may be found in recent legislation.[22] Mutual promises give rise to an obligation, and their breach to a right of action for damages. Time was when the (27) obligation and the remedy were unknown unless the promise was under seal.[23] Rights of action may be assigned, and the buyer prosecute them to judgment though he bought for purposes of suit. Time was when the assignment was impossible, and the maintenance of the suit a crime. It is no basis today for an action of deceit to show, without more, that there has been the breach of an executory promise; yet the breach of an executory promise came to have a remedy in our law because it was held to be a deceit.[24] These changes or most of them have been wrought by judges. The men who wrought them used the same tools as the judges of today. The changes, as they were made in this case or that, may not have seemed momentous in the making. The result, however, when the process was prolonged throughout the years, has been not merely to supplement or modify; it has been to revolu- (28) tionize and transform. For every tendency, one seems to see a counter-tendency; for every rule its antinomy. Nothing is stable. Nothing absolute. All is fluid and changeable. There is an endless "becoming." We are back with Heraclitus. That, I mean, is the average or aggregate impression which the picture leaves upon the mind. Doubtless in the last three centuries, some lines, once wavering, have become rigid. We leave more to legislatures today, and less perhaps to judges.[25] Yet even now there is change from decade to decade. The glacier still moves.

In this perpetual flux, the problem which confronts the judge is in reality a twofold one: he must first extract from the precedents the underlying principle, the *ratio decidendi;* he must then determine the path or direction along which the principle is to move and develop, if it is not to wither and die.

The first branch of the problem is the one to which we are accustomed to address ourselves (29) more consciously than to the other. Cases do not unfold their principles for the asking. They yield up their kernel slowly and painfully. The instance cannot lead to a generalization till we know it as it is. That in itself is no easy task. For the thing adjudged comes to us oftentimes swathed in obscuring dicta, which must be stripped off and cast aside. Judges differ greatly in their reverence for the illustrations and comments and side-remarks of their predecessors, to make no mention of their own. All agree that there may be dissent when the opinion is filed. Some would seem to hold that there must be none a moment thereafter. Plenary inspiration has then descended upon the work of the majority. No one, of course, avows such a belief, and yet sometimes there is an approach to it in conduct. I own that it is a good deal of a mystery to me how judges, of all persons in the world, should put their faith in dicta. A brief experience on the bench was enough to reveal to me all sorts of cracks and crevices and loopholes in my own opinions when picked up a few months after de (30) livery, and reread with due contrition. The persuasion that one's own infallibility is a myth leads by easy stages and with somewhat greater satisfaction to a refusal to ascribe infallibility to others. But dicta are not always ticketed as such, and one does not recognize them always at a glance. There is the constant need, as every law student knows, to separate the accidental and the non-essential from the essential and inherent. Let us assume, however, that this task has been achieved, and that the precedent is known as it really is. Let us assume too that the principle, latent within it, has been skillfully extracted and accurately stated. Only half or less than half of the work has yet been done. The problem remains to fix the bounds and the tendencies of development and growth, to set the directive force in motion along the right path at the parting of the ways.

The directive force of a principle may be exerted along the line of logical progression; this I will call the rule of analogy or the method of philosophy; along the line of historical de (31) velopment; this I will call the method of evolution; along the line of the customs of the community; this I will call the method of tradition; along the lines of justice, morals and social welfare, the *mores* of the day; and this I will call the method of sociology.

I have put first among the principles of selection to guide our choice of paths, the rule of analogy or the method of philosophy. In putting it first, I do not mean to rate it as most important. On the contrary, it is often sacrificed to others. I have put it first because it has, I think, a certain presumption in its favor. Given a mass of particulars, a congeries of judgments on related topics, the principle that unifies and rationalizes them has a tendency, and a legitimate one, to project and extend itself to new cases within the limits of its capacity to unify and rationalize. It has the primacy that comes from natural and orderly and logical succession. Homage is due to it over every competing principle that is unable by appeal to history or tradition or policy or justice to make out a (32) better right. All sorts of deflecting forces may appear to contest its sway and absorb its power. At least, it is the heir presumptive. A pretender to the title will have to fight his way.

Great judges have sometimes spoken as if the principle of philosophy, *i.e.,* of logical development, meant little or nothing in our law. Probably none of them in conduct was ever true to such a faith. Lord Halsbury said in Quinn v. Leathem, 1901, A. C. 495, 506: "A case is only an authority for what it actually decides. I entirely deny that it can be quoted for a proposition that may seem to follow logically from it. Such a mode of reasoning assumes that the law is necessarily a logical code, whereas every lawyer must acknowledge that the law is not always logical at all." [26] All this may be true but we must not press the truth too far. Logical consistency does not cease to be a good because it is not the supreme good. Holmes has told us (33) in a sentence which is now classic that "the life of the law has not been logic; it has been experience." [27] But Holmes did not tell us that logic is to be ignored when experience is silent. I am not to mar the symmetry of the legal structure by the introduction of inconsistencies and irrelevancies and artificial exceptions unless for some sufficient reason, which will commonly be some consideration of history or custom or policy or justice. Lacking such a reason, I must be logical, just as I must be impartial, and upon like grounds. It will not do to decide the same question one way between one set of litigants and the opposite way between another. "If a group of cases involves the same point, the parties expect the same decision. It would be a gross injustice to decide alternate cases on opposite principles. If a case was decided against me yesterday when I was defendant, I shall look for the same judgment today if I am plaintiff. To decide differently would raise a feeling of resentment and wrong in my breast; it would be an (34) infringement, material and moral, of my rights." [28] Everyone feels the force of this sentiment when two cases are the same. Adherence to precedent must then be the rule rather than the exception if litigants are to have faith in the even-handed administration of justice in the courts. A sentiment like in kind, though different in degree, is at the root of the tendency of precedent to extend itself along the lines of logical development.[29] No doubt the sentiment is powerfully reinforced by what is often nothing but an intellectual passion for *elegantia juris,* for symmetry of form and substance.[30] That is an ideal which can never fail to exert some measure of attraction upon the professional experts who make up the lawyer class. To the Roman lawyers, it meant much, more (35) than it has meant to English lawyers or to ours, certainly more than it has meant to clients. "The client," says Miller in his "Data of Jurisprudence," [31] "cares little for a 'beautiful' case! He wishes it settled somehow on the most favorable terms he can obtain." Even that is not always true. But as a system of case law develops, the sordid controversies of litigants are the stuff out of which great and shining truths will ultimately be shaped. The accidental and the transitory will yield the essential and the permanent. The judge who moulds the law by the method of philosophy may be satisfying an intellectual craving for symmetry of form and substance. But he is doing something more. He is keeping the law true in its response to a deep-seated and imperious sentiment. Only experts perhaps may be able to gauge the quality of his work and appraise its significance. But their judgment, the judgment of the lawyer class, will spread to others, and tinge the common consciousness and the common faith. In default of other tests, the method of philosophy must remain the organon of the courts if (36) chance and favor are to be excluded, and the affairs of men are to be governed with the serene and impartial uniformity which is of the essence of the idea of law.

You will say that there is an intolerable vagueness in all this. If the method of philosophy is to be employed in the absence of a better one, some test of comparative fitness should be furnished. I hope, before I have ended, to sketch, though only in the broadest outline, the fundamental considerations by which the choice of methods should be governed. In the nature of things they can never be catalogued with precision. Much must be left to that deftness in the use of tools which the practice of an art develops. A few hints, a few suggestions, the rest must be trusted to the feeling of the artist. But for the moment, I am satisfied to establish the method of philosophy as one organon among several, leaving the choice of one or the other to be talked of later. Very likely I have labored unduly to established its title to a place so modest. Above all, in the Law School of Yale University, the (37) title will not be challenged. I say that because in the work of a brilliant teacher of this school, the late Wesley Newcomb Hohfeld, I find impressive recognition of the importance of this method, when kept within due limits, and some of the happiest illustrations of its legitimate employment. His treatise on "Fundamental Conception Applied in Judicial Reasoning" is in reality a plea that fundamental conceptions be analyzed more clearly, and their philosophical implications, their logical conclusions, developed more consistently. I do not mean to represent him as holding to the view that logical conclusions must always follow the conceptions developed by analysis. "No one saw more clearly than he that while the analytical matter is an indispensable tool, it is not an all-sufficient one for the lawyer."[32] "He emphasized over and over again" that "analytical work merely paves the way for other branches of jurisprudence, and that without the aid of the latter, satisfactory solution of (38) legal problems cannot be reached."[33] We must know where logic and philosophy lead even though we may determine to abandon them for other guides. The times will be many when we can do no better than follow where they point.

Example, if not better than precept, may at least prove to be easier. We may get some sense of the class of questions to which a method is adapted when we have studied the class of questions to which it has been applied. Let me give some haphazard illustrations of conclusions adopted by our law through the development of legal conceptions to logical conclusions. A agrees to sell a chattel to B. Before title passes, the chattel is destroyed. The loss falls on the seller who has sued at law for the price.[34] A agrees to sell a house and lot. Before title passes, the house is destroyed. The seller sues in equity for specific performance. The loss falls upon the (39) buyer.[35] That is probably the prevailing view, though its wisdom has been sharply criticized.[36] These variant conclusions are not dictated by variant considerations of policy or justice. They are projections of a principle to its logical outcome, or the outcome supposed to be logical. Equity treats that as done which ought to be done. Contracts for the sale of land, unlike most contracts for the sale of chattels, are within the jurisdiction of equity. The vendee is in equity the owner from the beginning. Therefore, the burdens as well as the benefits of ownership shall be his. Let me take as another illustration of my meaning the cases which define the rights of assignees of choses in action. In the discussion of these cases, you will find much conflict of opinion about fundamental conceptions. Some tell us that the assignee has a legal ownership.[37] Others say that his right is purely equitable.[38] (40) Given, however, the fundamental conception, all agree in deducing its consequences by methods in which the preponderating element is the method of philosophy. We may find kindred illustrations in the law of trusts and contracts and in many other fields. It would be wearisome to accumulate them.

The directive force of logic does not always exert itself, however, along a single and unobstructed path. One principle or precedent, pushed to the limit of its logic, may point to one conclusion; another principle or precedent, followed with like logic, may point with equal certainty to another. In this conflict, we must choose between the two paths, selecting one or other, or perhaps striking out upon a third, which will be the resultant of the two forces in combination, or will represent the mean between extremes. Let me take as an illustration of such conflict the famous case of Riggs v. Palmer, 115 N. Y. 506. That case decided that a legatee who had murdered his testator would not be permitted by a court of equity to enjoy the benefits of the will. Con (41) flicting principles were there in competition for the mastery. One of them prevailed, and vanquished all the others. There was the principle of the binding force of a will disposing of the estate of a testator in conformity with law. That principle, pushed to the limit of its logic, seemed to uphold the title of the murderer. There was the principle that civil courts may not add to the pains and penalties of crimes. That, pushed to the limit of its logic, seemed again to uphold his title. But over against these was another principle, of greater generality, its roots deeply fastened in universal sentiments of justice, the principle that no man should profit from his own inequity or take advantage of his own wrong. The logic of this principle prevailed over the logic of the others. I say its logic prevailed. The thing which really interests us, however, is why and how the choice was made between one logic and another. In this instance, the reason is not obscure. One path was followed, another closed, because of the conviction in the judicial mind that the one selected led to justice. Analogies and (42) precedents and the principles behind them were brought together as rivals for precedence; in the end, the principle that was thought to be most fundamental, to represent the larger and deeper social interests, put its competitors to flight. I am not greatly concerned about the particular formula through which justice was attained. Consistency was preserved, logic received its tribute, by holding that the legal title passed, but that it was subjected to a constructive trust.[39] A constructive trust is nothing but "the formula through which the conscience of equity finds expression." [40] Property is acquired in such circumstances that the holder of the legal title may not in good conscience retain the beneficial interest. Equity, to express its disapproval of his conduct, converts him into a trustee.[41] Such formulas are merely the remedial devices by which a result conceived of as right and just is (43) made to square with principle and with the symmetry of the legal system. What concerns me now is not the remedial device, but rather the underlying motive, the indwelling, creative energy, which brings such devices into play. The murderer lost the legacy for which the murder was committed because the social interest served by refusing to permit the criminal to profit by his crime is greater than that served by the preservation and enforcement of legal rights of ownership. My illustration, indeed, has brought me ahead of my story. The judicial process is there in microcosm. We go forward with our logic, with our analogies, with our philosophies, till we reach a certain point. At first, we have no trouble with the paths; they follow the same lines. Then they begin to diverge, and we must make a choice between them. History or custom or social utility or some compelling sentiment of justice or sometimes perhaps a semi-intuitive apprehension of the pervading spirit of our law, must come to the rescue of the anxious judge, and tell him where to go.

(44) It is easy to accumulate examples of the process—of the constant checking and testing of philosophy by justice, and of justice by philosophy. Take the rule which permits recovery with compensation for defects in cases of substantial, though incomplete performance. We have often applied it for the protection of builders who in trifling details and without evil purpose have departed from their contracts. The courts had some trouble for a time, when they were deciding such cases, to square their justice with their logic. Even now, an uneasy feeling betrays itself in treatise and decision that the two fabrics do not fit. As I had occasion to say in a recent case: "Those who think more of symmetry and logic in the development of legal rules than of practical adaptation to the attainment of a just result" remain "troubled by a classification where the lines of division are

so wavering and blurred."[42] I have no doubt that the inspiration of the rule is a mere sentiment of justice. That sentiment asserting itself, we have proceeded to surround it (45) with the halo of conformity to precedent. Some judges saw the unifying principle in the law of quasi-contracts. Others saw it in the distinction between dependent and independent promises, or between promises and conditions. All found, however, in the end that there *was* a principle in the legal armory which, when taken down from the wall where it was rusting, was capable of furnishing a weapon for the fight and of hewing a path to justice. Justice reacted upon logic, sentiment upon reason, by guiding the choice to be made between one logic and another. Reason in its turn reacted upon sentiment by purging it of what is arbitrary, by checking it when it might otherwise have been extravagant, by relating it to method and order and coherence and tradition.[43]

In this conception of the method of logic or philosophy as one organon among several, I find nothing hostile to the teachings of continental jurists who would dethrone it from its place and (46) power in systems of jurisprudence other than our own. They have combated an evil which has touched the common law only here and there, and lightly. I do not mean that there are not fields where we have stood in need of the same lesson. In some part, however, we have been saved by the inductive process through which our case law has developed from evils and dangers inseparable from the development of law, upon the basis of the *jus scriptum*, by a process of deduction.[44] Yet even continental jurists who emphasize the need of other methods, do not ask us to abstract from legal principles all their fructifying power. The misuse of logic or philosophy begins when its method and its ends are treated as supreme and final. They can never be banished altogether. "Assuredly," says François Gény,[45] "there should be no question of banishing ratiocination and logical methods from the (47) science of positive law." Even general principles may sometimes be followed rigorously in the deduction of their consequences. "The abuse," he says, "consists, if I do not mistake, in envisaging ideal conceptions, provisional and purely subjective in their nature, as endowed with a permanent objective reality. And this false point of view, which, to my thinking, is a vestige of the absolute realism of the middle ages, ends in confining the entire system of positive law, *a priori,* within a limited number of logical categories, which are predetermined in essence, immovable in basis, governed by inflexible dogmas, and thus incapable of adapting themselves to the ever varied and changing exigencies of life."

In law, as in every other branch of knowledge, the truths given by induction tend to form the premises for new deductions. The lawyers and the judges of successive generations do not repeat for themselves the process of verification, any more than most of us repeat the demonstrations of the truths of astronomy or physics. A stock of juridical conceptions and formulas is (48) developed, and we take them, so to speak, ready-made. Such fundamental conceptions as contract and possession and ownership and testament and many others, are there, ready for use. How they came to be there, I do not need to inquire. I am writing, not a history of the evolution of law, but a sketch of the judicial process applied to law full grown. These fundamental conceptions once attained form the starting point from which are derived new consequences, which at first tentative and groping, gain by reiteration a new permanence and certainty. In the end, they become accepted themselves as fundamental and axiomatic. So it is with the growth from precedent to precedent. The implications of a decision may in the beginning be equivocal. New cases by commentary and exposition extract the essence. At last there emerges a rule or principle which becomes a datum, a point of departure, from which new lines will be run, from which new courses will be measured. Sometimes the rule or principle is found to have been formulated too narrowly or too broadly, and has to be reframed. (49) Sometimes it is accepted as a postulate of later reasoning, its origins are forgotten, it becomes a new stock of descent, its issue unite with other strains, and persisting permeate the law. You may call the process one of analogy or of logic or of philosophy as you please. Its essence in any event is the derivation of a consequence from a rule or a principle or a precedent which, accepted as a datum, contains implicitly within itself the germ of the conclusion. In all this, I do not use the word philosophy in any strict or formal sense. The method tapers down from the syllogism at one end to mere analogy at the other. Sometimes the extension of a precedent goes to the limit of its logic. Sometimes it does not go so far. Sometimes by a process of analogy it is carried even farther. That is a tool which no system of jurisprudence has been able to discard.[46] A rule which has worked well in one field, or which, in any event, is there whether its workings have been revealed or not, is carried over into another. Instances of such a process I group (50) under the same heading as those where the nexus of logic is closer and more binding.[47] At bottom and in their underlying motives, they are phases of the same method. They are inspired by the same yearning for consistency, for certainty, for uniformity of plan and structure. They have their roots in the constant striving of the mind for a larger and more inclusive unity, in which differences will be reconciled, and abnormalities will vanish.

REFERENCES

1. *Cf.* N. M. Butler, "Philosophy," pp. 18, 43.
2. "Human Nature in Politics," p. 138.
3. Sec. 370, p. 165.
4. *Cf.* Pound, "Courts and Legislation," 9 Modern Legal Philosophy Series, p. 226.
5. "Die Kunst der Rechtsanwendung," p. 72.
6. "Science of Legal Method," 9 Modern Legal Philosophy Series, pp. 4, 45, 65, 72, 124, 130, 159.
7. Gény, "Méthode d' Interprétation et Sources en droit privé positif," vol. II, p. 180, sec. 176, ed. 1919; transl. 9 Modern Legal Philosophy Series, p. 45.
8. P. 65, *supra;* "Freie Rechtsfindung und freie Rechtswissenschaft," 9 Modern Legal Philosophy Series.
9. *Cf.* Gnaeus Flavius (Kantorowicz), "Der Kampf um Rechtswissenschaft," p. 48: "Von der Kultur des Richters hängt im letzten Grunde aller Fortschritt der Rechtsentwicklung ab."
10. Gray, "Nature and Sources of the Law," sec. 395; Muirhead, "Roman Law," pp. 399, 400.
11. Introduction to Gierke's "Political Theories of the Middle Age," p. viii.
12. Saleilles, "Die la Personalité Juridique," p. 45; Ehrlich, "Grundlegung der Soziologie des Rechts," pp. 34, 35; Pound, "Proceedings of American Bar Assn. 1919," p. 455.
13. "Essay on Judicature."
14. Redlich, "The Case Method in American Law Schools," Bulletin No. 8, Carnegie Foundation, p. 37.
15. McDougall, "Social Psychology," p. 354; J. C. Gray, "Judicial Precedents," 9 *Harvard L. R.* 27.
16. Munroe Smith, "Jurisprudence," Columbia University Press, 1909, p. 21; *cf.* Pound, "Courts and Legislation," 7 Am. Pol. Science Rev. 361; 9 Modern Legal Philosophy Series, p. 214; Pollock, "Essays in Jurisprudence and Ethics," p. 246.
17. Cooley, "Torts," 1st ed., p. 93; Pollock, "Torts," 10th ed., p. 21.
18. Phelps v. Nowlen, 72 N. Y. 39; Rideout v. Knox, 148 Mass. 368.
19. Lamb v. Cheney, 227 N. Y. 418; Aikens v. Wisconsin, 195 U. S. 194, 204; Pollock, "Torts," *supra.*
20. Arnold, "Essays in Criticism," second series, p. 1.

21. Holdsworth, "History of English Law," 2, p. 41; Wigmore, "Responsibility for Tortious Acts," 7 *Harvard L. R.* 315, 383, 441; 3 Anglo-Am. Legal Essays 474; Smith "Liability for Damage to Land," 33 *Harvard L. R.* 551; Ames, "Law and Morals," 22 *Harvard L. R.* 97, 99; Isaacs, "Fault and Liability," 31 *Harvard L. R.* 954.

22. *Cf.* Duguit, "Les Transformations générales du droit privé depuis le Code Napoléon," Continental Legal Hist. Series, vol. XI, pp. 125, 126, secs. 40, 42.

23. Holdsworth, *supra,* 2, p. 72; Ames, "History of Parol Contracts prior to Assumpsit," 3 Anglo-Am. Legal Essays 304.

24. Holdsworth, *supra,* 3, pp. 330, 336; Ames, "History of Assumpsit," 3 Anglo-Am. Legal Essays 275, 276.

25. F. C. Montague in "A Sketch of Legal History" Maitland and Montague, p. 161.

26. *Cf.* Bailhache, J., in Belfast Ropewalk Co. v. Bushell, 1918, 1 K. B. 210, 213: "Unfortunately or fortunately, I am not sure which, our law is not a science."

27. "The Common Law," p. 1.

28. W. G. Miller, "The Data of Jurisprudence," p. 335; *cf.* Gray, "Nature and Sources of the Law," sec. 420; Salmond, "Jurisprudence," p. 170.

29. *Cf.* Gény, "Méthode d'Interprétation et Sources et droit privé positif," vol. 11, p. 119.

30. W. G. Miller, *supra,* p. 281; Bryce, "Studies in History and Jurisprudence," vol. II, p. 629.

31. P. 1.

32. Introduction to Hohfeld's Treatise by W. W. Cook.

33. Professor Cook's Introduction.

34. Higgins v. Murray, 73 N. Y. 252, 254; 2 Williston on Contracts, sec. 962; N. Y. Personal Prop. Law, sec. 103a.

35. Paine v. Meller, 6 Ves. 349, 352; Sewell v. Underhill, 197 N. Y. 168; 2 Williston on Contracts, sec. 931.

36. 2 Williston on Contracts, sec. 940.

37. Cook, 29 *Harvard L. R.* 816, 836.

38. Williston, 30 *Harvard L. R.* 97; 31 *ibid.* 822.

39. Ellerson v. Westcott, 148 N. Y. 149, 154; Ames, "Lectures on Legal History," pp. 313, 314.

40. Beatty v. Guggenheim Exploration Co., 225 N. Y. 380, 386.

41. Beatty v. Guggenheim Exploration Co., *supra;* Ames, *supra.*

42. Jacobs & Youngs, Inc. v. Kent, 230 N. Y. 239.

43. *Cf.* Hynes v. N. Y. Central R. R. Co., 231 N. Y. 229, 235.

44. "Notre droit public, comme notre droit privé est un *jus scriptum*" (Michoud, "La Responsibilité de l'état à raison des fautes de ses agents," Revue du droit public, 1895, p. 273, quoted by Gény, vol. I, p. 40, sec. 19).

45. *Op. cit.,* vol. I, p. 127, sec. 61.

46. Ehrlich "Die Juristische Logik," pp. 225, 227.

47. *Cf.* Gény, *op. cit.,* vol. II, p. 121, sec. 165; also vol. I, p. 304, sec. 107.

(51)

Lecture II. The Methods of History, Tradition and Sociology.

THE method of philosophy comes in competition, however, with other tendencies which find their outlet in other methods. One of these is the historical method, or the method of evolution. The tendency of a principle to expand itself to the limit of its logic may be counteracted by the tendency to confine itself within the limits of its history. I do not mean that even then the two methods are always in opposition. A classification which treats them as distinct is, doubtless, subject to the reproach that it involves a certain overlapping of the lines and principles of division. Very often, the effect of history is to make the path of logic clear.[1] Growth may be logical whether it is shaped by the principle (52) of consistency with the past or by that of consistency with some pre-established norm, some general conception, some "indwelling, and creative principle."[2] The directive force of the precedent may be found either in the events that made it what it is, or in some principle which enables us to say of it that it is what it ought to be. Development may involve either an investigation of origins or an effort of pure reason. Both methods have their logic. For the moment, however, it will be convenient to identify the method of history with the one, and to confine the method of logic or philosophy to the other. Some conceptions of the law owe their existing form almost exclusively to history. They are not to be understood except as historical growths. In the development of such principles, history is likely to predominate over logic or pure reason. Other conceptions, though they have, of course, a history, have taken form and shape to a larger extent under the influence of reason or of com (53) parative jurisprudence. They are part of the *jus gentium*. In the development of such principles logic is likely to predominate over history. An illustration is the conception of juristic or corporate personality with the long train of consequences which that conception has engendered. Sometimes the subject matter will lend itself as naturally to one method as to another. In such circumstances, considerations of custom or utility will often be present to regulate the choice. A residuum will be left where the personality of the judge, his taste, his training or his bent of mind, may prove the controlling factor. I do not mean that the directive force of history, even where its claims are most assertive, confines the law of the future to uninspired repetition of the law of the present and the past. I mean simply that history, in illuminating the past, illuminates the present, and in illuminating the present, illuminates the future. "If at one time it seemed likely," says Maitland,[3] "that the historical spirit (the spirit which strove to understand the classi (54) cal jurisprudence of Rome and the Twelve Tables, and the Lex Salica, and law of all ages and climes) was fatalistic and inimical to reform, that time already lies in the past. . . . Nowadays we may see the office of historical research as that of explaining, and therefore lightening, the pressure that the past must exercise upon the present and the present upon the future. Today we study the day before yesterday, in order that yesterday may not paralyze today, and today may not paralyze tomorrow."

Let me speak first of those fields where there can be no progress without history. I think the law of real property supplies the readiest example.[4] No lawgiver meditating a code of laws conceived the system of feudal tenures. History built up the system and the law that went with it. Never by a process of logical deduction from the idea of abstract ownership could we distinguish the incidents of an estate in fee simple from those of an estate for life, or those of an estate for life from those of an estate for years. Upon (55) these points, "a page of history is worth a volume of logic." [5] So it is wherever we turn in the forest of the law of land. Restraints upon alienation, the suspension of absolute ownership, contingent remainders, executory devises, private trusts and trusts for charities, all these heads of the law are intelligible only in the light of history, and get from history the impetus which must shape their subsequent development. I do not mean that even in this field, the method of philosophy plays no part at all. Some of the conceptions of the land law, once fixed, are pushed to their logical conclusions with inexorable severity. The point is rather that the conceptions themselves have come to us from without and not from within, that they embody the thought, not so much of the present as of the past, that separated from the past their form and meaning are unintelligible and arbitrary, and hence that their development, in order to be truly logical, must be mindful of their origins. In a measure that is true of most of the (56) conceptions of our law. Metaphysical principles have seldom been their life. If I emphasize the law of real estate, it is merely as a conspicuous example. Other illustrations, even though less conspicuous, abound. "The forms of action we have buried," says Maitland,[6] "but they still rule us from their graves." Holmes has the same thought: [7] "If we consider the law of contracts," he says, "we find it full of history. The distinctions between debt, covenant and assumpsit are merely historical. The classification of certain obligations to pay money, imposed by the law irrespective of any bargain as quasi-contracts, is merely historical. The doctrine of consideration is merely historical. The effect given to a seal is to be explained by history alone." The powers and functions of an executor, the distinctions between larceny and embezzlement, the rules of venue and the jurisdiction over foreign trespass, these are a few haphazard illustrations of growths which history has fostered, and which history (57) must tend to shape. There are times when the subject matter lends itself almost indifferently to the application of one method or another, and the predilection or training of the judge determines the choice of paths. The subject has been penetratingly discussed by Pound.[8] I borrow one of his illustrations. Is a gift of movables *inter vivos* effective without delivery? The controversy raged for many years before it was set at rest. Some judges relied on the analogy of the Roman Law. Others upon the history of forms of conveyance in our law. With some, it was the analysis of fundamental conceptions, followed by the extension of the results of analysis to logical conclusions. The declared will to give and to accept was to have that effect and no more which was consistent with some preestablished definition of a legal transaction, an act in the law. With others, the central thought was not consistency with a conception, the consideration of what logically ought to be done, but rather consistency with (58) history, the consideration of what had been done. I think the opinions in Lumley v. Gye, 2 El. & Bl. 216, which established a right of action against A for malicious interference with a contract between B and C, exhibit the same divergent strains, the same variance in emphasis. Often, the two methods supplement each other. Which method will predominate in any case, may depend at times upon intuitions of convenience or fitness too subtle to be formulated, too imponderable to be valued, too volatile to be localized or even fully apprehended. Sometimes the prevailing tendencies exhibited in the current writings of philosophical jurists may sway the balance. There are vogues and fashions in jurisprudence as in literature and art and dress. But of this there will be more to say when we deal with the forces that work subconsciously in the shaping of the law.

If history and philosophy do not serve to fix the direction of a principle, custom may step in. When we speak of custom, we may mean more things than one. "Consuetudo," says Coke, "is (59) one of the maine triangles of the lawes of England; these lawes being divided into common law, statute law and customs."[9] Here common law and custom are thought of as distinct. Not so, however, Blackstone: "This unwritten or Common Law is properly distinguishable into three kinds: (1) General customs, which are the universal rule of the whole Kingdom, and form the Common Law, in its stricter and more usual signification. (2) Particular customs, which for the most part affect only the inhabitants of particular districts. (3) Certain particular laws, which by custom are adopted and used by some particular courts of pretty general and extensive jurisdiction."[10]

Undoubtedly the creative energy of custom in the development of common law is less today than it was in bygone times.[11] Even in bygone (60) times, its energy was very likely exaggerated by Blackstone and his followers. "Today we recognize," in the words of Pound,[12] "that the custom is a custom of judicial decision, not of popular action." It is "doubtful," says Gray,[13] "whether at all stages of legal history, rules laid down by judges have not generated custom, rather than custom generated the rules." In these days, at all events, we look to custom, not so much for the creation of new rules, but for the tests and standards that are to determine how established rules shall be applied. When custom seeks to do more than this, there is a growing tendency in the law to leave development to legislation. Judges do not feel the same need of putting the *imprimatur* of law upon customs of recent growth, knocking for entrance into the legal system, and viewed askance because of some novel aspect of form or feature, as they would if legislatures were not in frequent session, capable of establishing a title that will be unimpeached and unimpeach (61) able. But the power is not lost because it is exercised with caution. "The law merchant," says an English judge, "is not fixed and stereotyped, it has not yet been arrested in its growth by being moulded into a code; it is, to use the words of Lord Chief Justice Cockburn in Goodwin v. Roberts, L. R. 10 Exch. 346, capable of being expanded and enlarged to meet the wants of trade."[14] In the absence of inconsistent statute, new classes of negotiable instruments may be created by mercantile practice.[15] The obligations of public and private corporations may retain the quality of negotiability, despite the presence of a seal, which at common law would destroy it. "There is nothing immoral or contrary to good policy in making them negotiable if the necessities of commerce require that they should be so. A mere technical dogma of the courts or the common law cannot prohibit the commercial world from inventing or issuing any species of (62) security not known in the last century."[16] So, in the memory of men yet living, the great inventions that embodied the power of steam and electricity, the railroad and the steamship, the telegraph and the telephone, have built up new customs and new law. Already there is a body of legal literature that deals with the legal problems of the air.

It is, however, not so much in the making of new rules as in the application of old ones that the creative energy of custom most often manifests itself today. General standards of right and duty are established. Custom must determine whether there has been adherence or departure. My partner has the powers that are usual in the trade. They may be so well known that the courts will notice them judicially. Such for illustration is the power of a member of a trading firm to make or indorse negotiable paper in the course of the firm's business.[17] They may be (63) such that the court will require evidence of their existence.[18] The master in the discharge of his duty to protect the servant against harm must exercise the degree of care that is commonly exercised in like circumstance by men of ordinary prudence. The triers of the facts in determining whether that standard has been attained, must consult the habits of life, the everyday beliefs and practices, of the men and women about them. Innumerable, also, are the cases where the course of dealing to be followed is defined by the customs, or, more properly speaking, the usages of a particular trade or market or profession.[19] The constant assumption runs throughout the law that the natural and spontaneous evolutions of habit fix the limits of right and wrong. A slight extension of custom identifies it with customary morality, the prevailing standard of right conduct, the *mores* of the time.[20] This is the point (64) of contact between the method of tradition and the method of sociology. They have their roots in the same soil. Each method maintains the interaction between conduct and order, between life and law. Life casts the moulds of conduct, which will some day become fixed as law. Law preserves the moulds, which have taken form and shape from life.

Three of the directive forces of our law, philosophy, history and custom, have now been seen at work. We have gone far enough to appreciate the complexity of the problem. We see that to determine to be loyal to precedents and to the principles back of precedents, does not carry us far upon the road. Principles are complex bundles. It is well enough to say that we shall be consistent, but consistent with what? Shall it be consistency with the origins of the rule, the course and tendency of development? Shall it be consistency with logic or philosophy or the fundamental conceptions of jurisprudence as disclosed by analysis of our own and foreign systems? All these loyalties are possible. All have (65) sometimes prevailed. How are we to choose between them? Putting that question aside, how do we choose between them? Some concepts of the law have been in a peculiar sense historical growths. In such departments, history will tend to give direction to development. In other departments, certain large and fundamental concepts, which comparative jurisprudence shows to be common to other highly developed systems, loom up above all others. In these we shall give a larger scope to logic and symmetry. A broad field there also is in which rules may, with approximately the same convenience, be settled one way or the other. Here custom tends to assert itself as the controlling force in guiding the choice of paths. Finally, when the social needs demand one settlement rather than another, there are times when we must bend symmetry, ignore history and sacrifice custom in the pursuit of other and larger ends.

From history and philosophy and custom, we pass, therefore, to the force which in our day and generation is becoming the greatest of them (66) all, the power of social justice which finds its outlet and expression in the method of sociology.

The final cause of law is the welfare of society. The rule that misses its aim cannot permanently justify its existence. "Ethical considerations can no more be excluded from the administration of justice which is the end and purpose of all civil laws than one can exclude the vital air from his room and live." [21] Logic and history and custom have their place. We will shape the law to conform to them when we may; but only within bounds. The end which the law serves will dominate them all. There is an old legend that on one occasion God prayed, and his prayer was "Be it my will that my justice be ruled by my mercy." That is a prayer which we all need to utter at times when the demon of formalism tempts the intellect with the lure of scientific order. I do not mean, of course, that judges are commissioned to set aside existing rules at pleasure in favor of any other (67) set of rules which they may hold to be expedient or wise. I mean that when they are called upon to say how far existing rules are to be extended or restricted, they must let the welfare of society fix the path, its direction and its distance. We are not to forget, said Sir George Jessel, in an often quoted judgment, that there is this paramount public policy, that we are not lightly to interfere with freedom of contract.[22] So in this field, there may be a paramount public policy, one that will prevail over temporary inconvenience or occasional hardship, not lightly to sacrifice certainty and uniformity and order and coherence. All these elements must be considered. They are to be given such weight as sound judgment dictates. They are constituents of that social welfare which it is our business to discover.[23] In a given instance we may find that they are constituents of preponderating value. In others, we may find that their value is subordinate. We must appraise them as best we can.

(68) I have said that judges are not commissioned to make and unmake rules at pleasure in accordance with changing views of expediency or wisdom. Our judges cannot say with

Hobbes: "Princes succeed one another, and one judge passeth, another cometh; nay heaven and earth shall pass, but not one tittle of the law of nature shall pass, for it is the eternal law of God. Therefore, all the sentences of precedent judges that have ever been, cannot altogether make a law contrary to natural equity, nor any examples of former judges can warrant an unreasonable sentence or discharge the present judge of the trouble of studying what is equity in the case he is to judge from the principles of his own natural reason." [24] Nearer to the truth for us are the words of an English judge: "Our common law system consists in applying to new combinations of circumstances those rules of law which we derive from legal principles and judicial precedents, and for the sake of attaining uniformity, con (69) sistency and certainty, we must apply those rules when they are not plainly unreasonable and inconvenient to all cases which arise; and we are not at liberty to reject them and to abandon all analogy to them in those in which they have not yet been judicially applied, because we think that the rules are not as convenient and reasonable as we ourselves could have devised." [25] This does not mean that there are not gaps, yet unfilled, within which judgment moves untrammeled. Mr. Justice Holmes has summed it up in one of his flashing epigrams: "I recognize without hesitation that judges must and do legislate, but they do so only interstitially; they are confined from molar to molecular motions. A common-law judge could not say, 'I think the doctrine of consideration a bit of historical nonsense and shall not enforce it in my court.'" [26] This conception of the legislative power of a judge as operating between spaces is akin to the theory of "gaps in the law" familiar (70) to foreign jurists.[27] "The general framework furnished by the statute is to be filled in for each case by means of interpretation, that is, by following out the principles of the statute. In every case, without exception, it is the business of the court to supply what the statute omits, but always by means of an interpretative function." [28] If the statute is interpreted by the method of "free decision," the process differs in degree rather than in kind from the process followed by the judges of England and America in the development of the common law. Indeed, Ehrlich in a recent book [29] quotes approvingly an English writer, who says [30] that "a code would not, except in a few cases, in which the law at present is obscure, limit any discretion now pos (71) sessed by the judges. It would simply change the form of the rules by which they are bound." I think that statement overshoots the mark. The fissures in the common law are wider than the fissures in a statute, at least in the form of statute common in England and the United States. In countries where statutes are oftener confined to the announcement of general principles, and there is no attempt to deal with details or particulars, legislation has less tendency to limit the freedom of the judge. That is why in our own law there is often greater freedom of choice in the construction of constitutions than in that of ordinary statutes. Constitutions are more likely to enunciate general principles, which must be worked out and applied thereafter to particular conditions. What concerns us now, however, is not the size of the gaps. It is rather the principle that shall determine how they are to be filled, whether their size be great or small. The method of sociology in filling the gaps, puts its emphasis on the social welfare.

Social welfare is a broad term. I use it to (72) cover many concepts more or less allied. It may mean what is commonly spoken of as public policy, the good of the collective body. In such cases, its demands are often those of mere expediency or prudence. It may mean on the other hand the social gain that is wrought by adherence to the standards of right conduct, which find expression in the *mores* of the community. In such cases, its demands are those of religion or of ethics or of the social sense of justice, whether formulated in creed or system, or immanent in the common mind. One does not readily find a single term to cover these and kindred aims which shade off into one another by imperceptible gradations. Perhaps we might fall back with Kohler [31] and Brütt [32] and Berolzheimer [33] on the indefinable, but comprehensive something known as Kultur if recent history had not discredited it and threatened odium for (73) those that use it. I have chosen in its stead a term which, if not precise enough for the philosopher, will at least be found sufficiently definite and inclusive to suit the purposes of the judge.

It is true, I think, today in every department of the law that the social value of a rule has become a test of growing power and importance. This truth is powerfully driven home to the lawyers of this country in the writings of Dean Pound. "Perhaps the most significant advance in the modern science of law is the change from the analytical to the functional attitude." [34] "The emphasis has changed from the content of the precept and the existence of the remedy to the effect of the precept in action and the availability and efficiency of the remedy to attain the ends for which the precept was devised." [35] Foreign jurists have the same thought: "The whole of the judicial function," says Gmelin,[36] (74) "has . . . been shifted. The will of the State, expressed in decision and judgment is to bring about a just determination by means of the subjective sense of justice inherent in the judge, guided by an effective weighing of the interests of the parties in the light of the opinions generally prevailing among the community regarding transactions like those in question. The determination should under all circumstances be in harmony with the requirements of good faith in business intercourse and the needs of practical life, unless a positive statute prevents it; and in weighing conflicting interests, the interest that is better founded in reason and more worthy of protection should be helped to achieve victory." [37] "On the one hand," says Gény,[38] "we are to interrogate reason and conscience, to discover in our inmost nature, the very basis of justice; on the other, we are to address ourselves to social (75) phenomena, to ascertain the laws of their harmony and the principles of order which they exact." And again: [39] "Justice and general utility, such will be the two objectives that will direct our course."

All departments of the law have been touched and elevated by this spirit. In some, however, the method of sociology works in harmony with the method of philosophy or of evolution or of tradition. Those, therefore, are the fields where logic and coherence and consistency must still be sought as ends. In others, it seems to displace the methods that compete with it. Those are the fields where the virtues of consistency must yield within those interstitial limits where judicial power moves. In a sense it is true that we are applying the method of sociology when we pursue logic and coherence and consistency as the greater social values. I am concerned for the moment with the fields in which the method is in antagonism to others rather than with those in which their action is in unison. Accurate divi (76) sion is, of course, impossible. A few broad areas may, however, be roughly marked as those in which the method of sociology has fruitful application. Let me seek some illustrations of its workings. I will look for them first of all in the field of constitutional law, where the primacy of this method is, I think, undoubted, then in certain branches of private law where public policy, having created rules, must have like capacity to alter them, and finally in other fields where the method, though less insistent and pervasive, stands ever in the background, and emerges to the front when technicality or logic or tradition may seem to press their claims unduly.

I speak first of the Constitution, and in particular of the great immunities with which it surrounds the individual. No one shall be deprived of liberty without due process of law. Here is a concept of the greatest generality. Yet it is put before the courts *en bloc*. Liberty is not defined. Its limits are not mapped and charted. How shall they be known? Does liberty mean the (77) same thing for successive generations? May restraints that were arbitrary yesterday be useful and rational and therefore lawful today? May restraints that are arbitrary today become useful and rational and therefore lawful tomorrow? I have no doubt that the answer to these questions must be yes. There were times in our judicial history when the answer might have been no. Liberty was conceived of at first as something static and absolute. The Declaration of Independence had enshrined it. The blood of Revolution had sanctified it. The political philosophy of Rousseau and of Locke and later of Herbert Spencer and of the Manchester school of economists had dignified and rationalized it. *Laissez faire* was not only a counsel of caution which statesmen would do well to heed. It was a categorical imperative which statesmen, as well as judges, must obey. The "nineteenth century theory" was "one of eternal legal conceptions involved in the very idea of justice and containing potentially an exact rule for every case to be reached by an absolute process of logical deduc- (78) tion." [40] The century had not closed, however, before a new political philosophy became reflected in the work of statesmen and ultimately in the decrees of courts. The transition is interestingly described by Dicey in his "Law and Opinion in England." [41] The movement from individualistic liberalism to unsystematic collectivism" had brought changes in the social order which carried with them the need of a new formulation of fundamental rights and duties. In our country, the need did not assert itself so soon. Courts still spoke in the phrases of a philosophy that had served its day.[42] Gradually, however, though not without frequent protest and intermittent movements backward, a new conception of the significance of constitutional limitations in the domain of individual liberty, emerged to recognition and to dominance. Judge Hough, in an interesting address, finds the dawn (79) of the new epoch in 1883, when Hurtado v. California, 110 U. S. 516, was argued.[43] If the new epoch had then dawned, it was still obscured by fog and cloud. Scattered rays of light may have heralded the coming day. They were not enough to blaze the path. Even as late as 1905, the decision in Lochner v. N. Y., 198 U. S. 45, still spoke in terms untouched by the light of the new spirit. It is the dissenting opinion of Justice Holmes, which men will turn to in the future as the beginning of an era.[44] In the instance, it was the voice of a minority. In principle, it has become the voice of a new dispensation, which has written itself into law. "The Fourteenth Amendment does not enact Mr. Herbert Spencer's Social Statics." [45] "A constitution is not intended to embody a particular economic theory, whether of paternalism and the organic relation of the citizen to the state, or of *laissez* (80) *faire*." [46] "The word liberty in the Fourteenth Amendment is perverted when it is held to prevent the natural outcome of a dominant opinion, unless it can be said that a rational and fair man necessarily would admit that the statute proposed would infringe fundamental principles as they have been understood by the traditions of our people and our law." [47] That is the conception of liberty which is dominant today.[48] It has its critics even yet,[49] but its dominance is, I think, assured. No doubt, there will at times be difference of opinion when a conception so delicate is applied to varying conditions.[50] At times, indeed, the conditions themselves are imperfectly disclosed and inadequately known. Many and insidious are the agencies by which opinion is poisoned at its sources. Courts have often been (81) led into error in passing upon the validity of a statute, not from misunderstanding of the law, but from misunderstanding of the facts. This happened in New York. A statute forbidding night work for women was declared arbitrary and void in 1907.[51] In 1915, with fuller knowledge of the investigations of social workers, a like statute was held to be reasonable and valid.[52] Courts know today that statutes are to be viewed, not in isolation or *in vacuo,* as pronouncements of abstract principles for the guidance of an ideal community, but in the setting and the framework of present-day conditions, as revealed by the labors of economists and students of the social sciences in our own country and abroad.[53] The same fluid and dynamic conception which underlies the modern notion of liberty, as secured to the individual by the constitutional immunity, (82) must also underlie the cognate notion of equality. No state shall deny to any person within its jurisdiction "the equal protection of the laws."[54] Restrictions, viewed narrowly, may seem to foster inequality. The same restrictions, when viewed broadly, may be seen "to be necessary in the long run in order to establish the equality of position between the parties in which liberty of contract begins."[55] Charmont in "La Renaissance du Droit Naturel,"[56] gives neat expression to the same thought: "On tend à considerer qu'il n'y a pas de contrat respectable si les parties n'ont pas été placées dans les conditions non seulement de liberté, mais d'égalité. Si l'un des contractants est sans abri, sans ressources, condamné à subir les exigences de l'autre, la liberté de fait est supprimée."[57]

From all this, it results that the content of (83) constitutional immunities is not constant, but varies from age to age. "The needs of successive generations may make restrictions imperative today, which were vain and capricious to the vision of times past."[58] "We must never forget," in Marshall's mighty phrase, "that it is a *constitution* we are expounding."[59] Statutes are designed to meet the fugitive exigencies of the hour. Amendment is easy as the exigencies change. In such cases, the meaning, once construed, tends legitimately to stereotype itself in the form first cast. A *constitution* states or ought to state not rules for the passing hour, but principles for an expanding future. In so far as it deviates from that standard, and descends into details and particulars, it loses its flexibility, the scope of interpretation contracts, the meaning (84) hardens. While it is true to its function, it maintains its power of adaptation, its suppleness, its play. I think it is interesting to note that even in the interpretation of ordinary statutes, there are jurists, at any rate abroad, who maintain that the meaning of today is not always the meaning of tomorrow. "The President of the highest French Court, M. Ballot-Beaupré, explained, a few years ago, that the provisions of the Napoleonic legislation had been adapted to modern conditions by a judicial interpretation in '*le sens évolutif.*' 'We do not inquire,' he said, 'what the legislator willed a century ago, but what he would have willed if he had known what our present conditions would be.' "[60] So Kohler: "It follows from all this that the interpretation of a statute must by no means of necessity remain the same forever. To speak of an exclusively correct interpretation, one which would be the true meaning of the statute from the begin (85) ning to the end of its day, is altogether erroneous.[61] I think the instances must be rare, if any can be found at all, in which this method of interpretation has been applied in English or American law to ordinary legislation. I have no doubt that it has been applied in the past and with increasing frequency will be applied in the future, to fix the scope and meaning of the broad precepts and immunities in state and national constitutions. I see no reason why it may not be applied to statutes framed upon lines similarly general, if any such there are. We are to read them, whether the result be contraction or expansion, in "*le sens évolutif.*" [62]

Apposite illustrations may be found in recent statutes and decisions. It was long ago held by the Supreme Court that the legislature had the power to control and regulate a business affected (86) with "a public use." [63] It is held by the Supreme Court today that there is a like power where the business is affected with "a public interest." [64] The business of fire insurance has been brought within that category.[65] A recent decision of an inferior court has put within the same category the business of the sale of coal where the emergency of war or of the dislocation that results from war brings hardship and oppression in the train of unfettered competition.[66] The advocates of the recent housing statutes in New York [67] profess to find in like principles the justification for new restraints upon ancient rights of property. I do not suggest any opinion upon the question whether those acts in any of their aspects may be held to go too far. I do no more than indicate the nature of the problem, and the method and spirit of approach.[68]

(87) Property, like liberty, though immune under the Constitution from destruction, is not immune from regulation essential for the common good. What that regulation shall be, every generation must work out for itself.[69] The generation which gave us Munn v. Illinois, 94 U. S. 113 (1876), and like cases, asserted the right of regulation whenever business was "affected with a public use." The phrase in its application meant little more than if it said, whenever the social need shall be imminent and pressing. Such a formulation of the principle may have been adequate for the exigencies of the time. Today there is a growing tendency in political and juristic thought to probe the principle more deeply and formulate it more broadly. Men are saying today that property, like every other social institution, has a social function to fulfill. Legislation which destroys the institution is one thing. Legislation which holds it true to its function is quite another. That is the dominant theme of a new and (88) forceful school of publicists and jurists on the continent of Europe, in England, and even here. Among the French, one may find the thought developed with great power and suggestiveness by Duguit in his "Transformations générales du droit privé depuis le Code Napoléon." [70] It is yet too early to say how far this new conception of function and its obligations will gain a lodgment in our law. Perhaps we shall find in the end that it is little more than Munn v. Illinois in the garb of a new philosophy. I do not attempt to predict the extent to which we shall adopt it, or even to assert that we shall adopt it at all. Enough for my purpose at present that new times and new manners may call for new standards and new rules.

The courts, then, are free in marking the limits of the individual's immunities to shape their judgments in accordance with reason and justice. That does not mean that in judging the validity of statutes they are free to substitute (89) their own ideas of reason and justice for those of the men and women whom they serve. Their standard must be an objective one. In such matters, the thing that counts is not what I believe to be right. It is what I may reasonably believe that some other man or normal intellect and conscience might reasonably look upon as right. "While the courts must exercise a judgment of their own, it by no means is true that every law is void which may seem to the judges who pass upon it excessive, unsuited to its ostensible end, or based upon conceptions of morality with which they disagree. Considerable latitude must be allowed for difference of view as well as for possible peculiar conditions which this court can know but imperfectly, if at all. Otherwise a constitution, instead of embodying only relatively fundamental rules of right, as generally understood by all English-speaking communities, would become the partisan of a particular set of ethical or economical opinions, which by no means are held *semper ubique et ab omnibus.*" [71] (90) Here as so often in the law, "the standard of conduct is external, and takes no account of the personal equation of the man concerned." [72] "The interpreter," says Brütt,[73] "must above all things put aside his estimate of political and legislative values, and must endeavor to ascertain in a purely objective spirit what ordering of the social life of the community comports best with the aim of the law in question in the circumstances before him." Some fields of the law there are, indeed, where there is freer scope for subjective vision. Of these we shall say more hereafter. The personal element, whatever its scope in other spheres, should have little, if any, sway in determining the limits of legislative power. One department of the government may not force upon another its own standards of propriety. "It must be remembered that legislatures are ultimate guardians of the liberties and welfare of the people in quite as great a degree as courts." [74]

(91) Some critics of our public law insist that the power of the courts to fix the limits of permissible encroachment by statute upon the liberty of the individual is one that ought to be withdrawn.[75] It means, they say, either too much or too little. If it is freely exercised, if it is made an excuse for imposing the individual beliefs and philosophies of the judges upon other branches of the government, if it stereotypes legislation within the forms and limits that were expedient in the nineteenth or perhaps the eighteenth century, it shackles progress and breeds distrust and suspicion of the courts. If, on the other hand, it is interpreted in the broad and variable sense which I believe to be the true one, if statutes are to be

sustained unless they are so plainly arbitrary and oppressive that right-minded men and women could not reasonably regard them otherwise, the right of supervision, it is said, is not worth the danger of abuse. "There no doubt comes a time when a statute is so obviously oppressive and ab (92) surd that it can have no justification in any sane polity." [76] Such times may indeed come, yet only seldom. The occasions must be few when legislatures will enact a statute that will merit condemnation upon the application of a test so liberal; and if carelessness or haste or momentary passion may at rare intervals bring such statutes into being with hardship to individuals or classes, we may trust to succeeding legislatures for the undoing of the wrong. That is the argument of the critics of the existing system. My own belief is that it lays too little stress on the value of the "imponderables." The utility of an external power restraining the legislative judgment is not to be measured by counting the occasions of its exercise. The great ideals of liberty and equality are preserved against the assaults of opportunism, the expediency of the passing hour, the erosion of small encroachments, the scorn and derision of those who have no patience with general principles, by enshrining them in constitutions, and (93) consecrating to the task of their protection a body of defenders. By conscious or subconscious influence, the presence of this restraining power, aloof in the background, but none the less always in reserve, tends to stabilize and rationalize the legislative judgment, to infuse it with the glow of principle, to hold the standard aloft and visible to those who must run the race and keep the faith.[77] I do not mean to deny that there have been times when the possibility of judicial review has worked the other way. Legislatures have sometimes disregarded their own responsibility, and passed it on to the courts. Such dangers must be balanced against those of independence from all restraint, independence on the part of public officers elected for brief terms, without the guiding force of a continuous tradition. On the whole, I believe the latter dangers to be the more formidable of the two. Great maxims, if they may be violated with impunity, are honored often with lip-service, which passes (94) easily into irreverence. The restraining power of the judiciary does not manifest its chief worth in the few cases in which the legislature has gone beyond the lines that mark the limits of discretion. Rather shall we find its chief worth in making vocal and audible the ideals that might otherwise be silenced, in giving them continuity of life and of expression, in guiding and directing choice within the limits where choice ranges. This function should preserve to the courts the power that now belongs to them, if only the power is exercised with insight into social values, and with suppleness of adaptation to changing social needs.

I pass to another field where the dominance of the method of sociology may be reckoned as assured. There are some rules of private law which have been shaped in their creation by public policy, and this, not merely silently or in conjunction with other forces, but avowedly, and almost, if not quite, exclusively. These, public policy, as determined by new conditions, is competent to change. I take as an illustration modern decisions (95) which have liberalized the common law rule condemning contracts in restraint of trade. The courts have here allowed themselves a freedom of action which in many branches of the law they might be reluctant to avow. Lord Watson put the matter bluntly in Nordenfeldt v. Maxim, Nordenfeldt Guns & Ammunition Co. L. R. 1894 App. Cas. 535, 553: "A series of decisions based upon grounds of public policy, however eminent the judges by whom they were delivered, cannot possess the same binding authority as decisions which deal with and formulate principles which are purely legal. The course of policy pursued by any country in relation to, and for promoting the interests of, its commerce must, as time advances and as its commerce thrives, undergo change and development from various causes which are altogether independent of the action of its courts. In England, at least, it is beyond the jurisdiction of her tribunals to mould and stereotype national policy. Their function, when a case like the present is brought before them, is, in my opinion, not necessarily to ac (96) cept what was held to have been the rule of policy a hundred or a hundred and fifty years ago, but to ascertain, with as near an approach to accuracy as circumstances permit, what is the rule of policy for the then present time. When that rule has been ascertained, it becomes their duty to refuse to give effect to a private contract which violates the rule, and would, if judicially enforced, prove injurious to the community." A like thought finds expression in the opinions of our own courts. "Arbitrary rules which were originally well founded have thus been made to yield to changed conditions, and underlying principles are applied to existing methods of doing business. The tendencies in most of the American courts are in the same direction."[78] I think we may trace a like development in the attitude of the courts toward the activities of labor unions. The suspicion and even hostility of an earlier generation found reflection in judicial decisions which a changing conception of social values (97) has made it necessary to recast.[79] Some remnants of the older point of view survive, but they are remnants only. The field is one where the law is yet in the making or better perhaps in the remaking. We cannot doubt that its new form will bear an impress of social needs and values which are emerging even now to recognition and to power.

REFERENCES

1. *Cf.* Holmes, "The Path of the Law," 10 *Harvard L. R.* 465.
2. Bryce, "Studies in History and Jurisprudence," vol. II, p. 609.
3. "Collected Papers," vol. III, p. 438.
4. Techt v. Hughes, 229 N. Y. 222, 240.
5. Holmes, J., in N. Y. Trust Co. v. Eisner, 256 U. S. 345, 349.
6. "Equity and Forms of Action," p. 296.
7. "The Path of the Law," 10 *Harvard L. R.* 472.
8. "Juristic Science and the Law," 31 *Harvard L. R.* 1047.
9. Coke on Littleton, 62a; Post v. Pearsall, 22 Wend. 440.
10. Blackstone, Comm., pp. 67, 68; Gray, "Nature and Sources of the Law," p. 266, sec. 598; Sadler, "The Relation of Custom to Law," p. 59.
11. *Cf.* Gray, *supra,* sec. 634; Salmond, "Jurisprudence," p. 143; Gény, *op. cit.,* vol. I, p. 324, sec. 111.
12. "Common Law and Legislation," 21 *Harvard L. R.* 383, 406.
13. *Supra,* sec. 634.
14. Edelstein v. Schuler 1902, 2 K. B. 144, 154; *cf.* Bechuanaland Exploration Co. v. London Trading Bank, 1898, 2 Q. B. 658.
15. Cases, *supra.*
16. Mercer County v. Hacket, 1 Wall. 83; *cf.* Chase Nat. Bank v. Faurot, 149 N. Y. 532.
17. Lewy v. Johnson, 2 Pet. 186.
18. First Nat. Bank v. Farson 226 N. Y. 218.
19. Irwin v. Williar, 110 U. S. 499, 513; Walls v. Bailey, 49 N. Y. 464; 2 Williston on Contracts, sec. 649.
20. Gény, *op. cit.,* vol. I, p. 319, sec. 110.
21. Dillon, "Laws and Jurisprudence of England and America," p. 18, quoted by Pound, 27 *Harvard L. R.* 731, 733.
22. Printing etc. Registering Co. v. Sampson, L. R. 19 Eq. 462. 465.
23. *Cf.* Brütt, *supra,* pp. 161, 163.
24. Hobbes, vol. II, p. 264; quoted by W. G. Miller, "The Data of Jurisprudence," p. 399.

25. Sir James Parke, afterwards Lord Wensleydale, in Mirehouse v. Russell, 1 Cl. & F. 527, 546, quoted by Ehrlich, "Grundlegung des Soziologie des Rechts" [1913], p. 234; *cf.* Pollock, "Jurisprudence," p. 323.

26. Southern Pacific Co. v. Jensen 244 U. S. 205, 221.

27. 9 Modern Legal Philosophy Series, pp. 159–163, 172–175; *cf.* Ehrlich, "Die juristische Logik," 215, 216; Zitelmann, "Lücken im Recht," 23; Brütt, "Die Kunst der Rechtsandwendung," p. 75; Stammler, "Lehre von dem Richtigen Rechts," p. 271.

28. Kiss, "Equity and Law," 9 Modern Legal Philosophy Series, p. 161.

29. "Grundlegung der Soziologie des Rechts" [1913], p. 234.

30. 19 L. Q. R. 15.

31. Enzyklopadie, Bd. 1, D. 10; Philosophy of Law, 12 Modern Legal Philosophy Series, p. 58.

32. *Supra,* p. 133, *et seq.*

33. "System des Rechts und Wirthschaftsphilosophie," Bd. 3, s. 28.

34. Pound, "Administrative Application of Legal Standards," Proceedings American Bar Association 1919, pp. 441, 449.

35. *Ibid.,* p. 451; *cf.* Pound, "Mechanical Jurisprudence," 8 *Columbia L. R.* 603.

36. "Sociological Method," transl., 9 Modern Legal Philosophy Series, p. 131.

37. Gmelin, *supra; cf.* Ehrlich, "Die juristische Logik," p. 187; Duguit, "Les Transformations du droit depuis le Code Napoléon," transl., Continental Legal Hist. Series, vol. XI, pp. 72, 79.

38. *Op. cit.,* vol. II, p. 92, sec. 159.

39. Vol. II, p. 91.

40. Pound, "Juristic Science and The Law," 31 *Harvard L. R.* 1047, 1048.

41. *Cf.* Duguit, *supra.*

42. Haines, "The Law of Nature in Federal Decisions," 25 *Yale L. J.* 617.

43. Hough, "Due Process of Law Today," 32 *Harvard L. R.* 218, 227.

44. *Cf.* Hough p. 232; also Frankfurter, "Const. Opinions of Holmes, J.," 29 *Harvard L. R.* 683, 687; Ehrlich, "Die juristische Logik," pp. 237, 239.

45. 198 U. S. 75.

46. P. 75.

47. P. 76.

48. Noble v. State Bank, 219 U. S. 104; Tanner v. Little, 240 U. S. 369; Hall v. Geiger Jones Co., 242 U. S. 539; Green v. Frazier, 253 U. S. 233; Frankfurter, *supra.*

49 Burgess, "Reconciliation of Government and Liberty."

50. Adams v. Tanner, 244 U. S. 590.

51. People v. Williams, 189 N. Y. 131.

52. People v. Schweinler Press, 214 N. Y. 395.

53. Muller v. Oregon, 208 U. S. 412; Pound, "Courts and Legislation," 9 Modern Legal Philosophy Series, p. 225; Pound, "Scope and Progress of Sociological Jurisprudence," 25 *Harvard L. R.* 513; *cf.* Brandeis, J., in Adams v. Tanner, 244 U. S. 590, 600.

54. U. S. Const., 14th Amendment.

55. Holmes, J., dissenting in Coppage v. Kansas, 236 U. S. 1, 27.

56. Montpellier, Coulet et fils, éditeurs, 1910.

57. "There is now a tendency to consider no contract worthy of respect unless the parties to it are in relations, not only of liberty, but of equality. If one of the parties be without defense or resources, compelled to comply with the demands of the other, the result is a suppression of true freedom."—Charmont, *supra,* p. 172; transl. in 7 Modern Legal Philosophy Series, p. 110, sec. 83.

58. Klein v. Maravelas, 219 N. Y. 383, 386.

59. *Cf.* Frankfurter, *supra;* McCulloch v. Maryland, 4 Wheat. 407.

60. Munroe Smith, "Jurisprudence," pp. 29, 30; *cf.* Vander Eycken, *supra,* pp. 383, 384; also Brütt, *supra,* p. 62.

61. Kohler. "Interpretation of Law," transl. in 9 Modern Legal Philosophy Series, 192; *cf.* the Report of Prof. Huber on the German Code, quoted by Gény, "Technic of Codes," 9 Modern Legal Philosophy Series, p. 548; also Gény, "Méthode et Sources en droit privé positif," vol. I, p. 273.

62. Munroe Smith, *supra.*

63. Munn v. Illinois, 94 U. S. 113.

64. German Alliance Ins. Co. v. Kansas, 233 U. S. 389.

65. German Alliance Ins. Co. v. Kansas, *supra.*

66. American Coal Mining Co. v. Coal & Food Commission, U. S. District Court, Indiana, Sept. 6, 1920.

67. L. 1920 chaps. 942 to 953.

68. Since these lectures were written, the statutes have been sustained: People *ex rel.* Durham Realty Co. v. La Fetra, 230 N. Y. 429; Marcus Brown Holding Co. v. Feldman, 256 U. S. 170.

69. Green v. Frazier, 253 U. S. 233.

70. Transl., Continental Legal Hist. Series, vol. XI, p. 74, sec. 6, *et seq.;* for a more extreme view, see R. H. Tawney, "The Acquisitive Society."

71. Otis v. Parker, 187 U. S. 608.

72. The Germanic, 196 U. S. 589, 596.

73. "Die Kunst der Rechtsanwendung," p. 57.

74. Missouri, K. & T. Co. v. May, 194 U. S. 267, 270; People v. Crane, 214 N. Y. 154, 173.

75. *Cf.* Collins, "The 14th Amendment and the States," pp. 158, 166.

76. Learned Hand, "Due Process of Law and the Eight Hour Day," 21 *Harvard L. R.* 495, 508.

77. *Cf.* Laski, "Authority in the Modern State," pp. 62, 63.

78. Knowlton, J., in Anchor Electric Co. v. Hawkes, 171 Mass. 101, 104.

79. *Cf.* Laski, "Authority in the Modern State," p. 39.

(98)

Lecture III. The Method of Sociology.
The Judge as a Legislator.

I HAVE chosen these branches of the law merely as conspicuous illustrations of the application by the courts of the method of sociology. But the truth is that there is no branch where the method is not fruitful. Even when it does not seem to dominate, it is always in reserve. It is the arbiter between other methods, determining in the last analysis the choice of each, weighing their competing claims, setting bounds to their pretensions, balancing and moderating and harmonizing them all. Few rules in our time are so well established that they may not be called upon any day to justify their existence as means adapted to an end. If they do not function they are diseased. If they are diseased, they must not propagate their kind. Sometimes they are cut out and extirpated altogether. Sometimes (99) they are left with the shadow of continued life, but sterilized, truncated, impotent for harm.

We get a striking illustration of the force of logical consistency, then of its gradual breaking down before the demands of practical convenience in isolated or exceptional instances, and finally of the generative force of the exceptions as a new stock, in the cases that deal with the right of a beneficiary to recover on a contract. England has been logically consistent and has refused the right of action altogether. New York and most states yielded to the demands of convenience and enforced the right of action, but at first only exceptionally and subject to many restrictions. Gradually the exceptions broadened till today they have left little of the rule.[1] It survives chiefly in those cases where intention would be frustrated or convenience impaired by the extension of the right of action to others than the contracting parties.[2] Rules derived by a process of logical deduction from pre-established (100) conceptions of contract and obligation have broken down before the slow and steady and erosive action of utility and justice.[3]

We see the same process at work in other fields. We no longer interpret contracts with meticulous adherence to the letter when in conflict with the spirit. We read covenants into them by implication when we find them "instinct with an obligation" imperfectly expressed. "The law has outgrown its primitive stage of formalism when the precise word was the sovereign talisman, and every slip was fatal." [4] Perhaps it is in the field of procedure that we have witnessed the chief changes; though greater ones must yet be wrought. Indictments and civil pleadings are viewed with indulgent eyes. Rulings upon questions of evidence are held with increasing frequency to come within the discretion of the judge presiding at the trial. Errors are no longer ground for the upsetting of judgments with the ensuing horror of new trials, unless the appellate court (101) is satisfied that they have affected the result. Legislation has sometimes been necessary to free us from the old fetters. Sometimes the conservatism of judges has threatened for an interval to rob the legislation of its efficacy.[5] This danger was disclosed in the attitude of the courts toward the reforms embodied in codes of practice, in the days when they were first enacted.[6] Precedents established in those times exert an unhappy influence even now. None the less, the tendency today is in th direction of a growing liberalism. The new spirit has made its way gradually; and its progress, unnoticed step by step, is visible in retrospect as we look back upon the distance traversed. The old forms remain, but they are filled with a new content. We are getting away from what Ehrlich calls "die spielerische und die mathematische Entscheidung," [7] the conception of a lawsuit either as a mathematical prob-(102) lem or as a sportsman's game. Our own Wigmore has done much to make that conception out of date.[8] We are thinking of the end which the law serves, and fitting its rules to the task of service.

This conception of the end of the law as determining the direction of its growth, which was Jhering's great contribution to the theory of jurisprudence,[9] finds its organon, its instrument, in the method of sociology. Not the origin, but the goal, is the main thing. There can be no wisdom in the choice of a path unless we know where it will lead. The teleological conception of his function must be ever in the judge's mind. This means, of course, that the juristic philosophy of the common law is at bottom the philosophy of pragmatism.[10] Its truth is relative, not absolute. The rule that functions well produces (103) a title deed to recognition.

Only in determining how it functions we must not view it too narrowly. We must not sacrifice the general to the particular. We must not throw to the winds the advantages of consistency and uniformity to do justice in the instance.[11] We must keep within those interstitial limits which precedent and custom and the long and silent and almost indefinable practice of other judges through the centuries of the common law have set to judge-made innovations. But within the limits thus set, within the range over which choice moves, the final principle of selection for judges, as for legislators, is one of fitness to an end. "Le but est la vie interne, l'âme cachée, mais génératrice, de tous les droits." [12] We do not pick our rules of law full-blossomed from the trees. Every judge consulting his own experience must be conscious of times when a free exercise of will, directed of (104) set purpose to the furtherance of the common good, determined the form and tendency of a rule which at that moment took its origin in one creative act. Savigny's conception of law as something realized without struggle or aim or purpose, a process of silent growth, the fruition in life and manners of a people's history and genius, gives a picture incomplete and partial. It is true if we understand it to mean that the judge in shaping the rules of law must heed the *mores* of his day. It is one-sided and therefore false in so far as it implies that the *mores* of the day automatically shape rules which, full grown and ready made, are handed to the judge.[13] Legal norms are confused with legal principles—*Entscheidungsnormen* with *Rechtssätze*.[14] Law is, indeed, an historical growth, for it is an expression of customary morality which develops silently and unconsciously from one age to an (105) other. That is the great truth in Savigny's theory of its origin. But law is also a conscious or purposed growth, for the expression of customary morality will be false unless the mind of the judge is directed to the attainment of the moral end and its embodiment in legal forms.[15] Nothing less than conscious effort will be adequate if the end in view is to prevail. The standards or patterns of utility and morals will be found by the judge in the life of the community. They will be found in the same way by the legislator. That does not mean, however, that the work of the one any more than that of the other is a replica of nature's forms.

There has been much debate among foreign jurists whether the norms of right and useful conduct, the patterns of social welfare, are to be found by the judge in conformity with an objective or a subjective standard. Opposing schools of thought have battled for each view.[16] At times, (106) the controversy has seemed to turn upon the use of words and little more. So far as the distinction has practical significance, the traditions of our jurisprudence commit us to the objective standard. I do not mean, of course, that this ideal of objective vision is ever perfectly attained. We cannot transcend the limitations of the *ego* and see anything as it really is. None the less, the ideal is one to be striven for within the limits of our capacity. This truth, when clearly perceived, tends to unify the judge's function. His duty to declare the law in accordance with reason and justice is seen to be a phase of his duty to declare it in accordance with custom. It is the customary morality of right-minded men and women which he is to enforce by his decree. A jurisprudence that is not constantly brought into relation to objective or external standards, incurs the risk of degenerating into what the Germans call "Die Gefühlsjurisprudenz," a jurisprudence of mere sentiment or feeling.[17] A judicial judgment, says Stammler, "should be a judgment of objective (107) right, and no subjective and free opinion; a verdict and not a mere personal fiat. Evil stands the case when it is to be said of a judicial decree as the saying goes in the play of the 'Two Gentlemen of Verona' (Act I, sc. ii):

" 'I have no other but a woman's reason;
I think him so, because I think him so.' "[18]

Scholars of distinction have argued for a more subjective standard. "We all agree," says Professor Gray,[19] "that many cases should be decided by the courts on notions of right and wrong and, of course, everyone will agree that a judge is likely to share the notions of right and wrong prevalent in the community in which he lives; but suppose in a case where there is nothing to guide him but notions of right and wrong, that his notions of right and wrong differ from those of the community—which ought he to follow—his own notions, or the notions of the community? Mr. Carter's theory ["Origin and Sources of Law," J. C. Carter] requires him to (108) say that the judge must follow the notions of the community. I believe that he should follow his own notions." The hypothesis that Professor Gray offers us, is not likely to be realized in practice. Rare indeed must be the case when, with conflicting notions of right conduct, there will be nothing else to sway the balance. If, however, the case supposed were here, a judge, I think, would err if he were to impose upon the community as a rule of life his own idiosyncrasies of conduct or belief. Let us, suppose, for illustration, a judge who looked upon theatre-going as a sin. Would he be doing right if, in a field where the rule of law was still unsettled, he permitted this conviction, though known to be in conflict with the dominant standard of right conduct, to govern his decision? My own notion is that he would be under a duty to conform to the accepted standards of the community, the *mores* of the times. This does not mean, however, that a judge is powerless to raise the level of prevailing conduct. In one field or another of activity, practices in opposition to the sentiments and (109) standards of the age may grow up and threaten to intrench themselves if not dislodged. Despite their temporary hold, they do not stand comparison with accepted norms of morals. Indolence or passivity has tolerated what the considerate judgment of the community condemns. In such cases, one of the highest functions of the judge is to establish the true relation between conduct and profession. There are even times, to speak somewhat paradoxically, when nothing less than a subjective measure will satisfy objective standards. Some relations in life impose a duty to act in accordance with the customary morality and nothing more. In those the customary morality must be the standard for the judge. *Caveat emptor* is a maxim that will often have to be followed when the morality which it expresses is not that of sensitive souls. Other relations in life, as, e.g., those of trustee and beneficiary, or principal and surety, impose a duty to act in accordance with the highest standards which a man of the most delicate conscience and the nicest sense of honor might impose upon (110) himself. In such cases, to enforce adherence to those standards becomes the duty of the judge. Whether novel situations are to be brought within one class of relations or within the other must be determined, as they arise, by considerations of analogy, of convenience, of fitness, and of justice.

The truth, indeed, is, as I have said, that the distinction

between the subjective or individual and the objective or general conscience, in the field where the judge is not limited by established rules, is shadowy and evanescent, and tends to become one of words and little more. For the casuist and the philosopher, it has its speculative interest. In the practical administration of justice, it will seldom be decisive for the judge. This is admitted by Brütt, one of the staunchest upholders of the theory of objective right.[20] The perception of objective right takes the color of the subjective mind. The conclusions of the subjective mind take the color of customary practices and objectified beliefs. There is con-
(111) stant and subtle interaction between what is without and what is within. We may hold, on the one side, with Tarde and his school, that all social innovations come "from individual inventions spread by imitation," [21] or on the other side, with Durkheim and his school, that all such innovations come "through the action of the social mind." [22] In either view, whether the impulse spreads from the individual or from society, from within or from without, neither the components nor the mass can work in independence of each other. The personal and the general mind and will are inseparably united. The difference, as one theory of judicial duty or the other prevails, involves at most a little change of emphasis, of the method of approach, of the point of view, the angle, from which problems are envisaged. Only dimly and by force of an influence subconscious, or nearly so, will the difference be reflected in the decisions of the courts.

(112) My analysis of the judicial process comes then to this, and little more: logic, and history, and custom, and utility, and the accepted standards of right conduct, are the forces which singly or in combination shape the progress of the law. Which of these forces shall dominate in any case, must depend largely upon the comparative importance or value of the social interests that will be thereby promoted or impaired.[23] One of the most fundamental social interests is that law shall be uniform and impartial. There must be nothing in its action that savors of prejudice or favor or even arbitrary whim or fitfulness. Therefore in the main there shall be adherence to precedent. There shall be symmetrical development, consistently with history or custom when history or custom has been the motive force, or the chief one,

in giving shape to existing rules, and with logic or philosophy when the motive power has been theirs. But symmetrical development may be bought at too high a price. Uni (113) formity ceases to be a good when it becomes uniformity of oppression. The social interest served by symmetry or certainty must then be balanced against the social interest served by equity and fairness or other elements of social welfare. These may enjoin upon the judge the duty of drawing the line at another angle, of staking the path along new courses, of marking a new point of departure from which others who come after him will set out upon their journey.

If you ask how he is to know when one interest outweighs another, I can only answer that he must get his knowledge just as the legislator gets it, from experience and study and reflection; in brief, from life itself. Here, indeed, is the point of contact between the legislator's work and his. The choice of methods, the appraisement of values, must in the end be guided by like considerations for the one as for the other. Each indeed is legislating within the limits of his competence. No doubt the limits for the judge are narrower. He legislates only between gaps. He fills the open spaces in the law. How far he (114) may go without traveling beyond the walls of the interstices cannot be staked out for him upon a chart. He must learn it for himself as he gains the sense of fitness and proportion that comes with years of habitude in the practice of an art. Even within the gaps, restrictions not easy to define, but felt, however impalpable they may be, by every judge and lawyer, hedge and circumscribe his action. They are established by the traditions of the centuries, by the example of other judges, his predecessors and his colleagues, by the collective judgment of the profession, and by the duty of adherence to the pervading spirit of the law. "Il ne peut intervenir," says Charmont,[24] "que pour suppléer les sources formelles, mais il n'a pas, dans cette mesure même, toute latitude pour créer des règles de droit. Il ne peut ni faire échec aux principes généraux de notre organisation juridique, explicitement on implicitement consacrés, no formuler une réglementation de detail pour l'exercise de certain droits, en établissant des (115) délais, des formalités, des règles de publicité."[25] None the less, within the confines of these open spaces and those of precedent and tradition, choice moves with a freedom which stamps its action as creative. The law which is the resulting product is not found, but made. The process, being legislative, demands the legislator's wisdom.

(116) There is in truth nothing revolutionary or even novel in this view of the judicial function.[26] It is the way that courts have gone about their business for centuries in the development of the common law. The difference from age to age is not so much in the recognition of the need that law shall conform itself to an end. It is rather in the nature of the end to which there has been need to conform. There have been periods when uniformity, even rigidity, the elimination of the personal element, were felt to be the paramount needs.[27] By a sort of paradox, the end was best served by disregarding it and thinking only of the means. Gradually the need of a more flexible system asserted itself. Often the gap between the old rule and the new was bridged by the pious fraud of a fiction.[28] The thing which concerns us here is that it was bridged whenever the (117) importance of the end was dominant. Today the use of fictions has declined; and the springs of action are disclosed where once they were concealed. Even now, they are not fully known, however, even to those whom they control. Much of the process has been unconscious or nearly so. The ends to which courts have addressed themselves, the reasons and motives that have guided them, have often been vaguely felt, intuitively or almost intuitively apprehended, seldom explicitly avowed. There has been little of deliberate introspection, of dissection, of analysis, of philosophizing. The result has been an amalgam of which the ingredients were unknown or forgotten. That is why there is something of a shock in the discovery that legislative policy has made the compound what it is. "We do not (118) realize," says Holmes,[29] "how large a part of our law is open to reconsideration upon a slight change in the habit of the public mind. No concrete proposition is self-evident, no matter how ready we may be to accept it, not even Mr. Herbert Spencer's every man has a right to do what he wills, provided he interferes not with a like right on the part of his neighbors." "Why," he continues, "is a false and injurious statement privileged, if it is made honestly in giving information about a servant? It is because it has been thought more important that information should be given freely, than that a man should be protected from

what under other circumstances would be an actionable wrong. Why is a man at liberty to set up a business which he knows will ruin his neighbor? It is because the public good is supposed to be best subserved by free competition. Obviously such judgments of relative importance may vary in different times and places. . . . I think that the judges themselves have failed adequately to recognize their (119) duty of weighing considerations of social advantage. The duty is inevitable, and the result of the often proclaimed judicial aversion to deal with such considerations is simply to leave the very ground and foundation of judgments inarticulate, and often unconscious, as I have said."

Not only in our common law system has this conception made its way. Even in other systems where the power of judicial initiative is more closely limited by statute, a like development is in the air. Everywhere there is growing emphasis on the analogy between the function of the judge and the function of the legislator. I may instance François Gény who has developed the analogy with boldness and suggestive power.[30] "A priori," he says, "the process of research *(la recherche)*, which is imposed upon the judge in finding the law seems to us very analogous to that incumbent on the legislator himself. Except for this circumstance, certainly not negligible, and yet of secondary importance, that the process (120) is set in motion by some concrete situation, and in order to adapt the law to that situation, the considerations which ought to guide it are, in respect of the final end to be attained, exactly of the same nature as those which ought to dominate legislative action itself, since it is a question in each case, of satisfying, as best may be, justice and social utility by an appropriate rule. Hence, I will not hesitate in the silence or inadequacy of formal sources, to indicate as the general line of direction for the judge the following: that he ought to shape his judgment of the law in obedience to the same aims which would be those of a legislator who was proposing to himself to regulate the question. None the less, an important distinction separates here judicial from legislative activity. While the legislator is not hampered by any limitations in the appreciation of a general situation, which he regulates in a manner altogether abstract, the judge, who decides in view of particular cases, and with reference to problems absolutely concrete, ought, in adherence to the spirit of our modern organiza (121) tion, and in order to escape the dangers of arbitrary action, to disengage himself, so far as possible, of every influence that is personal or that comes from the particular situation which is presented to him, and base his judicial decision on elements of an objective nature. And that is why the activity which is proper to him has seemed to me capable of being justly qualified: free scientific research, *libre recherche scientifique:* free, since it is here removed from the action of positive authority; scientific, at the same time, because it can find its solid foundations only in the objective elements which science alone is able to reveal to it." [31]

The rationale of the modern viewpoint has been admirably expressed by Vander Eycken [32] in his "Méthode positive de l'Interprétation juridique": [33] "Formerly men looked upon law as the product of the conscious will of the legislator. Today they see in it a natural force. (122) If, however, we can attribute to law the epithet 'natural', it is, as we have said, in a different sense from that which formerly attached to the expression 'natural law.' That expression then meant that nature had imprinted in us, as one of the very elements of reason, certain principles of which all the articles of the code were only the application. The same expression ought to mean today that law springs from the relations of fact which exist between things. Like those relations themselves, natural law is in perpetual travail. It is no longer in texts or in systems derived from reason that we must look for the source of law; it is in social utility, in the necessity that certain consequences shall be attached to given hypotheses. The legislator has only a fragmentary consciousness of this law; he translates it by the rules which he prescribes. When the question is one of fixing the meaning of those rules, where ought we to search? Manifestly at their source; that is to say, in the exigencies of social life. There resides the strongest probability of discovering the sense of the law. In the (123) same way when the question is one of supplying the gaps in the law, it is not of logical deductions, it is rather of social needs, that we are to ask the solution."

Many of the gaps have been filled in the development of the common law by borrowing from other systems. Whole titles in our jurisprudence have been taken from the law of Rome. Some of the greatest of our judges—Mansfield in

England, Kent and Story here—were never weary of supporting their judgments by citations from the Digest. We should be traveling too far afield if we were to attempt an estimate of the extent to which the law of Rome has modified the common law either in England or with us.[34] Authority it never had. The great historic movement of the Reception did not touch the British Isles.[35] Analogies have been supplied. Lines of thought have been suggested. Wise solutions (124) have been offered for problems otherwise insoluble. None the less, the function of the foreign system has been to advise rather than to command. It has not furnished a new method. It has given the raw material to be utilized by methods already considered—the methods of philosophy and history and sociology—in the moulding of their products. It is only one compartment in the great reservoir of social experience and truth and wisdom from which the judges of the common law must draw their inspiration and their knowledge.

In thus recognizing, as I do, that the power to declare the law carries with it the power, and within limits the duty, to make law when none exists, I do not mean to range myself with the jurists who seem to hold that in reality there is no law except the decisions of the courts. I think the truth is midway between the extremes that are represented at one end by Coke and Hale and Blackstone and at the other by such authors as Austin and Holland and Gray and Jethro Brown. The theory of the older writers (125) was that judges did not legislate at all. A pre-existing rule was there, imbedded, if concealed, in the body of the customary law. All that the judges did, was to throw off the wrappings, and expose the statute to our view.[36] Since the days of Bentham and Austin, no one, it is believed, has accepted this theory without deduction or reserve, though even in modern decisions we find traces of its lingering influence. Today there is rather danger of another though an opposite error. From holding that the law is never made by judges, the votaries of the Austinian analysis have been led at times to the conclusion that it is never made by anyone else. Customs, no matter how firmly established, are not law, they say, until adopted by the courts.[37] Even statutes are not law because the courts must fix their meaning. That is the view of Gray in his "Nature and Sources of the Law." [38] "The true view, as

I (126) submit," he says, "is that the Law is what the Judges declare; that statutes, precedents, the opinions of learned experts, customs and morality are the sources of the Law." [39] So, Jethro Brown in a paper on "Law and Evolution,"[40] tells us that a statute, till construed, is not real law. It is only "ostensible" law. Real law, he says, is not found anywhere except in the judgment of a court. In that view, even past decisions are not law. The courts may overrule them. For the same reason present decisions are not law, except for the parties litigant. Men go about their business from day to day, and govern their conduct by an *ignis fatuus*. The rules to which they yield obedience are in truth not law at all. Law never *is,* but is always about to be. It is realized only when embodied in a judgment, and in being realized, expires. There are no such things as rules or principles: there are only isolated dooms.

A definition of law which in effect denies the possibility of law since it denies the possibility of (127) rules of general operation,[41] must contain within itself the seeds of fallacy and error. Analysis is useless if it destroys what it is intended to explain. Law and obedience to law are facts confirmed every day to us all in our experience of life. If the result of a definition is to make them seem to be illusions, so much the worse for the definition; we must enlarge it till it is broad enough to answer to realities. The outstanding truths of life, the great and unquestioned phenomena of society, are not to be argued away as myths and vagaries when they do not fit within our little moulds. If necessary, we must remake the moulds. We must seek a conception of law which realism can accept as true. Statutes do not cease to be law because the power to fix their meaning in case of doubt or ambiguity has been confided to the courts. One might as well say for like reasons that contracts have no reality as expressions of a contracting will. The quality of law is not withdrawn from all precedents, however well established, because courts (128) sometimes exercise the privilege of overruling their own decisions. Those, I think, are the conclusions to which a sense of realism must lead us. No doubt there is a field within which judicial judgment moves untrammeled by fixed principles. Obscurity of statute or of precedent or of customs or of morals, or collision between some or all of them, may leave the law unsettled, and cast a duty upon the courts to declare it retrospectively in the exercise of a power frankly legislative in function. In such cases, all that the parties to the controversy can do is to forecast the declaration of the rule as best they can, and govern themselves accordingly. We must not let these occasional and relatively rare instances blind our eyes to the innumerable instances where there is neither obscurity nor collision nor opportunity for diverse judgment. Most of us live our lives in conscious submission to rules of law, yet without necessity of resort to the courts to ascertain our rights and duties. Lawsuits are rare and catastrophic experiences for the vast majority of men, and even when the (129) catastrophe ensues, the controversy relates most often not to the law, but to the facts. In countless litigations, the law is so clear that judges have no discretion. They have the right to legislate within gaps, but often there are no gaps. We shall have a false view of the landscape if we look at the waste spaces only, and refuse to see the acres already sown and fruitful. I think the difficulty has its origin in the failure to distinguish between right and power, between the command embodied in a judgment and the jural principle to which the obedience of the judge is due. Judges have, of course, the power, though not the right, to ignore the mandate of a statute, and render judgment in despite of it. They have the power, though not the right, to travel beyond the walls of the interstices, the bounds set to judicial innovation by precedent and custom. None the less, by that abuse of power, they violate the law. If they violate it willfully, i.e., with guilty and evil mind, they commit a legal wrong, and may be removed or punished even though the judgments which they have rendered stand. (130) In brief, there are jural principles which limit the freedom of the judge,[42] and, indeed, in the view of some writers, which we do not need to endorse, the freedom of the state itself.[43] Life may be lived, conduct may be ordered, it *is* lived and ordered, for unnumbered human beings without bringing them within the field where the law can be misread, unless indeed the misreading be accompanied by conscious abuse of power. Their conduct never touches the borderland, the penumbra, where controversy begins. They go from birth to death, their action restrained at every turn by the power of state, and not once do they appeal to judges to mark the boundaries between right and wrong. I am unable to withhold the name of law from rules which exercise this compulsion over the fortunes of mankind.[44]

(131) The old Blackstonian theory of pre-existing rules of law which judges found, but did not make, fitted in with a theory still more ancient, the theory of a law of nature. The growth of that conception forms a long and interesting chapter in the history of jurisprudence and political science.[45] The doctrine reached its highest development with the Stoics, has persisted in varying phases through the centuries, and imbedding itself deeply in common forms of speech and thought, has profoundly influenced the speculations and ideals of men in statecraft and in law. For a time, with the rise and dominance of the analytical school of jurists, it seemed discredited and abandoned.[46] Recent juristic thought has given it a new currency, though in a form so profoundly altered that the old theory survives (132) in little more than name.[47] The law of nature is no longer conceived of as something static and eternal. It does not override human or positive law. It is the stuff out of which human or positive law is to be woven, when other sources fail.[48] "The modern philosophy of law comes in contact with the natural law philosophy in that the one as well as the other seeks to be the science of the just. But the modern philosophy of law departs essentially from the natural-law philosophy in that the latter seeks a just, natural law outside of positive law, while the new philosophy of law desires to deduce and fix the element of the just in and out of the positive law—out of what it is and of what it is becoming. The natural law school seeks an absolute, ideal law, 'natural law,' the law κατ' ἐξοχῆν, by the side of which positive law has only secondary importance. The (133) modern philosophy of law recognizes that there is only *one* law, the positive law, but it seeks its ideal side, and its enduring idea." [49] I am not concerned to vindicate the accuracy of the nomenclature by which the dictates of reason and conscience which the judge is under a duty to obey, are given the name of law before he has embodied them in a judgment and set the *imprimatur* of the law upon them.[50] I shall not be troubled if we say with Austin and Holland and Gray and many others that till then they are moral precepts, and nothing more. Such verbal disputations do not greatly interest me. What really matters is this, that the judge is under a duty, within the limits of his power

of innovation, to maintain a relation between law and morals, between the precepts of jurisprudence (134) and those of reason and good conscience. I suppose it is true in a certain sense that this duty was never doubted.[51] One feels at times, however, that it was obscured by the analytical jurists, who, in stressing verbal niceties of definition, made a corresponding sacrifice of emphasis upon the deeper and finer realities of ends and aims and functions. The constant insistence that morality and justice are not law, has tended to breed distrust and contempt of law as something to which morality and justice are not merely alien, but hostile. The new development of "naturrecht" may be pardoned infelicities of phrase, if it introduces us to new felicities of methods and ideals. Not for us the barren logomachy that dwells upon the contrasts between law and justice, and forgets their deeper harmonies. For us rather the trumpet call of the French "code civil": [52] "Le juge, qui refusera de juger, sous prétexte du silence, de l'obscurité (135) ou de l'insuffisance de la loi, pourra être poursuivi comme coupable de déni de justice." [53] "It is the function of our courts," says an acute critic "to keep the doctrines up to date with the *mores* by continual restatement and by giving them a continually new content. This is judicial legislation, and the judge legislates at his peril. Nevertheless, it is the necessity and duty of such legislation that gives to judicial office its highest honor; and no brave and honest judge shirks the duty or fears the peril." [54]

You may say that there is no assurance that judges will interpret the *mores* of their day more wisely and truly than other men. I am not disposed to deny this but in my view it is quite beside the point. The point is rather that this power of interpretation must be lodged somewhere, and the custom of the constitution has lodged it in the judges. If they are to fulfill their (136) function as judges, it could hardly be lodged elsewhere. Their conclusions must, indeed, be subject to constant testing and retesting, revision and readjustment; but if they act with conscience and intelligence, they ought to attain in their conclusions a fair average of truth and wisdom. The recognition of this power and duty to shape the law in conformity with the customary morality, is something far removed from the destruction of all rules and the substitution in every instance of the individual sense of justice, the *arbitrium boni viri.*[55] That might result in a benevolent despotism if the judges were benevolent men. It would put an end to the reign of law. The method of sociology, even though applied with greater freedom than in the past, is heading us toward no such cataclysm. The form and structure of the organism are fixed. The cells in which there is motion do not change the proportions of the mass. Insignificant is the power of innovation of any judge, when compared with (137) the bulk and pressure of the rules that hedge him on every side. Innovate, however, to some extent, he must, for with new conditions there must be new rules. All that the method of sociology demands is that within this narrow range of choice, he shall search for social justice. There were stages in the history of the law when a method less psychological was needed. The old quantitative tests of truth did not fail in their day to serve the social needs.[56] Their day has long passed. Modern juristic thought, turning in upon itself, subjecting the judicial process to introspective scrutiny, may have given us a new terminology and a new emphasis. But in truth its method is not new. It is the method of the great chancellors, who without sacrificing uniformity and certainty, built up the system of equity with constant appeal to the teachings of right reason and conscience. It is the method by which the common law has renewed its life at (138) the hands of its great masters—the method of Mansfield and Marshall and Kent and Holmes.

There have, indeed, been movements, and in our own day, to make the individual sense of justice in law as well as in morals the sole criterion of right and wrong. We are invited, in Gény's phrase, to establish a system of "juridical anarchy" at worst, or of "judicial impressionism" at best.[57] The experiment, or something at least approaching it, was tried not long ago in France. There are sponsors of a like creed among the critics of our own courts.[58] The French experiment, which has become known as "le phénomène Magnaud," is the subject of a chapter in the epilogue to the last edition, published in 1919, of Gény's brilliant book.[59] Between 1889 and 1904, the tribunal of the first (139) instance of Château-Thierry, following the lead of its chief, le President Magnaud, initiated a revolt against the existing order in jurisprudence. Its members became known as the good judges, *"les bons juges."* They seem to have asked themselves in every instance what in the circumstances before them a good man would wish to do, and to have rendered judgment accordingly. Sometimes this was done in the face of inconsistent statutes. I do not profess to know their work at first hand. Gény condemns it, and says the movement has spent its force. Whatever the merits or demerits of such impressionism may be, that is not the judicial process as we know it in our law.[60] Our jurisprudence has held fast to Kant's categorical imperative, "Act on a maxim which thou canst will to be law universal." It has refused to sacrifice the larger and more inclusive good to the narrower and smaller. A contract is made. Performance is burdensome and perhaps oppressive. If we were to consider only the individual instance, we might be ready to (140) release the promisor. We look beyond the particular to the universal, and shape our judgment in obedience to the fundamental interest of society that contracts shall be fulfilled. There is a wide gap between the use of the individual sentiment of justice as a substitute for law, and its use as one of the tests and touchstones in construing or extending law. I think the tone and temper in which the modern judge should set about his task are well expressed in the first article of the Swiss Civil Code of 1907, an article around which there has grown up a large body of juristic commentary. "The statute," says the Swiss Code, "governs all matters within the letter or the spirit of any of its mandates. In default of an applicable statute, the judge is to pronounce judgment according to the customary law, and in default of a custom according to the rules which he would establish if he were to assume the part of a legislator. He is to draw his inspiration, however, from the solutions consecrated by the doctrine of the learned and the jurisprudence of the courts—par la doctrine et (141) la jurisprudence." [61] There, in the final precept, is the gist of the difference between "le phénomène Magnaud," and justice according to law. The judge, even when he is free, is still not wholly free. He is not to innovate at pleasure. He is not a knight-errant, roaming at will in pursuit of his own ideal of beauty or of goodness. He is to draw his inspiration from consecrated principles. He is not to yield to spasmodic sentiment, to vague and unregulated benevolence. He is to exercise a discretion informed by tradition, methodized by analogy, disciplined by system, and subordinated to "the primordial necessity of order in the social life." [62] Wide enough in all conscience is the field of discretion that remains.

REFERENCES

1. Seaver v. Ransom, 224 N. Y. 233.

2. Fosmire v. National Surety Co., 229 N. Y. 44.

3. *Cf.* Duguit, *op. cit.*, Continental Legal Hist. Series, vol. XI, p. 120, sec. 36.

4. Wood v. Duff Gordon, 222 N. Y. 88.

5. Kelso v. Ellis, 224 N. Y. 528, 536, 537; California Packing Co. v. Kelly S. & D. Co., 228 N. Y. 49.

6. Pound, "Common Law and Legislation," 21 Harvard L. R. 383, 387.

7. Ehrlich, "Die juristische Logik," p. 295; *cf.* pp. 294, 296.

8. See his Treatise on Evidence, *passim.*

9. Jhering, "Zweck im Recht," 5 Modern Legal Philosophy Series; also Gény, *op. cit.*, vol. I, p. 8; Pound, "Scope and Purpose of Sociological Jurisprudence," 25 Harvard L. R. 140, 141, 145; Pound, "Mechanical Jurisprudence," 8 Columbia L. R. 603, 610.

10. Pound, "Mechanical Jurisprudence," 8 Columbia L. R. 603, 609.

11. *Cf.* Brütt, *supra,* pp. 161, 163.

12. Saleilles, "De la Personnalité Juridique," p. 497. "Avec Jhering nous resterons des réalistes, mais avec lui aussi nous serons des idéalistes, attachés à l'idée de but et de finalité sociale."—Saleilles, p. 516.

13. *Cf.* Ehrlich, "Grundlegung der Soziologie des Rechts," pp. 366, 368; Pound, "Courts and Legislation," 9 Modern Legal Philosophy Series, p. 212; Gray, "Nature and Sources of Law," secs. 628, 650; Vinogradoff, "Outlines of Historical Jurisprudence," p. 135.

14. Ehrlich, *supra.*

15. *Cf.* Gény, *op. cit.*, vol. I, p. 263, sec. 92.

16. For a clear and interesting summary, see Brütt, *supra,* p. 101, *et seq.; cf.* Gény, *op. cit.*, vol. I, p. 221 and contrast Flavius, *op. cit.*, p. 87.

17. Brütt, *supra,* pp. 101–111.

18. Stammler, "Richtiges Recht," s. 162, quoted by Brütt, *supra.* p. 104.

19. "Nature and Sources of Law," sec. 610.

20. *Supra,* p. 139.

21. Barnes, "Durkheim's Political Theory," 35 Pol. Science Quarterly, p. 239.

22. *Ibid.; cf.* Barker, "Political Thought from Spencer to Today," pp. 151, 153, 175.

23. Vander Eycken, "Méthode Positive de l'Interprétation juridique," p. 59; Ehrlich, "Die juristische Logik," p. 187.

24. "La Renaissance du droit naturel," p. 181.

25. "He may intervene only to supplement the formal authorities, and even in that field there are limits to his discretion in establishing rules of law. He may neither restrict the scope of the general principles of our juridical organization, explicitly or implicitly sanctioned, nor may he lay down detailed regulations governing the exercise of given rights, by introducing delays, formalities, or rules of publicity."—Charmont, *supra,* transl. in 7 Modern Legal Philosophy Series, p. 120, sec. 91. *Cf.* Jhering, "Law as a Means to an End" (5 Modern Legal Philosophy Series: Introduction by W. M. Geldart, p. xlvi): "The purposes of law are embodied in legal conceptions which must develop in independence and cannot at every step be called upon to conform to particular needs. Otherwise system and certainty would be unattainable. But this autonomy of law, if it were only because of excess or defects of logic, will lead to a divergence between law and the needs of life, which from time to time calls for correction. . . . How far if at all the needful

changes can or ought to be carried out by judicial decisions or the development of legal theory, and how far the intervention of the legislator will be called for, is a matter that will vary from one legal territory to another according to the accepted traditions as to the binding force of precedents, the character of the enacted law, and the wider or narrower liberty of judicial interpretation."

26. *Cf.* Berolzheimer, 9 Modern Legal Philosophy Series, pp. 167, 168.

27. Flavius, *supra,* p. 49; 2 Pollock and Maitland, "History of English Law," p. 561.

28. Smith, "Surviving Fictions," 27 Yale L. J., 147, 317; Ehrlich, *supra,* pp. 227, 228; Saleilles, "De la Pérsonnalité Juridique," p. 382.

"Lorsque la loi sanctionne certains rapports juridiques, à l'exclusion de tels autres qui en différent, il arrive, pour tels ou tels rapports de droit plus ou moins similaires auxquels on sent le besoin d'étendre la protection légale, que l'on est tenté de procéder, soit par analogie, soit par fiction. La fiction est une analogie en peu amplifiée, ou plutôt dissimulée."—Saleilles, *supra.*

29. "The Path of the Law," 10 Harvard L. R. 466.

30. *Op. cit.,* vol. II, p. 77.

31. Ehrlich has the same thought, "Die juristische Logik," p. 312.

32. Professor in the University of Brussels.

33. P. 401, sec. 239.

34. On this subject, see Sherman, "Roman Law in the Modern World"; Scrutton, "Roman Law Influence," 1 Select Essays in Anglo-Am. Legal Hist. 208.

35. 1 Pollock and Maitland's "History of English Law," 88, 114; Maitland's "Introduction to Gierke," *supra,* p. xii.

36. *Cf.* Pound, 27 Harvard L. R. 731, 733.

37. Austin, "Jurisprudence," vol. I, 37, 104; Holland, "Jurisprudence," p. 54; W. Jethro Brown, "The Austinian Theory of Law," p. 311.

38. Sec. 602.

39. *Cf.* Gray, *supra,* secs. 276, 366, 369.

40. 29 Yale L. J. 394.

41. *Cf.* Beale, "Conflict of Laws," p. 153, sec. 129.

42. Salmond, "Jurisprudence," p. 157; Sadler, "Relation of Law to Custom," pp. 4, 6, 50; F. A. Geer, 9 L. Q. R. 153

43. Duguit, "Law and The State," 31 Harvard L. R. 1; Vinogradoff, "The Crisis of Modern Jurisprudence," 29 Yale L. J. 312; Laski, "Authority in the Modern State," pp. 41, 42.

44. "Law is the body of general principles and of particular rules in accordance with which civil rights are created and regulated, and wrongs prevented or redressed" (Beale, "Conflict of Laws," p. 132, sec. 114).

45. Salmond, "The Law of Nature," 11 L. Q. R. 121; Pollock, "The History of the Law of Nature," 1 Columbia L. R. 11; 2 Lowell, "The Government of England," 477, 478; Maitland's "Collected Papers," p. 23.

46. *Cf.* Ritchie, "Natural Rights."

47. Pound, 25 Harvard L. R. 162; Charmont, "La Renaissance du droit naturel," *passim;* also transl., 7 Modern Legal Philosophy Series, 106, 111; Demogue, "Analysis of Fundamental Notions," 7 Modern Legal Philosophy Series, p. 373, sec. 212; Laski, "Authority in the Modern State," p. 64.

48. Vander Eycken, *op. cit.,* p. 401.

49. Berolzheimer, "System der Rechts und Wirthschaftsphilosophie," vol. II, 27, quoted by Pound, "Scope and Purpose of Sociological Jurisprudence," 24 Harvard L. R. 607; also Isaacs, "The Schools of Jurisprudence," 31 Harvard L. R. 373, 389; and for the mediaeval view, Maitland's "Gierke, Political Theories of the Middle Age," pp. 75, 84, 93, 173.

50. Holland, "Jurisprudence," p. 54.

51. See Gray, *supra,* p. 286, secs. 644, 645.

52. Art. 4; Gray, *supra,* sec. 642; Gény, *op. cit.,* vol. II, p. 75, sec. 155; Gnaeus Flavius, "Der Kampf um die Rechtswissenschaft," p. 14.

53. "The judge who shall refuse to give judgment under pretext of the

silence, of the obscurity, or of the inadequacy of the law, shall be subject to prosecution as guilty of a denial of justice."

54. Arthur L. Corbin, 29 Yale L. J. 771.

55. *Cf.* Standard Chemical Corp. v. Waugh Corp., 231 N. Y. 51, 55.

56. Flavius, "Der Kampf um die Rechtswissenschaft," pp. 48, 49; Ehrlich, "Die juristische Logik," pp. 291, 292.

57. Gény, *op. cit.*, ed. of 1919, vol. II, p. 288, sec. 196; p. 305, sec. 200.

58. Bruce, "Judicial Buncombe in North Dakota and Other States," 88 Central L. J. 136; Judge Robinson's Reply, 88 *id.* 155; "Rule and Discretion in the Administration of Justice," 33 Harvard L. R. 792.

59. Gény, *op. cit.*, ed. of 1919, vol. II, p. 287, sec. 196, *et seq.*

60. Salmond, "Jurisprudence," pp. 19, 20.

61. Gény, *op. cit.*, II, p. 213; also Perick, "The Swiss Code," XI, Continental Legal Hist. Series, p. 238, sec. 5.

62. Gény, *op. cit.*, II, p. 303, sec. 200.

(142)

Lecture IV. Adherence to Precedent. The Subconscious Element in the Judicial Process. Conclusion.

THE system of law-making by judicial decisions which supply the rule for transactions closed before the decision was announced, would indeed be intolerable in its hardship and oppression if natural law, in the sense in which I have used the term, did not supply the main rule of judgment to the judge when precedent and custom fail or are displaced. Acquiescence in such a method has its basis in the belief that when the law has left the situation uncovered by any pre-existing rule, there is nothing to do except to have some impartial arbiter declare what fair and reasonable men, mindful of the habits of life of the community, and of the standards of justice and fair dealing prevalent among them, ought in such circumstances to do, with no rules except those of custom and con (143) science to regulate their conduct. The feeling is that nine times out of ten, if not oftener, the conduct of right-minded men would not have been different if the rule embodied in the decision had been announced by statute in advance. In the small minority of cases, where ignorance has counted, it is as likely to have affected one side as the other; and since a controversy has arisen and must be determined somehow, there is nothing to do, in default of a rule already made, but to constitute some authority which will make it after the event. Some one must be the loser; it is part of the game of life; we have to pay in countless ways for the absence of prophetic vision. No doubt the ideal system, if it were attainable, would be a code at once so flexible and so minute, as to supply in advance for every conceivable situation the just and fitting rule. But life is too complex to bring the attainment of this ideal within the compass of human powers. We must recognize the truth, says Gény,[1] that the will *(la volonté)* which inspires a statute (144) "extends only over a domain of concrete facts, very narrow and very limited. Almost always, a statute has only a single point of view. All history demonstrates that legislation intervenes only when a definite abuse has disclosed itself, through the excess of which public feeling has finally been aroused. When the legislator interposes, it is to put an end to such and such facts, very clearly determined, which have provoked his decision. And if, to reach his goal, he thinks it proper to proceed along the path of general ideas and abstract formulas, the principles that he announces have value, in his thought, only in the measure in which they are applicable to the evils which it was his effort to destroy, and to similar conditions which would tend to spring from them. As for other logical consequences to be deduced from these principles, the legislator has not suspected them; some, perhaps many, if he had foreseen, he would not have hesitated to repudiate. In consecrating them, no one can claim either to be following his will or to be bowing to his judgment. All that one does (145) thereby is to develop a principle, henceforth isolated and independent of the will which created it, to transform it into a new entity, which in turn develops of itself, and to give it an independent life, regardless of the will of the legislator and most often in despite of it." These are the words of a French jurist, writing of a legal system founded on a code. The gaps inevitable in such a system must, at least in equal measure, be inevitable in a system of case law built up, haphazard, through the controversies of litigants.[2] In each system, hardship must at times result from postponement of the rule of action till a time when action is complete. It is one of the consequences of the limitations of the human intellect and of the denial to legislators and judges of infinite prevision. But the truth is, as I have said, that even when there is ignorance of the rule, the cases are few in which ignorance has determined conduct. Most often the controversy arises about something that would (146) have happened anyhow. An automobile is manufactured with defective wheels. The question is whether the manufacturer owes a duty of inspection to anyone except the buyer.[3] The occupant of the car, injured because of the defect, presses one view upon the court; the manufacturer, another. There is small chance, whichever party prevails, that conduct would have been different if the rule had been known in advance. The manufacturer did not say to himself, "I will not inspect these wheels, because that is not my duty." Admittedly, it was his duty, at least toward the immediate buyer. A wrong in any event has been done. The question is to what extent it shall entail unpleasant consequences on the wrongdoer.

I say, therefore, that in the vast majority of cases the retrospective effect of judge-made law is felt either to involve no hardship or only such hardship as is inevitable where no rule has been declared. I think it is significant that when the hardship is felt to be too great or to be un (147) necessary, retrospective operation is withheld. Take the cases where a court of final appeal has declared a statute void, and afterwards, reversing itself, declares the statute valid. Intervening transactions have been governed by the first decision. What shall be said of the validity of such transactions when the decision is overruled? Most courts in a spirit of realism have held that the operation of the statute has been suspended in the interval.[4] It may be hard to square such a ruling with abstract dogmas and definitions. When so much else that a court does, is done with retroactive force, why draw the line here? The answer is, I think, that the line is drawn here, because the injustice and oppression of a refusal to draw it would be so great as to be intolerable. We will not help out the man who has (148) trusted to the judgment of some inferior court.[5] In his case, the chance of miscalculation is felt to be a fair risk of the game of life, not different in degree from the risk of any other misconception of right or duty. He knows that he has taken a chance, which caution often might have avoided. The judgment of a court of final appeal is felt to stand upon a different basis. I am not sure that any adequate distinction is to be drawn between a change of ruling in respect of the validity of a statute and a change of ruling in respect of the meaning or operation of a statute,[6] or even in respect of the meaning or operation of a rule of common law.[7] Where the line of division will some day be located, I will make no attempt to say. I feel assured, however, that its location, wherever it shall be, will be governed, not by metaphysical conceptions of the nature of judge-made law, nor by the fetich of some implacable tenet, such as that of the division of (149) governmental powers,[8] but by considerations of convenience, of utilitv, and of the deepest sentiments of justice.

In these days, there is a good deal of discussion whether the rule of adherence to precedent ought to be abandoned altogether.[9] I would not go so far myself. I think adherence to precedent should be the rule and not the exception. I have already had occasion to dwell upon some of the considerations that sustain it. To these I may add that the labor of judges would be increased almost to the breaking point if every past decision could be reopened in every case, and one could not lay one's own course of bricks on the secure foundation of the courses laid by others who had gone before him. Perhaps the constitution of my own court has tended to accentuate this belief. We have had ten judges, of whom (150) only seven sit at a time. It happens again and again, where the question is a close one, that a case which one week is decided one way might be decided another way the next if it were then heard for the first time. The situation would, however, be intolerable if the weekly changes in the composition of the court were accompanied by changes in its rulings. In such circumstances there is nothing to do except to stand by the errors of our brethren of the week before, whether we relish them or not. But I am ready to concede that the rule of adherence to precedent, though it ought not to be abandoned, ought to be in some degree relaxed. I think that when a rule, after it has been duly tested by experience, has been found to be inconsistent with the sense of justice or with the social welfare, there should be less hesitation in frank avowal and full abandonment. We have had to do this sometimes in the field of constitutional law.[10] Perhaps we should do so oftener in fields of private law where considerations of social utility are not so (151) aggressive and insistent. There should be greater readiness to abandon an untenable position when the rule to be discarded may not reasonably be supposed to have determined the conduct of the litigants, and particularly when in its origin it was the product of institutions or conditions which have gained a new significance or development with the progress of the years. In such circumstances, the words of Wheeler, J., in Dwy v. Connecticut Co., 89 Conn. 74, 99, express the tone and temper in which problems should be met: "That court best serves the law which recognizes that the rules of law which grew up in a remote generation may, in the fullness of experience, be found to serve another generation badly, and which discards the old rule when it finds that another rule of law represents what should be according to the established and settled judgment of society, and no considerable property rights have become vested in reliance upon the old rule. It is thus great writers upon the common law have discovered the source and method of its growth, and in its growth found its health and (152) life. It is not and it should not be stationary. Change of this character should not be left to the legislature." If judges have wofully misinterpreted the *mores* of their day, or if the *mores* of their day are no longer those of ours, they ought not to tie, in helpless submission, the hands of their successors.

Let me offer one or two examples to make my meaning plainer. I offer them tentatively and without assurance that they are apt. They will be helpful none the less. The instance may be rejected, but the principle abides.

It is a rule of the common law that a surety is discharged from liability if the time of payment is extended by contract between the principal debtor and the creditor without the surety's consent. Even an extension for a single day will be sufficient to bring about that result.[11] Without such an extension, the surety would have the privilege upon the maturity of the debt of making payment to the creditor, and demanding immediate subrogation to the latter's remedies (153) against the principal. He must, therefore, it is said, be deemed to have suffered prejudice if, by extension of the due date, the right has been postponed. I have no doubt that this rule may justly be applied whenever the surety can show that the extension has resulted in actual damage, as where the principal in the interval has become insolvent, or the value of the security has been impaired, though even in such circumstances the measure of exoneration ought in justice to be determined by the extent of the damage suffered. Perhaps there might be justice in permitting exoneration whenever the surety had tendered payment of the debt, and demanded subrogation to the remedies against the debtor. Perhaps the burden of disproving prejudice ought to be cast upon the creditor. No such limitations have been recognized. The rule applies to cases where neither tender nor actual damage is established or pretended. The law has shaped its judgments upon the fictitious assumption that a surety, who has probably lain awake at nights for fear that payment may some day be demanded, has (154) in truth been smarting under the repressed desire to force an unwelcome payment on a reluctant or capricious creditor. The extended period has gone by; the surety has made no move, has not even troubled himself to inquire; yet he is held to be released on the theory that were it not for the extension, of which he knew nothing, and by which his conduct could not have been controlled, he would have come forward voluntarily with a tender of the debt. Such rules are survivals of the days when commercial dealings were simpler, when surety companies were unknown, when sureties were commonly generous friends whose confidence had been abused, and when the main effort of the courts seems to have been to find some plausible excuse for letting them out of their engagements. Already I see some signs of a change of spirit in decisions of recent dates.[12] I think we may well ask ourselves whether courts are not under a duty to go (155) farther, and place this branch of the law upon a basis more consistent with the realities of business experience and the moralities of life.

It is another rule of the common law that a parol agreement, though subsequently made, is ineffective to vary or discharge a contract under seal.[13] In days when seals counted for a good deal, there may have been some reason in this recognition of a mystical solemnity. In our day, when the perfunctory initials "L. S." have replaced the heraldic devices, the law is conscious of its own absurdity when it preserves the rubrics of a vanished era.[14] Judges have made worthy, if shamefaced, efforts, while giving lip service to the rule, to riddle it with exceptions and by distinctions reduce it to a shadow.[15] A recent case suggests that timidity, and not reverence, has postponed the hour of dissolution.[16] The law (156) will have cause for gratitude to the deliverer who will strike the fatal blow.

I have drawn illustrations from the field of substantive law. The law of evidence and generally the whole subject of procedure supply fields where change may properly be made with a freedom even greater. The considerations of policy that dictate adherence to existing rules where substantive rights are involved, apply with diminished force when it is a question of the law of remedies. Let me take an illustration from the law of evidence. A man is prosecuted for rape. His defense is that the woman consented. He may show that her *reputation* for chastity is bad. He may not show specific, even though repeated, acts of unchastity with another man or other men.[17] The one thing that any sensible trier of the facts would wish to know above all others in estimating the truth of his defense, is held by an inflexible rule, to be something that must be excluded from the consideration of the jury. Even though the woman takes (157) the stand herself, the defendant is not greatly helped, for though he may then cross-examine her about other acts, he is concluded by her answer. Undoubtedly a judge should exercise a certain discretion in the admission of such evidence, should exclude it if too remote, and should be prompt by granting a continuance or otherwise to obviate any hardship resulting from surprise. That is not the effect of the present rule. The evidence is excluded altogether and always. Some courts, indeed, have taken a different view, but their number unfortunately is small. Here, as in many other branches of the law of evidence, we see an exaggerated reliance upon general reputation as a test for the ascertainment of the character of litigants or witnesses. Such a faith is a survival of more simple times. It was justified in days when men lived in small communities. Perhaps it has some justification even now in rural districts. In the life of great cities, it has made evidence of character a farce. Here, as in many other branches of adjective law, a spirit of realism should bring about a (158) harmony between present rules and present needs.

None the less, the rule of adherence to precedent is applied with less rigidity in the United States than in England, and, I think, with a rigidity that is diminishing even here. The House of Lords holds itself absolutely bound by its own prior decisions.[18] The United States Supreme Court and the highest courts of the several states overrule their own prior decisions when manifestly erroneous.[19] Pollock, in a paper entitled "The Science of Case Law," written more than forty years ago, spoke of the freedom with which this was done, as suggesting that the law was nothing more than a matter of individual opinion.[20] Since then the tendency has, if anything, increased. An extreme illustration may be (159) found in a recent decision of a federal court.[21] The plaintiff sued a manufacturer of automobiles to recover damages for personal injuries resulting from a defective car. On the first trial he had a verdict, which the Circuit Court of Appeals for the second circuit reversed on the ground that the manufacturer owed no duty to the plaintiff, the occupant of the car, since the latter was not the original purchaser, but had bought from some one else.[22] On a second trial, the judge, in obedience to this ruling, dismissed the complaint, and a writ of error brought the case before the same appellate court again. In the meantime, the New York Court of Appeals had held, in an action against another manufacturer, that there was a duty in such circumstances, irrespective of privity of contract.[23] The federal court followed that decision, overruled its prior ruling, and reversed the judgment of dismissal which had been entered in compliance with its mandate. The defendant in that case who first reversed the (160) judgment because the complaint had *not* been dismissed, and then suffered a reversal because on the same evidence the complaint *had* been dismissed, probably has some views of his own about the nature of the judicial process. I do not attempt to say whether departure from the rule of adherence to precedent was justified in such conditions. One judge dissenting held the view that the earlier decision should have been applied as the law of the case irrespective of its correctness, like the rule of *res adjudicata.* The conclusion of the majority of the court, whether right or wrong, is interesting as evidence of a spirit and a tendency to subordinate precedent to justice. How to reconcile that tendency, which is a growing and in the main a wholesome one, with the need of uniformity and certainty, is one of the great problems confronting the lawyers and judges of our day. We shall have to feel our way here as elsewhere in the law. Somewhere between worship of the past and exaltation of the present, the path of safety will be found.

(161) Our survey of judicial methods teaches us, I think, the lesson that the whole subject-matter of jurisprudence is more plastic, more malleable, the moulds less definitely cast, the bounds of right and wrong less preordained and constant, than most of us, without the aid of some such analysis, have been accustomed to believe. We like to picture to ourselves the field of the law as accurately mapped and plotted. We draw our little lines, and they are hardly down before we blur them. As in time and space, so here. Divisions are working hypotheses, adopted for convenience. We are tending more and more toward an appreciation of the truth that, after all, there are few rules; there are chiefly standards and degrees. It is a question of degree whether I have been

negligent. It is a question of degree whether in the use of my own land, I have created a nuisance which may be abated by my neighbor. It is a question of degree whether the law which takes my property and limits my conduct, impairs my liberty unduly. So also the duty of a judge becomes itself a question of degree, and (162) he is a useful judge or a poor one as he estimates the measure accurately or loosely. He must balance all his ingredients, his philosophy, his logic, his analogies, his history, his customs, his sense of right, and all the rest, and adding a little here and taking out a little there, must determine, as wisely as he can, which weight shall tip the scales. If this seems a weak and inconclusive summary, I am not sure that the fault is mine. I know he is a wise pharmacist who from a recipe so general can compound a fitting remedy. But the like criticism may be made of most attempts to formulate the principles which regulate the practice of an art. W. Jethro Brown reminds us in a recent paper on "Law and Evolution" [24] that "Sir Joshua Reynolds' book on painting, offers little or no guidance to those who wish to become famous painters. Books on literary styles are notoriously lacking, speaking as a rule, in practical utility." After the wearisome process of analysis has been finished, there must be for every judge a new synthesis which (163) he will have to make for himself. The most that he can hope for is that with long thought and study, with years of practice at the bar or on the bench, and with the aid of that inward grace which comes now and again to the elect of any calling, the analysis may help a little to make the synthesis a true one.

In what I have said, I have thrown, perhaps too much, into the background and the shadow the cases where the controversy turns not upon the rule of law, but upon its application to the facts. Those cases, after all, make up the bulk of the business of the courts. They are important for the litigants concerned in them. They call for intelligence and patience and reasonable discernment on the part of the judges who must decide them. But they leave jurisprudence where it stood before. As applied to such cases, the judicial process, as was said at the outset of these lectures, is a process of search and comparison, and little else. We have to distinguish between the precedents which are merely static, and those (164) which are dynamic.[25] Because the former outnumber the latter many times, a sketch of the judicial process which concerns itself almost exclusively with the creative or dynamic element, is likely to give a false impression, an overcolored picture, of uncertainty in the law and of free discretion in the judge. Of the cases that come before the court in which I sit, a majority, I think, could not, with semblance of reason, be decided in any way but one. The law and its application alike are plain. Such cases are predestined, so to speak, to affirmance without opinion. In another and considerable percentage, the rule of law is certain, and the application alone doubtful. A complicated record must be dissected, the narratives of witnesses, more or less incoherent and unintelligible, must be analyzed, to determine whether a given situation comes within one district or another upon the chart of rights and wrongs. The traveler who knows that a railroad crosses his path must look for approaching trains. That is at least the gen (165) eral rule. In numberless litigations the description of the landscape must be studied to see whether vision has been obstructed, whether something has been done or omitted to put the traveler off his guard. Often these cases and others like them provoke difference of opinion among judges. Jurisprudence remains untouched, however, regardless of the outcome. Finally there remains a percentage, not large indeed, and yet not so small as to be negligible, where a decision one way or the other, will count for the future, will advance or retard, sometimes much, sometimes little, the development of the law. These are the cases where the creative element in the judicial process finds its opportunity and power. It is with these cases that I have chiefly concerned myself in all that I have said to you. In a sense it is true of many of them that they might be decided either way. By that I mean that reasons plausible and fairly persuasive might be found for one conclusion as for another. Here come into play that balancing of judgment, that testing and sorting of considerations of analogy (166) and logic and utility and fairness, which I have been trying to describe. Here it is that the judge assumes the function of a lawgiver. I was much troubled in spirit, in my first years upon the bench, to find how trackless was the ocean on which I had embarked. I sought for certainty. I was oppressed and disheartened when I found that the quest for it was futile. I was trying to reach land, the solid land of fixed and settled rules the paradise of a justice that would declare itself by tokens plainer and more commanding than its pale and glimmering reflections in my own vacillating mind and conscience. I found "with the voyagers in Browning's 'Paracelsus' that the real heaven was always beyond."[26] As the years have gone by, and as I have reflected more and more upon the nature of the judicial process, I have become reconciled to the uncertainty, because I have grown to see it as inevitable. I have grown to see that the process in its highest reaches is not discovery, but creation; (167) and that the doubts and misgivings, the hopes and fears, are part of the travail of mind, the pangs of death and the pangs of birth, in which principles that have served their day expire, and new principles are born.

I have spoken of the forces of which judges avowedly avail to shape the form and content of their judgments. Even these forces are seldom fully in consciousness. They lie so near the surface, however, that their existence and influence are not likely to be disclaimed. But the subject is not exhausted with the recognition of their power. Deep below consciousness are other forces, the likes and the dislikes, the predilections and the prejudices, the complex of instincts and emotions and habits and convictions, which make the man, whether he be litigant or judge. I wish I might have found the time and opportunity to pursue this subject farther. I shall be able, as it is, to do little more than remind you of its existence.[27] There has been a certain lack of (168) candor in much of the discussion of the theme, or rather perhaps in the refusal to discuss it, as if judges must lose respect and confidence by the reminder that they are subject to human limitations. I do not doubt the grandeur of the conception which lifts them into the realm of pure reason, above and beyond the sweep of perturbing and deflecting forces. None the less, if there is anything of reality in my analysis of the judicial process, they do not stand aloof on these chill and distant heights; and we shall not help the cause of truth by acting and speaking as if they do. The great tides and currents which engulf the rest of men, do not turn aside in their course, and pass the judges by. We like to figure to ourselves the processes of justice as coldly objective and impersonal. The law, conceived of as a real existence, dwelling apart and alone, speaks, through the voices of priests and ministers, the words which they have no choice except to utter. That is an ideal of objective truth toward which (169) every system of jurisprudence tends. It is an ideal of which great publicists and judges have spoken as of something possible to attain. "The judges of the nation," says Montesquieu, "are only the mouths that pronounce the words of the law, inanimate beings, who can moderate neither its force nor its rigor." [28] So Marshall, in Osborne v. Bank of the United States, 9 Wheat. 738, 866: The judicial department "has no will in any case. . . . Judicial power is never exercised for the purpose of giving effect to the will of the judge; always for the purpose of giving effect to the will of the legislature; or in other words, to the will of the law." It has a lofty sound; it is well and finely said; but it can never be more than partly true. Marshall's own career is a conspicuous illustration of the fact that the ideal is beyond the reach of human faculties to attain. He gave to the constitution of the United States the impress of his own mind; and the form of (170) our constitutional law is what it is, because he moulded it while it was still plastic and malleable in the fire of his own intense convictions. At the opposite extreme are the words of the French jurist, Saleilles, in his treatise "De la Personnalité Juridique": [29] "One wills at the beginning the result; one finds the principle afterwards; such is the genesis of all juridical construction. Once accepted, the construction presents itself, doubtless, in the ensemble of legal doctrine, under the opposite aspect. The factors are inverted. The principle appears as an initial cause, from which one has drawn the result which is found deduced from it." I would not put the case thus broadly. So sweeping a statement exaggerates the element of free volition. It ignores the factors of determinism which cabin and confine within narrow bounds the range of unfettered choice. None the less, by its very excess of emphasis, it supplies the needed corrective of an ideal of impossible objectivity. Nearer to the truth, and midway between these (171) extremes, are the words of a man who was not a jurist, but whose intuitions and perceptions were deep and brilliant —the words of President Roosevelt in his message of December 8, 1908, to the Congress of the United States: [30] "The chief lawmakers in our country may be, and often are, the judges, because they are the final seat of authority. Every time they interpret contract, property, vested rights, due process of law, liberty, they necessarily enact into law parts of a system of social philosophy; and as such interpretation is fundamental they give direction to all law-making. The decisions of the courts on economic and social questions depend upon their economic and social philosophy; and for the peaceful progress of our people during the twentieth century we shall owe most to those judges who hold to a twentieth century economic and social philosophy and not to a long outgrown philosophy, which was itself the product of primitive economic conditions."

I remember that this statement when made, (172) aroused a storm of criticism. It betrayed ignorance, they said, of the nature of the judicial process. The business of the judge, they told us, was to discover objective truth. His own little individuality, his tiny stock of scattered and unco-ordinated philosophies, these, with all his weaknesses and unconscious prejudices, were to be laid aside and forgotten. What did men care for *his* reading of the eternal verities? It was not worth recording. What the world was seeking, was the eternal verities themselves. Far am I from denying that this is, indeed, the goal toward which all of us must strive. Something of Pascal's spirit of self-search and self-reproach must come at moments to the man who finds himself summoned to the duty of shaping the progress of the law. The very breadth and scope of the opportunity to give expression to his finer self, seem to point the accusing finger of disparagement and scorn. What am I that in these great movements onward, this rush and sweep of forces, my petty personality should deflect them by a hairbreadth? Why should the (173) pure light of truth be broken up and impregnated and colored with any element of my being? Such doubts and hesitations besiege one now and again. The truth is, however, that all these inward questionings are born of the hope and desire to transcend the limitations which hedge our human nature. Roosevelt, who knew men, had no illusions on this score. He was not positing an ideal. He was not fixing a goal. He was measuring the powers and the endurance of those by whom the race was to be run. My duty as judge may be to objectify in law, not my own aspirations and convictions and philosophies, but the aspirations and convictions and philosophies of the men and women of my time. Hardly shall I do this well if my own sympathies and beliefs and passionate devotions are with a time that is past. "We shall never be able to flatter ourselves, in any system of judicial interpretation, that we have eliminated altogether the personal measure of the interpreter. In the moral sciences, there is no method or procedure which entirely sup-(174) plants subjective reason." [31] We may figure the task of the judge, if we please, as the task of a translator, the reading of signs and symbols given from without. None the less, we will not set men to such a task, unless they have absorbed the spirit, and have filled themselves with a love, of the language they must read.

I have no quarrel, therefore, with the doctrine that judges ought to be in sympathy with the spirit of their times. Alas! assent to such a generality does not carry us far upon the road to truth. In every court there are likely to be as many estimates of the "Zeitgeist" as there are judges on its bench. Of the power of favor or prejudice in any sordid or vulgar or evil sense, I have found no trace, not even the faintest, among the judges whom I have known. But every day there is borne in on me a new conviction of the inescapable relation between the truth without us and the truth within. The spirit of the age, as it is revealed to each of us, is too often only (175) the spirit of the group in which the accidents of birth or education or occupation or fellowship have given us a place. No effort or revolution of the mind will overthrow utterly and at all times the empire of these subconscious loyalties. "Our beliefs and opinions," says James Harvey Robinson,[32] "like our standards of conduct come to us insensibly as products of our companionship with our fellow men, not as results of our personal experience and the inferences we individually make from our own observations. We are constantly misled by our extraordinary faculty of 'rationalizing'—that is, of devising plausible arguments for accepting what is imposed upon us by the traditions of the group to which we belong. We are abjectly credulous by nature, and instinctively accept the verdicts of the group. We are suggestible not merely when under the spell of an excited mob or a fervent revival, but we are ever and always listening to the still small voice of the herd, and are ever ready to defend and (176) justify its instructions and warnings, and accept them as the mature results of our own reasoning."

This was written, not of judges specially, but of men and women of all classes. The training of the judge, if coupled with what is styled the judicial temperament, will help in some degree to emancipate him from the suggestive power of individual dislikes and prepossessions. It will help to broaden the group to which his subconscious loyalties are due. Never will these loyalties be utterly extinguished while human nature is what it is. We may wonder sometimes how from the play of all these forces of individualism, there can come anything coherent, anything but chaos and the void. Those are the moments in which we exaggerate the elements of difference. In the end there emerges something which has a composite shape and truth and order. It has been said that "History, like mathematics, is obliged to assume that eccentricities more or less balance each other, so that something remains constant at last." [33] The like is true of the (177) work of courts. The eccentricities of judges balance one another. One judge looks at problems from the point of view of history, another from that of philosophy, another from that of social utility, one is a formalist, another a latitudinarian, one is timorous of change, another dissatisfied with the present; out of the attrition of diverse minds there is beaten something which has a constancy and uniformity and average value greater than its component elements. The same thing is true of the work of juries. I do not mean to suggest that the product in either case does not betray the flaws inherent in its origin. The flaws are there as in every human institution. Because they are not only there but visible, we have faith that they will be corrected. There is no assurance that the rule of the majority will be the expression of perfect reason when embodied in constitution or in statute. We ought not to expect more of it when embodied in the judgments of the courts. The tide rises and falls but the sands of error crumble.

(178) The work of a judge is in one sense enduring and in another sense ephemeral. What is good in it endures. What is erroneous is pretty sure to perish. The good remains the foundation on which new structures will be built. The bad will be rejected and cast off in the laboratory of the years. Little by little the old doctrine is undermined. Often the encroachments are so gradual that their significance is at first obscured. Finally we discover that the contour of the land-

scape has been changed, that the old maps must be cast aside, and the ground charted anew. The process, with all its silent yet inevitable power, has been described by Mr. Henderson with singular felicity:[34] "When an adherent of a systematic faith is brought continuously in touch with influences and exposed to desires inconsistent with that faith, a process of unconscious cerebration may take place, by which a growing store of hostile mental inclinations may accumulate, (179) strongly motivating action and decision, but seldom emerging clearly into consciousness. In the meantime the formulas of the old faith are retained and repeated by force of habit, until one day the realization comes that conduct and sympathies and fundamental desires have become so inconsistent with the logical framework that it must be discarded. Then begins the task of building up and rationalizing a new faith."

Ever in the making, as law develops through the centuries, is this new faith which silently and steadily effaces our mistakes and eccentricities. I sometimes think that we worry ourselves overmuch about the enduring consequences of our errors. They may work a little confusion for a time. In the end, they will be modified or corrected or their teachings ignored. The future takes care of such things. In the endless process of testing and retesting, there is a constant rejection of the dross, and a constant retention of whatever is pure and sound and fine.

The future, gentlemen, is yours. We have been called to do our parts in an ageless process. Long (180) after I am dead and gone, and my little part in it is forgotten, you will be here to do your share, and to carry the torch forward. I know that the flame will burn bright while the torch is in your keeping.

REFERENCES

1. *Op. cit.*, preface, p. xvi.

2. Pollock, "Essays in Jurisprudence and Ethics; The Science of Case Law," p. 241.

3. MacPherson v. Buick Motor Co., 217 N. Y. 382.

4. Harris v. Jex, 55 N. Y. 421; Gelpcke v. Dubuque, 1 Wall. 125; Holmes, J., in Kuhn v. Fairmount Coal Co., 215 U. S. 349, 371; 29 Harvard L. R. 80, 103; Danchey Co. v. Farmy, 105 Misc. 470; Freeman, "Retroactive Operation of Decisions," 18 Columbia L. R. p. 230; Gray, *supra*, secs. 547, 548; Carpenter, "Court Decisions and the Common Law," 17 Columbia L. R. 593.

5. Evans v. Supreme Council, 223 N. Y. 497, 503.

6. Douglass v. County of Pike, 101 U. S. 677.

7. *Cf.* Wigmore, "The Judicial Function," Preface to 9 Modern Legal Philosophy Series, pp. xxxvii, xxxviii.

8. Laski, "Authority in the Modern State," pp. 70, 71; Green, "Separation of Governmental Powers," 29 Yale L. J. 371.

9. "Rule and Discretion in the Administration of Justice," 33 Harvard L. R. 972; 29 Yale L. J. 909; 34 Harvard L. R. 74; 9 Modern Legal Philosophy Series, Preface, p. xxxvi.

10. Klein v. Maravelas, 219 N. Y. 383.

11. N. Y. Life Ins. Co. v. Casey, 178 N. Y. 381.

12. Wilkinson v. McKemmie, 229 U. S. 590, 593; U. S. v. McMullen, 222 U. S. 460, 468; Richardson v. County of Steuben, 226 N. Y. 13; Assets Realization Co. v. Roth, 226 N. Y. 370.

13. McCreery v. Day, 119 N. Y. 1; 3 Williston on Contracts, secs. 1835, 1836.

14. Harris v. Shorall, 230 N. Y. 343.

15. McCreery v. Day, *supra;* Thomson v. Poor, 147 N. Y. 402.

16. Harris v. Shorall, *supra.*

17. People v. Carey, 223 N. Y. 519.

18. Gray, *supra,* sec. 462; Salmond, "Jurisprudence," p. 164, sec. 64; Pound, "Juristic Science and the Law," 31 Harvard L. R. 1053; London Street Tramways Co. v. London County Council, 1898, A. C. 375, 379.

19. Pollock, "First Book of Jurisprudence," pp. 319, 320; Gray, "Judicial Precedents," 9 Harvard L. R. 27, 40.

20. "Essays in Jurisprudence and Ethics," p. 245.

21. Johnson v. Cadillac Motor Co., 261 Fed. 878.

22. 221 Fed. 801.

23. MacPherson v. Buick Motor Co., 217 N. Y. 382.

24. 29 Yale L. J. 394, 397.

25. *Cf.* Salmond, "Jurisprudence," p. 160.

26. G. Lowes Dickinson, "Religion and Immortality," p. 70.

27. An interesting study of this subject will be found in a book published since these lectures were written, "The Foundations of Social Science," by James Mickel Williams, p. 209 *et seq.*

28. Montesquieu, "Esprit des Lois," LIV, XI, chap. VI, quoted by Ehrlich, "Die juristische Logik," p. 101; Gény, *op. cit.,* p. 76; *cf.* Flavius, *supra,* p. 40.

29. Pp. 45, 46.

30. 43 Congressional Record, part 1, p. 21.

31. Gény, *op. cit.,* vol. II, p. 93, sec. 159; vol. II, p. 142, sec. 168; also Flavius, p. 43.

32. "The Still Small Voice of the Herd," 32 Political Science Quarterly 315.

33. Henry Adams, "The Degradation of the Democratic Dogma," pp. 291, 292.

34. "Foreign Corporations in American Constitutional Law," p. 164; *cf.* Powell, "The Changing Law of Foreign Corporations," 33 Pol. Science Quarterly, p. 569.

Complete Text

of

THE GROWTH OF THE LAW*

Introductory Note

These lectures, given at the Law School of Yale University in December, 1923, are to be regarded as a supplement to lectures given at the same University in 1921, and published by the Yale University Press under the title of "The Nature of the Judicial Process."

Some thoughts, imperfectly developed in the first series, seemed to call for fuller and more explicit statement in the second, even at some risk of repetition.

B. N. C.

New York, May 30, 1924.

---

* *The Growth of the Law.* Copyrighted by Yale University Press. Reprinted with the permission of Yale University Press and Columbia University, the residuary legatee of the literary estate of Benjamin Nathan Cardozo.

THE GROWTH OF THE LAW

Introduction. The Need of a Scientific Restatement as an Aid to Certainty.

(1)

THE law of our day faces a twofold need. The first is the need of some restatement that will bring certainty and order out of the wilderness of precedent. This is the task of legal science. The second is the need of a philosophy that will mediate between the conflicting claims of stability and progress, and supply a principle of growth. The first need is deeply felt and widely acknowledged. The American Law Institute, recently organized, is an attempt to meet it. The second, though less generally appreciated, is emerging year by year to fuller recognition. (2) My purpose in these lectures is to say something to you about both, but most of all about the second.

"Law must be stable, and yet it cannot stand still." [1] Here is the great antinomy confronting us at every turn. Rest and motion, unrelieved and unchecked, are equally destructive. The law, like human kind, if life is to continue, must find some path of compromise. Two distinct tendencies, pulling in different directions, must be harnessed together and made to work in unison. All depends on the wisdom with which the joinder is effected.[2] The subject has a literature that takes us back to Aristotle and earlier.[3] Νόμος is to be supplemented by ἐπιείκεια; the tables by the edict; law by equity; custom by statute; rule by discretion. "If we must choose," says Pound in his *Introduction to the Philosophy of Law* (p. 128), "if judicial administration of jus (3) tice must of necessity be wholly mechanical or else wholly administrative, it was a sound instinct of lawyers in the maturity of law that led them to prefer the former." Fusion in due proportion is the problem of the ages.

One does not need to expatiate upon the value of certainty in a developed legal system. Law as a guide to conduct is reduced to the level of mere futility if it is unknown and unknowable. Our law stands indicted for uncertainty, and the names of weighty witnesses are endorsed upon the bill.

If we seek for causes, there are many. Eight or more were enumerated by the American Law Institute at its organization meeting, adopting the report of a committee. There was the lack of agreement on the fundamental principles of the common law; lack of precision in the use of legal terms; conflicting and badly drawn statutory provisions; attempted distinction between cases where the facts present no distinction in the legal principles applicable; the great volume of recorded decisions; ignorance of judges and lawyers; the number and nature of novel legal (4) questions.[4] Of all these causes, the weightiest, I fancy, is the multiplication of decisions. The fecundity of our case law would make Malthus stand aghast. Adherence to precedent was once a steadying force, the guarantee, as it seemed, of stability and certainty. We would not sacrifice any of the brood, and now the spawning progeny, forgetful of our mercy, are rending those who spared them.[5] Increase of numbers has not made (5) for increase of respect. The output of a multitude of minds must be expected to contain its proportion of vagaries. So vast a brood includes the defective and the helpless. An avalanche of decisions by tribunals great and small is producing a situation where citation of precedent is tending to count for less, and appeal to an informing principle is tending to count for more. Crowded dockets make it impossible for judges, however able, to probe every case to its foundations. Even if time were adequate, the case, as it comes before a court, is specific, concrete, the general shrouded in particulars. With the mind directed to these particulars, inevitably it will happen, in view of the limitations of human vision, that the universal element will sometimes be lost sight of in its wrappings, the larger truth ignored, though it fills the background of the landscape, because our eyes are fixed upon the smaller one that lies before us at our feet. This danger, great as it has always been, grows greater every day as mass and maze increase. The very strength of our common law, its cautious advance (6) and retreat a few steps at a time [6] is turned into a weakness unless bearings are taken at frequent intervals, so that we may know the relation of the step to the movement as a whole. One line is run here; another there. We have a filigree of threads and cross-threads, radiating from the center, and dividing one another into sections and cross-sections. We shall be caught in the tentacles of the web, unless some superintending mind imparts the secret of the structure, lifting us to a height where the unity of the circle will be visible as it lies below. The perplexity of the judge becomes the scholar's opportunity.

A movement justifying the hope that the opportunity will not be lost is already under way. The American Law Institute, organized at Washington in February, 1923, is the first coöperative endeavor by all the groups engaged in the development of law to grapple with the monster of uncertainty and slay him. It proposes a scientific and accurate restatement of the law in specially (7) selected fields. The fields that have been marked for entry at the outset are contracts, torts, conflict of laws, and agency. Others will be chosen later. The restatement will consist, first, of a summary of principles stated with such fullness as will afford an adequate presentation of the subject, somewhat after the manner of Dicey's *Conflict of Laws* or Stephen's *Digest of the Law of Evidence;* and, second, of such amplification, illustration, and explanation as shall be necessary to the complete understanding and practical application of the principles, the same works that I have mentioned again supplying an approximate example. Accompanying each restatement there will be a treatise which is to consist of a complete exposition of the present condition of the law and a full citation of authorities. It is to analyze and discuss all the legal problems presented, and justify the statement of the law set forth in the principles.

Professor Williston of Harvard will draft the statement of the law of contracts, and the treatise to go with it. Among the critics of his work will be Professor Corbin (8) of Yale, Professor Page of Wisconsin, and Professor Oliphant of Columbia. Professor Bohlen of the University of Pennsylvania, assisted by Professor Young B. Smith of Columbia, Dean Hepburn of Indiana, Professor Goodrich of Michigan, and Professor Thurston of Yale will state the law of torts. Professor Beale of Harvard will deal with the conflict of laws after first reconciling his own conflicts with Professor Lorenzen of Yale, Professor Bigelow of Chicago, Professor Buchanan of Pittsburgh, and Professor Goodrich of Michigan. Professor Mechem of the University of Chicago will state the law of agency. The groups of critics and advisers are not constant, but from time to time, as occasion prompts, are varied or enlarged. The statement of the draftsman, tentative and provisional in its beginnings, will be subject to suggestion and revision at the hands of his associates, leaders, all, of juristic thought. It will then be submitted to the Council and the members of the Institute. After emerging from their scrutiny, it will be either accepted as adequate or referred back to (9) its authors. When, finally, it goes out under the name and with the sanction of the Institute, after all this testing and retesting, it will be something less than a code and something more than a treatise. It will be invested with unique authority, not to command, but to persuade. It will embody a composite thought and speak a composite voice. Universities and bench and bar will have had a part in its creation.

I have great faith in the power of such a restatement to unify our law. Of course, like anything else worthy of success, it must justify itself by the way in which it is done. Unless it is done with superlative skill, it will fail and ought to fail. None the less, the plan reduces to a minimum the likelihood of failure. If these men cannot restate the law, then the law is incapable of being restated by anyone. You must not think of the product as a code, invested with the binding force of statute. The only force it will possess, at least at the beginning, will be its inherent power of persuasion. Restatement is needed, "not to repress the forces through which judge- (10) made law develops, but to stimulate and free them."[7] "The judicial process is to be set in motion again, but with a new point of departure, a new impetus and direction. In breaking one set of shackles, we are not to substitute another. We are to set the judges free."[8] No doubt there will be a strong presumption in favor of the principle or the precept that can vouch such sponsors to its aid. The thought was happily stated by Mr. Root at the organization of the Institute in his address as chairman of the meeting: "Any lawyer, whose interest in litigation requires him to say that a different view of the law shall be taken, will have upon his shoulders the burden to overturn the statement. Instead of going back through ten thousand cases, it will have been done for him; there will not be a conclusive presumption, but a practical *prima facie* statement upon which, unless it is overturned, judgment may rest." We know how much can be done by one man, acting and speaking only (11) for himself, to build up a common law. Kent and Story did it in their day. Williston and Wigmore are doing it in ours. One dare not estimate the number of sane and sound judgments, useful members of society, that would have been brought into the world defective and deformed without the guidance of these masters. They have shown what can be done for law by a wise science of eugenics. If all this can be accomplished by individual initiative and endeavor, how much greater will be the authority of one who speaks, not merely in his own name, but in that of an organized profession.

More and more we are looking to the scholar in his study, to the jurist rather than to the judge or lawyer, for inspiration and for guidance. Historians tell us that in olden days the practice was much followed by the German courts "of sending up the documents of a case to the law faculty of a university of some standing—Halle, Greifswald, Jena—in order to obtain a consultation as to the proper decision."[9] A tendency dif(12)ferent from this, and yet recalling it in many ways, can be traced even now in the progress of our law. Extra-judicial agencies are assuming an importance that increases year by year. Chief of these agencies is the criticism and the suggestion of scholars in the universities and in other institutes of learning. Until the rise of the modern law school with its critical method, there was no organ through which professional opinion could disclose itself effectively and promptly. The bar was, indeed, there, but its reaction was slow and casual. It was too loosely organized and too busy at times about winning its own cases to be vigilant, in season and out, for the symmetry of legal science. Sometimes, it is true, when a court had gone woefully astray, there would develop in the course of years an undercurrent of hostile judgment which at intervals (13) would well up and emerge above the surface. The same thing might happen, and more promptly, if the case was a conspicuous one, exciting public interest. Criticism, however, was in the main sporadic and unorganized, and limited too often to muttered disapproval, hardly vocal or audible, and only slowly, if at all, communicated to those whose work was disapproved. The universities have given us for the first time a body of critics ever on the watch.

This new organ of expression is the university law review.

I have spoken of the words of Williston and Wigmore which took the rank of classics almost overnight. Hardly less notable are the studies in smaller fields which are made month by month in the columns of the reviews. In the preface to one of the supplements of his treatise on Evidence, Wigmore complains, writing in 1915, that the courts were unwilling, as it seemed, to refer to the masters of juristic thought unless the products of their labor were published in a volume. Anything *bound* might be cited, though wrought through no process more intel (14) lectual than the use of paste pot and scissors. Pamphlets were anathema. It is perhaps significant that in the preface to the last edition he omits the caustic comment. Judges have at last awakened, or at all events a number of them not wholly negligible, to the treasures buried in the law reviews. A recent case in New York will illustrate my meaning, and show the power of the universities to guide the course of judgment. We had a series of decisions dealing with a supposed rule that in actions for specific performance there must be mutuality of remedy, and mutuality, not merely at the time of the decree, but at the making of the contract. Some cases, repeating the words of Fry and Pomeroy, went pretty far in exalting the supposed rule into one of general application. I have little doubt that if the university professors had not intervened, the rule would have been extended by a process of purely logical deduction, and things would have gone from bad to worse. In the meantime the professors in the universities became busy, and pointed out where we were tending. Ames (15) started the crusade in an early number of the *Columbia Law Review*.[10] Lewis of Pennsylvania strengthened the attack, advancing from a somewhat different angle, in a series of papers in the *American Law Register*.[11] More recently Dean Stone of Columbia, writing in the *Columbia Law Review*,[12] exposed the dangers of the course that many of the courts were following. Finally Professor Williston summarized the arguments and the precedents in his treasury of learning.[13] Only the other day, the Court of Appeals reconsidered the whole subject, and put it on a basis which will be found consistent, so, at least, I hope, with equity and justice.[14] But the interesting thing about the episode is the part that was played by extra-judicial agencies. Without the critical labors of Ames and Lewis and

Stone and Williston, the heresy, instead of dying out, would (16) probably have persisted, and even spread. It would have gained new vitality with every judgment that confirmed it. Inevitably, too, the process of logic or of development by analogy would have pushed it forward into new fields. What saved the day was criticism from without

I have little doubt, therefore, that the proposed restatement will prove a potent force in bringing certainty and order out of our wilderness of precedent. "He who has not a copy of Azo's books," ran the proverb of the Middle Ages, "need not go to the Courts of Justice." [15] So men will come in time to speak of the publications of the Institute. We shall turn to their pages before turning anywhere else. Often we shall go no farther. They will accumulate with the years a power and prestige that will level opposition. Little by little the courts, even though nonconformist at the beginning, will tend to conformity and unity. Two words of caution, however, we must keep with us. In our worship of certainty, we must distinguish between the (17) sound certainty and the sham, between what is gold and what is tinsel; and then, when certainty is attained, we must remember that it is not the only good; that we can buy it at too high a price; that there is danger in perpetual quiescence as well as in perpetual motion; and that a compromise must be found in a principle of growth.

I have said that there is a certainty that is genuine and a certainty that is illusory, a symmetry that is worth attaining and a symmetry to be shunned. One of the reasons why our law needs to be restated is that judges strive at times after the certainty that is sham instead of the certainty that is genuine. They strive after a certainty that will keep the law consistent within their own parish, their little territorial jurisdictions, instead of the certainty that will keep it consistent with verities and principles as broad as the common law itself, and as deep and fundamental as the postulates of justice. The tendency is insidious and to some extent inevitable. Particular precedents are carried to con (18) clusions which are thought to be their logical development. The end is not foreseen. Every new decision brings the judge a little farther. Before long he finds himself in a dilemma. He does not like the spot where he is placed, yet he is unwilling and perhaps unable to retreat from it. The certainty that is arrived at by adherence to precedent is attained, but there is a sacrifice of another certainty that is larger and more vital. This latter certainty is lost if we view the law in shreds and patches, not steadily and whole with a sweep that reaches the horizon. Often a spurious consistency is preserved by artificial and unreal distinctions. The idol is discredited, but he is honored with lip service, the rubrics of the ancient ritual. We must have the courage to unmask pretense if we are to reach a peace that will abide beyond the fleeting hour. The law's uncertainties are to be corrected, but so also are its deformities. Often they go together, and the remedy that cures the one will be found to cure the other. Restatement must include revision when the vestiges of organs, atrophied (19) by disuse, will become centers of infection if left within the social body.

My second caution, however, is the weightier. Overemphasis of certainty may carry us to the worship of an intolerable rigidity. If we were to state the law today as well as human minds can state it, new problems, arising almost overnight, would encumber the ground again. "As in other sciences, so in politics, it is impossible that all things should be precisely set down in writing; for enactments must be universal, but actions are concerned with particulars." [16] Restatement will clear the ground of débris. It will enable us to reckon our gains and losses, strike a balance, and start afresh. This is an important, an almost inestimably important, service. But hereafter, as before, the changing combinations of events will beat upon the walls of ancient categories. "Life has relations not capable of division into inflexible compartments. The moulds expand and shrink."[17] Existing rules and principles can give (20) us our present location, our bearings, our latitude and longitude. The inn that shelters for the night is not the journey's end. The law, like the traveler, must be ready for the morrow. It must have the principle of growth.

REFERENCES

1. Pound, *Interpretations of Legal History*, p. 1.

2. Vinogradoff, *Common Sense in Law*, p. 122; Coudert, *Certainty and Justice*, p. 1.

3. Vinogradoff, *Historical Jurisprudence*, vol. II, p. 64; *Common Sense in Law*, p. 209.

4. It is interesting to match this catalogue of grievances against the catalogue made by Bacon in his proposal for amending the laws of Eng-

land, some three hundred years ago (Bacon, Law Tracts, p. 5) "Certain it is, that our laws, as they now stand, are subject to great incertainties, and variety of opinion, delays and evasions; whereof ensueth, (1) That the multiplicity and length of suits is great; (2) That the contentious person, is armed, and the honest subject wearied and oppressed; (3) that the judge is more absolute; who, in doubtful cases, hath a greater stroke and liberty; (4) that the chancery courts are more filled, the remedy of law being often obscure and doubtful; (5) that the ignorant lawyer shroudeth his ignorance of law, in that, doubts are frequent and many; (6) That men's assurances of their lands and estates by patents, deeds, wills, are often subject to question, and hollow; and many the like inconveniences."

5. Stone "Some Aspects of the Problem of Law Simplification," 23 *Columbia Law Review* 319; Salmond, "The Literature of Law," 22 *Columbia Law Review* 197, 199.

6. Pound, "Courts and Legislation," 7 *Am. Pol. Science Rev.* 361; IX Modern Legal Philosophy Series, p. 214.

7. 35 *Harv. L. R.* 113, 117.

8. 35 *Harv. L. R., supra.*

9. Vinogradoff, *Common Sense in Law,* p. 203; Stammler, "Modern Jurisprudence," 21 *Michigan Law Rev.* 877, 878; cf. the *Responsa Prudentium of Roman Law;* Muirhead, *Roman Law,* pp. 291, 293; J. M. Gest, "Notes upon Legal Continental Literature," 69 *Univ. of Pennsylvania Law Rev.* 128, 129; Hadley, *Rome and the World Today* 238, 242, recalling Shakespeare's "Merchant of Venice."

10. 3 *Col. L. R.* 1; *Lectures on Legal History,* p. 370.

11. 40 *Am. Law Register,* N.S., 270, 382, 447, 507, 559; 42 *id.* 591.

12. 16 *Col. L. R.* 443.

13. 3 Williston, *Contracts,* secs. 1433, 1436, 1440.

14. Epstein v. Gluckin, 233 N. Y. 490.

15. Vinogradoff, *Common Sense in Law,* p. 202.

16. Aristotle, *Politics,* Book II, Jowett's translation.

17. Glanzer v. Shepard, 233 N. Y. 236, 241.

(21)

— II —

The Need of a Philosophy of Law as an Aid to Growth. The Problems of Legal Philosophy. The Meaning and Genesis of Law.

I AM brought thus to the second phase of my discourse, the need of a philosophy of law. The theorist has a hard time to make his way in an ungrateful world. He is supposed to be indifferent to realities; yet his life is spent in the exposure of realities which, till illumined by his searchlight, were hidden and unknown. He is contrasted, and to his great disfavor, with the strenuous man of action, who ploughs or builds or navigates or trades, yet, in moments of meditation he takes the consoling knowledge to his heart that the action of his favored brothers would be futile unless informed and inspired by (22) thoughts that came from him. Of the lot of all theorists, that of the philosopher is the sorriest. He is the theorist κατ' ἐξοχήν. Let us heave a stone at him, say his enemies, and thus stigmatize his tribe. "I thought the man had sense," said the Duchess of Marlborough when she quarreled with Voltaire; "but I find him at bottom either a fool or a philosopher."[1] General truths are hard to grasp. Most of us have all we can do in accumulating by dint of toil the knowledge of a few particulars. A troublesome lot, these men who are searching always for the ultimate. If we cannot understand, let us show that the superiority is ours by combining to deride.

I have made myself today the self-appointed spokesman and defender of the philosopher in the field of law. I am not concerned to vindicate philosophy, either in jurisprudence or outside of it, as an inquiry of cultural value or speculative interest. Pretensions, thus limited, would perhaps be feebly contested, or even grudgingly allowed. My concern is with the relation of phi (23) losophy to life. The significance of this relation should be brought home to the student while he is yet standing on the threshold. You think perhaps of philosophy as dwelling in the clouds. I hope you may see that she is able to descend to earth. You think that in stopping to pay court to her, when you should be hastening forward on your journey, you are loitering in bypaths and wasting precious hours. I hope you may share my faith that you are on the highway to the goal. Here you will find the key for the unlocking of bolts and combinations that shall never be pried open by clumsier or grosser tools. You think there is nothing practical in a theory that is concerned with ultimate conceptions. That is true perhaps while you are doing the journeyman's work of your profession. You may find in the end, when you pass to higher problems, that instead of its being true that the study of the ultimate is profitless, there is little that is profitable in the study of anything else.[2]

(24) At the outset, let us try to get some notion of what a philosophy of law includes. There is no need to mark its content by unvarying or rigid lines. It is enough to indicate some things that are certain to fall within its limits. We shall thus evade difficulties of definition which a philosophy of law shares with philosophy in general. "The moment you attempt to define its subject matter," says Windelband in his recent *Introduction to Philosophy,*[3] "you find the philosophers themselves failing you. There is no such thing as a generally received definition of philosophy, and it would be useless to reproduce the innumerable attempts that have been made to provide one." [4] Description may serve where definition would be hazardous. A philosophy of law will tell us how law comes into being, how it grows, and whither it tends. Genesis and development and end or function, these things, if no others, will be dealt within its pages. To (25) these it will probably add a description of the genesis and growth and function, not only of law itself, but also of some of those conceptions that are fundamental in the legal framework. One who wishes to get a notion of the contour of the field can do no better than consult the brilliant *Introduction to a Philosophy of Law* by the Dean of the Harvard Law School. One will find there little of merely abstract definition, of diagrams and maps and charts. One will see the fields as they are tilled, and gain a sense of their value by tasting of their fruits.

The genesis, the growth, the function, and the end of law—the terms seem general and abstract, too far dissevered from realities, raised too high above the ground, to interest the legal wayfarer. But believe me, it is not so. It is these generalities and abstractions that give direction to legal thinking, that sway the minds of judges, that determine, when the balance wavers, the outcome of the doubtful lawsuit. Implicit in every decision where the question is, so to speak, at large, is a philosophy of the origin and aim of (26) law, a philosophy which, however veiled, is in truth the final arbiter. It accepts one set of arguments, modifies another, rejects a third, standing ever in reserve as a court of ultimate appeal. Often the philosophy is ill coördinated and fragmentary. Its empire is not always suspected even by its subjects. Neither lawyer nor judge, pressing forward along one line or retreating along another, is conscious at all times that it is philosophy which is impelling him to the front or driving him to the rear. None the less, the goad is there. If we cannot escape the Furies, we shall do well to understand them.

My approach to the subject will be by asking you to consider at the outset the nature of the judicial process. The lawyer cannot rise to the full measure of his power in persuading, nor the judge to the full measure of *his* power in deciding, without an understanding of the process which the one attempts to control and the other to pursue. Analysis of the judicial process involves analysis of the genesis and growth of law, and this involves a study of functions and of (27) ends. What do we mean by law, and how is it created? After it is created, how is it extended or developed? What are the principles that guide the choice of paths when the judge, without controlling precedent, finds himself standing uncertain at the parting of the ways? What are the directive forces to be obeyed, the methods to be applied, the ends to be sought? These are problems of philosophy. Every decision, where the judicial process is creative, and not merely static or declaratory, is a reflection of the problem and an expression of the answer. The philosophy may be inconsistent or unsound or distorted. The answers will share the vice, and be perverse or unwise or contradictory. The problem is always present. We shall not find the solution by acting as if there were nothing to be solved.

Let me first consider what we are to understand by "law," at least for the purpose of the inquiry on which we are embarking. We must know what law is, or at any rate what we mean by it, before we can know how it develops.

Isolate or try to isolate this little patch upon the (28) web of human thought, and you will be given some hint of the unifying threads that are shot through the fabric of our knowledge. Queries that were propounded in the beginnings of recorded thought turn up in unexpected regions and press us for an answer. Philosophy has her feuds that heed no truce of God. For several thousand years she has been trying to compose them, yet it is only with indifferent success that she has kept the peace within her borders. The tyro in legal studies may thus be pardoned some surprise and petulance when he finds the borders trenching upon the precincts of the law. Here at least, he has said to himself, here at least is a quiet nook where my ears will not be assailed with the babble of contending schools. The chatter of nominalist and realist, waging their never ending war of words, will not penetrate these sheltered fields. Platonist and Aristotelian will here know themselves as brothers. Vain is his thought. The promised haven is not found. At the very threshold of his study, when he seeks a definition of law itself, the ancient factions are (29) before him, already at each other's throats. Is there any law beyond the precept of isolated judgments? Must we surrender the quest for the universal, and content ourselves with what is merely a succession of particulars? Back of the changing phenomena are we to posit a substratum which gives coherence and reality? These are not questions suggested by the study of mediaeval schoolmen. They were not propounded by Aquinas. The student will have to grapple with them if he would understand his Blackstone. Every now and then he will be reminded of their bearing upon present-day realities. He tries to console himself with the thought that peace awaits him later. All this, he argues, is but preliminary. When I am fairly launched upon my subject, I shall gain the open sea. He opens a book on corporations, and seeks to understand the nature of juristic persons. Nominalist and realist are at each other's throats again. One of the factions has it that the corporation is but a name or symbol for an aggregate of men and women. The other faction tells him that beyond (30) the name and the components there is in very truth a *tertium quid*. Some of the bitterest controversies of the law preserve the ancient feud today.[5] Platonist and Aristotelian flock to the standards of their leaders. The air resounds again with the slogans of the schools.

Our concern for the moment is with conflicting theories of the nature of law itself. With all the bitterness of the conflict, it is in part a war of words. A good deal of the warfare has its origin in the confusion that arises when a single term of broad and ill-defined content is made to do duty without discrimination for two or more (31) ideas. Dean Pound in a recent essay[6] bewails "the ambiguity of the term 'law' that requires us to use one word for the legal precepts which are actually recognized and applied in the tribunals of a given time and place and for the more general body of doctrine and tradition from which those precepts are chiefly drawn, and by which we criticize them." The attempt of some jurists to confine law in its proper sense to the first of these meanings, involving a refusal to extend it to the second, ends in a sceptical nihilism which is the negation of all law. What is left is not a body of rules of general application, but mere isolated judgments, binding upon the parties only, and losing their quality of law in the very moment that they gain it. I have had occasion elsewhere to develop this point more fully.[7] I have shown, too, how varying views of the nature and origin of law may lead to varying decisions upon the merits of a lawsuit. What are (32) the rights of litigants who have acted upon a judgment of the highest court of a state to the effect that a statute is invalid, if a controversy between them comes before the same court after the earlier judgment has been overruled? You will find it hard to reach a solution of such a problem without wandering into a philosophical dissertation upon the nature of law in general. Some difficulties and ambiguities that beset the jurists of continental Europe have, indeed, been spared us. We do not need to spend pages in an attempted demonstration that *Gesetz* is not co-terminous with *Recht,*[8] that *la loi* is narrower than *le droit,*[9] that law is something more than statute. We are saved from all this because in action every day about us is the process by which forms of conduct are stamped in the judicial mint as law, and thereafter circulate freely as part of the coinage of the realm. But even before that stage is reached there has not been lacking altogether the element of coercive power. (33) Men go about their business, and regulate their affairs with serenity and safety, though the principle or rule or standard to which they adhere for guidance or enlightenment is without the sanction of a judgment, and even more frequently without the sanction of a statute. At some point back of definitive adjudication, of perfect or unfailing certainty, we reach the stage of law.

If you ask what degree of assurance must attach to a principle or a rule or a standard not yet embodied in a judgment before the name law may properly be affixed to it, I can only fall back upon a thought which I shall have occasion to develop farther, the thought that law, like other branches of social science, must be satisfied to test the validity of its conclusions by the logic of probabilities rather than the logic of certainty. When there is such a degree of probability as to lead to a reasonable assurance that a given conclusion ought to be and will be embodied in a judgment, we speak of the conclusion as law, though the judgment has not yet (34) been rendered, and though, conceivably, when rendered, it may disappoint our expectation. I think it is interesting to reflect that such a use of the term law strengthens the analogy between the law which is the concern of jurisprudence, and those principles of order, the natural or moral laws, which are the concern of natural or moral science. The pendulum has swung back and forth a good many times, but the tendency of juristic thought today involves emphasis upon the elements of agreement rather than the elements of difference.[10]

It was not always so. In the days, now too remote, of my study in a law school, authors and teachers delighted to dwell on the antithesis between law that was truly law, and law masquerading in borrowed plumes, with no better claim of title than metaphor or remote analogy. Law that was truly law was to be the subject of our study. We were not to look for it anywhere except in statute or decision, and hardly perhaps in statute. Its personification was the sheriff, and (35) the test of its reality a writ. Law by metaphor or analogy was merely a principle of order. We might recognize the kinship if we chose, but always in the spirit of condescension that is due to poor relations. It would do no harm to humor the planets, or gratify their sense of pride, by saying it was law that governed their majestic movements. All the time, however, we should remember that the poor relations must know their place, and keep within the bounds of moderation the claims of distant kinship. Tide and eclipse and the changing seasons of the year display, we were told, a uniformity of their own. We were not to confuse it with the sequence revealed to faithful eyes after long and patient scrutiny in the judgments of the courts. The uniformities of the equinoxes might be deeper and more obvious than those of the decisions construing the statute of frauds in its fourth and seventeenth sections. None the less, coherence, if lacking in the commentary, was balanced and compensated by the presence of something else. The product of judicial exegesis might seethe (36) and teem with incongruities. We were consoled at least by the assurance that it had something more important. It had the quality of law.

The passing years have not brought to me the gift of wisdom, but they have at least opened my eyes to the perception that distinctions which in those early days seemed sharp and obvious are in truth shadowy and blurred, the walls of the compartments in no wise water-tight or rigid. In particular, I see that the relationship is closer than I fancied between the principles of order which, to my early thinking, were laws by brevet or courtesy, and the Simon-pure creations of state power, functioning in all the plenitude of sovereignty through its appointed agencies, the courts. If once I figured the two families as distant kinsmen, tracing their lines perhaps to a common ancestor, but so remotely and obscurely that the call of blood might be ignored, I have now arrived at the belief that they are cousins german, if not brothers.

Law is something more than a succession of isolated judgments which spend their force as (37) law when they have composed the controversies that led to them. "The general body of doctrine and tradition" from which the judgments were derived, and "by which we criticize them" [11] must be ranked as law also, not merely because it is the chief subject of our study, but because also the limits which it imposes upon a judge's liberty of choice are not purely advisory, but involve in greater or less degree an element of coercive power. At all events, if this is not law, some other word must be invented to describe it; and to it we shall then transfer the major portion of our interest. Judgments themselves have importance for the student so far, and so far only, as they permit a reasonable prediction that like judgments will be rendered if like situations are repeated. The study of the law is thus seen to be the study of principles of order revealing themselves in uniformities of antecedents and consequents. When the uniformities are sufficiently constant to be the subject of prediction (38) with reasonable certainty, we say that law exists. Indeed, they may be so persuasive and compelling as to lead us to say, if the prediction miscarries, that the judgment which disappoints us is error, or false law—at all events, if we have the hardihood to disregard the warning of Holland and others that false law is a misnomer, and that law, like grammar, is superlative. We may even hazard a new prediction that the judgment which gives momentary currency to error will some day be reversed. On the other hand, situations may exist where the uniformities are so inconstant, the analogies so doubtful, the body of principles and tradition so equivocal in their directions, that we are unable to predict. We can at most argue or suggest. No doubt there is difficulty, upon occasion, in fixing the point of time at which one process shades into the other. When does a mere hypothesis become transformed into a principle or a rule, and when does the principle or rule put off the vestments of authority, and become a shattered or deposed hypothesis? Falling back upon my logic of (39) probabilities, I can do not better than point my meaning by the aid of concrete illustrations.

We speak of it as a rule of law today that mutual promises give rise to a contract, and their breach to a right of action for damages. We know this was not always so.[12] We can name the case whereby the rule as we know it was established.[13] Until the judgment in Strangborough v. Warner, 4 Leon 3, decided in 1588, there had been in English law the most fragmentary and imperfect development of contract by mere consent. Before the rendition of that judgment, we cannot say with justice that there was a preëxisting principle or rule which the judges were extending or applying. They formulated the principle or rule themselves, and gave it potency thereafter by a process of creation. Suppose some court today should refuse to accept the judgment in Strangborough's case, (40) and hold the contract void. The ruling might involve an abuse of power, or flagrant error, but the judgment, unless reversed upon appeal, would, none the less, be binding upon the parties, and express the law for them. With this possibility before us, with the power residing in the court to nullify all our predictions, why do we, none the less, declare with assurance that this case is still to be accepted as a statement of the law? We do so because the observation of recorded instances almost without number induces a belief which has the certainty of conviction that the rule will be acted on as law by the agencies of government. As in the processes of nature, we give the name of law to uniformity of succession.[14]

Let me pass now to an illustration where the answer is more doubtful. A maker of automobiles is sued by the victim of an accident. The plaintiff bought the vehicle, not from the maker, but from someone else. He asserts that there was (41) negligence in the process of manufacture and that privity of contract is unnecessary to confer a right of action. Since the decision in MacPherson v. Buick Mfg. Co. 217 N. Y. 382, decided in 1916, the law of New York must be said to be in accordance with the plaintiff's claim. What, however, was the posture of affairs before the Buick case had been determined? Was there any law on the subject? A mass of judgments, more or less relevant, had been rendered by the same and other courts. A body of particulars existed on which an hypothesis might be reared. None the less, their implications were equivocal. We see this in the fact that the judgment of the court was not rendered without dissent. Whether the law can be said to have existed in advance of the decision, will depend upon the varying estimates of the nexus between the conclusion and existing principle and precedent.

Let me take another case where the problem was yet more doubtful. Suppose a decision frankly new, covering a virgin field,[15] or a deci (42) sion reached as the result of the upsetting of another judgment.[16] Klein v. Maravelas held valid the sales in bulk act, and in so doing overruled an earlier decision which held it void. People v. Schweinler Press held valid the statute limiting hours of work for women, overruling an earlier decision to the contrary. Epstein v. Gluckin qualified the scope of earlier decisions which had made mutuality of remedy a condition of equitable relief, and did this in recognition of extra-judicial criticism of the earlier and narrower view. In all these qualifying or overruling judgments, appeal was made to a body either of judicial or of professional opinion which displayed uniformities at variance with the judgment to be nullified or limited. A wrong answer was set right by the substitution of the true one. The quality of law was maintained as the expression through the courts of a principle of order.

Now, we must note that in all these cases (43) there was present the possibility that the prediction would miscarry. The distinction in that respect between one case and another is one merely of degree. So, indeed, it must always be. The court may reverse itself, and unsettle what seemed settled. It may ignore or misapply established rules through carelessness or ignorance or in rare instances corruption. What permits us to say that the principles are law is the force or persuasiveness of the prediction that they will or ought to be applied. Even when the conclusion upon a special state of facts is in doubt, as in the case of the manufacturer of the Buick car, there is little doubt that the conclusion will be drawn from a stock of principles and rules which will be treated as invested with legal obligation. The court will not roam at large, and light upon one conclusion or another as the result of favor or caprice. This stock of rules and principles is what for most purposes we mean by law. We may not draw the same deductions from them as the court does in this case or in that. There will be little difference in our premises. (44) We shall unite in viewing as law that body of principle and dogma which with a reasonable measure of probability may be predicted as the basis for judgment in pending or in future controversies. When the prediction reaches a high degree of certainty or assurance, we speak of the law as settled, though, no matter how great the apparent settlement, the possibility of error in the prediction is always present. When the prediction does not reach so high a standard, we speak of the law as doubtful or uncertain. Farther down is the vanishing point where law does not exist, and must be brought into being, if at all, by an act of free creation.

I wrote these words before I had seen an interesting article by Dr. John C. H. Wu on the "Juristic Philosophy of Mr. Justice Holmes."[17] My thought, it will be seen, is in close approach to theirs. "The prophecies of what the courts will do in fact, and nothing more pretentious," says Holmes, "are what I mean by the (45) law." [18] Dr. Wu develops with acuteness the implications of the statement. "Law is, thus, a matter of prediction. It does not even consist of the rules already recognized and acted on, as Salmond would define it; [19] it consists of the rules which the courts will probably recognize or act on. . . . Psychologically, law is a science of prediction *par excellence.* It concerns primarily our future interest; people do not study cases for pleasure, but generally with a view to anticipating what the courts will do when future cases arise. One constantly refers, it is true, to past cases as so many depositaries of the law, but in the last analysis that is done almost always with the intention of showing that there is sufficient ground for believing that the courts will act in such and such a way in the future." Analysis of right and duty exposes the same core within them. "For legal purposes," says Holmes, *Collected Papers* (p. 313), "a right is only the (46) hypostasis of prophecy—the imagination of a substance supporting the fact that the public force will be brought to bear upon those who do things said to contravene it—just as we talk of the force of gravitation accounting for the conduct of bodies in space." "A legal duty so called is nothing but a prediction that if a man does or omits certain things, he will be made to suffer in this or that way by judgment of the court." [20]

I know there is a vagueness in all this that may dissatisfy the seeker for inflexible categories, clean-cut and definite compartments, ticketed and labeled and capable of being recognized at sight. The quest is constant and persistent, but it is doomed to disappointment. I do not need to enter into a discussion of the meaning of truth itself.[21] The reality that is absolute and unconditioned may exist, but man must know it, if at all, through its manifestations in the conditioned and the relative. Pragmatism is at least a working rule by which truth is to be (47) tested, and its attainment known.[22] If philosophy has not yet been able to penetrate the mystery of substance, if it has not yet been able to tell us wherein consists the identity of things,[23] we ought not to feel surprise that it is still baffled by the products of conceptual thought, the never ending struggle over universals, their content and identity.[24] I am not concerned to inquire whether back of these uniformities which have their flower and fruit in judgments, there may be others still higher and broader, revelations of a social order, norms of right and justice, to which the lower and narrower uniformities must conform, and after which they must be patterned, if they are to be effective and enduring. I doubt whether these types or patterns, except to the extent that they are consistent with statute or decision, should receive the name of (48) law, though in the view of Duguit and others,[25] statute or decision is law only to the extent that it is a sharer in their essence, an expression of their spirit. "The more I advance in age," writes Duguit,[26] "and seek to penetrate the problem of law, the more I am convinced that law is not a creation of the state, that it exists without the state, that the notion of law is altogether independent of the state, and that the rule of law imposes itself on the state as it does upon individuals." Legal obligation, as he views it, is not an "obligation modifying the individual will, but an obligation purely social, that is to say, of such a nature that if it is not satisfied, it produces a disturbance of equilibrium in the constituent elements of the social group, and, as a consequence, a social reaction, that is to say, a spontaneous effort to reëstablish equilibrium." [27] Speculations of this kind, however interesting in themselves, are alien, after all, to the subject of (49) our study. If there is any law which is back of the sovereignty of the state, and superior thereto, it is not law in such a sense as to concern the judge or the lawyer, however much it concerns the statesman or the moralist. The courts are creatures of the state and of its power, and while their life as courts continues, they must obey the law of their creator.[28] This seems to be recognized by Duguit himself. He draws a distinction between "la règle de droit normative," and "la règle de droit constructive," which comes pretty close to throwing his whole theory overboard except for the student of statecraft or of ethics. A normative rule or juridical norm exists when the mass of the individuals composing the social group comprehend and admit that a reaction against the violators of the rule can be socially organized.[29] A constructive rule is a rule established to assure the enforcement, so far as possible, of a normative rule,[30] and implies the (50) existence of a state.[31] "The great mass of our positive laws," he writes,[32] "are composed of constructive or technical rules which imply a more or less developed political organization.

They are addressed in reality to government and its agents. . . . Although they imply the existence of a state, they may be simply customary. They are obligatory for government and for the representatives of government." The norms are little more than those prevailing habits and convictions which cannot safely be ignored if law in its administration is to win obedience and respect.[33] (51) "I have no difficulty in acknowledging," he continues,[34] "that a juridical norm taken by itself and independently of the means of putting it in force, is a view of the mind rather than a concrete reality. One would find with difficulty either in primitive or in civilized societies juridical norms unaccompanied by legal instrumentalities for putting them in force, created either by custom or by the written law. One can cite the *'leges imperfectae'* of Roman law. But aside from the fact that they were very rare, it seems that they were accompanied in one way or another at least by indirect sanctions. However that may be, almost always the normative rule is enveloped in constructive rules, which create an organization, sometimes altogether rudimentary, sometimes very developed and very scientific, and which open up instrumentalities tending to sanction directly or indirectly the obligations negative or positive resulting from the norm." "Normative rules" cease to be law for the advocate or the judge when they are over (52) ridden by "constructive rules." They are then merely standards or ideals which in time may win their way. Advocate or judge must reject them as law till their day of triumph has been reached, and the state is ready to support them through its courts and other agencies with the sanction of its power.

A principle or rule of conduct so established as to justify a prediction with reasonable certainty that it will be enforced by the courts if its authority is challenged, is, then, for the purpose of our study, a principle or rule of law. In speaking of principles and rules of conduct, I include those norms or standards of behavior which, if not strictly rules or principles, since they have not been formally declared in statute or decision,[35] are none the less the types or patterns to which statute or decision may be expected to conform. All that I mean to deny them is a potency superior to that of the established organs of the state. They have their roots in the

(53) customary forms and methods of business and of fellowship, the prevalent convictions of equity and justice, the complex of belief and practice which we style the *mores* of the day. They may lack an official *imprimatur*,[36] but this will not always hinder us from resting securely on the assumption that the omission will be supplied when occasion so demands.[37] Unless and until our expectation is disappointed, a standard or rule or principle so verified is treated as law in the governance of conduct, and may fairly be characterized as law in the governance of speech. The uniformity that issues in a reasonable prediction of continuance is the uniformity obeyed.

I have not embarked on this inquiry as a mere exercise in dialectics. I am persuaded that at the root of any satisfactory philosophy of growth, there must be an understanding of what it is that is to grow, a philosophy of genesis or birth. We (54) must get away at one extreme from the notion that law is fixed and immutable, that the conclusion which the judge declares, instead of being itself a more or less tentative hypothesis, an approximate formulation of a uniformity and an order inductively apprehended, has a genuine preëxistence, that judgment is a process of discovery, and not in any degree a process of creation. This is the extreme of which Blackstone is the most eminent exponent. On the other hand, we must avoid another extreme, which, if not the view of Austin, is a version of his thought, or perhaps a perversion, much developed by his successors,—the conception of law as a series of isolated dooms, the general merged in the particular, the principle dethroned and the instance exalted as supreme. Each extreme has a tendency, though for a different reason, to stifle the creative element. The one teaches the lesson that there is nothing to create. The other teaches the lesson that the thing created is a finality, and that the duty is to reproduce. The apotheosis of *stare decisis* is the result. The judgment is the (55) thing. There is no law behind it or apart from it. Let us worship at the shrine of the literal and the actual. What has been held has a significance so unique that, in addition to accepting it as a datum, we are to accept its logical implications as supplying the sole instruments of advance. Between these two extremes we have the conception of law as a body of rules and principles and standards which in their extension to new combinations of events are to be sorted, selected, moulded, and adapted in subordination to an end. A process of trial and error brings judgments into being. A process of trial and error determines their right to reproduce their kind.

REFERENCES

1. Quoted by Strachey, *Books and Characters,* p. 125.
2. *Cf.* Tourtoulon, *Philosophy in the Development of Law,* vol. XIII, Modern Legal Philosophy Series, Professor Cohen's Introduction, p. 24.
3. *Introduction to Philosophy,* by Wm. Windelband, translated by Joseph McCabe, p. 20.
4. *Cf.* Wm. James, *Some Problems of Philosophy,* p. 29; Royce, *The Spirit of Modern Philosophy,* p. 1.
5. Saleilles, *De la personnalité juridique;* Vinogradoff, *Common Sense in Law,* p. 77; Barker, *Political Thought from Spencer to Today,* p. 175; Maitland, Introduction to Gierke's *Political Theories of the Middle Age,* XVIII; Maitland, *Coll. Papers,* 3, pp. 304, 314; Buckland, *Roman Law,* pp. 175, 176; Henderson, *The Position of Foreign Corporations in American Constitutional Law,* p. 3 "The problem of the one and the many lies at the bottom of all logic, of all ethics, of all economics, and of all politics," Nicholas Murray Butler, address at the Hague on "The Development of the International Mind," July 20, 1923, vol. IX, *Am. Bar Assn. Jour.,* p. 520.
6. Judge Holmes's "Contributions to the Science of Law," 34 *Harv. L. R.* 449, 452.
7. *Nature of the Judicial Process,* p. 126.
8. Ehrlich, *Grundlegung der Soziologie des Rechts.*
9. Duguit, *Traité de droit constitutionnel.*
10. *Cf.* Charmont, *Renaissance du droit naturel.*
11. Pound, *supra.*
12. Holdsworth, *History of English Law,* vol. II, p. 72; Ames, *History of Parol Contracts Prior to Assumpsit,* III Anglo-Am. Legal Essays 304.
13. Sweet, *Foundations of Legal Liability,* vol. II, p. 55.
14. *Cf.* Vinogradoff, *Common Sense in Law,* pp. 206, 207.
15. Hynes v. N. Y. Central R. R. Co., 231 N. Y. 229.
16. Klein v. Maravelas, 219 N. Y. 383; People v. Schweinler Press, 214 N. Y. 395; *cf.* Epstein v. Gluckin, 233 N. Y. 490.
17. 21 *Mich. L. R.* 523, 530, March, 1923.
18. 21 *Mich. L. R.* 530, citing Holmes, *Collected Papers,* p. 173.
19. Salmond, *Jurisprudence,* p. 9, 4th ed.
20. *Collected Papers,* p. 169.
21. James, *Pragmatism;* James, *The Nature of Truth.*
22. In this sense at least, we may say with Comte: "Tout est relatif, voilà le seul principe absolu" (Windelband, *Introduction to Philosophy,* p. 38; *cf. ibid.,* pp. 45, 179).
23. Windelband, *supra,* pp. 52, 55, *et seq.*
24. Windelband, p. 186.
25. *Cf.* H. Krabbe, *The Modern Idea of the State.*
26. *Traité de droit constitutionnel,* 2d ed., vol. I, p. 33.
27. Vol. I, p. 20; *cf.* pp. 87, 88.
28. *Cf.* Sabine & Shepard, Introduction to H. Krabbe's *The Modern Idea of the State,* p. xlv.
29. *Traité de droit constitutionnel,* vol. I, p. 36; also p. 41.
30. P. 38.
31. P. 39.
32. P. 41.

33. This subject is well treated by A. R. Lord, *The Principles of Politics,* pp. 69, 70, 81, 91, 193, 197, 278, 295.

"The sovereign does not create justice in an ethical sense to be sure, and there may be cases in which it would not dare to deny that justice for fear of war or revolution. Sovereignty is a question of power, and no human power is unlimited. Carino v. Insular Government of the Philippine Islands, 212 U. S. 449, 458. But from the necessary point of view of the sovereign and its organs whatever is enforced by it as law is enforced as the expression of its will. Kawananakoa v. Polyblank, 205 U. S. 349, 353" (Holmes, J., in the *Western Maid,* 257 U. S. 432). *Cf.* Haldane, *The Reign of Relativity,* p. 378.

34. Vol. 1, p. 134.

35. Ehrlich, *Grundlegung der Soziologie des Rechts,* p. 368.

36. Holland, *Elements of Jurisprudence,* p. 54.

37. *Cf.* Ehrlich, *Grundlegung der Soziologie des Rechts,* p. 8. For illustrations of customs recently recognized by a court as invested with the force of law, see McKee v. Gratz, 260 U. S. 127, 136, and Walker v. Gish, 260 U. S. 447, 450.

— III —

(56)

The Growth of Law, and the Method of Judging.

FROM genesis I pass to growth. In what I have to say I propose to limit myself to growth through the judicial process. There may also, of course, be growth through legislation, but the science of legislation is no part of the field of my inquiry. How does the judge develop and extend the body of uniformities which we have named the law when changing combinations of events make development or extension needful? Is there only one method at his call, or is there a choice of methods, and if so, how do they differ, and what are the principles that are to regulate the choice between them? Some reasoned knowledge of these things is an important part of our equipment for service at the bar or on the bench. I confess that only late in life did (57) a sense of its importance come to me. While I was in practice at the bar, I tried to find the pertinent authority, and fit it to the case at hand. I was not much concerned whether it was right if I was sure that it was pertinent, and I had a blind faith which persisted in the face of reverses and discouragements, that if its pertinency was established, if it fitted well and truly, the courts would follow it inexorably to the limit of its logic. I learned by sad experience that they failed, now and again, to come out where I expected. I thought, however, in my simplicity that they had missed the road or carelessly misread the signposts; the divagations never had the aspect of willful adventures into the land of the unknown. The problem stood before me in a new light when I had to cope with it as judge. I found that the creative element was greater than I had fancied; the forks in the road more frequent; the signposts less complete. "We are not bound to believe," says Pound,[1] "that they [the judges] make legal precepts and set up (58) legal institutions out of whole cloth. Except as an act of Omnipotence, creation does not mean the making of something out of nothing. Creative activity takes materials and gives them form so that they may be put to uses for which the materials unformed are adapted." Some cases, of course, there are where one route and only one is possible. They are the cases where the law is fixed and settled. They make up in bulk what they lack in interest. Other cases present a genuine opportunity for choice—not a choice between two decisions, one of which may be said to be almost certainly right and the other almost certainly wrong, but a choice so nicely balanced that when once it is announced, a new right and a new wrong will emerge in the announcement. I do not mean, of course, that even in those cases, the preference is blind or arbitrary. The balance is swayed, not by gusts of fancy, but by reason. The judge who chooses believes with varying intensity of conviction that he has chosen well and wisely. None the less, even in his mind, there has been a genuine, not (59) merely a nominal alternative. There have been two paths, each open, though leading to different goals. The fork in the road has not been neutralized for the traveler by a barrier across one of the prongs with the label of "no thoroughfare." He must gather his wits, pluck up his courage, go forward one way or the other, and pray that he may be walking, not into ambush, morass, and darkness, but into safety, the open spaces, and the light.

In the opening pages of his book on pragmatism,[2] William James quotes a remark of Chesterton's to the effect that the most important thing about a man is his philosophy. The more I reflect about a judge's work, the more I am impressed with the belief that this, if not true for everyone, is true at least for judges. Of course, it is easy to misunderstand such a statement—to press it too far—and to make it an untruth. Ignorance or indolence may take shelter behind generalities of this kind. Lawyers who are unwilling to study the law as it is, may discover, (60) as they think, that study is unnecessary; sentiment or benevolence or some vague notion of social welfare becomes the only equipment needed. I hardly need to say that this is not my point of view. Nothing can take the place of rigorous and accurate and profound study of the law as already developed by the wisdom of the past. This is the raw material which we are to mould. Without it, no philosophy will amount to much, any more than a theory of aesthetics will help the sculptor who would mould the statue without clay. Nine-tenths, perhaps more, of the cases that come before a court are predetermined—predetermined in the sense that they are predestined—their fate preëstablished by inevitable laws that follow them from birth to death. The range of free activity is relatively small. We may easily seem to exaggerate it through excess of emphasis. None the less, those are the fields where the judicial function gains its largest opportunity and power. Those are the fields, too, where the process is of the largest interest. Given freedom of choice, how shall the (61) choice be guided? Complete freedom—unfettered and undirected—there never is. A thousand limitations—the product some of statute, some of precedent, some of vague tradition or of an immemorial technique,—encompass and hedge us even when we think of ourselves as ranging freely and at large. The inscrutable force of professional opinion presses upon us like the atmosphere, though we are heedless of its weight. Narrow at best is any freedom that is allotted to us. How shall we make the most of it in service to mankind?

A year or so ago, I was rash enough to publish some lectures on "The Nature of the Judicial Process" as I found it working in our law. I attempted then a fourfold division of the forces to be obeyed and the methods to be applied. The division, as I was at pains to point out, involved some overlapping of the lines,[3] but it seemed, for purposes of rough classification, to be helpful (62) and perhaps sufficient. I adhere to it now, in obedience to the law of parsimony of effort, since it is easier to follow the beaten track than it is to clear another. In doing this, I shall be treading in the footsteps of my predecessors, and illustrating the process that I am seeking to describe, since the power of precedent, when analyzed, is the power of the beaten track. Our fourfold division separates the force of logic or analogy, which gives us the method of philosophy, the force of history, which gives us the historical method, or the method of evolution; the force of custom, which yields the method of tradition; and the force of justice, morals and social welfare, the *mores* of the day, with its outlet or expression in the method of sociology. No doubt there is ground for criticism when logic is represented as a method in opposition to the others. In reality, it is a tool that cannot be ignored by any of them.[4] The thing that counts chiefly is the nature of the premises. We may take as our premise some preëstablished concep (63) tion or principle or precedent, and work it up by an effort of pure reason to its ultimate development, the limit of its logic. We may supplement the conception or principle or precedent by reference to extrinsic sources, and apply the tool of our logic to the premise as thus modified or corrected. The difference between the function of logic in the one case and in the other is in reality a difference of emphasis. The tool is treated on the one hand as a sufficient instrument of growth, and on the other as an instrument to coöperate with others. The principle of division is a difference, not of kind, but of degree. With this reservation, the fourfold classification of methods has sufficient correspondence with realities to supply a basis of distinction. The judicial process will not be rationalized until these methods have been valued, their functions apportioned, their results appraised, until a standard has been established whereby choice may be directed between one method and another. We may find the subject to be such that the hope to rationalize it fully, at all events in our day, will have to be dismissed (64) as futile. That is not a reason for refusing to do the best we can.

Now, the analysis of the forces and methods which do in fact govern the decision of the doubtful case is the task of that part of the philosophy of law which deals with development and growth, and the fixing of the standards by which choice should be directed is the task of that part which deals with functions and with ends. In the nature of things, the latter branch of the inquiry is the more delicate and uncertain. No recipe for the mingling of the ingredients has yet been formulated. Perhaps none can be formulated, unless it be as a hint, an illustration, a suggestion. But if we were never to reach the stage of synthesis, the process of analysis would of itself be worth the labor. The mere recognition of the truth that there are more methods to be applied than one, that there is more than one string to harp upon, is in itself a forward step and a long one upon the highway to salvation. We must spread the gospel, writes Professor Powell in a private letter from which I quote (65) with his permission, we must "spread the gospel that there is no gospel that will save us from the pain of choosing at every step."[5] There are times when precedents seem to lead to harsh or bizarre conclusions, at war with social needs. The law assumes the aspect of a scholastic exercise, divorced from the realities of life. In such junctures, judges would do well to keep before them as a living faith that a choice of methods is theirs in the shaping of their judgments. I do not mean to say that any one method has ever been consistently pursued in a whole department of the law to the exclusion of the others. Interaction has been inevitable, even when unconscious. I mean that particular causes have been determined and particular rules established or extended in submission to a technique which was supposed to coerce when it was intended to advise. We have not yet been able to orient ourselves with all our opportunities for experiment in centuries of experience. We do not know (66) where we should face. Judges march at times to pitiless conclusions under the prod of a remorseless logic which is supposed to leave them no alternative. They deplore the sacrificial rite. They perform it, none the less, with averted gaze, convinced as they plunge the knife that they obey the bidding of their office. The victim is offered up to the gods of jurisprudence on the altar of regularity. One who seeks examples may be referred to Dean Pound's illuminating paper on "Mechanical Jurisprudence."[6] I suspect that many of these sacrifices would have been discovered to be needless if a sounder analysis of the growth of law, a deeper and truer comprehension of its methods, had opened the priestly ears to the call of other voices. We should know, if thus informed, that magic words and incantations are as fatal to our science as they are to any other. Methods, when classified and separated, acquire their true bearing and perspective as means to an end, not as ends in themselves. We seek to find peace of mind in the word, the (67) formula, the ritual. The hope is an illusion.[7] We think we shall be satisfied to match the situation to the rule, and, finding correspondence, to declare it without flinching. Hardly is the ink dry upon our formula before the call of an unsuspected equity—the urge of a new group of facts, a new combination of events—bids us blur and blot and qualify and even, it may be, erase. The counterdrive—–the tug of emotion—is too strong to be resisted. What Professor Dewey says of problems of morals[8] is true, not in like degree, but, none the less, in large measure, of the deepest problems of the law; the situations which they present, so far as they are real problems, are almost always unique. There is nothing that can relieve us of "the pain of choosing at every step."

I do not underrate the yearning for mechanical and formal tests. They are possible and use (68) ful in zones upon the legal sphere. The pain of choosing is the pain of marking off such zones from others. It is a pain we must endure, for uniformity of method will carry us upon the rocks. The curse of this fluidity, of an ever shifting approximation, is one that law must bear, or other curses yet more dreadful will be invited in exchange. We can hardly hope to have it otherwise when we see how law develops. There are some thoughts in Keynes's recent book on the logic of probabilities which have their significance in this connection for lawyer and for judge. "In most branches of academic logic," says Keynes, "such as the theory of the syllogism or the geometry of ideal space, all the arguments aim at demonstrative certainty. They claim to be *conclusive.*. But many other arguments are rational and claim some weight without pretending to be certain. In Metaphysics, in Science, and in Conduct, most of the arguments upon which we habitually base our rational beliefs, are admitted to be inconclusive in a greater or less degree. Thus for a philosophical treat (69) ment of these branches of knowledge, the study of probability is required. The course which the history of thought has led Logic to follow has encouraged the view that doubtful arguments are not within its scope. But in the actual exercise of reason we do not wait on certainty, or deem it irrational to depend on a doubtful argument. If logic investigates the general principles of valid thought, the study of arguments, to which it is rational to attach *some* weight, is as much a part of it as the study of those which are demonstrative." [9] This is a distinction to be taken to heart by all of us who have a part in the development of law. We tend sometimes, in determining the growth of a principle or a precedent, to treat it as if it represented the outcome of a quest for certainty. That is to mistake its origin. Only in the rarest instances, if ever, was certainty either possible or expected. The principle or the precedent was the outcome of a quest for probabilities. Principles and precedents, (70) thus generated, carry throughout their lives the birthmarks of their origin. They are in truth provisional hypotheses, born in doubt and travail, expressing the adjustment which commended itself at the moment between competing possibilities.[10] We need not wonder that there is disappointment, ending in rebellion, when the effort is made to deduce the absolute and eternal from premises which in their origin were relative and transitory. The more we study law in its making, at least in its present stages of development, the more we gain the sense of a gradual striving toward an end, shaped by a logic which, eschewing the quest for certainty, must be satisfied if its conclusions are rooted in the probable.[11]

(71) I have spoken of generalities. Let me point my meaning by example. My search is for a case where there was an opportunity for diverse methods, and where the choice controlled the outcome. Perhaps as good a one as any is the decision of the Court of Appeals of New York in Ives v. The South Buffalo Railway Co.[12] That is the case, you will remember, where the Workmen's Compensation Act of 1910 was adjudged unconstitutional. The act required an employer to contribute to an insurance fund for the benefit of employees injured in the course of their employment. Property was held to have been taken without due process when a contribution was thus levied regardless of the employer's fault. Now, here was a case where a choice of methods was possible. It is quite aside (72) from my purpose to inquire whether the choice as made was right. The decision has been superseded by amendment of the constitution so far as it involves a problem in the constitutional law of the state.[13] It has been rejected by the Supreme Court of the United States in so far as it involves a problem in the constitutional law of the nation.[14] What interests me at the moment is that a problem in the choice of methods lay back of the problem of law, and determined its solution. On the one hand, the right of property, as it was known to the fathers of the republic, was posited as permanent and absolute. Impairment was not to be suffered except within narraw limits of history and precedent. No experiment was to be made along new lines of social betterment. The image was a perfect sphere. The least dent or abrasion was a subtraction from its essence. Given such premises, the conclusion is inevitable. The statute becomes an illegitimate assault upon rights (73) assured to the individual against the encroachments of society. The method of logic or philoso-

phy is at work in all its plenitude. The opposing view, if it is to be accepted, must be reached through other avenues of approach. The right which the assailants of the statute posit as absolute or permanent is conceived of by the supporters of the statute as conditioned by varying circumstances of time and space and environment and degree. The limitations appropriate to one stage of development may be inadequate for another. Not logic alone, but logic supplemented by the social sciences becomes the instrument of advance. We may frame our conclusions for convenience as universal propositions. We are to remember that in truth they are working hypotheses.[15] The catalogue of causes will be incomplete if the material and the formal and the efficient are enumerated to the exclusion of the final. The truth is not always to be reached by looking back to the beginning and (74) deducing from the source. The end may be frustrated unless we look forward to the goal.

The same divergent strains, the same opposition in the selected method, will be found in other cases which have become landmarks of the law. To go back but a few years or months, we may trace it in such decisions as the rent cases,[16] the case of the Arizona statute limiting the remedy of injunction in controversies between capital and labor,[17] and the minimum wage case.[18] One group erects within the mind a norm or standard of reasonable or traditional immunity, and from that deduces a conclusion as to the minimum acceptable in a given situation. The other group seeks the standard, not so much within, as without, and "among the important facts deserving consideration" includes "the prevailing public opinion concerning the evils and the remedy." [19] Of course, in the end, the differ (75) ence is a difference of degree. No absolutist is so intransigent as to assert that there can be literal adherence to a standard of equality or liberty. Some compromise is inevitable between liberty and license, between uniformity and diversity. The necessity for exceptions being conceded, the important thing is to determine the principle that shall govern their allowance. Shall we look for it within ourselves, in some mental pattern of an ideal community? Shall we look for it in the past, admitting no encroachment not sanctified by time? Or shall we look for it in the needs of the present, in "the exigencies of social life?" [20] Shall our standard be a metaphysical conception, or an historic datum, or a living need? As you give one answer or the other, you will reach different results. The trouble often arises from assuming that one method is supreme, from assuming that the truth or apparent truth yielded to us by one of them is to be accepted (76) without checking it and testing it by the truth yielded by the others. We are not to bow down before our metaphysical conception or our historic datum, and shut our eyes to living needs, and yet we are not to find a living need in every gust of fancy that would blow to earth the patterns of history and reason.[21]

My illustrations have been taken from the field of public law, but the field of private law also will yield one crop or another with the method which the husbandman applies. What are the rights of a stranger to a contract? Shall the development of the subject be guided by the image of the perfect sphere? Shall indentation or protuberance, no matter how convenient, be forbidden as deformities? Cling- to the conception of a contractual tie, shall we say that the parties linked together by the tie, and no one else, shall have a remedy in the courts when the tie has wrongfully been severed? The English courts have been faithful to the preëstab (77) lished conception, and have permitted no conclusion at war with logical deduction. At all events, the deviations, if any, have been few and doubtful. We in the United States have been readier to subordinate logic to utility, so that the remedies of third parties, beneficiaries of a contract, at first grudgingly allowed, are now multiplying and expanding.[22] The development is merely a phase of the assault, now extending along the entire line, upon the ancient citadel of privity. In New York, there is a remedy in tort, regardless of privity, against the negligent manufacturer, where the subject of the manufacture is likely to be dangerous to life.[23] The things classified as dangerous have been steadily extended with a corresponding extension of the application of the remedy. They began with Thomas v. Winchester [24] and the sale of poisons. They have been widened till they include a scaffold [25] or an automobile [26] or even pies and cakes (78) when nails and other foreign substances have supplied ingredients not mentioned in the recipes of cook books. From the field of torts, exceptions have spread to other fields on the borderland between tort and contract. Lack of privity will not defeat a right of action against a public weigher who certifies a weight at the order of one with the intent that the certificate shall guide the conduct of another.[27] Even in the United States, however, the current is not uniform. Recent decisions in Massachusetts have enforced the requirement of privity where a manufacturer has been sued by the victim of his negligence.[28] Logic and utility still struggle for the mastery.

In this analysis of the principles that shape the genesis and growth of law, I have striven to warn against the notion that any one of them is sovereign, that any one is invariably to be preferred over the others, that logic must always yield to history, or history to custom, or all to justice or utility as constituents of the social (79) welfare. Even if it be true that social welfare is the final test, "certainty and order are themselves constituents of the welfare which it is our business to discover." [29] My effort till now has been to analyze rather than to choose, to show that varying methods lead to varying results, not to fix the criteria by which preference is to be governed. The principles that are to determine choice must be formulated by that branch of the philosophy of law which is concerned with ends and functions. We have (let us assume) a group of precedents before us covering fields more or less analogous to the field of the problem to be solved. Sometimes the analogies are competitive. Shall we adopt this one or that? Shall we press forward on one line or on another? If logic is to be our guide, shall it be the logic of one analogy, the deduction from one principle, or the logic and the deduction that have their origin in others? You must not think of the choice as solely between logic and history, or logic and custom, or logic and justice. Often (80) the strife will be one of civil war between the logics, the analogies, themselves, with social utility stepping in as the arbiter between them. A choice must be made. In order that it may be made intelligently, two things must be known. Given a problem whether the directive force of a principle or a rule or a precedent is to be exerted along this path or along that, we must know how the principle or the rule or the precedent is functioning, and what is the end which ought to be attained. The two inquiries coalesce. Let me speak first of ends or aims, reserving till later what I may say of function, in so far as the two inquiries are distinct.

REFERENCES

1. *Interpretations of Legal History,* p. 127.
2. James, *Pragmatism,* pp. 1, 2.
3. *Nature of the Judicial Process,* p. 51; *cf.* Professor Cohen's Introduction, pp. 29, 30; Tourtoulon's *Philosophy in the Development of Law,* vol. XIII, Modern Legal Philosophy Series.
4. Cohen, *supra.*
5. *Cf.* Dewey, *Human Nature and Conduct,* pp. 239, 241.
6. 8 *Col. L. R.* 603.
7. Holmes, "The Path of the Law," *Collected Papers,* pp. 167, 180; Pound, *Criminal Justice in Cleveland,* p. 562.
8. *Reconstruction in Philosophy; Human Nature and Conduct.*
9. J. M. Keynes, *A Treatise on Probability,* p. 3. *Cf.* Charles S. Pierce, *Chance, Love and Logic,* p. 64.
10. *Cf.* Holmes, vol. I, *Continental Legal History Series,* p. 46.
11. I have been interested to find that Tourtoulon in his work on *Philosophy in the Development of Law* (recently translated in the Modern Legal Philosophy Series) has seen these variable and tentative forces working throughout history. "The philosophy of chance," he says (p. 634, vol. XIII, Modern Legal Philosophy Series), "seems to me the most natural conclusion of a philosophy of legal history. It substitutes the search for probability for the search for certainty. It shows the complexity of causes where others wish to see only a deceptive simplicity. It permits man to utilize so far as possible, his own ignorance. It inspires a salutary scepticism, not that of negation, but that of prudence; the kindly, scrupulous and searching scepticism which might well be the best instrument of progress for humanity."
12. 201 N. Y. 271.
13. Southern Pacific Ry. Co. v. Jensen, 215 N. Y. 514.
14. N. Y. C. R. R. Co. v. White, 243 U. S. 188.
15. *Cf.* Dewey, *Human Nature and Conduct* "The Nature of Principles," p. 239.
16. Block v. Hirsch, 256 U. S. 135; Marcus Brown Holding Co. v. Feldman, 256 U. S. 170.
17. Truax v. Corrigan, 257 U. S. 312.
18. Adkins v. The Children's Hospital of the District of Columbia, 261 U. S. 525.
19. Brandeis, J., in Truax v. Corrigan, *supra.*
20. Vander-Eycken, *Méthode Positive de l'interprétation juridique,* p. 401; see my *Nature of the Judicial Process,* p. 122; Pound, 44 *Reports Am. Bar Assn.* for 1919, p. 457.
21. *Cf.* Meyer v. Nebraska, 262 U. S. 390; Bartels v. Iowa, 262 U. S. 404.
22. *Nature of the Judicial Process,* p. 99.
23. MacPherson v. Buick Mfg. Co., 217 N. Y. 382.
24. 6 N. Y. 397.
25. Devlin v. Smith, 89 N. Y. 470.
26. MacPherson v. Buick Mfg. Co., *supra.*
27. Glanzer v. Shepard, 233 N. Y. 236.
28. Pitman v. Lynn Gas & Electric Co. 235 Mass. 322.
29. See my *Nature of the Judicial Process,* p. 67.

(81)

— IV —

The Function and the Ends of Law.

"MAKING or finding law, call it what you will, presupposes," says Pound,[1] "a mental picture of what one is doing, and of why he is doing it." If conflicting methods are applicable, our understanding of the significance of the process will regulate the preference. To state the ends of law would be the subject matter of a treatise. I shall not attempt to crowd the treatment within the limits of a lecture. Lack of time is a sufficient excuse, though I shall be prepared to plead others, if others were required. My present purpose will be attained if I arouse in you a sense of the bond between law and its philosophy. In the analysis of ends, the most fruitful generalizations yet reached, at least in Anglo-American law, are those of Roscoe Pound. Certain branches of the law call in conspicuous (82) measures for certainty and order, for an administration of justice that is strict and in a sense mechanical. He places here inheritance and succession, definition of interests in property and the conveyance thereof, matters of commercial law, and the creation incidents and transfers of obligations.[2] If he were to apportion methods in accordance with the scheme of division which I have followed, he would say that the methods applicable here are those of logic, history, and custom. Other branches of the law are better served where flexible standards, capable of being individualized to meet the needs of varying conditions, supersede the rigid rule with its mechanical application. He places here the law of torts, of public utilities, of fiduciary relations, and generally those branches that deal immediately with conduct.[3] If he were to apportion methods in accordance with my division, he would give precedence in this sphere to the method of sociology. A recent paper by Professor Sunderland (83) of the University of Michigan develops with much suggestive power the distinction between substantive law and the law of procedure in respect of their several claims to flexibility and to certainty.[4] No doubt, there is a borderland, a penumbra, where methods blend into one another without perceptible division. The apportionment of the relative value of certainty on the one side and justice on the other, of adherence to logic and advancement of utility, involves an appraisement of the social interest which each is capable of promoting. That is a calculus which has not yet been definitely made by any master of juristic theory.[5] Fruitful and penetrating suggestions have been contributed by Pound,[6] (84) but they do not profess to be more than provisional and tentative. Sociological jurisprudence, in the words of Dean Stone, has yet to develop the formulas and principles "which can be taught and expounded so as to make it a methodological guide either to the student of law or to the judge." [7] Its value at present is largely negative.[8] "It warns the judge and the student of law that logic and history cannot and ought not to have full sway when the dynamic judgment is to be rendered. It points out that in the choice of the particular device determining the result—social utility—the *mores* of the time, objectively determined, may properly turn the scale in favor of one against the other." [9] If classification were ever to become complete for any time and place, there is little chance that it would be final. The good of one generation is not always the good of its successor. For the lawyer as for the moralist, (85) the generalizations that result from the study of social phenomena are "not fixed rules for deciding doubtful cases, but instrumentalities for their investigation, methods by which the value of past experience is rendered available for present scrutiny of new perplexities." [10] Sociology would petrify with a rigidity more fatal than that of logic, or rather, perhaps, with a logic of its own, if its hypotheses were treated as finalities. "The problem," in the words of Dewey, "is one of continuous, vital readaptation." [11]

In the present state of our knowledge, the estimate of the comparative value of one social interest and another, when they come, two or more of them, into collision, will be shaped for the judge, as it is for the legislator, in accordance with an act of judgment in which many elements coöperate. It will be shaped by his experience of life; his understanding of the prevailing canons of justice and morality; his study of the social (86) sciences; at times, in the end, by his intuitions, his guesses, even his ignorance or prejudice. The web is tangled and obscure, shot through with a multitude of shades and colors, the skeins irregular and broken. Many hues that seem to be simple, are found, when analyzed, to be a complex and uncertain blend. Justice itself, which we are wont to appeal to as a test as well as an ideal, may mean different things to different minds and at different times. Attempts to objectify its standards, or even to describe them, have never wholly succeeded.[12] Aristotle distinguishes between corrective justice (διορθωτικόν), distributive justice (διανεμητικόν), and general justice (τὸ καθόλον δίκαιον).[13] Such a classification does (87) not carry us far. What we are seeking is not merely the justice that one receives when his rights and duties are determined by the law as it is; what we are seeking is the justice to which law in its making should conform. Justice in this sense is a concept by far more subtle and indefinite than any that is yielded by mere obedience to a rule. It remains to some extent, when all is said and done, the synonym of an aspiration, a mood of exaltation, a yearning for what is fine or high. "Justice," says Stammler in a recent paper,[14] "is the directing of a particular legal volition according to the conception of a pure community." Perhaps we shall even find at times that when talking about justice, the quality we have in mind is charity, and this though the one quality is often contrasted with the other.[15] The ingredient which sours if left alone, is preserved by an infusion, sweetening the product without changing its identity. You may give what re (88) cipes you will. A trained sense of taste approving or rejecting, will pass judgment on the whole.

The precept that emerges from this flux seems barren enough indeed, till the transfiguring process of creation has proved it to be fertile. "You shall not for some slight profit of convenience or utility depart from standards set by history or logic; the loss will be greater than the gain. You shall not drag in the dust the standards set by equity and justice to win some slight conformity to symmetry and order; the gain will be unequal to the loss." This and little more will be found inscribed upon the tables. We shall learn, none the less, that the commandment, jejune and vague upon its face, has unsuspected implications, hidden and unknown energies, that are revealed to the devout, to those who seek in very truth and with all their might to follow and obey. Between these poles there is room for an infinitude of nice adjustments, all swayed in some degree by the attraction of the force that radiates from either end. As new problems arise, (89) equity and justice will direct the mind to solutions which will be found, when they are scrutinized, to be consistent with symmetry and order, or even to be the starting points of a symmetry and order theretofore unknown. Logic and history, the countless analogies suggested by the recorded wisdom of the past, will in turn inspire new expedients for the attainment of equity and justice. We find a kindred phenomenon in literature, alike in poetry and in prose. The search is for the just word, the happy phrase, that will give expression to the thought, but somehow the thought itself is transfigured by the phrase when found. There is emancipation in our very bonds. The restraints of rhyme or metre, the exigencies of period or balance, liberate at times the thought which they confine, and in imprisoning release.

The truth, of course, is that in the development of law, as in other fields of thought, we can never rid ourselves of our dependence upon intuitions or flashes of insight transcending and transforming the contributions of mere experi-(90) ence. "The great historians," says Windelband,[16] "had no need to wait for the experiments and research of our psychophysicists. The psychology they used was that of daily life. It was the knowledge of men, the experience of life, of the common man, coupled with the insight of the genius and the poet. No one has ever yet succeeded in making a science of this psychology of intuitive understanding." What is here said of the historian is true also of the lawyer. A perception, more or less dim, of this truth underlies the remark of Graham Wallas,[17] that in some of the judges of our highest court there should be a touch of the qualities which make the poet. The scrutiny and dissection of social facts may supply us with the data upon which the creative spirit broods, but in the process of creation something is given out in excess of what is taken in. Gény, in his *Science and Technique of Law,* reminds us how this notion of the development of law fits into the general scheme of recent philosophical thought, and in particular with the (91) philosophy of Bergson and Bergson's school. "It is necessary, they tell us, to complete and correct the rigidity of the intellect by the suppleness of instinct, in a way to auscultate the mystery of the universe by means of a sort of intellectual sympathy." [18] "The new philosophy preaches under the name of 'intuition' a mode of knowledge more subtle than pure intellect, a mode of knowledge which instals itself in the very heart of reality," and penetrates, not from without, but from within.[19] We do not need to become the disciples of any theory of epistemology, Bergson's or any other, to perceive the force of the analogy between the creative process here described, and the process at work in the development of law. The mechanism displays the same diversity of form and parts and combinations.[20] Analysis alternates with synthesis; deduction with induction; reasoning with intuition. (92) The whole in Gény's words [21] is "a procedure extremely complex, and full of delicate nuances, all penetrated with casuistry and dialectics, a constant mixture of analysis and synthesis, in which the *a posteriori* processes which furnish adequate solutions presuppose directions *a priori*, proposed by reason and by will." The handling of examples, of concrete instances, will develop the skill proper to the art. Repetition of the precept without more will yield at best a bungling workman. "The artistic activity exhibits a mutual play of conscious and unconscious processes which can never be rationally explained. . . . The creation is accompanied by conscious criticism, but the positive element of achievement is not a matter of cunning and calculation; it comes as a fortunate chance from the unconscious depths of life." [22] So Pound: [23] "The in (93) stinct of the experienced workman operates with assurance. Innumerable details and minute discriminations have entered into it, and it has been gained by long experience which has made the proper inclusions and exclusions by trial and error until the effective line of action has become a habit." And again: [24] "It is an everyday experience of those who study judicial decisions that the results are usually sound, whether the reasoning from which the results purport to flow is sound or not. The trained intuition of the judge continually leads him to right results for which he is puzzled to give unimpeachable legal reasons." This does not mean in law, any more than in art generally, that the precept is to be condemned as useless. The key that methodology gives us will not release and expose the mystery by the mere turning of the hand. It is perhaps not so much a key as a clew, a something to be worked up and developed by ourselves if we would extract the essence of its virtue.

The analysis of social interests and their rela (94) tive importance is one of the clews, then, that the lawyer and the judge must utilize in the solution of their problems. The study has developed a science of its own. We may not clarify a subject when we give it a special name, but perhaps, in the eyes of some, we give it added dignity, if the name selected is a hard one. A terminology, recondite enough to satisfy these conditions, has grown up in the field which is the subject of our survey. Philosophers have given the name of axiology, or the science of values, to the study that busies itself with the estimate of comparative values in ethical, social, or aesthetic problems.[25] The conclusions of this science must, from time to time, be appropriated by the judge, yet they must be appropriated subject to restrictions which limit his freedom to accept or to reject. When the legislature has spoken, and declared one interest superior to another, the judge must subordinate his personal or subjective estimate of value to the estimate thus declared. He may not nullify or pervert a (95) statute because convinced that an erroneous axiology is reflected in its terms. Even when the legislature has not spoken, he is to regulate his estimate of values by objective rather than subjective standards, by the thought and will of the community rather than by his own idiosyncrasies of conduct and belief.[26] Often the two standards will be identical. At all events, if the communal thought or will is different, there will be neither statute nor custom nor other external token to declare or define the difference. The judge will then have no standard of value available except his own. In such circumstances, the objective will for him be merged in the subjective; the axiology that is to guide him will be his own and not another's.

We need have no fear in thus subordinating the individual to the community that great minds and great souls will be without an opportunity to reveal themselves. The search, indeed, is for something external, a norm which finds (96) expression in custom or convictions, but, in the very act of declaring what is found, there springs into being a new norm, a new standard, to which custom and convictions tend thereafter to conform. Who can doubt that courts of equity in enforcing the great principle that a trustee shall not profit by his trust nor even place himself in a position where his private interest may collide with his fiduciary duty, have raised the level of business honor, and kept awake a conscience that might otherwise have slumbered? Penetrating thoughts on this subject have been contributed by Duguit. The judge is to scrutinize the aggregate of social facts of which "the juridical norm" is to be regarded as a product. Chief among these are "the positive laws, the usages actually obeyed, the economic needs, the aspirations toward the realization of the just." [27] But the scrutiny, though an essential part of his function, is not the whole.[28] The judge interprets the (97) social conscience, and gives effect to it in law, but in so doing he helps to form and modify the conscience he interprets. Discovery and creation react upon each other.

I have been trying to give some notion of the kind of problems that must be met by a philosophy concerning itself with the final causes of the law. I have done this merely as a preface, though the preface has been a long one. What I have wished to lead up to is the bearing of such a philosophy upon the problems that must be met in practice by the lawyer or the judge. In emphasizing the importance of its aid, I have not meant, of course, to convey the suggestion that, left alone, it is all-sufficient. Resort to a philosophy of law in the development of rules and principles presupposes knowledge of the principles and rules which it is our business to develop. Here, as so often, the right word is said by Holmes. "When a man," says Holmes, "has a working knowledge of his business, he can spend his leisure better than in reading all the reported cases he has time for. They are apt to (98) be only the small change of legal thought." [29] Many things must be learned as facts in law as in other sciences. They are the coin which we must have in our pocket if we are to pay our way with legal tender. Until we are provided with a plentiful supply of it, we shall do better to stay at home, and not go forth upon our journey. I assume, then, what Holmes calls a working knowledge of the business. We must talk as one lawyer to another, or we shall be talking at cross-purposes. When this common ground is gained, we shall not go very far before beginning to philosophize.

Let me assume a case where authority is silent. You, gentlemen, or as many of you as may be lucky enough to receive a retainer, are the lawyers. I am the distracted judge. You have ransacked the digests, the cyclopaedias, the treatises, the law reviews. The decision on all fours which counsel love to produce with a latent note of triumph, cowing with authority the sceptic (99) on the bench, this buried treasure of the law books, refuses to come forth. The vigils and the quest yield at most a few remote analogies, which can be turned as easily to the service of one side as to the service of the other. What are you going to do to persuade? What am I going to do to decide? Perhaps we shall, neither of us, be fully conscious of the implications of the process. Much that goes on in the mind is subconscious or nearly so. But if, when the task is finished, we ask ourselves what we have done, we shall find, if we are frank in the answer, that with such equipment as we have, we have been playing the philosopher.

We had in my court a year or more ago a case that points my meaning.[30] A boy was bathing in a river. He climbed upon a springboard which projected from a bank. As he stood there, at the end of the board, poised for his dive into the stream, electric wires fell upon him, and swept him to his death below. In the suit for damages that followed, competitive analogies were in (100) voked by counsel for the administratrix and counsel for the railroad company, the owner of the upland. The administratrix found the analogy that suited her in the position of travelers on a highway. The boy was a bather in navigable waters; his rights were not lessened because his feet were on the board. The owner found the analogy to its liking in the position of a trespasser on land. The springboard, though it projected into the water, was, none the less, a fixture, and as a fixture it was constructively a part of the land to which it was annexed. The boy was thus a trespasser upon land in private ownership; the only duty of the owner was to refrain from wanton and malicious injury; if these elements were lacking, the death must go without requital. Now, the truth is that, as a mere bit of dialectics, these analogies would bring a judge to an impasse. No process of merely logical deduction could determine the choice between them. Neither analogy is precise, though each is apposite. There had arisen a new situation which could not force itself without (101) mutilation into any of the existing moulds. When we find a situation of this kind, the choice that will approve itself to this judge or to that, will be determined largely by his conception of the end of the law, the function of legal liability; and this question of ends and functions is a question of philosophy.

In the case that I have instanced, a majority of the court believed that liability should be adjudged. The deductions that might have been made from preëstablished definitions were subordinated and adapted to the fundamental principles that determine, or ought to determine, liability for conduct in a system of law wherein liability is adjusted to the ends which law should serve.[31] Hynes v. The New York Central Rail Road Co. was decided in May, 1921. Dean Pound's *Introduction to the Philosophy of Law* had not yet been published. It appeared in 1922. In these lectures, he advances a theory of liability which it may be interesting to compare with (102) the theory of liability reflected in our decision. "The law," he says,[32] "enforces the reasonable expectations arising out of conduct, relations and situations." I shall leave it to others to say whether the cause of the boy diving from the springboard would be helped or hindered by resort to such a test. This much I cannot doubt. *Some* theory of liability, some philosophy of the end to be served by tightening or enlarging the circle of rights and remedies, is at the root of any decision in novel situations when analogies are equivocal and precedents are silent. As it stands today, the judge is often left to improvise such a theory, such a philosophy, when confronted overnight by the exigencies of the case before him. Often he fumbles about, feeling in a vague way that some such problem is involved, but missing the universal element which would have quickened his decision with the inspiration of a principle. If he lacks an adequate philosophy, he either goes astray altogether, or at best does not rise above the empiricism that pro (103) nounces judgment upon particulars. We must learn that all methods are to be viewed not as idols but as tools. We must test one of them by the others, supplementing and reënforcing where there is weakness, so that what is strong and best in each will be at our service in the hour of need. Thus viewing them we shall often find that they are not antagonists but allies.

The truth, indeed, is that many a worker in the law who flies the flag of one school is giving aid and comfort unwittingly to another, and should be flying its flag instead. The historical school of jurisprudence is often contrasted with the sociological school, and there are important elements of difference between them, yet many who profess to use the historical method in the adjudication of a cause are in truth less loyal to the significance of the historical school than those who profess the method of sociology, and look more freely to the prevailing standards of welfare and utility. In the view of the historical school, "it it not the law-giver that makes the law; the folk-spirit does it. The law-giver has (104) only to write down what the spirit of the people dictates. To this end it is necessary that he be adequately instructed by systematic studies as to the true meaning of the folk-spirit." [33] "Law is *not a product of human will,* but is *a common conviction.*" [34] In all likelihood the historical school has exaggerated the unconscious, the unvolitional, element in the development of law. If, however, its assumptions be accepted, they exact, not blind reproduction of the past, but searching scrutiny of the present, for law, by the very terms of the hypothesis, is the expression of the convictions of the present, not the convictions of the past. Where then shall we look for the revelations of the folk-spirit if not in the prevailing standards of utility and welfare? We take a false and one-sided view of history when we ignore its dynamic aspects. The year books can teach us how a principle or a rule had its (105) beginnings. They cannot teach us that what was the beginning shall also be the end.

I find again in a recent judgment of my own court the case that points my meaning. We held a little while ago in Oppenheim v. Kridel, 236 N. Y. 156, that a woman, as well as a man, may maintain an action for criminal conversation. The court of intermediate appeal had ruled that the action would not lie. To make out the woman's disability, precedents were cited from the time of Lord Coke. Stress was laid upon pronouncements in those days that a man had a property right in the body of his wife. A wife, it was said, had none in the body of her husband. Stress was laid also upon rulings made in days when the wife was unable, unless the husband joined with her as plaintiff, to sue for any wrong. We did not ignore these precedents, but we held them inconclusive. Social, political, and legal reforms had changed the relations between the sexes, and put woman and man upon a plane of equality. Decisions founded upon the assumption of a bygone inequality were unrelated to (106) present-day realities, and ought not to be permitted to prescribe a rule of life.[35] The historical method was the organon of judgment in each court, but its application led in each to opposite results. One court, in its interpretation of legal history, was satisfied to treat as finalities the precedents of ancient year books. The other found a stream of thought, a tendency, a movement forward to a goal. Which, then, is the truer use of the historical method? Which exhibits the saner and the sounder loyalty? Shall the significance of events be determined by transporting them to our own time and viewing them as if they were the product of our own day and thought, or by viewing them as of the time of their occurrence, the product of their era, the expression of its beliefs and habits?

We need a selective process if history is to be read as history, and not merely as a barren chronicle. The several methods of approach, rightly understood and applied, correct and prove each other. An appeal to origins will be (107) futile, their significance perverted, unless tested and illumined by an appeal to ends. We must learn to handle our tools, to use our methods and our processes, not singly, but together. They are instruments of advance to be employed in combination. The failure to combine them, the use of this method or that as if one were exclusive of the other, has been the parent of many wrongs. Only precariously and doubtfully shall we arrive at the needed combination without the understanding that comes of accurate analysis—the analysis that is the essential preliminary to any sound and truthful synthesis. "Much will be gained," says Dean Pound,[36] "when courts have perceived what it is that they are doing, and are thus enabled to address themselves consciously to doing it the best that they may." This much, if no more, the study of the philosophy of law will teach us. It will teach the great commandment, "Thou shalt not make unto thyself any graven image—of maxims or formulas (108) to wit."[37] At times, indeed, we shall seem to have learned nothing, and shall wonder whether there was profit in the labor and the sacrifice. We shall say to ourselves that it is vain to seek a sovereign talisman; that the treasure box does not spring open at the magic of a whispered word; that there is no one method of judging, supreme over its competitors, but only a choice of methods changing with the changing problem; and that the choice and the attendant travail, far from being transitory phases of the process, are its inseparable conditions, the primal curse which it must suffer. But this, after all, will itself be a philosophy, and one that, taken to heart, may save us many blunders.

REFERENCES

1. *Introduction to Philosophy,* p. 59.
2. *Introduction to Philosophy of Law,* p. 139; *cf.* Stammler, 21 *Mich. L. R.* 873.
3. Pp. 138, 140.
4. 5 *Am. Law School Rev.,* p. 73, Mar., 1923; 29 *W. Va. Law Quart.* 77.
5. Albertsworth, "Program of Sociological Jurisprudence," VIII *Am. Bar Assn. Jour.* 393, 396; *cf.* Bentham, *Principles of Morals and Legislation;* Windelband, *Introduction to Philosophy,* 227, 229; Vander-Eycken, *Méthode positive de l'interprétation juridique;* Tourtoulon, *Philosophy in the Development of Law,* XIII Modern Legal Philosophical Series, pp. 479, 486.
6. Pound, "A Study of Social Interests," vol. XV, *Papers and Proceedings of American Sociological Society,* May 1921.
7. 22 *Col. L. R.* 382, 384.
8. Albertsworth, *supra.*
9. Stone, *supra,* also 23 *Col. L. R.* 328; *cf.* Lepaulle, "The Function of Comparative Law," 35 *Harv. L. R.* 838.
10. Dewey, *Human Nature and Conduct,* pp. 240, 241.
11. Dewey, *op. cit.,* p. 240.
12. Gény, *Science et Technique en droit privé positif,* vol. I, pp. 49, 50; vol. II, p. 389, § 171; Gény, *Méthode l'interprétation,* etc., vol. II, pp. 107–110; Vinogradoff, *Historical Jurisprudence,* vol. II, p. 45; Duguit, *Traité de droit constitutionnel,* vol. I, pp. 49–53; H. Spencer, Justice, *The Principles of Ethics,* vol. II, § 272, p. 45; Tourtoulon, *Philosophy in the Development of Law,* vol. XIII, Modern Legal Philosophical Series, pp. 266, 479, 492; also p. 36 of Professor Cohen's Introduction; Pollock, *First Book of Jurisprudence,* p. 30.
13. Vinogradoff, *Historical Jurisprudence,* vol. II, pp. 45–57.
14. 21 *Mich. L. R.* 889.
15. Tourtoulon, *supra;* Professor Cohen's Introduction, pp. 36, 39.
16. *Introduction to Philosophy,* pp. 206, 207.
17. Wallas, *Our Social Heritage,* p. 194.
18. Gény, *Science et Technique en droit privé positif,* vol. I, p. 80, § 26.
19. Gény, *supra; cf.* Pound, "The Theory of Judicial Decision," 36 *Harv. L. R.* 951.
20. We have that interaction between impulses and habits which Professor Dewey has recently described in his book on *Human Nature and Conduct.*
21. *Ibid.,* vol. I, p. 211, § 67.
22. Windelband, *op. cit.,* pp. 321, 322. "Si la connaissance du droit est une science, il est permis d'affirmer sans présomption que la manière de l'appliquer constitue véritablement un art" (Ransson, *"Essai sur l'art de juger,"* p. 21).
23. "The Theory of Judicial Decision," 36 *Harv. L. R.* 952.
24. Pp. 9, 51.
25. Windelband, *op. cit.,* pp. 209, 217.
26. *Cf.* H. Krabbe, *The Modern Idea of the State,* pp. 99, 100.

27. Duguit, *Traité de droit constitutionnel*, vol. I, pp. 79, 83.

28. Pp. 80, 83.

29. *Introduction to a General Survey of Continental Legal History*, vol. I, Continental Legal History Series, p. xlvi.

30. Hynes v. N. Y. Central R. R. Co., 231 N. Y. 229.

31. *Cf.* F. H. Bohlen, "Mixed Questions of Law a Fact," 72 *Univ. of Penn. L. R.*, pp. 111, 120.

32. P. 189.

33. Stammler, "Fundamental Tendencies in Modern Jurisprudence," 21 *Mich. L. R.* 647.

34. *Ibid.*, p. 650; *cf.* Duguit, *Traité de droit constitutionnel*, vol. I, pp. 56, 72.

35. *Cf.* R. v. Jackson, 1891, 1 Q.B. 671.

36. 36 *Harv. L. R.* 959.

37. Sir Frederick Pollock, 39 *Law Quarterly Review* 169.

(109)

— V —

Functions and Ends (Continued). Conclusion.

I HAVE shown juristic methods sorted and handled by their users in adaptation to the ends which each is capable of serving. The examples I have given may seem to stress the worth of change, the virtue of flexibility, as contrasted with the worth of certainty. To keep the balance true, let me put before you other cases where certainty was founded to be the larger good when mobility was weighed against it. A manufacturer of paper made a contract with the publisher of a newspaper to furnish paper in monthly installments of stated quantities for a stated term of years. During the first three months of the term, the price was fixed in advance. During the residue, it was to be such a price, continuing for such a time, as buyer and seller might agree, (110) subject, however, to the proviso that the price to be named for this undesignated period should not be more than that then charged to large consumers by another manufacturer. When the initial period expired, the buyer demanded monthly deliveries at the price established as the maximum. The seller, refusing to comply with the demand, took the ground that the contract was abortive for the reason that there had been no agreement upon the time during which this price was to continue. The Court of Appeals of New York upheld this position, and ruled that the seller's right was unaffected by his motive.[1] Here was a case where advantage had been taken of the strict letter of a contract to avoid an onerous engagement. Not inconceivably a sensitive conscience would have rejected such an outlet of escape. We thought this immaterial. The court subordinated the equity of a particular situation (111) to the overmastering need of certainty in the transactions of commercial life. The end to be attained in the development of the law of contract is the supremacy, not of some hypothetical, imaginary will, apart from external manifestations, but of will outwardly revealed in the spoken or the written word. The loss to business would in the long run be greater than the gain if judges were clothed with power to revise as well as to interpret. Perhaps, with a higher conception of business and its needs,[2] the time will come when even revision will be permitted if it is revision in consonance with established standards of fair dealing, but the time is not yet. In this department of activity, the current axiology still places stability and certainty in the forefront of the virtues. "The field is one where the law should hold fast to fundamental conceptions of contract and of duty, and follow them with loyalty to logical conclusions."[3] One could cite other instances without number.[4]

(112) I have spoken thus far of ends. I must give a word to functions. To some extent, the two subjects are coterminous. Our philosophy will tell us the proper function of law in telling us the ends that law should endeavor to attain; but closely related to such a study is the inquiry whether law, as it has developed in this subject or in that, does in truth fulfill its function—is functioning well or ill. The latter inquiry is perhaps a branch of social science, calling for a survey of social facts, rather than a branch of philosophy itself, yet the two subjects converge, and one will seldom be fruitful unless supplemented by the other. "Consequences cannot alter statutes, but may help to fix their meaning."[5] We test the rule by its results.

The point of view seems obvious, yet it wins its way slowly, and with hesitant avowal.[6] A difference has been noted between the attitude of mind of the scientist who studies a problem of (113) the social life of man, and the attitude of mind of scientists in other fields. James Harvey Robinson has a telling passage on the subject in his recent book on *The Mind in the Making* (p. 11). The scientist in other fields asks himself dispassionately, how does the precept work? If he finds that it works ill, he casts it aside as error. The student of society has been disposed to take institutions as he finds them, and, indeed, if he studies them as a judge, he will learn that to a large extent he cannot take them otherwise. Only at long intervals have judges asked themselves the question, How does the precept work? Is it a sensible rule for the governance of mankind? They have not asked the question, for they have looked upon the answer as more or less irrelevant. They have generally been content with the inquiry, Is it a rule that exists? What are its logical presuppositions or its logical developments?

The method of sociology, in stressing ends and functions, involves with growing frequency the approach from other angles. The judge in the (114) effort to decide, the lawyer in the effort to persuade, is driven, as he adopts this method, to test a rule by its results. Of course, there are times, now as in the past, when the inquiry must stop with the answer to the question, Is it a rule that exists? Function becomes important in those cases chiefly where the problem is one of direction or extension. In such circumstances, the choice of a path is blind and unintelligent without a survey of the route which has been traveled and of the place to which the route has brought us.

A recent case in the Supreme Court supplies the needed illustration. The case was a prosecution for murder.[7] The trial judge had charged that the defendant, though attacked with a deadly weapon, was not at liberty to stand his ground if a man of reasonable prudence would have seen a possibility of flight. Support is not lacking for such a statement of the law. The Supreme Court, speaking by Holmes, J., refused to accept a rule so unrelated to normal human (115) conduct under stress of strong emotion. "The law," said Judge Holmes, "has grown, and even if historical mistakes have contributed to its growth it has tended in the direction of rules consistent with human nature. . . . Detached reflection cannot be demanded in the presence of an uplifted knife. Therefore in this court, at least, it is not a condition of immunity that one in that situation should pause to consider whether a reasonable man might not think it possible to fly with safety or to disable his assailant rather than to kill him." Enough that he reasonably believes the danger to be imminent. The failure to retreat is, indeed, a circumstance to be considered in determining whether the belief is genuine. Given the belief, based on reasonable grounds, immunity is not withdrawn because some other reasonable man might have perceived the possibility of flight. We do not need to inquire whether it is possible to find in this decision a departure from precedents enshrined in the reports. In some states, *e.g.*, New York, the rule is hardened to some extent by the (116) provisions of a statute.[8] What interests us now is not so much the decision itself as its animating spirit. It is built on the assumption that function is perverted if a rule is unrelated to the realities of conduct, and the rule itself is moulded to effect the needed adaptation.

The growing power of this spirit declares itself in many fields. A school of thinkers of increasing weight and number is today stressing the relation between a rule and its effects, between the soundness of the one and the benefits of the other. This has been brought out sharply in the preliminary discussions as to the proposed restatement of the law. We have been reminded that where decisions are conflicting, a choice will be unintelligent unless we are informed which one of the conflicting rules has proved, in its operation, the most workable and useful.[9] Some of the errors of courts have their origin in im (117) perfect knowledge of the economic and social consequences of a decision, or of the economic and social needs to which a decision will respond. In the complexities of modern life there is a constantly increasing need for resort by the judges to some fact-finding agency which will substitute exact knowledge of factual conditions for conjecture and impression. A study of the opinions of Mr. Justice Brandeis will prove an impressive lesson in the capacity of the law to refresh itself from extrinsic sources, and thus vitalize its growth. His opinions are replete with references to "the contemporary conditions, social, industrial, and political, of the community affected." [10]

Sooner or later, if the demands of social utility are sufficiently urgent, if the operation of an existing rule is sufficiently productive of hardship or inconvenience, utility will tend to triumph. "The view of the legal system as a closed book was never anything but a purely theoretical (118) dogma of the schools. Jurisprudence has never been able in the long run to resist successfully a social or economic need that was strong and just." [11] We have a conspicuous illustration in the law of waters in our western states. "Two systems of water law are in force within the United States—the riparian and the appropriation systems." [12] The system first named prevails in thirty-one of the forty-eight states. Its fundamental principle is "that each riparian proprietor has an equal right to make a reasonable use of the waters of the stream, subject to the equal right of the other riparian proprietors likewise to make a reasonable use." [13] Some of the arid states of the west found this system unsuited to their needs. Division of the water "into small quantities among the various water users and on the general principle of equality of right" would be a division "so minute as not to be of (119) advantage to anybody." [14] "It is better in such a region that some have enough and others go without, than that the division should be so minute as to be of no real economic value." The appropriation system is built upon the recognition of this truth. Its fundamental principle is "that the water user who first puts to beneficial use—irrigation, mining, manufacturing, power, household, or other economic use——the water of a stream, acquires thereby the first right to the water, to the extent reasonably necessary to his use, and that he who is the second to put the water of the stream to beneficial use, acquires the second right, a right similar to the first right, but subordinate thereto, and he who is the third to put it to use acquires the third right, a right subordinate to the other two, and so on throughout the entire series of uses." [15] Here we have the conscious departure from a known rule, and the deliberate adoption of a new one, in obedience to the promptings of a social need so obvious (120) and so insistent as to overrun the ancient channel and cut a new one for itself.

The whole subject of the philosophy of function is, indeed, closely related to the vexed and perplexing problem of the authority of precedent. Through one agency or another, either by statute or by decision, rules, however well established, must be revised when they are found after fair trial to be inconsistent in their workings with an attainment of the ends which law is meant to serve. The revision is a delicate task, not to be undertaken by gross or adventurous hands, lest certainty and order be unduly sacrificed, yet a task also not to be shirked through timidity or sloth. I have had occasion elsewhere to indicate a few of the anachronisms that might be eradicated from the legal system.[16] Many others could be instanced. Some of this cleansing of ancient plague spots, the judges ought to do themselves. To the extent that they are unwilling or unable, there must be resort to legislation. The difficulty here is to establish some channel (121) of communication between legislature and courts. The channel is essential, first, that the needs of the courts may be known to the legislature, and, second, that the needs, when known, may be intelligently and promptly met. I have suggested a ministry of justice,[17] though I am not insensible of the imperfections of the plan. More hopeful in its promise of success is the project of the American Law Institute, already outlined in these lectures. The Institute will, of course, be national in scope. None the less, its recommendations may be applied with slight modification to different localities. The local bar associations or the local ministries of justice will thus be supplied with standards by which their own judgment will be guided, their own hesitations overcome, their own diversities corrected. No doubt there are many rules of property or conduct which could not be changed retroactively without hardship or oppression, and this whether wise or unwise in their origin. So far as I am aware, no judge ever thinks of changing them. (122) The picture of the bewildered litigant lured into a course of action by the false light of a decision, only to meet ruin when the light is extinguished and the decision is overruled, is for the most part a figment of excited brains. The only rules there is ever any thought of changing are those that are invoked by injustice after the event to shelter and intrench itself. In the rarest instances, if ever, would conduct have been different if the rule had been known and the change foreseen.[18] At times the change means the imposition of a bill of costs that might otherwise have been saved. That is a cheap price to pay for the uprooting of an ancient wrong. One man is made a victim to the extent of a few dollars in return for a readjustment that will save many victims in the future. If change, however, cannot be made through the judicial process, unaided from without, some external agency there must be through which the aid will be supplied. There are times when we can learn whether a rule functions well or ill by compari (123) son with a standard of justice or equity, known, or capable of being known, to us all through a scrutiny of conscience or through appeal to everyday experience. There are times when the manner of its functioning will be unknown without the recorded observations, the collected facts and figures, the patient and systematic studies, of scientists and social workers. "One of the most important functions of any vocational body," says Graham Wallas,[19] "is the continuous revision and increase of the heritage of knowledge and thought which comes within its sphere. In the case of law this function is peculiarly important. Law is the framework of the social machine, and if a sufficient number of instructed, free and fertile thinkers could set themselves to ask in the light of our modern knowledge of history, politics and psychology, what are the purposes of law, and by what means those purposes can be attained, an incalculable improvement in human relations might result."

Law is thus in touch with all the political and (124) social sciences.[20] The question is, let us say, whether the hours of labor for women may be regulated by statute. That question came before the Supreme Court in Muller v. Oregon, 208 U. S. 412. The brief submitted by Mr. Justice Brandeis, then at the bar, in support of the validity of the statute, supplied a new technique. It is the sociological method in action. The brief did not concern itself to any considerable extent with decisions or juristic conceptions or abstract arguments. It showed by copious references to authorities in economic and social science all over the world that unrestricted hours of labor for women had been felt to be an evil, and that almost everywhere statutes had been found necessary that the evil might be curbed. In these and like cases, the problem was at once ethical and social. But the same method is capable of adaptation to problems of a different order. Often the question before the court is concerned with the rule that is to regulate some business enterprise or transaction. The facts of economic (125) and business life are then relevant considerations. Lord Mansfield heeded them when he built up the law merchant. He did not exhaust their possibilities. The law of bills of lading, of sales, of partnership, or corporations, is still guided, though at times inadequately, by considerations of practical efficiency. The subject has been well considered by Professor Llewellyn of your own law school in a recent address before the Academy of Political Science in the City of New York.[21] "The law," he says, in summing up his conclusions, "needs to act far more quickly than it does in recognizing and giving effect to new business institutions as they arise; it needs to permit to those institutions far greater flexibility than at present in the modification from case to case of their lesser details; it needs to do both of these things with an earnest view to the economic function, and not to the legal incrustations, of the institutions concerned; and the restatement of the law, to satisfy business needs, (126) must work, and work vigorously, toward these ends." The Institute is not, however, the only agency that is tending toward the fuller ascertainment of the needs of economic life. The Federal Trade Commission is building up a body of precedent which will fix the proprieties of commercial usage. Comparative law, too, is furnishing example and suggestion, and the points of contact are many between it and jurisprudence.

To the influence of the social sciences, of political economy, of business usage in the development of law, we must add the influence of philosophy. I am speaking now, let it be recalled, not of a philosophy *of* law, not of a theory of the genesis of law, its growth, its end, its function, but of rules and concepts *within* the legal system, and the reaction of general theories of philosophy upon their form and content. The two subjects tend to coalesce. We shall find, for instance, that our theory of the genesis of law has philosophical implications which do not spend their force in determining our notion of (127) the origin of law in general, but spread out and affect our judgment in specific controversies. On the other hand, some problems of philosophy which seem in their general nature to be unrelated to a theory of law, are found, to our surprise, to lie at the root of problems which, at least upon the surface, are purely legalistic. Where shall we find an inquiry more abstract, more divorced, it would seem, from practice, than the metaphysical problem of the nature of truth itself? Who would think offhand that pragmatism had a message for the judge on the bench or the lawyer at the bar? I cannot doubt, however, that the message has been heard. By emphasizing standards of utility, by setting up the adaptation to an end as a test and evidence of verity, pragmatism is profoundly affecting the development of juristic thought. Its truth, if not genuine for the metaphysician, is genuine at least for those whose thought must be translated into action, who are not merely scientists, but craftsmen, and who must ever be satisfied with something less than the perfect and complete ideal. (128) It teaches each of us to be tolerant of the inevitable compromise. "If by the word 'truth'," says Santayana, "we designate not the actual order of the facts, nor the exact description of them, but some minor symbol of reconciliation with reality on our own part, bringing comfort, safety and assurance, then truth also will lie in compromise; truth will be partly truth to ourself, partly workable convention and plausibility." [22]

Take again the metaphysical problem of substance and the identity of material things. Law contents herself for the most part with those tests and standards of identity that are accepted by the average mind, untrained in metaphysics. Every now and then, however, she goes farther, though perhaps beyond her depth. A tree grows on a dividing line, its roots in the soil of one owner, and its branches over the soil of another. Dean Pound has shown us the philosophy of Aristotle establishing the identity of the tree and (129) adjusting the claims of the contending owners.[23] Grain is sold by a wrongdoer, and after its delivery to an innocent buyer is converted into whiskey.[24] Problems of identity again arise.[25] The whole subject of the confusion of goods is lined with the furrows of Greek philosophers and mediaeval schoolmen. The essential is marked off from the accidental, the constitutive from the derivative, the attribute from the *modi*.[26] There are times, too, when judges have had to struggle with problems of causation.[27] Even more notable has been the influence of theories of metaphysics upon the law of corporations and the theory of juristic persons.

I do not say that the intrusion of philosophy into these fields has been attended always with the happiest results. Some of her exploits may stand as warnings rather than as examples. If (130) that is so, the undivided blame is not to be put upon the lawyers. A sounder conception of the scope and function of philosophy on the part of the philosophers themselves would have served, in all likelihood, to guide us to a wiser outcome. We should then have concentrated our thought less on abstract conceptions and more on practical results. Professor Dewey tells us that philosophy, once a contemplative study, has suffered a change, and is becoming operative and practical.[28] More and more, he says,[29] it is facing "the great social and moral defects and troubles from which humanity suffers." It is concentrating "its attention upon clearing up the causes and exact nature of these evils and upon developing a clear idea of better social possibilities; in short, upon projecting an idea or ideal which, instead of expressing the notion of another world, or some far-away unrealizable goal, would be used as a method of understanding and rectifying specific social ills." What is this but to (131) say that the sociological method, which is making itself felt in law, is at work in other fields, and even on those exalted planes which philosophy has reserved as her own peculiar province? If some of the applications of philosophy to law may not incite to emulation, the fault has been, not in supposing that philosophy is a helpful guide, but in the conception of philosophy as alien to experience and life. One must select one's guide with care, even though the candidates for employment are decked in the regalia of the schools. The student does not need to be warned against fertilizing law with the teachings of philosophy. The warning must rather be to be on the watch for the philosophy which, disguised or unavowed, is latent in existing law, to extricate it when it is hidden, to test its truth and value, and to be ready to correct or discard it when it is defective or outworn. The more he knows of philosophy, past and present, the quicker his eyes will be to detect and his judgment to appraise.

There are those who, dismayed by the diffi (132) culties of the judicial process when it becomes a creative agency, would keep it to the sphere of imitative reproduction, and leave creation to the statutes. I am not sure but that I should be prepared to join them if statutes had proved adequate in the past to the bearing of such a burden, or gave promise of being adequate within any future now in sight. I have been surprised to see how many partisans the notion of a separation of powers rigid and perpetual—the judges the interpreters, the legislature the creator—is able even in our day to muster at the bar. Some months ago the *New York Law Journal* published letters of its readers, some in praise, some in criticism, of a decision recently announced. The critics, or some of them, went upon the theory that the rule of *stare decisis* was imbedded in the constitution, and that judges, when they departed from it, were usurpers, though the precedent ignored was as mouldy as the grave from which counsel had brought it forth to face the light of a new age. *Stare decisis* is not in the constitution, but I should be half (133) ready to put it there, and to add thereto the requirement of mechanical and literal reproduction, if only it were true that legislation is a sufficient agency of growth. The centuries, if they have proved anything, have proved the need of something more. These tentative and uncertain gropings may be deplored, but they are inevitable, none the less, if we are not to rush blindly into darkness. Unique situations can never have their answers ready made as in the complete letter-writing guides or the manuals of the art of conversation. Justice is not to be taken by storm. She is to be wooed by slow advances. Substitute statute for decision, and you shift the center of authority, but add no quota of inspired wisdom. If legislation is to take the place of the creative action of the courts, a legislative committee must stand back of us at every session, a sort of supercourt itself. No guarantee is given us that a choice thus made will be wiser than our own, yet its form will give it a rigidity that will make retreat or compromise impossible. We shall be exchanging a (134) process of trial and error at the hands of judges who make it the business of their lives for a process of trial and error at the hands of a legislative committee who will give it such spare moments as they can find amid multifarious demands. Even if we could believe that the amateurs would be wiser than the professionals, their remedy would be prescribed too late to help the patient whose disease they had observed. Administered to another, without reckoning a change of symptoms, it might do more harm than good. I do not mean to depreciate unduly the value of the statute as an instrument of reform. Legislation can eradicate a cancer, right some hoary wrong, correct some definitely established evil, which defies the feebler remedies, the distinctions and the fictions, familiar to the judicial process.[30] Legislation, too, can sum up at times and simplify the conclusions reached by courts, and give them new validity. Even then, its relief is provisional and temporary. The cycle is unending. "Code is followed by com (135) mentary, and commentary by revision, and thus the task is never done." [31] The adaptation of rule or principle to changing combinations of events demands the creative action of the judge. You may praise our work or criticize it. You may leave us with the name we have, or tag us with some other label, arbitrators or assessors. The process is here to stay.

Not a little of the suspicion and hostility enveloping the creative activity of the courts in the minds of laymen, if not of lawyers, is due to the prevalent assumption that statute is the typical law, and that the business of the judge is to apply to the facts as found a mandate which to be understood has only to be read. The courts, in the words of Professor Frankfurter, "become the interpreters of self-determining words with fixed content, yielding their meaning to a process of inexorable reasoning." [32] This view of the judicial process would be untenable even if statute did in truth make up the great body of our (136) law. The truth is, however, that it makes up the smaller part. Lord Bryce reminds us in *The American Commonwealth* that the average man in the everyday transactions of life is subject to constraints imposed by the law of the states rather than by the federal government, the law of the nation.[33] That is perhaps not so accurate a statement of ordinary conditions as it was when the *American Commonwealth* was written,[34] but it still approximates to the truth. In like manner, we may say that in the everyday transactions of life the average man is governed, not by statute, but by common law, or at most by statute built upon a substratum of common law, modifying, in details only, the common law foundation.[35] Failure to appreciate this truth has bred distrust of a creative activity which would otherwise have been seen to be appropriate and normal. A rule which in its origin was the creation of the courts themselves, and was (137) supposed in the making to express the *mores* of the day, may be abrogated by courts when the *mores* have so changed that perpetuation of the rule would do violence to the social conscience. No doubt there is need to consider whether men have acted in good faith on the assumption that the rule will be continued. If they have, retrospective change may be forbidden by the same social conscience to which appeal is made for its allowance. Such cases of legitimate reliance upon established wrong—its roots so spreading and so deep that it is to be tolerated, if not respected—are rarer in my judgment than some of us suppose. If abrogation is permissible in cases of extremity, still more plainly permissible at all times is continuing adaptation to varying conditions. This is not usurpation. It is not even innovation. It is the reservation for ourselves of the same power of creation that built up the common law through its exercise by the judges of the past.

This power of creation, if it is to be exercised with vision and understanding, exacts a philoso (138) phy of law, a theory of its genesis and growth and aim. Only thus shall we be saved from the empiricism which finds in an opinion, not a prophecy to inspire, but a command to be obeyed. The true point of view has been admirably stated by Mr. Justice Brandeis in his dissenting opinion in State of Washington v. Dawson & Co., 264 U. S. 219, 236. Arguing for the restriction of a rule which had proved itself unworkable, he says: "Such limitations of principles previously announced and such express disapproval of *dicta* are often necessary. It is an unavoidable incident of the search by courts of last resort for the true rule. The process of inclusion and exclusion, so often applied in developing a rule, cannot end with its first enunciation. The rule as announced must be deemed tentative. For the many and varying facts to which it will be applied cannot be foreseen. Modification implies growth. It is the life of the law." Human nature predisposes us to fight against this method, so exhausting in its demands upon strength or mind and body, and (139) to rest on tests mechanical. The delusive hope of certainty satisfies the conscience, only too ready to approve what inertia suggests. Inertia rather than malice was the moving force behind the method practiced by Judge Bridlegoose, the hero of one of Rabelais' satires, who carried mechanical tests to the summit of achievement. Judge Gest of the Orphans' Court of Philadelphia has revived him for us in an interesting address.[36] He decided four thousand cases during his judgeship and all of them by casting lots. Twenty-three hundred and nine of these were appealed, and in every instance on appeal the judgment was affirmed. Here is a fifth method to be added to these already unfolded in our scrutiny of the judicial process. If this be rejected as inadequate, the others will call for an equipment as rich and as varied as the culture of the race. We shall have to be on our guard, none the less, against a state of mind that will lead us to be too distrustful of ourselves. There is danger of a judge's becoming like Pitt's minister who was (140) so irresolute and vacillating that he was constantly late at entertainments because he could not make up his mind in proper time whether to go out or to stay at home.[37] The truth, of course, is that every doubtful decision involves a choice between a nicely balanced alternative, and no matter how long we debate or how carefully we ponder, we shall never arrive at certitude. "In electing a government," says Santayana,[38] "as in selecting a wife, only two or three candidates are commonly available, and the freeman's modest privilege is to declare hopefully which one he wants and then to put up with the one he gets." It is in this spirit of resignation that judges must decide and lawyers must submit.

For the task in truth is one to baffle the wisdom of the wisest. Law is the expression of a principle of order to which men must conform in their conduct and relations as members of society, if friction and waste are to be avoided (141) among the units of the aggregate, the atoms of the mass.[39] The expression may be false if those who formulate it, lawyer and judge and legislator, are blind to any phase of the life whose inner harmony they are commissioner to interpret and maintain.[40] No one of us has a vision at once so keen and so broad as to penetrate these unsounded depths and gather in its sweep this enveloping horizon. We can only cling for the most part to the accumulated experience of the past, and to the maxims and principles and rules and standards in which that experience is embodied. Little is the positive contribution that any one of us can hope to make, the impetus that any one of us can give, to the movement forward through the ages. That little will call for the straining of every faculty, the bending of every energy, the appeal to every available resource, within us or without. "Jurisprudence," (142) says Ulpian, "is the knowledge of things human and divine, the science of the just and the unjust." The definition, famous to the point of triteness though it is, has been scoffed at, not a little, as empty declamation. We have learned to doubt whether the derision was timely as it seemed. Sir Frederick Pollock has reminded us in a stimulating essay[41] that there may be more of honest truth in the inspiring generality than in many an arid phrase of a colder, if exacter, science. Perhaps our little glimpse into the ultimate, our peep together into the empyrean whence philosophy and law derive their eternal essence, will fill you as it fills me with something of a kindred faith. We shall be spared, at least, the blunder of thinking meanly of our calling. We shall see that our little parish has its vistas that lie open to the infinite. We shall know that the process of judging is a phase of a never ending movement, and that something more is exacted of those who are to play their part in it (143) than imitative reproduction, the lifeless repetition of a mechanical routine.

I come back in the end to the text with which I started: "Law must be stable, and yet it cannot stand still." The mystery of change and motion still vexes the minds of men as it baffled the Eleatics of old in the beginnings of recorded thought. I make no pretense of having given you the key that will solve the riddle, the larger and deeper principle that will harmonize two precepts which on their face may seem to conflict, and thus to result in an antinomy. I can only warn you that those who heed the one without honoring the other, will be worshiping false gods and leading their followers astray. The victory is not for the partisans of an inflexible logic nor yet for the levelers of all rule and all precedent, but the victory is for those who shall know how to fuse these two tendencies together in adaptation to an end as yet imperfectly discerned. I shall not take it amiss if you complain that I have done little more than state the existence of a problem. It is the best that I can do. (144) We are not yet in agreement about the answer, though in truth it is fundamental and at the basis of our work. We have had courts and recorded judgments for centuries, but for lack of an accepted philosophy of law, we have not yet laid down for our judges the underlying and controlling principles that are to shape the manner of their judging. We do not yet know either our powers or our duties. The tendency that is distinctive good to some is to some distinctive error. What one judge most earnestly believes to be the right method is met by the challenge of men as able and conscientious who say it is the wrong one. I feel very profoundly that at the root of many of our troubles is the need of a better understanding of the existence of this problem, if it is too much to hope just now for a better understanding of the answer. I feel very profoundly that much of the criticism of courts and many of the blunders of courts have their origin in false conceptions, or at any rate in varying conceptions, of the limits of judicial power, the essence of the judicial function, the (145) nature of the judicial process. We may not hope to eliminate impatience of judicial restraint, and even revolutionary encroachments upon the integrity of judicial power, till we settle down to some agreement about the things that are fundamental.

The summons to this better understanding still presses for an answer.

REFERENCES

1. Sun Printing & Publishing Co. v. Remington Pulp & Paper Company, 235 N. Y. 338. Of course, a different result may be reached if the omitted term is of subsidiary importance (1 Williston, *Contracts*, § 48), but ordinarily the price to be paid, if reserved for subsequent agreement, is to be ranked as fundamental.

2. Fosdick, *Christianity and Progress*, p. 111.

3. Imperator Realty Co. v. Tull, 228 N. Y. 447, 455.

4. See, *e.g.*, St. Regis Paper Co. v. Hubbs & Hastings Paper Co., 235 N. Y. 30; Murray v. Cunard S. S. Co., 235 N. Y 162.

5. Matter of Rouss, 221 N. Y. 81, 91.

6. *Cf.* Holmes, *The Common Law*, pp. 1, 2.

7. Brown v. U. S., 256 U. S. 335.

8. Penal Law, §§ 42, 1055; People v. Johnson, 139 N. Y. 358; and *cf.* People v. Tomlins, 213 N. Y. 240; People v. Fiori, 123 N. Y. App. Div. 178, 188, 189, 190.

9. Professor Herman Oliphant, *The Problems of Logical Method*, vol. X, Proceedings of Academy of Political Science in New York, p. 18.

10. Truax v. Corrigan, 257 U. S. 312; *cf.* Adams v. Tanner, 244 U. S. 590, 600.

11. Ehrlich, *Grundlegung der Soziologie des Rechts*, p. 346.

12. Bannister, "Interstate Rights in Interstate Streams in the Arid West," 36 *Harv. L. R.* 960.

13. Bannister, *supra*.

14. Bannister, *supra*, p. 962.

15. Bannister, *supra*, p. 961; Wyoming v. Colorado, 259 U. S. 419.

16. 35 *Harv. L. R.* 113.

17. 35 *Harv. L. R.* 113.

18. *Cf. The Nature of the Judicial Process*, p. 146.

19. *Our Social Heritage*, p. 126.

20. Vinogradoff, *Historical Jurisprudence*, vol. I.

21. X Proceedings Academy of Political Science, pp. 24, 32.

22. Santayana, *Soliloquies in England and Later Soliloquies*, p. 83.

23. Pound, "Juristic Science and Law," 31 *Harv. L. R.* 1049, 1050.

24. Silsbury v. McCoon, 3 N. Y. 379.

25. *Cf.* Buckland, *Roman Law*, pp. 210, 216.

26. Windelband, *op. cit.*, pp. 52, 66.

27. Bird v. Ins. Co., 224 N. Y. 47; Lewis v. Acc. Ins. Co., 224 N. Y. 18.

28. Dewey, *Reconstruction in Philosophy*, p. 122.

29. P. 124.

30. "A Ministry of Justice," 35 *Harv. L. R.* 113.

31. 35 *Harv. L. R.*, 113, 117.

32. Frankfurter, "Mr. Justice Holmes' Constitutional Opinions," 36 *Harv. L. R.* 912.

33. Bryce, *American Commonwealth*, vol. I, chap. 36, pp. 411, 412.

34. See Pierson, *Our Changing Constitution*.

35. *Cf.* Pound, *The Spirit of the Common Law*, ch. 1

36. Pennsylvania State Bar Association, June 26, 1923.

37. John Morley, *Burke*, p. 195.

38. *Soliloquies in England and Later Soliloquies*, p. 175.

39. Pound, *Criminal Justice in Cleveland*, pp. 563, 564; *cf.* Gény, *Méthode d'interprétation en droit privé positif*, vol. II, p. 221.

40. See Ehrlich, *Grundlegung der Soziologie des Rechts*, p. 384.

41. Pollock, Oxford Lectures, *The Methods of Jurisprudence*, p. 5.

Complete Text

of

THE PARADOXES OF LEGAL SCIENCE*

Columbia University Lectures
James S. Carpentier Foundation

April 10 1928

Hon. Benjamin N. Cardozo
16 West 75th Street
New York City

My dear Chief Judge

This is just a line to express my pleasure at finding on my table this morning your lectures on the Carpentier Foundation. I heard the first one with great satsifacton and shall be delighted to study the entire volume.

With congratulations and warm regard, I am

Faithfully yours,
NICHOLAS MURRAY BUTLER

BAR BUILDING
36 WEST 44TH STREET
NEW YORK CITY

April 14, 1928

Dr. Nicholas Murray Butler,
Broadway at 116th Street,
New York City.

Dear Dr. Butler:

Your pleasant note was found upon my desk on my return from Albany.

I have a wretched, sinking feeling as I survey the bound volumes. How did I ever bring myself to believe that the lectures were worth publishing? That is always my feeling at the beginning. I can only hope that time will soften it.

With thanks for your kindness, I am

Faithfully yours,
BENJAMIN N. CARDOZO

---

* *The Paradoxes of Legal Science.* Copyrighted 1928 by Columbia University Press. Reprinted by permission of Columbia University Press and with the permission of Columbia University, the residuary legatee of the literary estate of Benjamin Nathan Cardozo.

(1)

— I —

Introduction—Rest and Motion—Stability and Progress.

"THEY do things better with logarithms." The wail escapes me now and again when after putting forth the best that is in me, I look upon the finished product, and cannot say that it is good. In these moments of disquietude, I figure to myself the peace of mind that must come, let us say, to the designer of a mighty bridge. The finished product of his work is there before his eyes with all the beauty and simplicity and inevitableness of truth. He is not harrowed by misgivings whether the towers and piers and cables will stand the stress and strain. His business is to know. If his bridge were to fall, he would go down with it in disgrace and ruin. Yet withal, he has never a fear. No mere experiment has he wrought, but a highway to carry men and women from shore to shore, to carry them secure and unafraid, though the floods rage and boil below.

So I cry out at times in rebellion, "why cannot I do as much, or at least something measurably as much, to bridge with my rules of law the torrents of life?" I have given my years to the task, and behind me are untold generations, the judges and lawgivers (2) of old, who strove with a passion as burning. Code and commentary, manor-roll and year-book, treatise and law-report, reveal the processes of trial and error by which they struggled to attain the truth, enshrine their blunders and their trumphs for warning and example. All these memorials are mine; yet unwritten is my table of logarithms, the index of the power to which a precedent must be raised to produce the formula of justice. My bridges are experiments. I cannot span the tiniest stream in a region unexplored by judges or lawgivers before me, and go to rest in the secure belief that the span is wisely laid.

Let me not seem to cavil at the difficulties that learning can subdue. They are trying enough in all conscience, yet what industry can master, it would be weakness to lament. I am not thinking of the multitude of precedents and the labor of making them our own. The pangs that convulse are born of other trials. Diligence and memory and normal powers of reasoning may suffice to guide us truly in those fields where the judicial function is imitative or static, where known rules are to be applied to combinations of facts identical with present patterns, or, at worst, but slightly different. The travail comes when the judicial function is dynamic or creative. The rule must be announced for a novel situation where competitive analogies supply a hint or clew, but where precedents are lacking with authoritative commands.

I know the common answer to these and like laments. The law is not an exact science, we are told, (3) and there the matter ends, if we are willing there to end it. One does not appease the rebellion of the intellect by the reaffirmance of the evil against which intellect rebels. Exactness may be impossible, but this is not enough to cause the mind to acquiesce in a predestined incoherence. Jurisprudence will be the gainer in the long run by fanning the fires of mental insurrection instead of smothering them with platitudes. "If science," says Whitehead,[1] "is not to degenerate into a medley of *ad hoc* hypotheses, it must become philosophical and must enter upon a thorough criticism of its own foundation." We may say the like of law.

So I keep reaching out and groping for a pathway to the light. The outlet may not be found. At least there may be glimmerings that will deny themselves to a craven *non possumus,* the sterility of ignoble ease. Somewhere beneath the welter, there may be a rationalizing principle revealing system and harmony in what passes for discord and disorder. Modern science is tending to revolutionize our ideas of motion within the atom, and so of motion generally. We had thought of radiation as continuous and flowing. We are told that in truth it is discrete and irregular.[2] The electron does not glide from point to point. The goal is gained *per saltum.* "There is a possibility that the old laws, which represented mo (4) tion as a continuous smooth process, may be only statistical averages, and that when we come down to a sufficiently minute scale, everything really proceeds by jumps, like the cinema, which produces a misleading appearance of continuous motion by means of a succession of separate pictures." [3] Is it possible that in rationalizing the development of law, in measuring the radiating energy of principle and precedent, we have been hampered by a like illusion? We have sought for a formula consistent with steady advance through a continuum. The continuum does not exist.

Instead there are leaps from point to point. We have been beguiled by the ideal of an harmonious progression. Centres of energy exist, of attraction and repulsion. A landing-place is found between them. We make these landing places for ourselves through the methods of the judicial process. How shall they be wrought? Where shall they be found?

The reconciliation of the irreconcilable, the merger of antitheses, the synthesis of opposites, these are the great problems of the law. "Nomos," one might fairly say, is the child of antinomies, and is born of them in travail. We fancy ourselves to be dealing with some ultra-modern controversy, the product of the class of interests in an industrial society. The problem is laid bare, and at its core are the ancient mysteries crying out for understanding—rest and motion, the one and the many, the (5) self and the not-self, freedom and necessity, reality and appearance, the absolute and the relative. We have the claims of stability to be harmonized with those of progress. We are to reconcile liberty with equality, and both of them with order. The property rights of the individual we are to respect, yet we are not to press them to the point at which they threaten the welfare or the security of the many. We must preserve to justice its universal quality, and yet leave to it the capacity to be individual and particular. The precedent or the statute, though harsh, is to be obeyed, yet obeyed also, at the sacrifice not seldom of the written word, are to be the meliorating precepts of equity and conscience. Events are to be traced to causes, yet since causes are infinite in number, there must be a process of selection by which the cause to be assigned as operative will vary with the end in view. Is this dream land or reality? The ground seems to slip beneath our feet, yet a foothold must be found. "Fundamental opposites," I quote from a different context the words of Lytton Strachey in his essay on Pope, "fundamental opposites clash and are reconciled."

The problem points the method. The goal of juridical effort, says Demogue, is not logical synthesis, but compromise. "Of course," he adds, "this makes the law a subtle science, but it cannot be avoided." [4] A like bifurcation, the opposition between static and (6) dynamic, divides the universe.[5] So at least it seems to us today, though the truth of the division may be one that is relative to our own imperfect minds, unable to penetrate to the unity in which diversity is lost.[6] Until deeper insight is imparted to us, we must be content with many a makeshift compromise, with many a truth that is approximate and relative, when we are yearning for the absolute. "To bring about reconciliations," I quote Demogue again, "is the great work of jurists." [7]

Let us summon a few of these antithesis before us and watch the process of compromise as it mediates between them. Rest competes with motion, permanence with flux, stability with progress. Where shall compromise draw the line? The "one" is in rivalry with the "many," the individual with the group, the group with the community, liberty with restraint. Where is the line that we shall call the jural median? "Perfect security," says Demogue,[8] "would mean the infinite immobility of society," to which we add that perfect certainty would mean the same. The friends of constitutional government are prompt to repel encroachments upon liberty, yet liberty in the literal sense is desired only by the anarchists,[9] with whom the friends of constitutional government (7) would scorn to claim accord. Deep beneath the surface of the legal system, hidden in the structure of the constituent atoms, are these attractions and repulsions, uniting and dissevering as in one unending paradox. "Fundamental opposites clash and are reconciled."

In my studies of antinomies, I start with the antithesis between rest and motion, stability and progress. "There are two principles," says Whitehead,[10] "inherent in the very nature of things, recurring in some particular embodiments whatever field we explore—the spirit of change, and the spirit of conservation. There can be nothing real without both. Mere change without conservation is a passage from nothing to nothing. Its final integration yields mere transient non-entity. Mere conservation without change cannot conserve. For after all, there is a flux of circumstance, and the freshness of being evaporates under mere repetition." If life feels the tug of these opposing tendencies, so also must the law which is to prescribe the rule of life. We are told at times that change must be the work of statute, and that the function of the judicial process is one of conservation merely. But this is historically untrue, and were it true, would be unfortunate. Violent breaks with the past must come, indeed, from legislation, but manifold are the occasions when advance or retrogression is within the competence of judges as their competence has been determined by practice and tra (8) dition. The law has its formulas, and its methods of judging, appropriate to conservation, and its methods and formulas appropriate to change. If we figure stability and progress as opposite poles, then at one pole we have the maxim of *stare decisis* and the method of decision by the tool of a deductive logic; at the other we have the method which subordinates origins to ends. The one emphasizes considerations of uniformity and symmetry, and follows fundamental conceptions to ultimate conclusions. The other gives freer play to considerations of equity and justice, and the value to society of the interests affected. The one searches for the analogy that is nearest in point of similarity, and adheres to it inflexibly. The other, in its choice of the analogy that shall govern, finds community of spirit more significant than resemblance in externals. "Much of the administration of justice," says Pound,[11] "is a compromise between the tendency to treat each case as one of a generalized type of case, and the tendency to treat each case as unique."[12] Each method has its value, and for each in the changes of litigation there will come the hour for use. A wise eclecticism employs them both. Often the motivating force behind a choice will seem to be nothing more rational than mere empirical opportunism. This does not mean that the study of the process of selection yields nothing of utility. We may hit upon uniformities that will (9) help us in the course of time to the formulation of a principle. If the generalizations of jurisprudence are imperfect and provisional, so also, at least in the early stages of development, are those of science everywhere. "The things directly observed," it has been said,[13] "are, almost always, only samples. We want to conclude that the abstract conditions which hold for the samples, also hold for all other entities which, for some reason or other, appear to us to be of the same sort. This process of reasoning from the sample to the whole species is Induction. The theory of Induction is the despair of philosophy—and yet all our activities are based upon it." The jurist must have the patience and the faith that have inspired the meditations of the physicist, and have crowned experiment with triumph.

At the outset, there is need to delimit the subject matter

of our study. Our concern is with the law as it is shaped by the judicial process. Statutes may be put aside except in so far as they require the work of judges to expound them, for to the extent that their commands are unmistakable their interest is not so much for jurisprudence as for the science of legislation. I do not mean to suggest that the study of the process of legislation may not be fruitful of results. The truth is that many of us, bred in common law traditions, view statutes with a distrust which we may deplore, but not deny. This had led, as you know, to the maxim of construction that stat (10) utes derogating from the common law are to be strictly construed, a maxim which recalls what has been said by Sir Frederick Pollock of rules of statutory construction generally: they cannot well be accounted for except on the theory that the legislature generally changes the law for the worse, and that the business of judges is to keep the mischief of its interference within the narrowest possible bounds.[14] I do not forget a trenchant article by Roscoe Pound in which he exhibits this distrust as narrow minded in its origin and pernicious in its tendency.[15] I do not dwell upon his criticism now, for it is foreign to my theme. Perhaps a scientific study of legislation, its capacities and limitations, would bring us to a saner attitude. The point I wish to make is that our concern for the moment is with the work of judges only, and with law as it issues from their hands. So far as they are the mere mouthpiece of a legislature, speaking thoughts and enforcing commands that have been unmistakably set down, their activity is in its essence administrative and not judicial. Where doubt enters in, there enters the judicial function.

I come back to the antithesis between rest and motion. We live in a world of change. If a body of law were in existence adequate for the civilization of today, it could not meet the demands of the civilization of tomorrow. Society is inconstand. So long as (11) it is inconstant, and to the extent of such inconstancy, there can be no constancy in law. The kinetic forces are too strong for us. We may think the law is the same if we refuse to change the formulas. The identity is verbal only. The formula has no longer the same correspondence with reality. Translated into conduct, it means something other than it did. Law defines a relation not always between fixed points, but often, indeed oftenest, between points of varying position. The acts and situations to be regulated have a motion of their own. There is change whether we will it or not.[16]

One is reminded of the Einstein theory and the relativity of motion. "Stated generally, the teaching of Einstein is that absolute rest and motion are meaningless for physical science, and that motion can signify only the changing position of bodies relatively to each other." [17] If there were infinite space with only one object in it, motion for that object would have no meaning to our minds. If in infinite space there were only two objects, motion would still be without meaning so long as relatively to each other the positions were the same. There is need to import some of this same conception of relativity into our conception of the development of (12) law.[18] We render judgment by establishing a relation between moving objects—moving at different speeds and in different directions. If we fix the relation between them upon the assumption that they are stationary, the result will often be to exaggerate the distance. True constancy consists in fitting our statement of the relation to the new position of the objects and the new interval between them.

I find an illustration of my thought in the development of the law governing ocean bills of lading. One will see the history of the development well and graphically portrayed in an article in the *Yale Law Journal* by Mr. Chester B. McLaughlin, Jr., a member of the New York bar.[19] At first a bill of lading imported the delivery of merchandise on board a designated ship. The time came, however, with the upheavals of the Great War when the goings and comings of ships were too uncertain to be known or stated in advance. Goods were left at the dock, and all that the steamship company would undertake was to send them forward when it could. "During the war the whole routine of transoceanic shipments was destroyed, and no steamship company was able to predict even within months when it would be able to ship goods or on what steamer." [20] The documents issued to its shippers conformed to these necessities. (13) They no longer acknowledged receipt on a designated vessel. The acknowledgment was merely that the goods had been received for shipment on a named vessel "and/or on a following steamer." When the war was over, the change that had thus been born of necessity was continued for convenience.

"The necessities of proper stowage and the irregularity in arrival of shipments combined with the great accumulation of cargo, both inward and outward, on the piers and for different steamers" were thought to "render it physically impossible either to guarantee loading by a particular vessel, or to determine until after a steamer is loaded and the dock checked up whether any specific cargo had been loaded." [21] The old form of document thus came to be supplanted by a new one which omitted an acknowledgment once recognized as vital. The question was still open as to the extent to which the courts would effectuate the change. A bank was to pay for goods against a draft and a bill of lading. Was a document in the new form a bill of lading against which payment might be made? To have said "no" would have kept the law consistent with ancient definitions. To have said "yes" kept it consistent with the realities of usage and the needs of ocean commerce. In this dilemma, the courts preferred to answer "yes." [22] The truth, of course, was that there had been a change in methods of transportation which necessitated a revision (14) of the legal formula if the relation defined by law was to maintain its former correspondence with the relation to be regulated, *i.e.*, the relation known to business. Refusal to change the statement of the rule would have given to the change of events an exaggerated movement. Revision of the legal formula by keeping it in pace with the movement of events preserved its correspondence with existing norms of conduct.

I find another illustration in the capacity of the law merchant to extend the quality of negotiability to novel forms of documents if negotiable by custom.[23] This capacity may, of course, be arrested by statute, as in New York and other states.[24] In the absence of such restraint, there are few tendencies of growth more persistent and effective. The parallelism is maintained between the movement of legal concepts and that of mercantile expedients.

From these and kindred illustrations a working rule emerges. In default of a better name, I may style it the principle of relativity in the adaptation of the law to conduct. When changes of manners or business have brought it about that a rule of law which corresponded to previously existing norms or standards of behavior, corresponds no longer to the present norms or standards, but on the contrary departs from them, then those same forces or tend (15) encies of development that brought the law into adaptation to the old norms and standards are effective, without legislation, but by the inherent energies of the judicial process, to restore the equilibrium.

In formulating this canon I do not mean that it is capable of slavish application. No rule of thumb will tell us in advance when events in their movement have traversed such a distance that to avoid undue disparity we must reformulate the rule of law. Many factors of convenience must be counted. Many observations from different angles must be made before the survey will be accurate. Then, when distances have been measured, the canon may be borne in mind. Precedent or formal logic may seem to be pointing to stability. The principle of relativity in the adaptation of the law to conduct may point the way to change.

My illustrations have been drawn from changing forms of business. What is true of motion there is true, and for like reasons, of motion in the realm of morals. Manners and customs (if we may not label them as law itself) are at least a source of law. The judge, so far as freedom of choice is given to him, tends to a result that attaches legal obligation to the folkways, the norms or standards of behavior exemplified in the life about him.[25] Manners and customs are equally a source of morals. One has only to (16) glance at such a book as Sumner's *Folkways* or Hobhouse's *Morals in Evolution* to have this truth brought home with superabundant demonstration. Not that morals in our own day are compact of custom and nothing else. Undoubtedly, as Hobhouse has well brought out, reflection has combined with imitation, reasoning with mere mechanical repetition, philosophy with tradition, in the forming of the compound.[26] "As we follow the ethical movement in its advance, we shall find more and more that the interest shifts from the tradition which men follow half mechanically to the deliberate attempt to reorganize conduct on the basis of some distinct theory of life."[27] "In ethics, custom and theory are in constant and close interaction, and our subject, the comparative study of ethics, must embrace them both. It would include, were it within one man's power to treat it exhaustively, at one extreme the quasi-instinctive judgment based on the unthinking acceptance of tradition; at the other the profoundest theory of the thinker seeking a rational basis of conduct and an intelligible formula to express the end of life, and between these two the influences, rational and half rational, which are at work with increasing assiduity as civilization advances, remodelling custom and substituting deliberately accepted principle, whether true, half (17) true or false, for blind tradition." [28] "Our subject must include the ideal of the apostle as well as the working rule of the lawyer. Its upper limit is the philosopher's reasoned and rounded theory of life. Between these extremes all the judgments that men form about conduct fall within its scope." [29] "Blind adherence to custom is modified by an intelligent perception of the welfare of society, and moral obligation is set upon a rational basis. These changes react upon the actual contents of the moral law itself, what is just and good in custom being sifted out from what is indifferent or bad; and the purified moral code reacts in turn on the legislation by which advanced societies model their structure." [30] It reacts on legislation, but it reacts on judge-made law as well. The moral code of each generation, this amalgam of custom and philosophy and many an intermediate grade of conduct and belief, supplies a norm or standard of behavior which struggles to make itself articulate in law. The sanction or source of obligation for moral rules, it has been said,[31] is the pressure of society on the individual mind.[32] The same pressure is ever at work in the making of the law declared by courts. The state in commissioning its judges has commanded them to judge, but neither (18) in constitution nor in statute has it formulated a code to define the manner of their judging. The pressure of society invests new forms of conduct in the minds of the multitude with the sanction of moral obligation, and the same pressure working upon the mind of the judge invests them finally through his action with the sanction of the law.

Let me seek some illustrations of the movement of judge-made law in accord with changing *mores*. The law of domestic relations supplies the readiest examples. The husband at common law might restrain his wife by force if there was danger of her leaving him. There has been formal adjudication, if adjudication was needed to enlighten him, that the right is gone today.[33] Gone is it with the yet more ancient right, of which it was a phase, the right to maintain the marital authority by moderate castigation. The *mores* in their growth have imposed the restraint of law upon these grosser acts of tyranny, and from these has moved to others subtler and more elusive. Cruelty was once identified with physical abuse. Insult and derision, mental torture as well as physical, have come within its range.[34]

For society at large as well as for the family, the changing *mores* have brought changing law. A new sense of the significance of social solidarity has engendered a new conception of the duty to refrain from anti-social conduct. Ancient precedents gave (19) support to the view that conduct harmful to one's neighbor did not depend for its legality upon the animating motive. Modern decisions have set bounds to the license theretofore accorded to "disinterested malevolence."[35] A growing altruism, or if not this, a growing sense of social interdependence, is at the bottom of the change. Power might be exercised with brutal indifference to the many when society was organized on a basis of special privilege for the few. Democracy has brought in its wake a new outlook, and with the new outlook a new law. The social forces contributing to the change did not write their message down into the set paragraphs of a statute. They left it in the air where the pressure was more effective because felt by all alike. At last, the message became law.

One gains the sense of an epic movement unifying the legal process,—the picture and the promise of a plot majestically unfolding itself amid all the interludes and diversions —when one reads the history of English law in its birthplace and across the seas. A study of Holdsworth's narrative in its monumental comprehensiveness has brought this sharply home to me. The latent energies within the legal system— what the ancients would have called its "entelechy"—are revealed in all their vigor. Some (20) chapters have been told so often as to be familiar or no longer strange. We have grown accustomed to the significance of the forms of actions, and are no longer surprised to hear that the doctrine of consideration might have been different if assumpsit had not developed out of tort.[36] But there are other principles, and weighty ones, where something other than the forms of actions, more deliberate and conscious, has been the generative force. Take the rule that a master is liable for the contracts and torts of a servant within the scope of the apparent authority. Could anything be more typical of the common law as we know it? One has a shock of surprise when one is told for the first time that as late as the seventeenth century the law was very different.[37] "Except in those cases in which from motives of public policy a more extended liability was allowed, a master was only liable for the acts of his agent if he had actually ordered him to act, or if he had, by words or conduct, subsequently ratified his acts." [38] There was indeed a heavier liability for common carriers; for householders whose servants had caused damage by fire; and for the man who had undertaken to do something, and by his servant had done it badly.[39] But these and other instances of like liability were departures from the general rule. Only about two hundred years ago, at the end of the seventeenth (21) century, did judges awake to the fact that "the strict common law principles which governed the liability of masters or principals for the acts of their servants or agents were wholly unsuited to the commercial condition of the country." [40] They did not wait for legislation. Chief Justice Holt found in civil law principles, which had already been adopted by the Court of Admiralty, the analogies that were needed to smooth the path of progress. By borrowings from another system, with some infiltration of ideas from common law instances of exceptional liability, and if not thus, then at least by innovation of some sort, from whatever source derived, there came into English law the modern principle whereby the scope of the employer's liability is measured by the authority implicit in the nature of the business.[41] Only antiquarians recall that it is not as ancient as the law itself.

The powers inherent in the judicial office when Holt was Lord Chief Justice exist in undiminished force today. One does not extinguish them by saying that the earlier centuries were formative, and that there has followed a modern age in which the law is a closed book. Every age is modern to those who are living in it. True, of course, it is that in the centuries since Holt's time many lines once weak and wavering have become permanent and rigid. Principles and rules that were malleable in his day have petrified (22) with the accumulated weight of precedent on precedent. Land within the territory of the law that was then unsettled or uncultivated has been peopled or reclaimed. Frontiers, however, there still are, and will always be, where the lines of demarcation are uncertain and debatable, where occupation, if any, has been provisional and timid,—borderlands and marches where minds impatient of injustice refuse to be held back, but point the pathway of advance into regions unexplored beyond. It may hearten spirits such as these to bear in mind the creative energies that dwelt within the legal system at the threshold of the modern era, two centuries ago.

The example supplied by Holt would have slight significance if it were singular. One can match it by many others. Take a case decided a century later, in 1789, the great case of Pasley v. Freeman.[42] The ruling was then made that an action in tort might be maintained for "a false and fraudulent statement which caused damage to another, though there was no contractual relation between deceiver and the person deceived." [43] One judge, Grose, J., dissented upon the ground that no precedent existed for "an action upon a false affirmation, except against a party to a contract, and where there is a promise, either express or implied, that the fact is true which is misrepresented." Coming down to recent days, take the changes that have been wrought in the law (23) of defamation, of which two instances will suffice among many that could be cited. Anciently the law was that the mere repetition of a slander was not actionable if the repetition was accompanied by a designation of the author.[44] The common law world was then a paradise for gossips. "This was long regarded as settled law [45] and was not overruled till the beginning of the nineteenth century." [46] Within the field of defamation, a second instance, yet more recent, is furnished by the law of privilege. The fair and true report of a judicial or other public proceeding has long been held to be a privilege of the press. At first, however, proceedings in courts not of record were at times excluded from the privilege.[47] So were *ex parte* proceedings. So were such proceedings as the filing of a complaint or answer, at least until the stage was reached when they laid a basis for judicial actions. One by one these exceptions dropped away. Proceedings in the lower courts were put on the same footing as proceedings in the higher ones.[48] *Ex parte* proceedings might be reported as freely as those that were contentious.[49] Finally, only the other day, the Court of Appeals of New York extended the privilege to the report of statements in a pleading (24) before the stage of trial.[50] "We may as well disregard the overwhelming weight of authority elsewhere," said Judge Pound, "and start with a rule of our own consistent with practical experience."[51] For example not less striking, take the group of decisions, the chief of them very recent, that revolutionized the law of blasphemy and the law of superstitious uses as they had stood in the English courts for three centuries and more.[52] "It is obvious," says Holdsworth, commenting on these decisions,[53] "that the dominant factor in the various trains of legal reasoning which have justified the abolition of the older doctrines of law and equity, and, with the assistance of the Legislature, have impelled them in the direction of universal toleration, has been the influence of public opinion as to the proper relation of the state and its law to religion." There are observations in Lord Sumner's judgment in Bowman v. The Secular Society, *supra,* that may seem to disguise the transformation, or belittle its significance. "After all," he says,[54] "the question whether a given opinion is a danger to society is a question of the times, and is a question of fact." One may call it a question of fact if one will, for it is from the fact (25) that law emerges. "Ex facto jus oritur."[55] The truth is that a changing sense of the exactions of utility and justice has evoked a changing law.

Other illustrations are not lacking.[56] At times the new ethos does not mean that there has come into being a new conception of right and wrong. It may mean nothing more than a new impatience, a new restiveness, in the face of old abuses long recognized as wrong. Transition stages there are also when an observer can mark the law in the very process of "becoming." It is throwing off a crippling dogma, and struggling for freer motion. For years there has been a dogma of the books that in the absence of a special duty of protection, one may stand by with indifference and see another perish, by drowning, say, or fire, though there would be no peril in a rescue. A rule so divorced from morals was sure to breed misgivings. We need not be surprised to find that in cases of recent date, a tendency is manifest to narrow it or even whittle it away.[57] We cannot say today that the old rule has been supplanted. The rulings are too meagre. Sown, however, are the seeds of scepticism, the precursor often of decay. Some day (26) we may awake to find that the old tissues are dissolved. Then will come a new generalization, and with it a new law.[58]

Our course of advance, therefore is neither a straight line nor a curve. It is a series of dots and (27) dashes. Progress comes *per saltum,* by successive compromises between extremes, compromises often, if I may borrow Professor Cohen's phrase, between "positivism and idealism." "The notion that a jurist can dispense with any consideration as to what the law ought to be arises from the fiction that the law is a complete and closed system, and that judges and jurists are mere automata to record its will or phonographs to pronounce its provisions." [59] Ideas of justice will no more submit to be "banished from the theory of law" than "from its administration." [60] "What has happened," we are told, "is simply that ideas of justice have lost prestige among jurists and are pursued in an unavowed form." [61]

I take leave to doubt whether the prestige of idealism as one of the motive forces of the law is indeed at so low an ebb. If I were to state the case in terms of the tides, I would say that a flood season is at hand, if not already here.[62] Juristic idealism, as I view the scene, is more conscious of itself than it has been for many years. Jurists such as Stammler in Germany and Gény in France have brought it forth into the open when once it was concealed. Whatever its prestige, and however unavowed its processes, there can be little doubt as to its power. You may (28) chain the law down with all manner of clamps and bonds. The wizard Justice has a queer way of setting the victim free. This is true even in systems founded upon codes. It is more plainly true of a system such as ours. Even in code systems, the law leaves many things unsaid. It states a general principle, and turns over to the judge the task of filling up the gaps.[63] His guide is then the just law, the law, that is to say, whereby justice is attained. The positive law may indeed override the law of justice. "We must always remember" says Stammler "that the judge has a right to introduce and exercise just law directly, only in those cases where the positive law directs him to do so." [64] The direction may be implied, however, as well as express. "The positive law may lay this duty upon him by explicit instruction or by silence." [65] In case of the law's silence, we must have recourse to the fundamental idea of law itself, "an endeavor to realize justice by force." [66] Often, however, the reference to the just law is explicit and unmistakable. Take, for instance, the provisions of Sec. 242 of the German Civil Code:[67] "The debtor is obliged to perform his service as good faith and (29) regard to business custom dictate." There is a like provision in the French Code Civil.[68] We must not think of the just law, when it prevails, as something distinct from the positive law, or in antagonism to it. It is itself a phase, a subdivision, a compartment, of positive law. As to this Stammler is at pains to develop his thesis with precision. There is a very general "misapprehension," he says,[69] "of the concepts positive and just law." "It seems" to many "that there is a distinction between positive law and a certain 'ethical something' which, at any rate, is not law. This is not true. The distinction we are making is within law itself. It refers to the difference in the *manner* in which the 'content' of 'positive' law is to be determined. They are merely different means with which the one positive law intends to carry out its fundamental purpose. Accordingly 'good faith' is not outside of positive law; much less is it opposed to it; but it is an instrument of the positive law which the latter employs to determine its content."

If a code does not escape the need of supplementing its mandates by reference to the norms of morals, we may be sure that the same instrument of growth in the hands of common law judges will be used with greater freedom. The whole system which they develop has been built on the assumption that it is an expression of the *mores*. What has once been settled by a precedent will not be unsettled over night, for (30) certainty and uniformity are gains not lightly to be sacrificed. Above all is this true when honest men have shaped their conduct upon the faith of the pronouncement. On the other hand, conformity is not to be turned into a fetich. The disparity between precedent and ethos may so lengthen with the years that only covin and chicanery would be disappointed if the separation were to end. There are many intermediate stages, moreover, between adherence and reversal. The pressure of the *mores*, if inadequate to obliterate the past, may fix direction for the future. The evil precedent may live, but so sterilized and truncated as to have small capacity for harm. It will be prudently ignored when invoked as an apposite analogy in novel situations, though the novel element be small. There will be brought forward other analogies, less precise, it may be, but more apposite to the needs of morals. The weights are constantly shifted to restore the equilibrium between precedent and justice.

REFERENCES

1. *Science and the Modern World*, p. 24.
2. Whitehead, *op. cit.*, pp. 50, 181; Bertrand Russell, *The A.B.C. of Atoms*, pp. 9, 54, 55, and the same author's "Philosophy," pp. 101, 107.
3. Bertrand Russell, *The A.B.C. of Atoms*, p. 9; *cf.* Bertrand Russell, "Mathematics and Metaphysics," in *Mysticism and Logic*, p. 84.
4. Demogue, *Analysis of Fundamental Notions*, vol. 7, Modern Legal Philosophy Series, p. 570. *Cf.* Bryce, *Studies in History and Jurisprudence*, quoted by Andrews, "Recent Decisions of the Court of Appeals," 12 *Cornell Law Quarterly*, 433.
5. Demogue, *op. cit.*, pp. 429, 430, 448.
6. Haldane, *The Reign of Relativity*, pp. 11, 37, 63; Dewey, *Experience and Nature*, p. 46.
7. Demogue, *op. cit.*, p. 570.
8. *Op. cit.*, p. 445.
9. G. Lowes Dickinson, *Justice and Liberty*, p. 142.
10. *Science and the Modern World*, p. 281.
11. Article "Jurisprudence" in the *History and Prospects of the Social Sciences*, by Harry Elmer, Barnes, and others, p. 472.
12. *Cf.* Cardozo, *The Growth of the Law*, p. 67.
13. Whitehead, *op. cit.*, p. 34.
14. Pollock, *Essays in Jurisprudence and Ethics*, p. 85.
15. Pound, "Common Law and Legislation," 21 *Harvard L. R.* 383.
16. *Cf.* M. R. Cohen, "The Place of Logic in the Law," 29 *Harvard Law Review*, 629; Frankfurter, "Hours of Labor and Realism," 29 *H. L. R.* 369.
17. Haldane, *The Reign of Relativity*, p. 55; *cf.* p. 92; Bertrand Russell, *The A. B. C. of Relativity*, pp. 24, 69.
18. *Cf.* Lippmann, *The Phantom Public*, p. 89; W. F. Ogburn, *Social Change*, p. 199; Sorokin, *Social Mobility*, p. 4.
19. "The Evolution of the Ocean Bill of Lading," 35 *Yale Law Journal* 549.
20. McLaughlin, *supra*, p. 559.
21. McLaughlin, *supra*, p. 560.
22. Vietor v. National City Bank, 200 App. Div. 557, 1923; 237 N. Y. 538.
23. See, *e.g.*, Goodwin v. Roberts, *L. R.*, 10 Ex. 346; Bechuan Land Exploration Co. v. London Trading Co., 1898, 2 Q. B.. 658; Edelstein v. Schuler, 1902, 2 K. B. 144, 154.
24. Bank of Manhattan Company v. Morgan, 1926, 242 N. Y. 38.
25. Willis, J., in Millar v. Taylor, 1769, 4 Burr. 2303, 2312, quoted by Lefroy, 32 *L. Q. R.* 294.
26. *Cf.* MacIver, *Community*, pp. 149, 150; Vinogradoff, *Custom and Right*, p. 34; "A comparative survey of western European customs discloses, as it seems to me, three main factors: business practice, tradition, and reflective formulation."—Vinogradoff, *op. cit.*
27. Hobhouse, *Morals in Evolution*, p. 18.
28. Hobhouse, *supra*, p. 18.
29. Hobhouse, *supra*, p. 25.
30. Hobhouse, *supra*, p. 30.
31. Dewey, *Human Nature and Conduct*, pp. 326, 327; also pp. 75, 81.
32. *Cf.* Korkunov, *General Theory of Law*, Modern Legal Phil. Series, p. 45; Dewey and Tufts, *Ethics*, p. 360.
33. R. v. Jackson, 1891, 1 Q. B. 671.

34. Pearson v. Pearson, 1920, 230 N. Y. 141.

35. American Bank & Trust Co. v. Federal Reserve Bank, 1921, 256 U. S. 350, 358; Beardsley v. Kilmer, 1923, 236 N. Y. 80; Ames, *Lectures on Legal History*, p. 398; *cf.* however, Sorrell v. Smith, 1925, A. C. 700; Stammler, *The Theory of Justice*, Modern Legal Phil. Series, p. 253.

36. Holdsworth, *History of English Law*, vol. 8, pp. 7, 42, 47.

37. Holdsworth, *op. cit.*, vol. 8, p. 227, 228, 229, 252, 474, 476.

38. Holdsworth, *op. cit.*, vol. 8, p. 227.

39. Holdsworth, *op. cit.*, vol. 8, p. 476; vol. 3, p. 385.

40. Holdsworth, *op. cit.*, vol. 8, p. 252.

41. Holdsworth, *op. cit.*, vol. 8, pp. 229, 252, 474, 475; vol. 6, p. 520.

42. 3 T. R. 51.

43. Holdsworth, *op. cit.*, vol. 8, p. 426.

44. Earl of Northampton's Case, 1613, 2 Co. Rep. 134.

45. Davis v. Lewis, 1796, 7 T. R. 17.

46. McPherson v. Daniels, 1829, 10 B. & C. 263; Holdsworth, *op. cit.*, vol. 8, p. 357.

47. Odgers, *Libel and Slander*, 5th ed., p. 308.

48. Odgers, *supra.*

49. Usill v. Hales, 3 C. P. D. 324, 325; Wilson v. Walter, L. R., 4 Q. B. 93.

50. Campbell v. N. Y. Evening Post, 1927, 245 N. Y. 320.

51. 245 N. Y. at p. 328; *cf.* remarks of Cockburn, C. J., in Wasson v. Walter, 1868, L. R., 4 Q. B. 73.

52. R. v. Ramsay, 1883, 15 Cox, C. C. 231; Bowman v. The Secular Society, 1917, A. C. 406; Bowne v. Keane, 1919, A. C. 815; Holdsworth, *op. cit.*, vol. 8, pp. 415–420.

53. P. 418.

54. 1917, A. C. 466, 467.

55. *Cf.* Brandeis, J., in Adams v. Tanner, 1917, 244 U. S. 590, 600.

56. One may find many of them in Lefroy, "The Basis of Case Law," 22 *L. Q. R.* 293, and Andrews, "Recent Decisions of the Court of Appeals," 12 *Cornell Law Quarterly* 433.

57. Pound, *Law and Morals*, pp. 72, 73; and *cf.* his citation of Bentham, *Principles of Morals and Legislation*, ch. 17, sec. 19, Clarendon Press Edition, p. 323; Lefroy, "The Basis of Case Law," 22 *L. Q. R.* 293; Queen v. Instan, 1893, 1 Q. B. 450.

58. A significant case is Queen v. Instan, 1893, 1 Q. B. 450. There, the defendant, a woman of full age and having no means of her own, lived alone with her aunt, a woman of seventy-three, who maintained her. The aunt for the last ten days of her life suffered from a disease which made her perfectly helpless. During this time the defendant lived in the house, and took in the food supplied by the tradesmen, but gave none of it to the sick woman, and procured neither nursing nor medical attendance. Death was accelerated by lack of food and care. The Queen's Bench Division unanimously decided that a duty was imposed on the defendant under the circumstances to supply her aunt with sufficient food to maintain life, and she was convicted of manslaughter. Lord Coleridge, C. J., said (p. 453): "It would not be correct to say that every moral obligation involves a legal duty; but every legal duty is founded on a moral obligation. A legal common law duty is nothing else than the enforcing by law of that which is a moral obligation without legal enforcement. There can be no question in this case that it was the clear duty of the prisoner to impart to the deceased so much as was necessary to sustain life of the food which she from time to time took in and which was paid for by the deceased's own money for the purpose of maintenance of herself and the prisoner; it was only through the instrumentality of the prisoner that the deceased could get the food. There was therefore a common law duty imposed upon the prisoner which she did not discharge. . . . There is no case directly in point; but it would be a slur upon and a discredit to the administration of justice in this country if there were any doubt as to the legal principle or as to

the present case being within it. The prisoner was under a moral obligation to the deceased from which arose a legal duty towards her."

Casuistry will discover reasons why the holding in that case falls short of a decision that a stranger to one in danger may be charged with a legal duty of succor or of rescue. The holding is none the less significant of a tendency of thought which is gaining year by year in power and momentum.

59. Morris R. Cohen, "Positivism and the Limits of Idealism in the Law," 27 *Columbia Law Review* 237, 238.

60. *Ibid.*

61. *Ibid.*, p. 237.

62. *Cf.* Cardozo, "A Ministry of Justice, 35 *Harv. L. Rev.* 113, at p. 126.

63. Stammler, *Theory of Justice,* Modern Legal Phil. Series, 198, 199· Vinogradoff, *Historical Jurisprudence,* vol. 2, pp. 64, 65, citing Aristotle's *Rhetoric.*

64. P. 240; *cf.* Brütt, *Die Kunst der Rechtsanwendung,* p. 147.

65. P. 241.

66. P. 209; *cf.* Brütt, *op. cit.,* p. 163: "Sehr zahlreich sind die Fälle, in denen unser Recht unmittelbar auf richtiges Recht Bezug nimmt."

67. *Bürgerliches Gesetzbuch.*

68. Sections 1134, 1359.

69. P. 259.

(31)

—II—

The Meaning of Justice—The Science of Values.

IF justice has this place in shaping the pathway of the law, it will profit us to know what justice means. "What we are seeking is not merely the justice that one receives when his rights and duties are determined by the law as it is; what we are seeking is the justice to which law in its making should conform." [70] Stammler in his *Theory of Justice* draws a sharp distinction between the law of justice and morality. His view is the Kantian one that morality is concerned with the purity of the will.[71] The just law, on the contrary, has relation to acts. From this it follows, he argues,[72] that "no matter how far the ethical perfection of the human race may in the course of time advance, there will always remain the right rule of social life as a specific object of investigation. The technical possibilities, the changing qualities and capabilities, the external conditions of life in the different regions of the world,—all of these offer a peculiar basis for coöperation, which must be regulated. And this regulation forms the object of an (32) independent method and study. A merely technical economy cannot be managed directly by the principles of good intention and perfection of character if we are to obtain final results. Our problems are of such a nature that we must first master them by means of rules for external conduct." There are, of course, other students of ethics who reject the Kantian principle that acts have no ethical quality in and of themselves apart from the will of the actor. "Most people," says Spencer,[73] "regard the subject matter of Ethics as being conduct considered as calling forth approbation or reprobation. But the primary subject matter of Ethics is conduct considered objectively as producing good or bad results to self or others or both." This was Bentham's thesis: "If motives are good or bad, it is only on account of their effects." [74] So today in the school of thinkers known as the English neo-realists, of whom George E. Moore is a notable example, goodness is held to be an ultimate and objectively subsisting entity.[75] In this view, the just law as Stammler conceives it becomes identified with the moral law, or with so much of the moral law as defines the quality of justice.

I must leave it to students of ethics to choose between these conflicting schools of thought, or to trace, as some have tried to do, a reconciling path of (33) compromise that will utilize what is true in each, and avoid their common error.[76] The student of legal science will fall back upon a method familiar to the law, and not unknown to philosophy. A German philosopher, Hans Vaihinger, has written a book which he has called *The Philosophy of As If, Die Philosophie des Als Ob*. "I called this work," he says,[77] "*The Philosophy of As If* because it seemed to me to express more convincingly than any other possible title what I wanted to say, namely, that 'As If,' *i.e.*, appearance, the consciously false, plays an enormous part in science, in world philosophies and in life. I wanted to give a complete enumeration of all the methods in which we operate intentionally with consciously false ideas, or rather judgments. I wanted to reveal the secret life of these extraordinary methods. I wanted to give a complete theory, an anatomy and physiology, so to speak, or rather a biology of 'As If.'" Adam Smith, for illustration, was a disciple of the philosophy of "As If" when he built a science of political economy on the assumption of an economic man, animated by egoism to the exclusion of all other impulses, and by that particular aspect of egoism which aims at economic good. There is no occasion, however, for going afield, and gathering illustrations from sciences other than our own. The law is no stranger to the philosophy of "As If." It has built up many of its doctrines by a make- (34) believe that things are other than they are. I put aside for the moment the crasser forms of fiction that have played a part upon the legal scene; for example, an allegation in a pleading not subject to be traversed, and yet known to be untrue. For the most part they were devices to advance the ends of justice, yet clumsy and at times offensive. Indeed, the father of Sir Matthew Hale gave up the practice of the law "because he could not reconcile his conscience to the system of adding untrue allegations to pleadings so as to 'lend colour' to the proceedings."[78] These forms are out of date, but we have with us even now, the quasi-contract, the adopted child, the constructive trust, all of flourishing vitality, to attest the empire of "as if" today.

What I have in mind more particularly, however, is a class of fictions of another order, the fiction which is a working tool of thought, but which at times hides itself from view till reflection and analysis have brought it to the light. As political economy has its economic man, so jurisprudence has its reasonable man, its negligent man, and, what is more in point for us just now, its moral man. Professor Edgerton in a recent paper has reviewed the authorities that bear upon the distinction between subjective and objective negligence. With a wealth of illustration he has developed the thesis that "negligence neither is nor involves ('presupposes') either indifference or inadvertence, or any other mental characteristic, qual (35) ity, state or process. Negligence is unreasonably dangerous conduct—*i.e.*, conduct abnormally likely to cause harm. Freedom from negligence (commonly called 'due care') does not require care, or any other mental phenomenon, but requires only that one's conduct be reasonably safe —as little likely to cause harm as the conduct of a normal person would be." [79] The law maintains this objective outlook upon morals to the extent that it appropriates the norms of morals as its own. The pure will may serve as an *excuse* when will or intention is the essence of a wrong.[80] It is not equivalent without more to the attainment of the moral ideal so far as that ideal is also the criterion of law. The jural pattern of moral values is the conduct that is moral in any given situation when the actor is viewed "als ob," as if, endowed with normal powers of will and understanding. The law may be satisfied with less. It does not aspire to less. It looks to nothing lower, but also perhaps to nothing higher, in framing its ideal.

I come back then to the definition of justice considered as a jural norm. It may be narrower or broader than the specific quality of justice as known to ethical theory. I hold it for my part to be so much of morality as juristic thought discovers to be wisely and efficiently enforcible by the aid of jural sanctions. I have little help here from Stammler's ex (36) position and analysis. Summary of his theory would be profitless, for the meaning is unintelligible without ample illustration.[81] His definition when developed is not lacking in suggestive power. It is too vague, however, and too abstract, to be a crutch for limping minds.[82] I think the law does better when it adopts another method of approach more pragmatic and inductive. One who seeks examples of this method will find them in the writings of Lévy-Bruhl among the French and in those of Hobhouse among the English.[83] "The morals of any given society at any given epoch," says Lévy-Bruhl,[84] "are determined by the totality of its conditions both from a static and a dynamic view point." "Social justice is a 'becoming,' if not a continuous progress." [85] "The content of the moral ideal is thus a compound of imagination, tradition and observation of social realities." [86] We have already followed the same thought in Hobhouse. The standards are the product of an interaction between impulse and habit,[87] and again between custom and reflection.

It comes down to this. There are certain forms of (37) conduct which at any given place and epoch are commonly accepted under the combined influence of reason, practice and tradition, as moral or immoral. If we were asked to define the precise quality that leads them to be so characterized, we might find it troublesome to make answer, yet the same difficulty is found in defining other abstract qualities, even those the most familiar. The forms of conduct thus discriminated are not the same at all times or in all places. Law accepts as the pattern of its justice the morality of the community whose conduct it assumes to regulate. In saying this, we are not to blind ourselves to the truth that uncertainty is far from banished. Morality is not merely different in different communities. Its level is not the same for all the component groups within the same community. A choice must still be made between one group standard and another. We have still to face the problem, at which one of these levels does the social pressure become strong enough to convert the moral norm into a jural one? All that we can say is that the line will be higher than the lowest level of moral principle and practice, and lower than the highest. The law will not hold the crowd to the morality of saints and seers. It will follow, or strive to follow, the principle and practice of the men and women of the community whom the social mind would rank as intelligent and virtuous.

The question then is whether the justice to which the law aspires is to be identified with virtue generally or only with some phase of it. Many attempts (38) have been made to isolate the quality of justice, and, stripped of other forms of virtue, to make it the ideal of law.[88] Plato saw in justice the harmony of the soul, which made it one with virtue generally.[89] Aristotle identified virtue with the mean between extremes, and saw in justice only a phase of it, the quality of virtue whereby every man receives his due. The difficulty is only cloaked, for what is due must be defined.[90] Yet Aristotle did not stop with the notion of mere legality. The jural ideal was felt even then to be justice thus limited and also something more. What is most significant in Aristotle's treatment of the subject is his chapter on a kind of justice which he describes as a justice outside legality,[91] δικαιοσύνη is to be supplemented by ἐπιείκεια, law by equity, the rule by the humane exception. "The teaching on this department of justice forms one of the most instructive parts of Greek jurisprudence; it has had a long history and a great influence on modern developments of the theory of law."[92] We get the same thought in the chapters of the *Ethics* that deal with other virtues. "That principle," says Aristotle, "which is most truly just is thought to partake of the (39) nature of friendship."[93] The stranger within the gates becomes a neighbor or a friend.

Among the moderns, Spencer announced a formula of justice, "Every man is free to do that which he wills, provided he infringes not the equal freedom of any other man."[94] This is in effect to make justice one with liberty. Stammler in his analysis of Justice[95] introduces the conception of grace or leniency as Aristotle had done before him, but ends with the Kantian ideal of a freely developed and freely acting personality. So, in our own body of law, the standard to which we appeal is sometimes characterized as that of justice, but also as the equitable, the fair, the thing consistent with good conscience.[96]

An ideal so expansive is no longer capable of being compressed within the analogy of an account between a debtor and a creditor with justice as the *quid pro quo*. The jural as well as the moral norm of justice, or even more perhaps than the moral norm, has in it an infusion of qualities with which justice is at times contrasted, such as charity or compas-(40) sion.[97] One who makes a payment carelessly has himself to blame for his plight if the payment is too large. Even so, the bank paying by mistake a check drawn by its customer in excess of the balance in his account, may at times get the money back from a payee, a third party, who acted in good faith.[98] Ownership is divested out of pity for negligence or error. One who sells his inheritance improvidently under the pressure of immediate need, knows that by the terms of the sale he gives up the expectancy forever. Even so, the buyer may be compelled (at least in many jurisdictions) to exhibit an involuntary charity and refrain from taking advantage of the necessities of the seller.[99] One who is in lawful possession of land may expel the unwelcome visitor, who, when bidden to depart, remains, and still more the intruder who has entered without leave. Even so, the privilege may vanish if the visitor is ill so that expulsion would be dangerous, or if the intruder has moored his boat at the dock to seek shelter in a storm.[100] One who holds over in possession of a building after the expiration of a term of years may be deemed at the election of the landlord to be a tenant for another (41) year.[101] Even so, the holding-over may be unavailing to lay a basis for the election when the tenant has been ill so that it would have been dangerous to leave.[102] Shylock appealed to justice, yet Portia made us know that the jural norm, however much it might disguise itself under a strict construction of the bond, did not in truth ignore the quality of mercy.[103] If this is true at times when the remedies are legal and enforcible of right, it is true even oftener when the remedies are equitable and enforcible at discretion. At the basis of the law of contract is the maxim *"uti lingua nuncupassit, ita jus esto."* [104] This is the foundation, yet many pages have been written to show the remedies available when the tongue has made a slip. There are other situations in which there figures even more plainly the element of grace. A contract is made without fraud or oppression. Change of circumstances brings hardship. The Chancellor withholds his remedies, and remits the suitor to a claim for damages which is known to be futile. Justice again is done by making charity a duty.

There must be flexibility for the formula that will hold within its walls this thing of changing content. Justice as a jural norm is not a fixed or determinate phase of the totality of moral conduct in a given situation. On the other hand, it is not morality as a (42) whole, even objectively considered. It is so much of morality as the thought and practice of a given epoch shall conceive to be appropriately invested with a legal sanction, and thereby marked off from morality in general.[105] This is not unlike the doctrine taught by Jellinek, though there are elements of difference. "Law" in his teaching "is a minimum ethics, that is to say the whole combined requirements of morals, whose observance, at a given stage of social development is absolutely indispensable."[106] If for "law" we substitute some such term as "the jural norm of justice," we shall not be far away from truth. I do not mean that judges have it in their power at one sweep to bring the law as it exists into conformity with this provisional ideal. Advance even so far may mean innovation too radical to be effected in a day without the aid of legislation. I mean that the ideal is nothing less, though the law of any epoch will always be behind it. If I may borrow a metaphor from the law of waters, the process by which judges work is one of erosion rather than avulsion. Here a little and there a little. We look about us later, and behold, the waste places are reclaimed.[107] Legal custom develops by the same forces and methods that (43) build up custom generally. "We know," says Hobhouse in his *Morals in Evolution*,[108] "how customs change and grow and disappear unconsciously as an individual stretches a point here or makes a new application of a precedent there. We can see how the interaction of multitudinous forces transmutes custom and produces a new tradition before any one has been aware of the change." So with the growth of law. The judge stretches a point here in response to a moral urge, or makes a new application of a precedent there. Before long a new tradition has arisen. Duties that had been conceived of as moral only, without other human sanction than the opinion of society, are found to be such that they may effectively and wisely be subjected to another form of sanction, the power of society. The moral norm and the jural have been brought together, and are one.

With some elements of difference, this conception of justice as legally organized or organizable morality is akin to the idea of justice as it has been analyzed by Mill. "Now it is known," he says in his essay "Utilitarianism,"[109] "that ethical writers divide moral duties into two classes, denoted by the ill-chosen expressions, duties of perfect and of imperfect obligation; the later being those in which, though the act is obligatory, the particular occasions of performing it are left to our choice; as in the case (44) of charity or beneficence, which we are indeed bound to practice, but not towards any definite person, nor at any prescribed time. In the more precise language of philosophic jurists, duties of perfect obligation are those duties in virtue of which a correlative *right* resides in some person or persons; duties of imperfect obligation are those moral obligations which do not give rise to any right. I think it will be found that this distinction exactly coincides with that which exists between justice and the other obligations of morality. In our survey of the various popular acceptations of justice, the term appeared generally to involve the idea of a personal right—a claim on the part of one or more individuals, like that which the law gives when it confers a proprietary or other legal right. Whether the injustice consists in depriving a person of a possession, or in breaking faith with him, or in treating him worse than he deserves, or worse than other people who have no greater claims, in each case the supposition implies two things—a wrong done and some assignable person who is wronged. Injustice may also be done by treating a person better than others; but the wrong in this case is to his competitors, who are also assignable persons. It seems to me that this feature in the case—a right in some person correlative to the moral obligation—constitutes the specific difference between justice and generosity or beneficence. Justice implies something which it is not only right to do, and wrong not to do, but which some individual (45) person can claim from us as his moral right." Mill goes on to point out that "no one has a moral right to our generosity or beneficence, because we are not morally bound to practice those virtues toward any given individual." There are times, however, as I have sought to show, when we are so bound—when the virtue of benevolence loses its indeterminate quality, and connotes the existence of a correlative claim of right. To that extent it is annexed to the domain of justice, and is incorporated into the jural norm.

Whenever a relation between human beings becomes organized into one that is specifically jural, the duties attached to it by law are assimilated more and more to those attached to it by morals. The law will not command the rich to give alms to the indigent. On occasion, none the less, it will impose restraints upon power taking advantage of necessity. The law will not enforce a duty of kindness to a neighbor. It will enforce a duty of kindness to wife or child or pupil. Observe, however, that relations, once so vague and unorganized as to lack a jural quality, may become organized and definite with the result that thereafter rights and duties will belong to them. A new relation may be established, or at times an existing one extended. For many years, there was stress upon a relation known as privity. In default of that connecting bond, there were times when the law would not recognize duties that were recognized in morals. Decisions of recent date have (46) made the bond of diminishing importance, and have broadened the relations to one's fellows from which duties are engendered.[110] The scope of legal duty has expanded in obedience to the urge of morals. We see the same urge in decisions that charge an owner of land with special duties to the young and heedless.[111] We see it in the inroad made by recent cases upon the concept of an infant's disability where injustice would be wrought if the concept were maintained in all its rigorous simplicity.[112] We see it in a tendency, still almost in embryo, and yet perceptible, to enlarge the duties owing to licensees and even trespassers by a gradual extension of the class of invitees.[113] We see it in the striking growth of the concept of duress, a concept broad enough today to supply a remedy against unfairness and oppression in forms long ranked as guiltless.[114] At times, indeed, the movement has been helped by legislation. The land owner was without redress at common law if (47) his neighbor cut off his light and air for the mere purpose of annoyance.[115] Statutes against spite fences have made neighborliness a duty.[116] Yet there are fields not far removed where statutes have been needless. In economic rivalry, the trader or the merchant may be ungenerous toward his competitor to promote his own advancement. He goes too far if the animating motive is unadulterated malice, the mere desire to destroy.[117]

Such are present-day distinctions. We must be on our guard against supposing that they have the attribute of finality. Stammler in his discussion of the German Civil Code [118] insists that the rule of justice should do more than forbid the unneighborly act that is animated by malice. In his view there should be a positive duty of generous conduct when there would be no loss to the doer or loss proportionately trivial. Undoubtedly the moral norm is not satisfied with less. The time may come when the jural norm will be able to exact as much. For the transformation that comes from the steady pressure of the *mores* is like the fabled transformation of the poet's dream. He awoke and found it truth. The standards of legal justice have been moved while we were dreaming of them, and planted in new soil. I speak of the standards as those of justice, yet it is justice in a large (48) sense, δικαιύνη modified by ἐπιείκεια, by the softer virtue of grace or leniency. The jural norm is identified with so much of the moral norm as exerts upon the social mind a pressure too strong to be satisfied with the sanction of mere opinion. A response or reaction is evoked in the form of social sentiment and conviction from which emerges a demand that the sanction of the opinion of society shall be fortified by the sanction of its power. When this pressure has gone so far that it may no longer be resisted, the judges are to say. For that they are interpreters of the social mind, its will, its expectation, its desires."[119] They tell us when the norms and standards of behavior and opinion have become so organized through the forces of custom or of morals as to have become translated into law. "Claims," says Vinogradoff in his lectures on Custom and Right,[120] "are made every day in all possible directions, and out of claims there arise sometimes what may be called natural claims, or moral rights. A man who has conferred a benefit on another person, even if he has no kind of written and valid acknowledgment in regard to the obligee, may rightly say that he has a claim to the gratitude or to reciprocal services of the other party. In order that such a moral claim should become juridical, it must pass through a second stage, the stage of declaration of right. A declaration of right is the admission by organized society (49) that the claim is justified from the public point of view."[121] Organized society may speak in such matters by the voice of its representatives in legislative assemblies. It may speak, at least in our Anglo-American system, by the voice of its judges. "The gradual consolidation of opinions and habits."[122] will then have done its work, and to the sanction of their pressure will be added the sanction of the law.

I have spoken of judges as the interpreters of the "social mind." There are possibilities of much logomachy in such a form of words. I have no desire to invite them. Among students of social theory there are some who view the mind of society as something super-added to the minds of the component members.[123] Other students tell us that the social mind, if we are to use the term at all, is merely the sum of individuals minds acting in society.[124] My own point of view will become clearer perhaps when I shall have occasion to discuss the antithesis between the individual and the group. I put aside for the moment the endless conflict between the monists and the pluralists, between the nominalists and the real (50) ists, obtruding itself here as upon so many scenes of carnage. We can be indifferent for present purposes whether the social mind is to be reckoned as unitary or multiple. Let it stand for nothing more than the organ or organs, whether they be multiple or unitary, out of which public opinion emerges as a product. Mr. Lippmann has taught us that the product is often put before us with spurious marks and symbols, so that recognition of its quality is at times no easy task.[125] Still more recently Dr. Dewey in his lectures, "The Public and Its Problems," has been preaching the same lesson. Indeed, there is an ambiguity in the very word "public," for the thought to be appraised and heeded is not the hasty or unconsidered impressions of the crowd; it is the thought of those sections of the crowd whose impressions have ripened into genuine opinion.[126] "The public is not, as I see it," says Mr. Lippmann, "a fixed body of individuals." [127] So it is that Giddings bids us to distinguish sharply "between public opinion and popular opinions and beliefs, and defines public opinion as critically thought out social judgments." [128] Opinion is not the commonplace,—at (51) least not by any law inherent in its being. "One mind in the right, whether in statesmanship, science, morals, or what not, may raise all other minds to its own point of view." [129] We do not strike an average between the thoughts of ability and folly.[130] If it is not the commonplace, still less is it the hasty prepossession, the whim or humor of the hour. Rather are we to identify it with that "strong and preponderant opinion" which has capacity at times to turn desire into law.[131] The common will must have made itself known for so long a time as well as in so distinct a manner as to have gained stability and authority.[132]

I do not underrate the blindness of the manuscript, the

need of circumspection in deciphering its characters, the manifold possibilities of error when every precept of caution has been formulated and followed. The task, however difficult, is here, and one must discharge it as one can. Legislators, confronted with a problem that differs in degree rather than in kind, solve or attempt to solve it day by day, with varying success, but at least with no thought to give it up at the beginning. Read such a book as the *Rise of American Civilization,* by Charles and Mary Beard, and see how the surge of social forces has (52) swept aside the little eddies of faction, the currents of party politics, or caught them in its larger movement.[133] Measures the most distinctive and important have taken form in obedience to a pressure that has overwhelmed the lines of sect or party; they are the emanation of a will which has become composite and impersonal. Not less clamorous at times is the summons to the courts to scan the scroll of life and announce their readings to the world.

In my discussion of the legal norms and of their gradual discovery and erection through the methods of the judicial process, I have isolated the quality of justice, and viewed it as if the search to understand and declare it were something singular and special. In truth the search is but a phase of a wider effort, a stage of a longer movement, a fragment of a larger whole. We read the quality of legal justice in the disclosures of the social mind. We read in the same book the values of all the social interests, moral, economic, educational, scientific, or aesthetic. A new science, the science of values or axiology is teaching students of social problems to read the book aright. A copious literature is already at their service. Such books as Bouglé's *Evolution of Values* (well translated by Mrs. Sellars), Perry's *General Theory of Value,* and Urban's *Valuation, Its Nature and Laws,* to name a few among many, are analyzing and explaining and classifying and grading the values that social man attaches or should attach to the conflicting and com (53) peting interests that enrich the fullness of his days.

Disagreement not unnaturally, there is here, as in almost every science, at least in early stages. So far as value is merely subjective, one finds it hard to dispute about it just as one does in respect of taste.[134] Even in its subjective aspect, however, it is shaped in large degree by the pressure of external forces. Value, when seemingly the most personal, is, at least in part, a social product, the product of collective life. Some writers there are, indeed, such as Durkheim and Bouglé, who ascribe the leading rôle at all times to the creative power of society, no matter how subjective at first sight the estimate of worth may seem. Society, in Bouglé's words, "is essentially creator of ideals." [135] "By its properties, by the peculiar forces which emerge from the assembling of men, are to be explained the characteristics of those great magnets which are called values." [136] "Judgments of value have for function to formulate, not the natural properties of things, but the desires of men living in society." [137] Other writers, though giving heed to the motive forces that are external, lay greater emphasis upon forces that are individual and personal.[138] On the other hand, when the value to be appraised is value objectively considered, and particularly when the question is one of the preference (54) to be given to diverse or competing values, the social element emerges everywhere to fuller recognition. "A subjective value," we are told by Urban,[139] "is said to be actual, to have objective grounds, when it is in some sense continuous with, or convertible into, the social value." He argues, it is true, that this is not a final test, yet he concedes that for the most part subjective worths that are real have capacity of substitution with worths that are social, may be translated into terms of social objectivity.[140] For Bouglé, the social element is even more insistent. "Values," he tells us, adopting Durkheim's thought, "values are objective because *imperative,* and imperative because *collective.*" [141]

There is significance in all this, it seems to me, for students of the judicial process. The judge who finds his moral value through his readings of the social mind, goes to the same source from which values generally are born, consults the same book that is spread open to us all. But a second point to be observed is this, that justice or moral value is only one value among many that must be appraised by the some method. Other values, not moral, values of expediency or of convenience or of economic or cultural advancement, a host of values that are not final, but merely means to others, are to be ascertained and assessed and equilibrated, the less sacrificed to the greater, all in subjection to like tests, the (55) thought and the will and the desires of society as the judge perceives and interprets them supplying the measure and the scale. The aim of the jurist, we are told by Pound, "at all times and in all the compromises and adjustments and reconciliations involved in the legal order" should be "to give effect to as much of the whole body of social interests as possible. . . . The compromises and adjustments that will achieve the largest security of social interests with the least sacrifice, must be sought through a process of trial and error." [142] In all this, one must beware of an axiology that is merely personal and subjective. A judge is to give effect in general not to his own scale of values, but to the scale of values revealed to him in his readings of the social mind. In particular he may not substitute his own reading for one established by the legislature, acting within constitutional limitations, through the pronouncements of a statute.[143] We may suspect that there have been times when statutes have been condemned as void under the influence of an axiology that failed in this objective quality. Many are the times, however, when there are no legislative pronouncements to give direction to a judge's reading of the book of life and manners. At those times, he must put himself as best he can within the heart and mind of others, and frame his estimate of values by the truth as thus revealed. Objective tests may fail him, or may be so (56) confused as to bewilder. He must then look within himself.[144]

I have spoken of the process as one of compromise between stability and motion. Like the Aristotelian mean between extremes, the path of compromise will not be found by figuring the mean proportional as in an exercise in mathematics.[145] If two extremes present themselves as possible solutions of any given controversy, we do not reach the true solution by rejecting both extremes as certainly unacceptable, and seeking a middle course. There will be many situations in which one of the extremes will mark the course to be selected. What has been spoken of as a compromise is perhaps more accurately described as a concordance. A choice is arrived at by a balancing of interests, an appraisal of their value with reference to jural ends. It is a choice, even then, not between stability and unrestrained motion, but between stability and motion moderated and tempered by the immemorial traditions of a professional technique; it is erosion, not avulsion.[146]

Thinkers have complained with justice of the lack (57) of any formula whereby preference can be determined when values are conflicting. There is no common denominator to which it is possible to reduce them. In general we may say that where conflict exists, moral values are to be preferred to economic, and economic to aesthetic. Yet casuistry will discover overlappings and exceptions. We build skyscrapers, though smaller dwellings might be safer for the builders. We run railroads, though lives might be saved if we were satisfied to travel slowly. We experiment with airplanes, though pilots run the risk of death. Yet even in these cases, indifference to moral values is not as clear as it may seem upon the surface. Moral or cultural gains, cultural in a large sense, are often indirectly served, or will be in the years to come. The skyscraper gives economic opportunity to many who without it might feel the pinch of want. The railroad brings foods and medi (58) cine and knowledge and many other forms of worth when worth would evaporate with delay. The airplane has possibilities so many that fancy cannot limit them. At all events a judge in his search for objective estimates of value is helpless to establish standards that will block the onward movement of civilization as civilization is conceived of at any given place or epoch. Individual predilections must yield to a social pressure so resistless. Bouglé, indeed, insists that there can be found in what he calls "polytelism,"[147] a reconciliation of apparent conflicts between one value and another. The same means has capacity to serve a multiplicity of ends.[148] In the present stage of the science of axiology, the picture may seem to have an over-roseate hue. Yet the judge, if he may not halt the march of civilization, may do something at times to moderate its pace, to mitigate its ruthless quality. The law will not prevent the erection of skyscrapers. It may call for safety devices that will reduce the toll of lives. The law will not prevent the operation of railroads. It may call for signals and watchmen, and may raise or depress the roadbed at the crossing of a highway. An adjustment may even be effected between economic and aesthetic values. The landowner will not be compelled to forego every profitable use of his land, but in some jurisdictions it is at least an open question whether a restriction may not be placed upon the (59) construction of unsightly signs.[149] Here as so often it is a question of degree. "The laws are silent amid arms." The decree of a court will not stay the clash of war, but it can halt the riot or the brawl or the brutal and debasing prize-fight.[150] Our function as judges is not to transform civilization, but to regulate and order it. The book of life changes, and the values revealed to us today may be different from those that will be revealed to us tomorrow.

I said not long ago that the choice to be made is not between stability and unrestrained motion, but between stability and motion moderated and tempered by the immemorial traditions of a professional technique. In the midst of these restraints the worker in the law is impressed ever and again with the wealth of weapons in the legal armory. Repeatedly, when one is hard beset, there are principles and precedents and analogies which may be pressed into the service of justice if one has the perceiving eye to use them. It is not unlike the divinations of the scientist. His experiments must be made significant by the flash of a luminous hypothesis. For the creative process in law, and indeed in science generally, has a kinship to the creative process in art. Imagination, whether you call it scientific or artistic, is for each the faculty that creates. There are the successive (60) stages of preparation, incubation and illumination described with so much insight by Graham Wallas in his analysis of the art of thought.[151] Learning is indeed necessary, but learning (to paraphrase what has been said of Keats) is the springboard by which imagination leaps to truth.[152] The law has its piercing intuitions, its tense, apocalyptic moments. We gather together our principles and precedents and analogies, even at times our fictions, and summon them to yield the energy that will best attain the jural end. If our wand has the divining touch, it will seldom knock in vain. So it is that the conclusion, however deliberate and labored, has often the aspect in the end of nothing but a lucky find.[153] "When I once asked the best administrator whom I knew," writes Mr. Wallas,[154] "how he formed his decisions, he laughed, and with the aid of letting out for the first time a guilty secret, said: 'Oh, I always decide by feeling. So and so always decides by calculation, and that is no good.' When, again, I asked an American judge, who is widely admired both for his skill and for his impartiality, how he and his fellows formed their conclusions, he also laughed, and said that he should be stoned in the street if it were known that, after listening with full consciousness to all the evidence, and following as carefully as he (61) could all the arguments, he waited until he 'felt' one way or the other." He had elided the preparation and the brooding, or at least had come to think of them as processes of faint kinship with the state of mind that followed. "When the conclusion is there," says William James,[155] "we have always forgotten most of the steps preceding its attainment."

One may think it strange that the material in the legal storehouse has a capacity so varied to combine and recombine in accordance with the forms of justice. The reason is not far to seek. A fruitful parent of injustice is the tyranny of concepts.[156] They are tyrants rather than servants when treated as real existences and developed with merciless disregard of consequences to the limit of their logic.[157] For the most part we should deal with them as provisional hypotheses to be reformulated and restrained when they have an outcome in oppression or injustice. But their empire, even when greatest, is never without limits. Here as elsewhere, tyranny breeds rebellion, and rebellion an emancipator. The concept, overgrown, and swollen with excess of power, is matched in the end by other concepts which put a curb on its pretensions. This interplay of concepts (62) has been developed with great clarity and power by Professor Dickinson of Princeton University in his recent book on *Administrative Justice and the Supremacy of Law in the United States.* "Almost every legal concept or principle," he writes,[158] "is found to be but the terminal of a scale which shades at its opposite extremity into another of exactly contrary tendency, and the line between the two oscillates from specific case to case according to the context. Thus the law of nuisance plays between the principle that every person is entitled to use his property for any purpose that he sees fit, and the opposing principle that every man is bound to use his property in such a manner as not to injure the property of his neighbor." Again the task of judging is found to be a choice between antithetical extremes. We seem to see the workings of an Hegelian philosophy of history whereby the tendency of every principle is to create its own antithesis or rival.[159]

Concepts are useful, indeed indispensable, if kept within their place. We will press them quite a distance. Many a time they will give rise to rules which might just as well be the opposite were it not that in giving adherence to the opposite we should mutilate the symmetry of the legal order, the relation of its parts, its logical coherence.[160] These are values deeply imbedded in our law and its philosophy. "If we have not identities to work upon, we have at least resemblances; (63) and on their basis can be constructed a legal system which, although far from attaining the inexorable and absolute certainty once thought possible, yet introduces a degree of beneficial order into a world that would be much worse without it." [161] A time comes, however, when the concepts carry us too far, or farther than we are ready to go with them, and behold, some other concept, with capacity to serve our needs, is waiting at the gate. "It is a peculiar virtue of our system of law,[162] that the process of inclusion and exclusion, so often employed in developing a rule is not allowed to end with its enunciation, and that an expression in an opinion yields later to the impact of facts unforeseen."

The impact may come from a new fact. It may come from a changing estimate of policy or justice, which is to say the same thing in other words, since the current thought as to such matters is as much a fact as any other. What was ruled or next to ruled was well enough often according to the wisdom of its day. The light of a new day has set it forth as folly. "The difficulty is," I quote Professor Dickinson again,[163] "that the contemporary view of public policy shifts with successive generations, and what was once the goal of policy ceases in time to be so." [164] We must look around then for some avenue of re (64) lease. "What is needed is not arbitrary discretion, but a rule for making exceptions—a rule for breaking a rule—and of such rules the law is of course full." [165] Sometimes the commitment to an outworn policy is too firm to be broken by the tools of the judicial process, at least without greater relaxation of the doctrine of *stare decisis* than has yet commended itself to judges.[166] This is why I have pleaded and still plead for a more intimate channel of connection between legislatures and courts, bodies which move today in stately isolation.[167] Even without this aid, much may still be done within the bounds of the traditional technique if only origins are thought of as subordinate to ends, and symmetry of formulas to symmetry of life.

There is nothing new in this notion of the subordination of legal concepts to expediency and justice, though as with many an old truth there is need to restate it now and again. What is new perhaps is the readiness to avow what has always been practiced, but practiced more or less intermittently, and at times with scant appreciation of the nature of the motive force.[168] Hesitant avowal has begotten conduct that is spasmodic and irregular: there has been a feeling, inarticulate to some extent, that the conduct was something to be deprecated, something calling for excuse. Instructive it is to observe the tri (65) umphs of the *mores* in the face of this resistance. Let me take such a concept as that of corporate personality. Holdsworth has some illuminating remarks upon the development of that concept in the history of English Law. He points out [169] that at first when the idea of a corporation was new, "the lawyers were inclined to lay more stress upon wide general deductions" from the concept corporation. "Thus they said that a corporation could not be seised to a use, either because a corporation had no conscience, or because the process of the court of Chancery could not issue against it, or because it had no capacity to take to another's use; and Blackstone stated that it could not be a trustee. Because it could hold only in its corporate capacity for the purpose of the corporation, it was said that a gift to a corporation and another person or another corporation jointly, would create, not a joint tenancy, but a tenancy in common; for in such a case the two co-owners held in different capacities." "No doubt," continues Holdsworth, "these were legitimate deductions from the vague and wide premises on which they were founded. But they were found to be inconvenient in practice. And so, on grounds of practical convenience, they have been evaded or altered. Equity, contrary to Blackstone's dictum, found no difficulty in ruling that a corporation could be trustee; and the legislature has recently enabled a corporation to hold jointly with another person or corporation. In (66) fact, though these wide deductions drawn from the nature of corporate personality have called attention to salient incapacities of corporations as compared with natural persons, they have never been able to stand any severe strain. Practical convenience rather than theoretical considerations have, from the days of the Year Books onward, determined what activities are possible, and what are impossible to a corporation." There was fresh example of this truth when a metaphysical theory of corporate personality was found to be in conflict with the necessities of war. A corporation organized in England and subject to its law, but controlled by German shareholders, was held to be an enemy alien, when the question to be determined was its capacity to trade, though its metaphysical spirit was as English as any spirit could well be.[170] "The limited liability," said Lord Halsbury,[171] "was a very useful introduction into our system, and there was no reason why foreigners should not, while dealing honestly with us, partake of the benefit of that institution; but it seems to me too monstrous to suppose that for an unlawful (because, after the declaration of war, a hostile) purpose the forms of that institution should be used and enemies of the state while actually at war with us should be allowed to continue trading and actually to sue for their profits of trade in any English Court of Justice."

REFERENCES

70. Cardozo, *Growth of the Law,* p. 87.
71. Stammler, *op. cit.,* pp. 40, 54, 58.
72. P. 55.
73. *Principles of Ethics,* part ii, "Justice," sec. 246.
74. *Principles of Morals and Legislation,* ch. x, sec. 2.
75. Moore, *Ethics,* Home University Library; A. K. Rogers, *English and American Philosophy Since 1800,* p. 143.
76. Dewey and Tufts, *Ethics,* pp. 237, 238.
77. Ogden's Translations, *The Philosophy of As If,* p. xli.
78. Birkenhead, *Fourteen English Judges,* p. 53.
79. Edgerton, "Negligence, Inadvertence and Indifference," 39 *Harv. L. R.* 849.
80. See *e.g.,* "Director of Public Prosecutions v. Beard," 1920, A. C. 479; Holdsworth, *op. cit.,* vol. 8, p. 443.
81. One will find a useful summary of Stammler's thought in Hocking, *Law and Rights.*
82. *Cf.* Kaufmann, "Der Kritik der Neukantischen Rechtsphilosophie," pp. 11, 16, *Tübingen,* 1921.
83. Lévy-Bruhl, *La Morale et la Science des Moeurs;* Hobhouse, *Morals in Evolution; cf.,* Demogue, *op. cit.,* 7 Modern Legal Phil. Series, pp. 376, 378.
84. *Op. cit.,* p. 197.
85. P. 213.
86. P. 151.
87. Dewey, *Human Nature and Conduct.*
88. Cardozo, *The Growth of the Law,* p. 86.
89. Hobhouse, *Morals in Evolution,* p. 554; Archibald Alexander, *A Short*

History of Philosophy, p. 57; Plato, *The Republic,* Book iv, sec. 443 (p. 149, Golden Treasury ed.).

90. *Cf.* Cohen, "Positivism and the Limits of Idealism in the Law," 27 *Col. L. R.* 237, 240.

91. Vinogradoff, *Historical Jurisprudence,* vol. ii, p. 63; Aristotle, *Nicomachean Ethics,* Everyman's ed., pp. 126, 127.

92. Vinogradoff, *op. cit.,* p. 63.

93. *Nichomachean Ethics,* Bk. viii, Everyman's ed., p. 183; *cf.* p. 197.

94. *Principles of Ethics,* part ii, "Justice," sec. 272; *cf.* Small, *General Sociology,* p. 603. For other definitions, see Demogue, *Analysis of Fundamental Notions,* vol. 7, Modern Legal Philosophy Series, pp. 481, 482, 483, 493, 494; Cardozo, *The Growth of the Law,* pp. 86, 87.

95. *Op. cit.,* pp. 94, 193.

96. Haines, "The Law of Natuie in Federal Decisions," 25 *Yale Law Journal* 617. For a recent illustration, see Yome v. Gorman, 1926, 242 N. Y. 396, 402, 404.

97. *Cf.* Dewey and Tufts, *Ethics,* p. 415.

98. F. N. Bk. v. Carnegie Trust Co., 1915, 213 N. Y. 301, 306; Mt. Morris Bank v. 23rd Ward Bank, 1902, 172 N. Y. 244.

99. Pomeroy. *Equity Jurisprudence,* sec. 953.

100. Depue v. Flatau, 100 Minn. 299; Ploff v. Putnam, 81 Vt. 471; Vincent v. Lake Erie Transp. Co., 109 Minn. 456; Bohlen, "Incomplete Privilege to Commit Intention Invasions of Property and Personality," 39 *Harvard L. R.* 301.

101. Schuyler v. Smith, 1873, 51 N. Y. 309.

102. Herter v. Mullen, 1899, 159 N. Y. 28.

103. *Cf* Jhering, *The Struggle for Law,* Lalor's translation, p. 81.

104. Stammler, *op. cit.,* p. 300.

105. *Cf.* Pound, *Law and Morals,* p. 111; Duguit, *Traité de Droit Constitutionnel,* vol. i, pp. 36, 41; Cardozo, *Growth of the Law,* p. 49.

106. Korkunov, *General Theory of Law,* p. 61; Pound, *Law and Morals,* p. 110.

107. The thought is happily expressed by Street, *Foundation of Legal Liability,* vol. i, p. 499: "Development there must be. But it cannot take place by leaps and bounds. There must be no ellipsis of any intermediate process. In the course of legal growth older principles are transcended, but this must take place by steps so natural and inevitable as to be in a measure unconscious."

108. P. 616.

109. Everyman's edition, p. 46.

110. Cardozo, *The Growth of the Law,* p. 77; *cf.* Int. Prod. Co. v. Erie R. R. Co., 1927, 244 N. Y. 331.

111. R. R. Co. v. Stout, 17 Wall. 657; U. P. R. Co. v. McDonald, 152 U. S. 262; Glasgow Corp. v. Taylor, 1922, A. C. 1; Perry v. Rochester Line Co., 1916, 219 N. Y. 60, 65; *contra,* Walsh v. Fitchburgh R. R. Co., 1895, 145 N. Y. 301; and *cf.* United Zinc & Capital Co. v. Britt, 1922, 258 U. S. 268.

112. Rice v. Butler, 1899, 160 N. Y. 578; Myers v. Hurley Motor Co., 1927, 273 U. S. 18; *contra,* McCarthy v. Henderson, 138 Mass. 310.

113. Pompana v. N. Y. Ry. Co., 66 Conn. 538, 539; Glasgow Corp. v. Taylor, 1922, A. C. 1; Shearman and Redfield, *Negligence,* 6th ed., sec. 706.

114. See, *e.g.,* Buckley v. Mayor, 30 App. Div. 463; 1899, 159 N. Y. 558.

115. Phelps v. Nowlen, 1878, 72 N. Y. 39.

116. Rideout v. Knox, 148 Mass. 368.

117. *Ante,* p. 14; *cf.* Exchange Bakery v. Rifpin, 1927, 245 N. Y. 260, 263.

118. *Op. cit.,* p. 253.

119. Lefroy, "The Basis of Case Law," 22 *Law Quart. Rev.* 293, 302, 303.

120. P. 68.

121. *Cf.* Duguit, *Traité de Droit Constitutionnel,* vol. 1, p. 361.

122. Vinogradoff, *op. cit.,* p. 21.

123. Cooley, *Social Organization;* Maitland, Introduction to Gierke's *Political Theory of the Middle Age,* xviii; *cf.* Hocking, *Man and the State,* p. 351; Borchard, "Government Responsibility in Tort," 36 *Yale L. J.* 757, 774.

124. Perry, *General Theory of Value,* pp. 461, 462, 465, 467; MacIver, *The Modern State,* pp. 449, 452, 474; Laski, *Grammar of Politics,* p. 32; Hobhouse, *Social Evolution and Political Theory,* p. 87; Giddings, *The Principles of Sociology,* p. 132.

125. Lippmann, "Public Opinion," "Liberty and the News," "The Phantom Public," *passim.*

126. *Cf.* Cardozo, *The Nature of the Judicial Process,* pp. 108–111.

127. Lippmann, *The Phantom Public,* p. 77; *cf.* pp. 168, 198; Hobhouse, *supra;* also Dewey, *The Public and Its Problems,* pp. 116, 117, 123, 126, 177; and Lowell, *Public Opinion and Popular Government,* pp. 13, 15; C. H. Cooley, *Social Organizations,* p. 121.

128. Giddings, *Inductive Sociology,* quoted by Barnes, *Sociology and Political Theory,* p. 202.

129. Cooley, *op. cit.,* p. 124; Hobhouse, *supra.*

130. "Quid turpius quam sapientis vitam ex insipientium sermone pendere?" Cicero, *De Finibus,* Book II, xv (Loeb's *Classical Library,* p. 138).

131. Holmes, J., in Noble State Bank v. Haskell, 219 U. S. 104.

132. *Cf.,* W. H. Taft, *Popular Government,* quoted by Dickinson, *Administrative Justice and the Supremacy of Law in the United States,* p. 103; also Lowell, *op. cit., pp.* 13, 15, 24, 46.

133. Beard, *Rise of American Civilization,* vol. 2, p. 589.

134. Perry, *op. cit.,* sec. 12.

135. Bouglé's *Evolution of Values,* Sellars' translation, p. 16.

136. Bouglé, *op. cit.,* p. 16.

137. Bouglé, *op. cit.,* p. 147.

138. Urban, *op. cit.;* Perry, *op. cit.*

139. *Op. cit.,* p. 388.

140. P. 408.

141. Bouglé, *op. cit.,* p. 16.

142. Pound, article "Jurisprudence," in the *History and Prospects of the Social Sciences,* by Harry Elmer Barnes and others, p. 472.

143. *Cf.* Cardozo, *The Growth of the Law,* p. 94.

144. Cardozo, *The Nature of the Judicial Process,* p. 110; Brütt, *Die Kunst der Rechtsanwendund,* pp. 101, 139.

145. *Cf.* Givler, "Ethics," in the *History and Prospects of the Social Sciences,* by Harry Elmer Barnes and others, p. 487; Aristotle, *Nicomachean Ethics,* Book vi, Everyman's ed., p. 130.

146. "In thus showing that judges do and must make law, I do not, of course, wish to maintain that they are in no wise bound and can make any law they please. Every one who is engaged in making or creating something is limited by the rules of the process and the nature of the material."—M. R. Cohen, "Legal Theories and Social Science," *The International Journal of Ethics,* July, 1915, pp. 476, 477.

We may say of law what Royce says of philosophy: "Our common dependence upon the history of thought for all our reflective undertakings is unquestionable. Our best originality, if we ever get any originality, must spring from this very dependence. Doctrines of genuinely revolutionary significance are rare indeed in the history of speculation, and they ought to be. Of lesser surprises, of marvels, of beautifully novel insights, all the greater highways of speculation are full; and yet even most of the marvels are only such in so far as they are set off upon a very large background of the historically familiar. Only a very few times in the history of thought is the continuity of the evolution distinctly broken. The novelties are elsewhere only relative, and get their very value from the fact that they are so."—Royce, *The Spirit of Modern Philosophy,* Preface, p. vii.

147. *Op. cit.,* p. 84.

148. Pp. 84, 257.

149. See, however, Peo. *ex rel.* Wineburgh Adv. Co. v. Murphy, 1909, 195 N. Y. 126; and *cf.* Matter of Wulfsohn v. Burden, 1925, 241 N. Y. 288, 300, and Welch v. Swasey, 1909, 214 U. S. 91, 108; Baker, "Municipal Aesthetics in the Law," *Ill. Law Rev.,* February, 1926.

150. *In re* Deb., 1895, 158 U. S. 564.

151. Wallas, *The Art of Thought*, pp. 80, 82, 94, 96.
152. Lowell's *Life of Keats*, vol. 1, p. 477; *cf.* Wallas, *op. cit.*, p. 124.
153. *Cf.* Cardozo, *The Growth of the Law*, pp. 92, 93.
154. *Op. cit.*, p. 119.
155. *Principles of Psychology*, vol. 1, p. 260, quoted by Wallas, *op. cit.*, p. 96.
156. Dickinson, *Administrative Justice and the Supremacy of Law in the United States*, p. 128; Cardozo, *Growth of the Law*, p. 100; Pound, *Interpretations of Legal History*, p. 119, *cf.* Hynes v. N. Y. Central R. R. Co., 1921, 231 N. Y. 229.
157. *Cf.* Taine's definition of the classic spirit in *L'Ancien Regime*, p. 262, quoted by Wallas, p. 175.
158. P. 135.
159. Royce, *The Spirit of Modern Philosophy*, Hegel, pp. 212, 213.
160. Dickinson, *op. cit.*, pp. 113, 119, 131, 141.
161. Dickinson, *op. cit.*, p. 131.
162. Brandeis, J., dissenting in Jaybird Mining Co. v. Weir, 1926, 271 U. S. 609.
163. *Op. cit.*, p. 131.
164. *Cf.* Brütt, *Die Kunst der Rechtsanwendung*, p. 183.
165. Dickinson, *op. cit.*, p. 139.
166. *Cf.* Wigmore, *Problems of Law*, pp. 79, 80.
167. "A Ministry of Justice," 35 *Harv. L. R.* 113.
168. Holmes, *The Common Law*, p. 1.
169. Holdsworth, *History of English Law*, vol. 9, pp. 51, 52.
170. Daimler Co. v. Continental Tyre Co., 1916, 2 A. C. 307.
171. P. 316.

(67)

—III —

The Equilibration of Interests—Cause and Effect—The Individual and Society—Liberty and Government.

I WOULD not seem to exaggerate the limits of fluidity either actual or desirable. The play of imagination upon the material in the legal store-room does not always evoke the spirit of change. There are times when it will yield the answer that rest should be preferred to motion. Fields there are in the domain of law where fundamental conceptions have been developed to their uttermost conclusions by the organon of logic. One finds this method of decision in much of the law of bills and notes. One finds it again in the law of real estate, though the presuppositions of the concepts, their logical implications, are not understandable unless the concepts are interpreted in the revealing light of history. One finds it again in one of the most baffling subjects of legal science, the so-called *Conflict of Law*. We deal there with the application of law in space. The walls of the compartments must be firm, the lines of demarcation plain, or there will be overlappings and encroachments with incongruities and clashes. In such circumstances, the finality of the rule is in itself a jural end. I do not mean that even in this sphere the (68) judge who seeks to reach the heart of a concept, its inmost implications, may not find, when he has gained the core, that the concept is one with policy and justice. All this may be true, yet when I view the subject as a whole, I find logic to have been more remorseless here, more blind to final causes, than it has been in other fields. Very likely it has been too remorseless. If it has, that is beside my present point, which is not criticism, but description. I survey the legal scene, and report what I discover.

The tendency of principle and rule to conform to moral standards, which is a true avenue of growth for law, is not to be confounded with the suspension of all principle and rule and the substitution of sentiment or unregulated benevolence, which, pushed to an extreme, is the negation

of all law. Every system of law has within it artificial devices which are deemed in the main and on the average to promote convenience or security or other forms of public good. These devices take the shape of rules or standards to which the individual though he be careless or ignorant, must at his peril conform. If they were to be abandoned by the law whenever they had been disregarded by the litigant affected, there would be no sense in making them. The individual must subscribe his will, and acknowledge its execution in the presence of witnesses. The gift *inter vivos* must be consummated by delivery, and will fail if it rest in mere executory in-
(69) tention.[172] The purchase by an infant of something not a necessity will be voidable though the infant is close to man's estate. The suit will fail unless begun with the term prescribed by law, though it be postponed but a day beyond. This does not mean that pressure is not exerted even in such cases to soften the rigor of undeviating conformity. At times the pressure is so great that courts have felt unable to withstand it. Witness the more or less insincere pretexts by which courts of equity avoid at times the enforcement of the statute of frauds upon some theory of part performance or of the breach of a constructive trust. This instance is the more noteworthy because there the court has struggled against the compulsion of a statute. The fact remains, however, that law, like social institutions generally, attains its aim as a device for promoting order and reducing waste at the price of occasional hardship when its mandate is disregarded or forgotten.[173] This without more does not defeat its binding force. There may be some clearing and pruning even then. There will be no tearing up of roots. The time may come, however, when hardship is so acute and general that the good of the device, submerged in the evil, is forgotten and invisible. The rule survives, if at all, as
(70) nothing more than a vestigial relic.[174] When this stage arrives, its days of life are numbered.

Two cases recently determined in my own court will illustrate my thought. The rule was settled at common law that an undisclosed principal might not be held to liability upon a contract which had been executed under seal. Much of the law as to seals has small relation in society as now organized to present-day realities. The question came up whether we would adhere to the rule that I have mentioned, or hold it to have faded away with the fading significance of seals. The decision was that the old rule would be enforced.[175] Precedents of recent date made departure difficult if *stare decisis* was not to be abandoned altogether, but there were other and deeper grounds of policy. Contracts had been made and transactions closed on the faith of the law as it had been theretofore declared. Men had taken title in the names of "dummies," and through them executed deeds and mortgages with the understanding, shared by the covenantees, that liability on the covenant would be confined to the apparent principal. They had done this honestly and without concealment. Something might be said, too, in favor of the social utility of a device by which the liability of the apparent principal could be substituted without elaborate forms for the liability of another back of him who was to reap the profits of the transaction. The law has like devices for limiting liability in other (71) situations, as, *e.g.*, in joint stock associations, corporations, and limited partnerships. In any event retrospective change would be unjust. The evil, if it was one, was to be eradicated by statute.

Not long after, there came another case in which the ancient law of seals was again the controlling factor.[176] The question then was whether we would adhere to the old rule that a parol contract was ineffective to modify a contract under seal. We had already abandoned this rule where the later contract, though parol, had been followed by performance. We had even intimated that it ought to be abandoned though the later contract was executory.[177] There was authority for such a holding in other jurisdictions.[178] When the question came before us squarely, we held the other way, though by a closely divided vote. I do not challenge the learning and power of the majority opinion. There is no gainsaying its conclusion if the judicial function is merely static. What seemed to be a division as to the law was in truth a difference of philosophy. Conceiving the judicial function as dynamic, I am still impressed with the conviction that there was here a fitting opportunity to uproot an ancient evil. It is safe to say that the later contract was not signed in the belief that the omission of a seal had reduced it to an empty form. If there was any such reservation in the mind of one of the signers, he was dealing unfairly (72) by the other signer when he made delivery of the instrument as of something authentic and effective. But the truth is, of course, that he had no such reservation. The suggestion that there was need of a seal was transparently an afterthought, a pretext for the avoidance of a burdensome engagement. The displacement of the ancient rule would have done violence to no interest that was worthy of protection. It would have kept the movement of the law in pace with the movement of events. The displacement would not even have been attended by the shock of surprise, for earlier decisions had shown forth the absurdity of the rule and predicted in guarded terms that it would soon be decently interred with all the rites appropriate to venerable but departed dogma. Here, I venture to believe, is a situation in which stability was unwisely chosen to the sacrifice of progress. Let us hope that through the aid of statute a better justice will prevail.

In problems such as these, the need is fairly obvious for a balancing of social interests and a choice proportioned to the value. One is surprised at every turn to find that the same need is present, lurking beneath the surface, when other processes and methods, at least upon a hasty view, might seem predominant or perhaps exclusive. Take such a legal concept as the familiar one of negligence. Involved at every turn is the equilibrium of social interests, moral and economic. Negligence as a term of legal art is, strictly speaking, misnomer, for negligence (73) connotes to the ordinary man the notion of lack of care, and yet one can be negligent in the view of the law though one has taken what one has supposed to be extraordinary care, and not negligent though one has taken no care at all.[179] Moreover, one can deliberately choose to be indifferent to the greatest peril, and yet avoid the charge of negligence for all one's scorn of prudence.[180]

Two factors, both social, contribute to the paradox. The first is the conception of the "reasonable man," the man who conforms in conduct to the common standards of society. If the individual falls short of the standards of the group, he does so at his peril. He must then answer for his negligence though his attention never flagged. Enough that a reasonable man would have appreciated the peril which because of stupidity or ignorance may have been hidden to the actor. The standard may be different for infants. It may be different also for those whose ignorance or stupidity is carried to such a point as to put them in the class of the abnormal,—the insane or the defective—though as to this the law is still unsettled.[181] On the other hand, if one acts at one's peril when one falls below the common (74) standard, one may have protection at the other extreme; one may not need to go beyond it. There may be occasions when an individual charged with negligence has taken no care at all or at all events very little, and yet by luck has conformed in overt act to the standard of conduct exacted of the diligent. In such a case, his mere subjective delinquency, the mere negligence of his thought, will not avail without more to put liability upon him.[182] Very likely the law has not been wholly consistent in their field any more than it has been in others. The standard of common care as measured by the conduct of a reasonable man is at times the expression of a minimum of duty rather than a maximum. If the individual has special skill or opportunities for knowledge, he may be required to do whatever a reasonable man would do if equally favored by nature and occasion.[183] By and large, however, with whatever allowance may be made for deviation or exception, the test of liability is external and objective.

There is, however, a second factor that contributes to the paradox. I may call it the calculus of interests. The measure of care imputed to that standardized being, the reasonable man, is one dependent upon the value of the interests involved. As to this I have learned much from Professor Bohlen, a great master of the law of Torts. The law measures the risks that a man may legitimately take by measuring the value (75) of the interests furthered by his conduct. I may accumulate explosives for the purpose of doing some work of construction that is important for mankind when I should be culpably reckless in accumulating them for pleasure or caprice. I may risk my life by plunging into turbulent ocean to save a drowning man when I should be culpably reckless if I were to make the plunge for sport or mere bravado. Inquiries that seem at the first glance the most simple and unitary—was this or that conduct negligent or the opposite? —turn out in the end to be multiple and complex. Back of the answers is a measurement of interests, a balancing of values, an appeal to the experience and sentiments and moral and economic judgments of the community, the group, the trade. Of course, some of these valuations become standardized with the lapse of years, and thus instantaneous or, as it were, intuitive. We know at once that it is negligence to drive at breakneck pace through a crowded street, with children playing in the centre, at least where the motive of the drive is the mere pleasure of the race. On the other hand, a judgment even so obvious as this yields quickly to the pressure of new facts with new social implications. We assign a different value to the movement of the fire engine or the ambulance. Constant and inevitable, even when half concealed, is the relation between the legality of the act and its value to society. We are balancing and compromising and adjusting every moment that we judge.

(76) The endless variety of the process is indeed a source of never-ceasing wonder. One would suppose after all these centuries of judging that the frontier would have vanished, that there would no longer be unsettled soil, no longer nebulae and star dust, but only peopled worlds. Yet in truth it is not so. There are topics where the law is still unformed and void. Some hint or premonition of coming shapes and moulds, it betrays amid the flux, yet it is so amorphous, so indeterminate, that formulation, if attempted, would be the prophecy of what is to be rather than the statement of what is. Matter, in Spencer's famous, if obsolete, definition of the process of evolution, "passes from an indefinite, incoherent homogeneity to a definite, coherent heretogeneity." So it is with the growth of law. Every topic is coherent with reference to some incoherence that is past, and incoherent with reference to some coherence yet to be. I am struck by this, from day to day, in the course of my judicial work. I am struck by it again when following the work of the American Law Institute in the restatement of the law. One cannot have a part, however humble, in the execution of that project without a mounting sense of wonder that with all our centuries of common law development, with all our multitudinous courts and still more multitudinous decisions, there are so many questions, elementary in the sense of being primary and basic, that remain unsettled even now. If they were propounded to you (77) suddenly, you would say that of course there must be authorities in abundance for anything so fundamental. You might feel some pricks of conscience at your own ignorance in being unable to repeat the proper answer out of hand. You would have

your self-respect restored in some degree if you came to survey the field, and found that the answer, if there was any, was at best uncertain and obscure. I have noticed this particularly in connection with the law of torts. Rights and privileges at the root, it would seem, of life in civilized society, are discovered to be involved in doubt. One wonders how one has attained maturity without getting oneself in trouble when one has been so uncertain all along of the things that one might do in affairs of primary concern. Take such fundamental privileges or claims of privilege as these—the privilege to employ force against another who threatens one with bodily harm; the privilege to employ force to effect a recaption of chattels taken from one's custody; the privilege to employ force to effect an entry upon land. It is astonishing how obscure and confused are the pronouncements upon these fundamental claims of right. What is certain is that the gaps in the system will be filled, and filled with ever-growing consciousness of the implications of the process, by a balancing of social interests, an estimate of social values, a reading of the social mind.

I have no thought to underrate the tribulations of the process. They have been known these many years. (78) From the press of Cambridge University there has come of recent days a translation by an English scholar [184] of the manual of Roman Law known as the Ecloga. Leo III and Constantine V, Roman Emperors, published it at Constantinople in 726. They ordered a group of scholars to render into Greek parts of the Institutes, the Digests, the Code and the Novels of "the great Justinian," improving his commands, however, "in the direction of humanity." To the judges of the empire and to all who aspired to judicial office, the Emperors said this: "Let those, and those only, who participate in sense and reason, and know clearly what true justice is, exercise straight vision in their judgments, and without passion apportion to each his deserts." Perhaps with all my talk about the compromise between antithetical extremes, I have not improved a great deal upon this formula of the Byzantine Emperors, though 1200 years have passed between their effort and my own.

I suspect that the Emperors found it easier to give their advice than the judges did to follow it. Certain it is, at all events, that the contrast between exhortation and obedience has not lessened with the years. I question whether many of you appreciate the misgivings that afflict a judge's mind when he has done the best he can, and handed down his judgment to be enshrined in the reports. Some, of course, are blessed with a spirit more robust. In a memoir (79) of the Earl of Halsbury, Lord Birkenhead speaks of "his stubborn and unconquerable pertinacity of view alike in the legal and political fields." "I do not recall," says his biographer, "that he ever admitted that he had been wrong in either. Nor do I believe that he ever thought so." [185] My acquaintance with judges inclines me to the view that such self-sufficiency is rare, though perhaps to some extent I am jumping to the conclusion that they survey the scene of life through lenses of the same power that are fitted to my eyes. Yet the travail with all its pangs is not peculiar to the bench. The worker in other fields of intellectual effort shares it with the judge. I pick up at random a book by a philosopher and man of letters. It tells of his perturbed and unhappy state of mind when he goes over his old writings.[186] He is tempted, he says, to change them in new editions, and then he argues, that, if he does, some of his readers may prefer the first edition to the second, and perhaps, living a decade longer, he may come to a like preference himself. That is my state of mind, and there is my consolation. I go over the old opinions, and wonder whether they are right, and then I say to myself that if I had written the other way, I should be just as doubtful as before. I suppose the defeated counsel will be a little less philosophical about the matter than I have tried to be, and will wish that I had hazarded the experiment of a change, but then I (80) reflect that his adversary would wish otherwise, and so the *chose jugée* abides. I see no remedy for such agonies, though men have sought for it these many years. Bertrand Russell reminds us in his paper on "Mathematics and Metaphysics," [187] that "two hundred years ago, the philosopher Leibnitz conceived a plan for an art of formal reasoning from which he hoped for a solution of all problems and an end to all disputes. If controversies arose, there would be no more need of disputation between two philosophers than between two accountants, for it would suffice for them to take their pens in their hands, sit down at their tables, and say to each other, let us calculate." If only Leibnitz's dream could be realized in the law! In the meanwhile, we must be content to stumble along the path, and offer up thanksgiving that we have not fallen into the pit.

I have spoken of the misgivings that afflict a judge's mind. Yet I would not leave you with the impression that inevitably and always they survive the declaration of the judgment. The curious thing is that sometimes in the hardest cases, in cases where the misgivings have been greatest at the beginning, they are finally extinguished, and extinguished most completely. I have gone through periods of uncertainty so great, that I have sometimes said to myself, "I shall never be able to vote in this case either one way or the other." Then, suddenly the fog has lifted. I have reached a stage of mental peace. I know (81) in a vague way that there is doubt whether my conclusion is right. I must needs admit the doubt in view of the travail that I suffered before landing at the haven. I cannot quarrel with any one who refuses to go along with me; and yet, for me, however it may be for others, the judgment reached with so much pain has become the only possible conclusion, the antecedent doubts merged, and finally extinguished, in the calmness of conviction. I have little question that these recurrent stages of agitation and serenity are the common experience of other toilers in fields of intellectual effort. All the more precious is the final peace for the storm that went before it. A highly developed machine has been turned over to our keeping, a machine with intricate cogs and weights and balances, the work of many minds. Small wonder that we lie awake at nights in fear that some new apprentice, who was supposed to lubricate the joints, may turn out in the end to be either a bungler or an enemy, and set the whole appliance out of gear.

As we take leave of the antithesis of rest and motion and its solution in law, our dominant impression must be one of compromise, of adjustment, of a pragmatic adaptation of means to ends, of the relativity of legal truths. The same principle of relativity is at the root of the treatment in law of another age-long antithesis, the antithesis of cause and effect. The law has its problems of causation. It must trace events to causes, or say with Hume that there is no cause, but only juxta-position or succession. (82) If it recognizes causation, as it does, it must determine which antecedent shall be deemed to be the jural cause, the antecedent to be selected from an infinite series of antecedents as big with the event. We are told very often that the law concerns itself with proximate causes and no others. The statement is almost meaningless, or rather, to the extent that on the surface it has meaning, it is far away from truth. Sometimes in the search for the jural cause, the law stops close to the event, but sometimes and often, it goes many stages back. The principle of the relativity of causation tells us that its methods could not well be different. "Cause," says Lord Haldane in his book, *The Reign of Relativity*,[188] "is a very indefinite expression. Externality to the effect is of its essence, but its meaning is relative in all cases to the subject-matter. For the housemaid the cause of the fire is the match she lights and applies. For the physicist the cause of the fire is the conversion of potential into kinetic energy, through the combination of carbon atoms with those of oxygen and the formation of oxides in the shape of gases which become progressively oxidized. For the judge who is trying a case of arson it is the wicked action of the prisoner in the dock. In each case there is a different field of inquiry, determined from a different standpoint. But no such field is even approximately exhaustive. The complete cause, if it could be found, would extend to the entire ground of the phenomenon (83) that had to be explained, and this ground would reach, not only to the whole of the world, but the entirety of the universe. More than this: if the ground could be completely stated it would be indistinguishable from the effect itself, including, as it would do, the whole of the conditions of existence. Thus we see that when we speak of the cause of an event we are only picking out what is relevant to the standpoint of a special inquiry, and is determined in its scope by the particular concept which our purpose makes us have in view."[189]

Here is the key to the juridical treatment of the problems of causation. We pick out the cause which in our judgment ought to be treated as the dominant one with reference, not merely to the event itself, but to the jural consequences that ought to attach to the event. There is an opinion by Lord Shaw in the English House of Lords in which he refers to the common figure of speech whereby a succession of causes is represented as a chain. He reminds us that the figure, though convenient, is inadequate. "Causation," he says, "is not a chain, but a net. At each point, influences, forces, events, precedent and simultaneous meet, and the radiation from each point extends infinitely." [190] From this complex web the law picks out now this cause and now that one. Thus the same event may have one jural cause when it is considered as giving rise to a cause of action upon (84) contract, and another when it is considered as giving rise to a cause of action for a tort. The law accepts or rejects one or another as it measures its own ends and the social benefits or evils of rejection or acceptance.

A case will point my meaning. A fire occurred at Big Tom, New Jersey. The fire exploded dynamite. The explosion by its vibrations caused damage to a vessel standing out in the river half a mile away. A policy of insurance secured the owner of the vessel against loss proximately caused by fire. The court assumed that by the law in most jurisdictions the fire would be the jural cause if the action were in tort against a wrongdoer who had negligently spread the flames. Indisputably it would if he had acted with intent to cause the very damage that resulted. On the other hand, the court refused to find that the fire was the jural cause within the meaning of the contract.[191]

The reasoning that led to this conclusion is in close approach to Lord Haldane's, though rendition of the judgment preceded by some years the publication of his book. "In last analysis," we said, "it is something in the minds of men, in the will of the contracting parties, and not merely in the physical bond of union between events, which solves, at least for the jurist, this problem of causation. In all this, there is nothing anomalous. Everything in nature is cause and effect by turns. For the physicist, one thing is the cause; for the jurist, another. Even for the jurist, (85) the same cause is alternately proximate and remote as the parties choose to view it. A policy provides that the insurer shall not be liable for damage caused by the explosion of a boiler. The explosion causes a fire. If it were not for the exception in the policy, the fire would be the proximate cause of the loss and the explosion the remote one. By force of the contract, the explosion becomes proximate.[192] A collision occurs at sea and fire supervenes. The fire may be the proximate cause and the collision the remote one for the purpose of an action on the policy. The collision remains proximate for the purpose of suit against the colliding vessel.[193] There is nothing absolute in the legal estimate of causation. Proximity and remoteness are relative and changing concepts." [194]

We see then why so much of the discussion of proximate cause in case and in commentary is mystifying and futile. There is a striving to give absolute validity to doctrines that must be conceived and stated in terms of relativity. No doubt, the tests propounded have value and significance. The difficulty in applying them, however, has its origin in the failure to remember that they are in truth, not tests, but clews. They help to guide the judgment in laying emphasis upon one cause or another among the many (86) that are secreted in the tangles of the web.[195] I find the same idea prefigured in an illuminating discussion by Professor Edgerton of the meaning of legal cause. I do not say that I would follow him in all his conclusions as to the relative function of judge and jury. For present purposes it is enough to mark the discernment and understanding with which he penetrates to the heart and essence of the problem. "A legal cause," he says, [196] "is a justly-attachable cause; (or) a legal consequence is a justly-attachable consequence; (or) a legal cause is a cause which stands in such a relation to its consequence that it is just to give legal effect to the relation; meaning by 'just,' not merely fair as between the parties, but socially advantageous, as serving the most important of the competing individual and social interests involved." [197] The truth which the law seeks in tracing events to causes is truth pragmatically envisaged, truth relative to jural ends.

From rest and motion, cause and effect, I pass to other opposites, the one and the many, the individual and the group, the group and the community, liberty and government.

The individual person is the atom in the social structure. The atom does not exist in isolation. It (87) combines with other atoms in response to a persistent instinct. The force or tendency by which the individual is moved to associate with others is known by the name of syngenism.[198] To syngenism, we owe the group in all its phases, at the lowest range the family, at the uppermost the state. The group is not a constant quantity. It is subject to Protean changes. We have, along with others the clan, the church, the club, the guild, each evoking loyalties, but loyalties varying in intensity at different times and places. There are attractions and repulsions between one individual and another, between individuals and groups, and finally between groups themselves. Energies must be released and energies must be curbed. The reconciliation of these opposites is one of the outstanding problems of the law; it is the problem of liberty and government.

The state exists to subordinate to law, and thereby to order and coherence, the rivalries and struggles of its component groups and individuals. It is thus, in the words of Small [199] "a union of disunions, a conciliation of conflicts, a harmony of discords. There is combination and there is severance; there is the setting of bonds and there is the loosening of bonds; there is conservation and there is change; there is a 'stereotyping principle' and there is an 'innovating principle'." [200] For every strophe an antistrophe. (88) The metronome of the law prescribes the interval between them.

One of the strange things about syngenism is that in creating the group, it recreates or modifies the individual. The individual in the group—in the trade union or the political party or the state—is not the same as the individual out of the group. His will has been transfigured by association with the wills of others. This does not mean that there is a mystical common will which belongs to the group as a person separate from its members. All that it means is that the wills of individuals like their habits and desires are modified by the interaction between mind and mind. The social mind is indeed the sum of the individual minds, but it is the sum of them when associated, and not their sum when dissevered. Thus interpreted Rousseau's *volonté générale* corresponds to a deep truth. Press it to greater lengths, and it is turned into a confusing fiction. This, I think, at least among Anglo-American students of the social sciences, is today the dominant conception of the mental life of groups. Thus Laski in his *Grammar of Politics:* [201] "Corporate personality and the will that it embodies, is real in the sense that it makes those upon whom it acts different from what they were before. But it remains different from the uniqueness which makes me separate from the rest of the universe. The unity of England is in the historic tradition which orientates a vast number of wills in a (89) similar direction; it is not in some mystic super-will built from their fusion." So Hobhouse in his *Social Evolution and Political Theory:*[202] "What has been said may be sufficient to show that when we speak of social thought, social will or, more generally, of social mind we neither imply a mystical psychic unity nor a fully achieved consciousness of the social life on the part of the component members of society. Such a consciousness is in fact a developed product of the social mind, but its presence is not to be assumed wherever the term 'social mind' is used. This term is simply an expression for the mass of ideas operative in a society, communicable from man to man, and serving to direct the thoughts and actions of individuals." And again,[203] "By the social mind, then, we mean not necessarily a unity pervading any given society as a whole, but a tissue of operative psychological forces which in their higher developments crystallize into unity within unity, and into organism operating upon organism. We mean something essentially of psychological character that arises from the operations of masses of men, and molds and is in turn remolded by the operation of masses of men; which has no existence except in the minds of men, and yet is never fully realized in the mind of any one man; which depends on the social relations between man and man, but takes full cognizance of the relation only in the higher stages of (90) its development." The same thought is happily stated by Dr. Seligman:[204] "Thus the group is neither an organism nor a phantom. It is an entity which, although composed of individuals, is not only abstractly but concretely distinct from the individuals concerned as non-group members. In short, although the group is created by individuals, it, in part at least, recreates the individual. It is the expression of the way in which separate wants are transmuted into common wants; it is the realization of the method by which the satisfactions of the individual become possible only through, and in unison with, the satisfactions of other individuals; it is the embodiment of the process by which the ever-present and ineradicable self-interest of human beings is slowly permeated by the broader feeling which in the finest individuals grows into loyalty and unselfishness."[205]

It would carry me too far afield if I were to consider at any length the character of the group as a juristic person, though the problem is not unrelated to the antitheses of the law, seeing that it is a phase of the eternal riddle of nominalism and realism, phenomenon and noumenon, appearance and reality. In Anglo-American Law, the so-called concession theory was long supposed to be the accepted doctrine. (91) The group as a juristic person does not come into being, according to this theory, until the state by appointed organs has declared that he shall live. "Corporate life and form," says Holdsworth,[206] "cannot exist without the permission of the state, express, presumed or implied." [207] There are indeed distinguished students of jurisprudence who are sponsors for an opposing theory.[208] The group in their view is a "real living thing," quite independent of any permission to exist as an incorporated person that may have been given by the state.[209] I may digress long enough to point out that this real living thing has made some curious breaches only lately in the doctrine held for orthodox. He has succeeded very recently in causing his existence to be recognized in advance of official declaration, though he has made his entrance upon the legal scene in a rather shame-faced sort of way, and, as it were, by the back door. The general rule may still be that corporate personality is a legislative gift rather than a (92) quality inherent in the very nature of a group. It seems, however, that at times even in our law a group has a solidarity so obvious as to evoke judicial recognition of its corporate or quasi-corporate existence, though no charter to act as a corporation has been either given or desired.[210] By the judgment of the Supreme Court of the United States in United Workers of America v. Coronado Coal Co., 259 U. S. 344, 385, 387, 388, an unincorporated trade union was held subject to suit as a *persona ficta*.[211] The summary pronouncement of the opinion would give scant notice to the uninformed that behind it lay an age-long controversy and a prolific legal literature. Our English brethren have gone farther. By a recent ruling of the Judicial Committee of the Privy Council,[212] a wooden idol worshipped in India as divine, was recognized as a *persona* in England, since it was so recognized in India. Accordingly lest its rights might be infringed, the judgment was reversed, and a guardian was appointed to represent the sacred effigy. Here the quality of personality was attributed not to a man or an aggregate of men, but to a thing confessedly inanimate. Analogies may be found in the corporate personality of the *fiscus* long familiar to European law,[213] and again in the personality of (93) the "Stiftung" or foundation.[214] A remote analogy may be found in the recognition of foreign corporations as persons, capable, under many decisions, of suing and being sued in our courts, if such capacity is theirs in the jurisdiction of the domicile. There is no occasion at this time to approve or to condemn these extensions of the notion of corporate personality. Some can be explained as instances of the application of "comity" or some principle akin thereto in accordance with established doctrines of private international law.[215] Others suggest a developing *rapprochement* between jurisprudence and sociology in the decisions of our courts. We are taking over social concepts and setting the imprimatur of the law upon them.

I put aside, however, for the time as foreign to my major theme the fascinating subject of the reality of corporate personality. Reality at least there is in the sense that among the phenomena of society are groups, not haphazard and occasional, but persistent and pervasive, which change the needs and the interests of the individuals within them. The law could not ignore this if it would, for if the groups are figured as concentric circles, the outer one is the (94) state itself. When therefore the state by its judges attempts to mark the respective limits of liberty and government, it must draw the line in such a way that the individual and the group, and the life appropriate to each, may have scope and opportunity for harmonious development. The location of this line is the overshadowing problem of liberty and law.

Liberty as a legal concept contains an underlying paradox. Liberty in the most literal sense is the negation of law, for law is restraint, and the absence of restraint is anarchy. On the other hand, anarchy by destroying restraint would leave liberty the exclusive possession of the strong or the unscrupulous. "This is a world of compensation," said Lincoln,[216] "and he who would be no slave must consent to have no slave." So once more we face a paradox.

The paradox was long ago perceived by Locke who gave expression to it in terms that have not been bettered since his day.[217] "For law in its true notion," he said, "is not so much the limitation as the direction of a free and intelligent agent to his proper interest, and prescribes no farther than is for the general good of those under that law. . . . That ill deserves the name of confinement which hedges us in only from bogs and precipices. So that however it may be mistaken, the end of law is not to abolish or restrain, but to preserve and enlarge freedom. For in all the states of created beings, capable of laws, (95) where there is no law there is no freedom. For liberty is to be free from restraint and violence from others, which cannot be where there is no law; and is not, as we are told, 'liberty for every man to do what he lists.' For who could be free, when every other man's humour might domineer over him? But a liberty to dispose and order freely as he lists his person, actions, possessions, and his whole property within the allowance of those laws under which he is, and therein not to be subject to the arbitrary will of another, but freely follow his own." Modern research in social science has amplified the thought of Locke, but without changing its essentials.

"If liberty is a social conception," says Hobhouse,[218] "there can be no liberty without social restraint. For any one person, indeed, there might be a maximum of liberty if all social restraints were removed. Where physical strength alone prevails the strongest man has unlimited liberty to do what he likes with the weaker; but clearly the greater the freedom of the strong man, the less the freedom of the weaker. What we mean by liberty as a social conception is a right to be shared by all members of society, and very little consideration suffices to show that, in the absence of restraints enforced on or accepted by all members of a society, the liberty of some must involve the oppression of others. . . . Excess of liberty contradicts itself. In short there is no (96) such thing; there is only liberty for one and restraint for another."[219]

Is there then no path of compromise except such as may be marked by the opportunism of the hour? We find in state and national constitutions a pledge of individual liberty. By common consent this means at least immunity from slavery or serfdom. In so far as it seems to promise more, are we restricted to a choice between a rhetorical flourish and a canonization of what is? Is there no criterion of rationality to enlighten decision with the inspiration of a principle?

In delimiting the field of liberty, courts have professed for the most part to go about their work empirically and have rather prided themselves on doing so. They have said, we will not define due process of law. We will leave it to be "pricked out" by a process of inclusion and exclusion in individual cases.[220] That was to play safely, and very likely at the beginning to play wisely. The question is how long we are to be satisfied with a series of *ad hoc* conclusions. It is all very well to go on pricking the lines, but the time must come when we shall do prudently to look them over, and see whether they make a pattern or a medley of scraps and patches. I do not suggest that political or social science has formulated a conception of liberty so precise and accurate that, applied as a (97) touchstone by the courts, it will mechanically disclose the truth. I do suggest and believe that empirical solutions will be saner and sounder if in the background of the empiricism there is the study and the knowledge of what men have thought and written in the anxious search and groping for a co-ordinating principle.

Bills of rights give assurance to the individual of the preservation of his liberty. They do not define the liberty they promise. In the beginnings of constitutional government, the freedom that was uppermost in the minds of men was freedom of the body. The subject was not to be tortured or imprisoned at the mere pleasure of the ruler. There went along with this, or grew from it, a conception of a liberty that was broader than the physical. Liberty became identified with the reign of law. "Freedom of men under government," says Locke,[221] "is to have a standing rule to live by common to every one of that society and made by, the legislative power erected in it." The individual may not be singled out from among his fellows, and made the victim of the shafts of malice. Those who are put over him "are to govern by promulgated established law, not to be varied in particular cases, but to have one rule for rich and poor, for the favorite at court and the countryman at plough."[222]

Up to this, there is no restraint upon the scope or (98) force of law so long as it be law, *i.e.*, so long as it be general or equal, a rule as contrasted with an "extemporary decree."[223] Liberty means more than this, however, as a concept of social science. It has come to mean more, at least in our own system, as a concept of constitutional law. The concept in our constitutional development has undergone a steady and highly significant development. The individual may not only insist that the law which limits him in his activities shall impose like limits upon others in like circumstances. He will also be heard to say that there is a domain of free activity that may not be touched by government or law at all, whether the command be special against him or general against him and others. By express provision of the constitution, he is assured freedom of speech and freedom of conscience or religion. These latter immunities have thus the sanctions of a specific pledge, but they are merely phases of a larger immunity which finds expression in the comprehensive declaration that no one shall be deprived of liberty without due process of law. Such at least appears to be the more recent doctrine of the court that speaks the final word.[224] Apart from any enumerated phase of liberty and beyond it, this declaration gives immunity against "the play and action of purely personal and arbitrary (99) power." [225] What is personal and arbitrary in mandate and restraint does not gain rationality and coherence because it takes the form of statute. The legislature does not speak with finality as to the measure of its own powers. The final word is for the courts.

Time does not permit, and my aim does not require, that I should catalogue the cases in which statutes have been condemned as founded on no other basis than malice or caprice. A few typical instances will serve to point my meaning. The government may not prohibit the teaching of a foreign language in private schools and colleges.[226] For the same reason, we can safely say, it may not prohibit the teaching in such places of other branches of human learning. It may not take unto itself exclusively the instruction of the young and mould their minds to its own model by forbidding them to be taught in any schools except its own.[227] Restraints such as these are encroachments upon the free development of personality in a society that is organized on the basis of the family. We reach the penetralia of liberty when we throttle the mental life of a group so fundamental.[228] On a plane less exalted than these decisions that deal with the liberty of the spirit are those that limit the power of government in the field of economic liberty. The (100) legislature may not require the payment to women workers of a minimum wage, though the wage does not exceed what is essential for the needs of decent living; [229] it may not prohibit employers from discriminating against employes who are connected with a labor union; [230] it may not abolish the equitable remedy of an injunction in controversies between capital and labor; [231] it may not require the submission of industrial disputes to boards of arbitration; [232] it may not even regulate the weight of loaves of bread,[233] nor forbid the introduction of shoddy into mattresses.[234]

I have no purpose at this time to debate the much-debated question whether these cases or some of them might better have been decided differently. As to that the court has spoken with an authority all its own. My purpose is merely to inquire whether liberty may not have a meaning as a concept of social science which will have illumination for problems of this order as they come before the court hereafter. The search is for some co-ordinating principle, whether the principle be rooted in history or in philosophy, in a study of what has been or in some effort of pure reason to determine what ought to be. I shall leave it (101) to others to apply the pronouncements of social science to the specific cases I have mentioned. It would not detract from the importance of the inquiry though it were found that in some instances, or even in many, the application would yield results at variance with those accepted by the court. I am concerned with a method that may have value in the future. I may seem to quote overmuch. My excuse is the desire to make manifest the truth that back of what I write is the sanction of something stronger than my own unaided thought.

REFERENCES

172. F. L. & T. Co. v. Windthrop, 238 N. Y. 477.

173. Stammler, "Fundamental Tendencies in Modern Jurisprudence," 21 *Mich. L. R.* 873; also Wu, appendix to Stammler's *Theory of Justice*, Modern Legal Phil. Series, p. 581; Cardozo, *Nature of the Judicial Process*, p. 138.

174. *Cf.* Salmond, *Jurisprudence*, pp. 167, 168.

175. Crowley v. Lewis, 1924, 239 N. Y. 264.

176. Cammack v. Slattery & Bros., Inc., 1925, 241 N. Y. 39.

177. Harris v. Shorall, 230 N. Y. 343.

178. *Williston on Contracts*, vol. 3, sec. 1836.

179. Edgerton, "Negligence, Inadvertence and Indifference," 39 *Harv. L. R.* 849.

180. Wagner v. Int. Ry. Co., 232 N. Y. 176.

181. Bohlen, *Studies in the Law of Torts*, "Liability in Tort of Infants and Insane Persons," p. 543; Seavey, "Negligence; Subjective or Objective," 41 *Harvard L. R.* 1; see, however, Williams v. Hays, 143 N. Y. 442; 157 N. Y. 541; O'Connor v. Hickey, 156 N. E. Rep. 838.

182. Edgerton, *supra;* Seavey, *supra.*

183. Seavey, *supra.*
184. Edwin Hanson Freshfield.
185. Birkenhead, *Fourteen English Judges,* p. 360.
186. Santayana, Preface to the second edition of the *Life of Reason.*
187. *Mysticism and Logic,* p. 79.
188. Pp. 125, 126.
189. *Cf.* Kohler, *Phil. of Law,* 12 Modern Legal Phil. Series, p. 35.
190. Leland Shipping Co. v. Norwich Fire Ins. Society, *L. R.* 1918 A. C. 350, 369.
191. Bird v. Ins. Co., 1918, 224 N. Y. 47.
192. St. John v. Am. Mut. F. & M. Ins. Co., 1854, 11 N. Y. 516; Ins. Co. v. Tweed, 1868, 7 Wall. 44.
193. N. Y. & B. D. Ex. Co. v. Traders' & M. Ins. Co.. 132 Mass. 377. 382.
194. Bird v. Ins. Co., *supra,* at pp. 54, 55; Kerr S. S. Co. v. Radio Corp., 1927, 245 N. Y. 284, 290.
195. *Cf.* James Angell McLaughlin, "Proximate Cause," 39 *Harvard L. R.* 149; Henry W. Edgerton, "Legal Cause," 72 *Univ. of Penn. L. R.* 211, 343; Joseph H. Beale, "The Proximate Consequences of an Act," 83 *H. L. R.* 633.
196. 72 *Univ. of Penn. L. R.* 348.
197. *Cf.* Bohlen, "Mixed Questions of Law and Facts," 72 *Univ. of Penn. L. R.* 120; Studies in the Law of Torts, p. 601.
198. Barnes, *Sociology and Political Theory,* p. 53.
199. *General Sociology,* p. 252; *cf.* Barnes, *op. cit.,* p. 33.
200. Small, *op. cit.,* p. 257.
201. P. 32.
202. P. 96.
203. P. 97.
204. "The Social Theory of Fiscal Science," 41 *Pol. Sci. Q.* 210.
205. *Cf.* Ernest Barker, *Political Thought from Herbert Spencer to the Present Day,* Home University Library, p. 175; MacIver, *Community,* pp. 78, 79; Small, *General Sociology,* p. 142; Young, *Social Psychology in History and Prospects of the Social Sciences,* by H. E. Barnes and others, p. 156.
206. *History of English Law,* vol. 9, p. 48.
207. *Cf.* Henderson, *Foreign Corporations in American Constitutional Law.* pp. 165, 167; Kohler, *Phil. of Law,* 12 Modern Legal Phil. Series, p. 68.
208. Consult Holdsworth, *op. cit.,* vol. 9, p. 48; Dewey, "The Historic Background of Corporate Legal Personality," 35 *Yale L. J.,* p. 655; Maitland, Introduction to Gierke's *Political Theories of Middle Age;* Barker, *Political Thought from Spencer to Today,* pp. 175–180; Laski, "The Personality of Associations," 29 *H. L. R.* 404; Borchard, "Government Responsibility in Tort," 36 *Yale L. J.* 757, 774; Geldart, *Legal Personality;* Bijur, J., in F. L. T. Co. v. Pierson, 130 Misc. N. Y. 11.
209. Holdsworth, vol. 9, p. 47.
210. *Cf.* MacIver, *The Modern State,* p. 475.
211. *Cf.* Taff Vale Ry. Co. v. A. S. R. S., 1901, A. C. 426.
212. Mulleck v. Mulleck, 1925, *L. R.,* 52 Ind. App. 245; "The Personality of an Idol," P. W. Duff, 3 *Cambridge L. J.* 42.
213. Jones, "The Early History of the Fiscus," 43 *L. Q. R.* 499, 502; M. R. Cohen, "Communal Ghosts and Other Perils in Social Philosophy," vol. 16, *Journal Philosophy, Psychology and Scientific Method,* 679, 680.
214. Saleilles, *La Personalité Juridique, passim;* Roguin, *La Règle de Droit,* vol. 2, pp. 434, 460, *et seq.;* Gray, *Nature and Sources of Law,* sections 137–140; Wise's *Outlines of Jurisprudence,* 4th ed. by Oliver, p. 49.
215. Young, "The Legal Personality of a Foreign Corporation," 22 *L. Q. R.* 178, 187.
216. Sandburg's *Life of Lincoln,* vol. 2, p. 182.
217. *Treatises on Civil Government,* book 2, sec. 57.
218. *Social Evolution and Political Theory,* p. 189.
219. *Cf.* the same author's *Liberalism,* Home University Library, pp. 23, 139, 140, 144, 145.
220. Davidson v. New Orleans, 1877, 96 U. S. 97, 104; *cf.* Village of Euclid v. Ambler Realty Co., 1926, 272 U. S. 365.

221. *Treatises on Civil Government,* book 2, sec. 21.
222. Locke, *op. cit.,* book ii, sec. 142.
223. Locke, *op. cit.,* book ii, secs. 131, 136.
224. N. Y. v. Gitlow, 1925, 268 U. S. 652; Pierce v. Society of the Sisters of the Holy Name of Jesus and Mary, 1925, 268 U. S. 510; Whitney v. Cal., 1927, 274 U. S. 357; Warren, "The New 'Liberty' under the Fourteenth Amendment," 39 *Harv. L. R.* 431.
225. Yick Wu v. Hopkins, 1886, 118 U. S. 35, 369.
226. Meyer v. Nebraska, 1923, 262 U. S. 390; Bartels v. Iowa, 1923, 262 U. S. 404.
227. Pierce v. Society, etc., 1925, 268 U. S. 510.
228. *Cf.* Spinoza, *Tractatus Politicus,* ch. 8.
229. Adkins v. Children's Hospital, 1923, 261 U. S. 525.
230. Coppage v. Kansas, 1915, 236 U. S. 1.
231. Truax v. Corrigan, 1921, 257 U. S. 312.
232. Wolff Packing Co. v. Industrial Court, 1922, 262 U. S. 522; and, 267 U. S. 552.
233. Burns Baking Co. v. Bryan, 1923, 264 U. S. 504.
234. Weaver v. Palmer Bros. Co., 1926, 270 U. S. 402.

(102)

—IV—

Liberty and Government—Conclusion.

HISTORY and reason unite in the warning that "liberty" is impaired by statutes clogging or diverting the free development of personality, or, in other words, of mind or spirit. By history, I have in mind specifically our own history, our own institutional origins; by reason, the scientific interpretation of the ideal of social welfare in the light of universal history, psychology and ethics. Our own institutional origins give the angle of departure. "I have sworn upon the altar of the living God eternal hostility against every form of tyranny over the mind of man." The words are those of Jefferson, but the spirit was in the air. In that faith was organized what Professor Beard has called the great American tradition.[235] To the minds of the fathers of the nation repression of thought and speech, and above all repression of conscience, were vivid and portentous evils.[236] Liberty in its other phases was guaranteed (103) in generalities that were pregnant with uncertainty. The deliverance of the soul was proclaimed in the forefront of our bill of rights, where all might know it as a cornerstone of our political philosophy. Some doubtless there were even in those days who lost their hold upon these verities of the spirit when theory met the test of practice. Witness the Sedition Act of 1798.[237] Yet deeper and more overwhelming than the passing inroad upon principle was the backwash of the returning wave. True, indeed, it is that the tide was to ebb and flow thereafter. The article of the constitution which proclaimed the emancipation of the spirit was not phrased, nor could it be, in terms so definite and certain as to avoid the opportunity for conflicting interpretations when specific measures from time to time were subjected to its test. With all these allowances the underlying principle of our political philosophy—the great American tradition—has been for the life of the mind the principle of liberty. "Ye shall know the truth, and the truth shall make you free."

In unison with the voice of history as it spoke at our

national beginnings is the deeper voice of science, the science of social life, interpreting universal history and the fundamental needs of man. Personal (104) liberty is a poor and shrunken thing, incapable of satisfying our aspirations or our wants, if it does not exact as its minimal requirement that there shall be the maintenance of opportunity for the growth of personality.[238] "He is the free man," said Spinoza, "who lives according to the dictates of reason alone."[239] We are free only if we know, and so in proportion to our knowledge. There is no freedom without choice, and there is no choice without knowledge,—or none that is not illusory. Implicit, therefore, in the very notion of liberty is the liberty of the mind to absorb and to beget. Here is the fundamental privilege to be maintained in Lord Acton's words, "against the influence of authority and majorities, customs and opinion."[240] "His one belief," says Dr. Figgis, in summarizing Acton's character, "his one belief was the right of every man not to have but to be his best."[241] The mind is in chains when it is without the opportunity to choose. One may argue, if one please, that opportunity to choose is more an evil than a good. One is guilty of a contradiction if one says that the opportunity can be denied, and liberty subsist. At the root of all liberty is the liberty to know.

This freedom of the soul in some of its major postulates, the freedom to speak and write, had its (105) classic vindication by Milton nearly three centuries ago.[242] The vindication was aimed at a particular form of encroachment upon the free development of mind, but it has implications not to be confined to its immediate occasion. What is true of restrictions upon printing must be true of other restrictions upon the movement of ideas. They are all condemned by the same curse. The difficulty about them is that they presuppose a gift of prophecy in fields where history makes it plain that prophecy is futile. Galileo and Copernicus and Bruno have taught us many lessons, yet not the least is the lesson of intellectual humility. "Raised to Giordano Bruno by the generation which he foresaw,"—the inscription that commemorates his glory and his torment,[243] has disquieting reminders. It tells us that the burning of books, the holocaust of ideas, is likely to be as ineffective as the burning of bodies, and almost as odious for those who light the fires. Experimentation there may be in many things of deep concern, but not in setting boundaries to thought, for thought freely communicated is the indispensable condition of intelligent experimentation, the one test of its validity.[244] As to this minimal postulate of liberty, the concord of opinion among students of the social sciences is un (106) broken and impressive. Reason has combined with emotion, thought reacted upon custom, in the upbuilding of an ethos, after the manner described by Hobhouse in his analysis of the process.[245] "The struggle of reason against authority," says Dr. Bury, summing up his review of the history of the conflict,[246] "has ended in what appears now to be a decisive and permanent victory for liberty. In the most civilized and progressive countries, freedom of discussion is recognized as a fundamental principle. In fact, we may say it is accepted as a test of enlightenment, and the man in the street is forward in acknowledging that countries like Russia and Spain, where opinion is more or less fettered, must on that account be considered less civilized than their neighbors." The man in the street this time has the philosopher beside him. If political philosophy has any message to impart, the right of the individual, "not to have but to be his best," has been accredited by the voice of wisdom as an inexpugnable inheritance, the good that it secures one of the accepted treasures of mankind.

We begin with Spinoza whose *Tractatus Theologico-Politicus* was published anonymously in 1670, contemporaneously almost with Milton's plea for liberty. "The more obstinately freedom of speech has been denied the more resolutely have mankind striven against the restraint,—not flatterers and (107) sycophants indeed, . . . but those whom a liberal education and integrity of life have made more free. . . . Men in general are so constituted that they bear nothing more impatiently than to see opinions which they hold for true regarded as crimes, and all that moves them to piety towards God and charity towards man accounted for wickedness; whence it comes that laws are detested, and whatever can be adventured against authority is held to be not base and reprehensible, but brave and praiseworthy. . . . They . . . are the true disturbers of the state who in a free commonwealth refuse that liberty of opinion which cannot be repressed." [247]

Modern speculation in sociology and ethics has been able

to do little more than elaborate and fortify this triumphant declaration of the explosive power of mind.

"The value of liberty," says Hobhouse,[248] "is to build up the life of the mind while the value of state control lies in securing the external conditions, including the mutual restraint, whereby the life of the mind is rendered secure. In the former sphere, compulsion only defeats itself. In the latter liberty defeats itself. Hence in the main the extension of control does not impair liberty, but on the contrary is itself the means of extending liberty and may and should be conceived with that very object in view. (108) Thus it is that upon the whole we see a tendency to the removal of restraints in the sphere in which whatever there is of value to mankind depends on spontaneity of impulse, free interchange of ideas, and voluntary co-operation going along with the tendency to draw tighter the bonds which restrain men from acting directly or indirectly to the injury of their fellows and to enlarge the borders of the action of the state in response to a developing sense of collective responsibility. We are dealing with two conditions of harmonious development apparently opposed and requiring themselves to be rendered harmonious by careful appreciation of their respective functions, and the general direction in which harmony is to be sought may be expressed by saying that the further development of the state lies in such an extension of public control as makes for the fuller development of the life of the mind."

The same author recurs to the same theme in another of his books,[249] and develops it acutely.

"There is no true opposition," he says, "between liberty as such and control as such, for every liberty rests on a corresponding act of control. The true opposition is between the control that cramps the personal life and the spiritual order and the control that is aimed at securing the external and material conditions of their free and unimpeded development." And again: [250] "Liberalism applies the wis (109)dom of Gamaliel in no spirit of indifference, but in the full conviction of the potency of truth. If this thing be of man, *i.e.*, if it is not rooted in actual verity, it will come to nought. If it be of God, let us take care that we be not found fighting against God." [251]

So, Laski, in his *Grammar of Politics:* "What seems to be

of the permanent essence of freedom is that the personality of each individual should be so unhampered in its development, whether by authority or by custom, that it can make for itself a satisfactory harmonisation of its impulses." [252] "Where restraint becomes an invasion of liberty is where the given prohibition acts so as to destroy that harmony of impulses which comes when a man knows that he is doing something it is worth while to do. Restraint is felt as evil when it frustrates the life of spiritual enrichment." [253] "The freedoms I must possess to enjoy a general liberty are those which, in their sum, will constitute the path through which my best self is capable of attainment. That is not to say it will be attained. It is to say only that I alone can make that best self, and that without those freedoms I have not the means of manufacture at my disposal." [254] "Freedoms are therefore opportunities which history has shown to be essential to the development of personality." [255]

(110) Quotation may close with the words of a great apostle of liberty who foresaw that his plea for the free development of the spirit would be likely to survive when his other contributions to our knowledge of the life of the mind should be distanced in the march of thought.

"If all mankind," says Mill in his essay on *Liberty*,[256] "if all mankind minus one were of one opinion and only one person were of the contrary opinion, mankind would be no more justified in silencing that person than he, if he had the power, would be justified in silencing mankind. Were an opinion a personal possession of no value except to the owner; if to be obstructed in the enjoyment of it were simply a private injury, it would make some difference whether the injury was inflicted only on a few persons or on many. But the peculiar evil of silencing the expression of an opinion is, that it is robbing the human race; posterity as well as the existing generation; those who dissent from the opinion still more than those who hold it. If the opinion is right, they are deprived of the opportunity of exchanging error for truth; if wrong, they lose, what is almost as great a benefit, the clearer perception and livelier impression of truth, produced by its collision with error." [257]

The acceptance of this principle, like that of any other so general or abstract, does not mean, of (111) course, that application to particular cases is without the opportunity for error. What Stammler says of the process of subsumption is true here as elsewhere. "So far," he says,[258] "as there are still doubts remaining in carrying out the method of just law, this is due to the problem of subsumption generally. For the subordination of a particular case to a general proposition can never be carried out with absolute precision. For there is no mathematical basis on the one hand, and on the other hand, there are other things at stake than the mere logical arrangement of concepts."[259] The right of free development does not exclude the right of government to insure for the young a minimum of knowledge. There is, of course, an opportunity even here for illegitimate encroachment. The state under the guise of paternal supervision may attempt covertly and gradually to mould its members to its will. The difference as so often is a difference of degree. The world has a certain stock of knowledge which has been garnered through the toil of centuries. The value of this stock has been so tested and verified by successive generations that to shut the young out from the opportunity of sharing in it would be to shut them out from the opportunity of pushing the bonds of knowledge farther. If private schools do not reach a level of reasonable competence, the state may insist that the young shall be trained in its own schools till this level is attained. (112) That is a very different exercise of power from the suppression of private schools altogether, irrespective of their merit, in furtherance of a purpose to give to all within the state a cast and mode of thought established by itself. We may ask how we are to know when the required level has been reached. There is no other standard save the judgment of the elect, the judgment of skill and experience the judgment of those trained in pedagogics. To this the courts will refer, and by this, when ascertained, they will be bound, though the function of ascertaining it will, of course, be theirs. Like difficulties may be encountered in precincts not judicial, as, for example, in the universities with their ever recurring problem of academic freedom. There is general agreement that a teacher is not to be dismissed unless for some better reason than the fact that he has inculcated novel or heterodox or unpopular doctrine, yet novelty or heterodoxy or unpopularity may be so extreme as to be other names for ignorance. The stream of principle will seem to lose itself at times in all the maze of varying circumstance, yet it emerges in the end and pursues its shining course.

Troublesome, too, at times are the distinctions between thought and conduct. The liberty that is assured to us is not liberty to act. It is liberty to think and speak. Thought and speech in certain contexts may be equivalent to acts. When this boundary is reached, we reach the limit of immunity. "No one (113) pretends," says Mill,[260] "that acts should be as free as opinions. On the contrary, even opinions lose their immunity where the circumstances in which they are expressed are such as to constitute their expression a positive instigation to some mischievous act. An opinion that corn-dealers are starvers of the poor, or that private property is robbery, ought to be unmolested when simply circulated through the press, but may justly incure punishment when delivered orally to an excited mob assembled before the house of a corn-dealer, or when handed about among the same mob in the form of a placard. Acts, of whatever kind, which, without justifiable cause, do harm to others may be, and in the more important cases, absolutely require to be, controlled by unfavorable sentiments, and, when needful by the active interference of mankind." [261] So Hobhouse: [262] "Even in regard to matter of opinion it is only opinion and persuasion that can be absolutely free, and even here it must be admitted that there are forms of persuasion that are in fact coercive, and it is fair for the state to consider how far the liberty of the younger or weaker must be protected against forms of temptation which overcome the will. Apart from this when opinion leads, however conscientiously, to action, such action (114) may coerce others, and this would bring the state into play in the name of liberty itself." [263]

One will find it instructive to apply these pronouncements to some of the rulings of the courts. We may apply them, *e.g.*, to the ruling that the institution of polygamy is not protected by the constitution against abolition by the legislaure because the supposed virtue of the practice is a tenet of a church.[264] We may apply them again to limitations upon freedom of utterance that have been held to be permissible in the emergency of war, or, for the preservation of the state, in times of peace as well. Here restraint and immunity have troublesome gradations. "There may indeed be breaches of the peace," says Stephen in his *History of the*

Criminal Law,[265] "which may destroy or endanger life, limb or property, and there may be incitements to such offenses. But no imaginable censure of the government, short of a censure which has an immediate tendency to produce such a breach of the peace, ought to be regarded as criminal." [266] We may say the same of expressions of opinion generally. Yet the test is one that it is easier to state than to apply. There are rulings in recent cases as, *e.g.*, in Abrams v. U. S., 1919, 250 U. S. 616, and N. Y. v. Gitlow, 1925, 268 U. S. 652, (115) that have provoked a sharp division of opinion among the judges of our highest court.[267] The division is a warning that delicate must be the scales for the weighing of the interactions between behavior and belief. If the reading of the balance is doubtful, the presumption in favor of liberty should serve to tilt the beam. That lesson, if no other, stands out from the surrounding darkness. Aglow even yet, after the cooling time of a century and more, is the coal from the fire that was the mind of Voltaire: "I do not believe in a word that you say, but I will defend to the death your right to say it."

When we pass from liberty of mind or spirit to other forms of liberty, and particularly economic liberty, we are in the grip of other troubles. The problem may not be more delicate, but at least it is more intricate, less unified and isolated. Especially is this so when we view it as a legal rather than a social problem, for our constitutional law in its development of the idea of liberty may not press development so far as to trench upon an institution constitutionally protected, the institution of private property. Statutes may go down because impairing an essential incident of property, though by establishing a wider distribution of equality they might tend to economic liberty. The teachings of the social scientist must be corrected so as to make allowance for these deflecting forces before applying them to (116) law. This does not mean, however, that they are to be neglected altogether.

I find no clearer exposition of the trend of social thought in the domain of economic liberty than in Hobhouse's book on *Liberalism,* the chapter on "Laissez faire." At the outset, the Manchester school opposed the regulation of hours of labor for industrial workmen through governmental action. Regulation was thought to be inconsistent with liberty of contract. Before long the truth became evident that the liberty was verbal only. "Here was the owner of a mill employing five hundred hands. Here was an operative possessed of no alternative means of subsistence seeking employment. Suppose them to bargain as to terms. If the bargain failed, the employer lost one man and had four hundred and ninety-nine to keep his mill going. At worst, he might for a day or two, until another operative appeared, have a little difficulty in working a single machine. During the same days the operative might have nothing to eat and might see his children hungry. Where was the effective liberty in such an arrangement?" [268] Trade unionism developed in an effort to adjust the balance. The benefit that came thereby to workmen enforced an important lesson of far wider application. This was that "in the matter of contract true freedom postulates substantial equality between the parties. In proportion as one party is in a position of vantage, he is able to dictate (117) his terms. In proportion as the other party is in a weak position, he must accept unfavorable terms." [269]

De Tocqueville was impressed with the belief that the love of equality is stronger in most minds than the love of liberty. But the opposition is unreal. Equality is the necessary condition of liberty, or at any rate of social liberty as contrasted with liberty that is unsocial or anarchical. At the root of the preference of equality, there is thus a sound core of intuition. "Liberty without equality is a name of noble sound and squalid result." [270]

The perception of this truth has brought about a growing acceptance in our law of the power of the legislature to regulate industrial conditions—to establish some degree of equality of opportunity between the affluent and the needy. There was opposition to the movement, based upon an individualistic philosophy which permeated for a time the decisions of the courts, yet the movement gained an impetus that could not be withstood. We find, accordingly, that there may be legislation requiring the use of safety devices in tenements and factories; invalidating contracts whereby the workmen release the master from his statutory duty; limiting the hours of work for women, and at last, after much hesitation, the hours of work for men. England has established wages boards in "sweated industries" which fix wages paid to workers without limitation of age or (118) sex.[271]

A decision of our Supreme Court has drawn a distinction between regulation of hours and regulation of wages.[272] There surely is none when liberty is viewed, not negatively or selfishly as a mere absence of restraint, but positively and socially as an adjustment of restraints to the end of freedom of opportunity. The decision evoked sharp dissent among the members of the court and animated criticism by leaders of juristic thought.[273]

I have said that the answer of social science is not doubtful when met by problems of this order. "There emerges," says Hobhouse,[274] "a distinction between social and unsocial freedom. Unsocial freedom is the right of a man to use his powers without regard to the wishes and interests of any one except himself. Such freedom is theoretically possible for an individual. It is antithetic to all public control. It is theoretically impossible for a plurality of individuals living in mutual contact. Socially it is a contradiction unless the desires of all men were automatically attuned to social ends. Such freedom, then, for any epoch short of the millenium rests on restraint. It is a freedom that can be enjoyed by all the members of a community, and it is the freedom to choose among those lines of activity which do not involve injury to others. As experience of the social (119) effects of action ripens and as the social conscience is awakened, the conception of injury is widened and insight into its causes is deepened. The area of restraint is therefore increased."

"It might seem to the superficial observer," writes a thoughtful student of the social structure,[275] "as if the increase of control, inspection, regulation, under democracy meant a greater abrogation of personality. But it is necessary to weigh liberty against liberty, and then we see that on the whole (whatever criticisms and exceptions we may make) the newer restrictions on liberty are incidental, leaving the essential individuality free, as contrasted with the older restrictions which struck at the very heart of individuality."

I come back to the words of Hobhouse: "As experience of the social effects of action ripens and as the social conscience is awakened, the conception of injury is widened, and insight into its causes is deepened. The area of restraint is therefore increased." We must learn the lesson that the freedoms comprehended within the concept "liberty" are not the same at different places or at different epochs. Restrictions necessary in a dense and highly organized industrial community may be arbitrary and oppressive in a pioneer community of agriculturists or miners. The physical and geographical conditions, mountains, crops and weather, affect the manner of life, and so the rules and liberties of life.[276] Economic (120) conditions have, of course, a potency not easily obscured. Our statutes against monopoly and against combinations in restraint of trade bear witness to the underlying assumption of our law that liberty can be pushed to a point at which liberty is destroyed. The lesson, of course, is that in fixing the content of the constitutional immunity, we must test the validity of statutes with our eyes ever on the concrete fact. We must know how men work, and how they live, before we can say whether liberty will be increased or diminished by regulations affecting the manner of their living.

With all this knowledge gained, there will be chance enough for error. We shall have before us still "the everlasting enigma in law and life: when is far too far?" [277] Yet there are signposts on the way, if only we have skill to read them. Lord Acton tells us that "the example of the Hebrew nation laid down the parallel lines on which all freedom has been won, the doctrine of national tradition and the doctrine of the higher law; the principle that a constitution grows from a root by a process of development, and not of essential change; and the principle that all political authority must be tested and reformed according to a code which was not made by man." [278] To the test of these doctrines the concrete facts must be subjected, after they have been labor (121) iously gathered, before we shall be able to interpret their significance. The doctrine of traditional development will forbid far-reaching change, change revolutionary in the suddenness of its onset and the extent of its upheaval. Yet the censor will have need of caution and humility. In a representative democracy, the occasions will be rare indeed when a cataclysmic rupture of the existing legal order will have the approval of a legislature chosen from the body of the people. "Historic continuity in constitutional construction," it has been said, "does not necessarily mean historic stereotype in application. To what extent respect for continuity demands adherence merely to what was, involves the art of adjudication—raises those questions of more or less that ultimately decide cases."[279] Legislature as well as court is an interpreter and a guardian of constitutional immunities.[280] We are to beware of the insularity of mind that perceives in every inroad upon habit a catastrophic revolution. There remains, however, a second test. The doctrine of the higher law, which today has no theological implications, or none that are necessarily theological, but is rather Stammler's doctrine of a natural law with a changing content[281]—the doctrine of the higher law will test the validity (122) of change within the limits of national tradition by its tendency to advance or retard the free development of personality in the conditions of time and place prevailing when the change is made.

There is a modern doctrine of natural rights which retains the label, but only in a slight degree the content, of the doctrine of natural rights as it was developed a century and more ago. You will find the present view-point conveniently and clearly summarized in a little book, *The Ethical Basis of the Modern State,* by Professor Norman Wilde of the University of Minnesota. "The modern doctrine of natural rights is realistic and historic. It knows nothing of humanity as such and its abstract rights, but finds only a varying body of traditions as to what are the essential conditions of social welfare. At every stage in the development of a people are found certain standards of living that fix the terms upon which men are willing to endure a given order. As long as society meets these terms they are willing to go peaceably about their business, but if these terms are not met and their fundamental habits of living and acting are interfered with, they rebel and demand their rights. What these fundamental rights are is not determined by human nature in the abstract, but by the custom and expectations of a given age and people. We may speak vaguely of life, liberty, and the pursuit of property and happiness, but (123) these moving terms have no meaning save as interpreted as terms of particular men and times. In every growing society there is as much need for the revision and reinterpretation of its rights as there is in the growing child for the alteration of its clothes."[282]

The guaranty of liberty in the constitutional law of the nation and its constituent commonwealths is a guaranty that claims and immunities conceived of at any given stage of civilization as primary and basic shall be preserved against destruction or encroachment by the agencies of government. We may classify under this head some of the decisions defining those indispensable elements of justice that are essential to the attainment of due process of law. There must be judgment after notice and a hearing. There must be trial by an impartial judge without interest in the event. Only the other day this principle was held to invalidate a conviction by a justice of the peace whose fees were proportioned to the fines that he imposed.[283] There must be calmness and deliberation, or at least the fair opportunity for them. A trial is none in substance, whatever it may be in form, if the verdict does no more than register the bidding of a mob.[284] Here are illustrations of possible encroachments upon the precincts of a freedom (124) that is primary and basic. Encroachments have been adjudged at times when the inroad was less apparent to the eye of philosophy or justice. In particular this has been so in defining the bounds of liberty of contract. The duty of delimiting the sphere of exemption must be cast, however, upon some one. In our constitutional system it has been cast upon the courts. The power is not to be cheapened and made odious by trivial or hasty exercise. It is to be reserved for true emergencies. The urge of selfish groups, or more rarely passion or indifference, may drive the lawmaker at times to forgetfulness or disregard of interests more permanent and essential than those exalted by his statute. It is the theory of our polity that beneath the transitory flux the judge may be expected to discern the deeper principle, and to rescue it from submergence in what is passing and particular.

This conception of liberty and in particular of economic liberty as something fluid and inconstant implies a duty of the courts to look to time and place and circumstance in determining its content. In our day there has been much emphasis of the need that fact finding agencies be organized to the end that time and place and circumstance be exhibited as they are. The complexities of modern life are so great that in the absence of fuller information than is commonly available to judges the significance of apparent limitations upon liberty is likely to be lost. The result is the treatment of liberty as something (125) static and predetermined. The decision of the Supreme Court in the Chastleton case [285] may prove to be the entering wedge that will open up a new technique. The question was whether in the District of Columbia there had come an end to the emergency that had been thought to justify a statute limiting the rents of dwellings. The court said that if its own judicial knowledge were to be the sole basis of its action, it would hold that the emergency had passed. It refused, however, to be so limited, but remitted the case to the trial court to investigate and report. There is little doubt that according to the practice in vogue in many jurisdictions, the court would have dealt with the case upon the footing of judicial notice. We have here the germ of a method capable of expansion. Courts should feel freer than they have hitherto felt to inform their judgment by inquiry. On the other hand, the very need for such inquiry is warning that in default of full disclosure of the facts, there should be submission, readier than has sometimes been accorded, to the judgment of the law-makers. The presumption of validity should be more than a pious formula, to be sanctimoniously repeated at the opening of an opinion and forgotten at the end.

Often a liberal antidote of experience supplies a sovereign cure for a paralyzing abstraction built upon a theory. Many a statutory innovation that would seem of sinister or destructive aspect if it were considered in advance, has lost its terror with (126) its novelty. Take such a group of statutes as the zoning laws that have made their way to recognition and enforcement in so many of our states.[286] I have little doubt that a generation ago they would have been thrown out by the courts as illegitimate encroachments upon that freedom of use which is an attribute of property. I venture to express some doubt as to the fate they would have suffered even in our own day if they had come before the Supreme Court while they were yet novelties in legislation. The fact is, however, that by the time they were subjected to that challenge, they were in successful operation far and wide throughout the land. The test of experience had proved them to be forces that made for conservation rather than destruction. More than that, the values thus maintained were not merely personal or moral—the values of health and comfort and decency and order—though very likely these alone would have sufficed; they were property values too, and thus closely linked to the conservative tradition. The legislation that maintained them might be socialistic in its tendency, but upholders of the existing order could take comfort in the thought that it was neither proletarian nor radical. The ogre lost his talons and assumed the aspect of a friend.

If reasoning is vitiated at times by adhering to abstractions, it is vitiated also by starting with a prepossession and finding arguments to sustain it. (127) The weakness is inherent in the judicial process.[287] The important thing, however, is to rid our prepossessions, so far as may be, of what is merely individual or personal, to detach them in a measure from ourselves, to build them, not upon instinctive or intuitive likes and dislikes, but upon an informed and liberal culture, a knowledge (as Arnold would have said) of the best that has been thought and said in the world, so far as that best has relation to the social problem to be solved. Of course, when our utmost effort has been put forth, we shall be far from freeing ourselves from the empire of inarticulate emotion, of beliefs so ingrained and inveterate as to be a portion of our very nature. "I must paint what I see in front of me," said the elder Yeats to his son, the poet. "Of course, I shall really paint something different because my own nature will come in unconsciously." [288] There is nothing new in all this. The same lesson was taught us long ago by Bacon in his searching analysis of the idols of the mind. "The human mind resembles those uneven mirrors which impart their own properties to different objects . . . and distort and disfigure them." [289] Yet the lesson, if not new, is also not outworn. Our modern students of the processes of mind and of society do well to place it in the forefront of their teaching. "Psychol (128) ogy," says J. A. Hobson,[290] "has almost wiped out hypocrisy. Sincerity is a matter of degree." The weakness is not peculiar to reasoning in law; it extends to reasoning in all the social sciences, and in some degree to reasoning everywhere. In the words of Dewey, "Thoughts sprout and vegetate; ideas proliferate. They come from deep unconscious sources. . . . The stuff of belief is not originated by us. It comes to us from others, by education, tradition and the suggestions of the environment." [291] The best that we can hope for is that from the knowledge of our weakness there will come the exercise of strength.

I have said that in our constitutional law, the concept of liberty as formulated by social science must be so restrained and regulated that there shall be no undue impairment of rights of private property. When impairment becomes undue, it cannot easily be stated within the limits of a formula. Again there is the need for compromise; a median line is to be drawn between excesses, between an egoism too narrow to be endured and an altruism too broad to be attained. A like antithesis confronts us in morals as in law. "It would . . . be a contradictory state of things," writes Windelband in his *Introduction to Philosophy,*[292] "if the happiness of the individual were a value that all others had to respect, yet he (129) himself were forbidden to cultivate it." The institution of private property is the tribute that is paid by law to what is self-regarding in the mind of man. Human nature, however, is not selfishness alone. Judges and lawmakers have seen that private property, if it is to be moulded in response to human needs, must be the expression of an egoism that is shorn of brutality. Some play must be allowed for those altruistic impulses that in any given time and place are habitual and normal. The bundle of power and privileges to which we give the name of ownership is not constant through the ages. The faggots must be put together and rebound from time to time. As I have pointed out before, "Men are saying today that property like every other social institution has a social function to fulfill. Legislation which destroys the institution is one thing. Legislation which holds it true to its function is quite another." [293]

Back of the pronouncements of the courts, one finds a recognition of this truth, though at times there has been too great an emphasis upon the forms of restraint inherited from the past and a corresponding unwillingness to give heed to the necessities of the present. The social urge, even when mak (130) ing itself felt, has been covered and at times obscured under incomplete or question-begging formulas and phrases. The usual statement is that property rights may be limited whenever property is so circumstanced as to be "affected with a public use." [294] Under cover of that text, with its convenient, if deceptive, vagueness,[295] many a lesson of humility has been taught unto the pride of ownership. One business after another has been annexed, so to speak, to the public domain, which seemed at times to be capable of indefinite aggrandizement, until only the other day there came an unexpected check. The decision in the New York Theatre Ticket Brokers case,[296] rendered by a closely divided court, has set up a new breakwater in the form of a more rigid adherence to those restraints and those only that have become consecrated by the hand of time. In the meanwhile, however, the surveyor, marking the contour of the shore, will have set down in his note book many a change of line. There may be regulation of rates for the use of grain elevators, for transportation by sea and land, for the use of gas and water, for telegraphs and telephones, and even for insurance against fire.[297] Not only that, but a business strictly private in one set of conditions, may through other and new conditions become quasi- (131) public overnight. The owner of land and buildings may find himself restricted in the rent that he is free to charge if the emergency is pressing enough to make the restriction necessary as a means to social justice.[298] At such times, no antecedent contract will be permitted to stand in the way of the power of the state to promote the welfare of its citizens by protecting them against the encroachments of a rapacious individualism.[299] The zoning laws have gone still farther and have extended regulation to property held for private uses though emergency is absent. The national government, too, has felt the leash relaxed when the necessity was adequate. Congress in times of stress and strain may take to itself the power of fixing the wages of engineers and others upon interstate lines of transportation.[300] Even in times more placid, the railroads may have to submit to the recaption by the government of a share of their earnings beyond a maximum percentage.[301] Property, like liberty, has been taught that some of its most cherished immunities are not absolute, but relative. We shall have to learn as the years go by to distinguish more and more between what is essential in the concept of ownership and so invariable under the (132) constitution, and what is accidental or unessential, and so variable and severable at the call of social needs.

When we speak of law and liberty and the need of compromise between them, what is uppermost in our minds is commonly the kind of problem that is involved in the definition of the constitutional immunity. In essence, however, the problem is not different whenever a rule of law is extended into fields unoccupied before. "Shall A answer to B for the consequences of an act?" means this and nothing more, "Shall the freedom of A to work damage to B be restrained so as to preserve to B the freedom to be exempt from damage?" In determining whether it shall, we must again evaluate the social interests concerned. We have regard to the social interest of certainty. The force of precedent and analogy may lead us to refuse an extension that we would otherwise concede. If these guides are silent or inconclusive, we give heed to the prompting of justice or of expediency, which may shade down from considerations of supreme importance to those of mere convenience. "Das Recht," as Binding puts it, "ist eine Ordnung menschlicher Freiheit."[302] The opposites, liberty and restraint, the individual and the group, are phases of those wider opposites, the one and the many, rest and motion, at the heart of all being. Dichotomy is everywhere.

One of the marks by which we recognize a social (133) interest as worthy of protection is the spontaneity and persistence with which groups are established to conserve it.[303] The mark, of course, is not infallible. There are groups, spontaneous and persistent enough,—camorras, secret orders, revolutionary bands—whose aims are anti-social. Even so, spontaneity and persistence are tokens not to be ignored that the associative process is moving toward a social end. A striking instance of this truth is seen in the history of trade-unions. At first the law held them anathema. They were combinations in restraint of trade, pernicious, it was thought, in so far as they were effective, and, in the long run, as futile as they were pernicious, since economic "laws," then supposed to be inexorable, would nullify the gains of victory, and restore the pre-existing level.[304] The result belied the prophecy. The urge to associate and unify was too spontaneous and persistent for any interdict to stifle it. The courts perceived and yielded.[305] They were helped at times by legislation. In many jurisdictions, however, they reached the same result unaided. They gave up denouncing as lawless and unsocial a form of grouping that appeared and reappeared in response to a social pressure akin in steadiness and intensity to the pressure that makes law. Whether the unions were to be classified as jural persons was another question of quite subsidiary (134) importance. What mattered most was that they were lawful. The state would hold them in check as it would hold in check the individual and even the agencies of government.[306] It would not repudiate or destroy them. In the struggle between liberty and restraint, a new liberty, asserting itself persistently and clamorously in the minds and hearts of men, became a liberty secured by law. Out of the psychical urge there had been born the jural right. The peace of a new compromise had been declared between the warring opposites.

I have already quoted a sentence from Strachey's essay on Pope. I venture to repeat it now in the setting in which he placed it. "Antithesis," he says, "permeates the structure; it permeates the whole conception of his work. Fundamental opposites clash and are reconciled." The innominate authors of our common law method of judging might say the same about their handiwork. Antithesis permeates the structure. Here is the mystery of the legal process, and here also is its lure. These unending paradoxes tease us with the challenge of a riddle, the incitement of the chase. The law, like science generally, if it could be followed to its roots, would take us down beneath the veins and ridges to the unplumbed depths of being, the reality behind the veil. The jurist must not despair because his plummets do not reach the goal at which in vain for two thousand years and more the philosophers have been casting theirs. (135) Rather will he learn with some of the philosophers themselves in moderating his ambitions to recast to some extent his notion of philosophy and to think of it as a means for the truer estimate of values and the better ordering of life.[307] He will hope indeed that with study and reflections there may develop in the end some form of calculus less precarious than any that philosopher or lawyer has yet been able to devise. In the meantime, amid the maze of contingency and regularity, he will content himself as best he can with his little compromises and adjustments, the expedients of the fleeting hour. They will fret him sometimes with a sense of their uncertainty. It should hearten him to keep in mind that uncertainty is the lot of every branch of thought and knowledge when verging on the ultimate. "To whatever domain of intellectual activity you may address your inquiry," I quote the words of a distinguished judge, "you will find in the upper levels of research and judgment grave differences of opinion among the elect few." [308] There is tonic in that thought. There is even greater tonic in the thought that on our side are unseen and masterful allies, who are helping us to win the fight by a power not our own. For the process by which law grows is above all a social process. The individual intellect is not as desolate as it seems. The pressure that gives form to manners and morals (136) gives form in the end to law; to judge-made law often, and when on occasion that fails, to law declared by statute. Initiative, ingenuity, idealism will help. For a time the lack of them may deflect and hinder. But the steady pressure goes on, and finds in the end the responsive mind.

Strepsiades in the Greek play was eager to escape the payment of his debts. He was told that the Sophists, led by Socrates, had a good λόγος and a bad one, and that through the bad one injustice could be made to masquerade as justice. So he went expectantly to the school, and prayed to be made perfect in the logic that could cheat. He was old and dull-witted, and could not learn, and his son of quicker wit became the pupil in his stead. The son learned only too well the lesson of the wicked logic. He proved before long to the luckless father that it is the duty of a son to beat his parents and despoil them. So the play ends with Strepsiades disillusioned and repentant. The wicked logic must be abjured; the good one marks the path of happiness and peace.

I have faith with Aristophanes that it is so. Yet even as of old, the rival logics can be heard contending in the law courts of today, and the seeker after peace and happiness is still bewildered by the din.

REFERENCES

235. Beard, "The Great American Tradition," *The Nation*, vol. 123, no. 3183, p. 7, July 7, 1926; *cf.* Beard, *The Rise of American Civilization*, vol. 1, pp. 151, 152, 160, 185, 379, 449, 487.

236. See *e.g.*, Jefferson's *Bill for the Introduction of Religious Freedom in Virginia;* also his notes on Virginia, quoted by Hirst, *Life and Letters of Thomas Jefferson*, pp. 136, 138; Franklin, and the questions put to new members of his Academy, Beard, *op. cit.*, p. 169; Chafee, *Freedom of Speech in War Time*, pp. 4, 21, 23.

237. *Cf.* Whipple, *The History of Civil Liberty in the United States;* also address by Judge Irving Lehman on "Religious Liberty in New York," printed in *N. Y. L. J.* of May 6, 1927; Beard, *op. cit.*, p. 543.

238. *Cf.* Hobhouse, *Social Evolution and Political Theory*, p. 199.

239. Spinoza, *Ethics*, p. 187, Everyman's ed., also p. 158.

240. Lord Acton, *The History of Freedom and Other Essays,* p. 3.
241. *The History of Freedom and Other Essays,* Introduction, p. xxvii.
242. *The Areopagitica,* a plea for the liberty of unlicensed printing, 1644.
243. Robinson, *The Mind in the Making,* p. 219; White, *History of the Warfare of Science with Theology,* vol. 1, p. 57; *cf.* MacDonnell, *Historical Trials,* Bruno, pp. 66, 83.
244. *Cf.* Bury, *A History of Freedom of Thought,* pp. 233, 239.
245. *Ante.*
246. *Op. cit.,* p. 247.
247. Spinoza, *Tractatus Theologico-Politicus,* translation by Willis, published in London, 1868, pp. 348, 351; Frank Thilly, *Spinoza's Doctrine of the Freedom of Peace,* 1923, pp. 88, 102.
248. *Social Evolution and Political Theory,* p. 202.
249. *Liberalism,* p. 147.
250. P. 118.
251. *Cf.* Maitland, *Collected Papers,* Liberty, vol. 3, p. 90.
252. P. 102.
253. P. 143.
254. P. 144.
255. P. 144; *cf.* Dewey, *The Public and Its Problems,* p. 150.
256. P. 79, Everyman's ed.
257. *Cf.* MacIver, *The Modern State,* p. 153.
258. *Op. cit.,* p. 233.
259. See also *op. cit.,* p. 239.
260. *Liberty,* Everyman's ed., p. 114.
261. "The most stringent protection of free speech would not protect a man in falsely shouting fire in a theatre and causing a panic."—Holmes, J., in Scheneck v. U. S., 1916, 249 U. S. 47, 52.
262. *Social Evolution and Political Theory,* p. 200; *cf.* the same author's *Liberalism,* p. 148.
263. See the same author's *Liberalism,* p. 148, and his *Elements of Social Justice,* pp. 73, 74; but *cf.* Laski, *A Grammar of Politics,* p. 120, and the same author's *Authority in the Modern State,* p. 56.
264. Reynolds v. U. S., 1878, 98 U. S. 145.
265. Vol. 2, p. 300.
266. See also Holdsworth, *History of English Law,* vol. 8, p. 338.
267. *Cf.* Brandeis, J., in Whitney v. Cal., 1927, 274 U. S. 357, 372.
268. Hobhouse, *op. cit.,* pp. 83, 84.
269. *Ibid.,* p. 85.
270. Hobhouse, *Liberalism,* p. 86.
271. Hobhouse, *Liberalism,* p. 86.
272. Adkins v. Children's Hospital, 1923, 261 U. S. 525.
273. See the volume *The Supreme Court and Minimum Wage Legislation,* published by *New Republic, Inc.,* New York, 1925.
274. *Liberalism,* p. 91.
275. MacIver, *Community,* p. 317.
276. Barnes, *Sociology and Political Theory,* pp. 30, 66.
277. Frankfurter and Corcoran, "Petty Offences and Trial by Jury," 39 *Harvard L. R.* 981.
278. Acton, *History of Freedom and Other Essays,* "Freedom in Antiquity," p. 5.
279. Frankfurter and Corcoran, "Petty Federal Offences and Trial by Jury," 39 *H. L. R.* 922.
280. M. K. & T. Ry. Co. v. May, 1904, 194 U. S. 267, 270; People v. Crane, 1915, 214 N. Y. 154, 173.
281. See Cardozo, *Nature of the Judicial Process,* p. 132; also Laski, *English Political Theory,* Home University Library, p. 60; Charmont, *La Renaissance du Droit Naturel,* 7 Modern Legal Phil. Series, p. 111; Borchard, "Government Responsibility in Tort," 36 *Yale Law Journal.*
282. Wilde, *The Ethical Basis of the State,* p. 83; *cf.* M. R. Cohen, "Jus Naturale Redivivum," 25 *Phil. Rev.* 761; Laski, *Authority in the Modern State,* pp. 64, 65.

283. Tumey v. Ohio, 1927, 273 U. S. 510.
284. Moore v. Dempsey, 1923, 261 U. S. 86.
285. Chastleton Corporation v. Sinclair, 1924, 264 U. S. 543.
286. Village of Euclid v. Ambler Realty Co., 1926, 272 U. S. 365.
287. Laski, *A Grammar of Politics*, p. 544; and *cf.* Laski, "Judicial Review of Social Policy in England," 39 *Harv. L. R.* 832.
288. W. B. Yeats, *Autobiographies*, p. 101.
289. *Nov. Org.*, 1, 41.
290. *Free Thought in the Social Sciences*, p. 45.
291. Dewey, *Human Nature and Conduct*, p. 314; *cf.* Robinson, *The Mind in the Making*, pp. 59, 60.
292. P. 226.
293. Cardozo, *The Nature of the Judicial Process*, p. 87; *cf.* Duguit, *Transformations Generales du Droit Privé Depuis le Code Napoléon*, Continental Legal History Series, vol. xi, p. 74; M. R. Cohen, "Recent Philosophical Legal Literature," *The International Journal of Ethics*, July, 1916, p. 530; also the group of articles on "Property" in the volume of the *Rational Basis of Legal Institutions* in the Modern Legal Philosophy Series, p. 167, *et seq.*
294. Munn v. Illinois, 94 U. S. 113.
295. Stone, J., dissenting in the New York theatre brokers case, Tyson & Bro. v. Banton, 1927, 273 U. S. 418, 451.
296. *Supra.*
297. German Alliance Ins. Co. v. Kansas, 1914, 233 U. S. 389.
298. Marcus Brown Holding Co. v. Feldman, 1921, 256 U. S. 170; Block v. Hirsch, 1921, 256 U. S. 135; Levy Leasing Co. v. Siegel, 1922, 258 U. S. 242; Peo. *ex rel.* Durham Realty Co. v. La Fetra, 1921, 230 N. Y. 429.
299. Levy Leasing Co. v. Siegel, *supra;* Union Dry Goods Co. v. Georgia Public Serv. Corp., 1919, 248 U. S. 372.
300. Wilson v. New, 1917, 243 U. S. 332.
301. Dayton Goose Creek Ry. Co. v. U. S., 1924, 263 U. S. 456.
302. *Cf.* Korkunov, *General Theory of Law*, p. 61.
303. *Cf.* MacIver, *The Modern State*, p. 475.
304. J. A. Hobson, *Free Thought in the Social Sciences*, pp. 88, 89; Beard, *The Rise of American Civilization*, vol. 2, pp. 236, 237.
305. For a summary of the decisions see 16 *Ruling Case Law*, 418.
306. Barker, *Political Thought from Spencer to Today*, p. 179.
307. Dewey, *Experience and Nature*, pp. 394, 396, 398, 403, 404, 408; Dewey, *Reconstruction in Philosophy*, pp. 122, 124.
308. Chas. E. Hughes, address at the Sixtieth Convocation of the University of the State of New York, October 17, 1924.

Complete Text

of

LAW AND LITERATURE*

AND OTHER ESSAYS AND ADDRESSES

TO

THE SACRED MEMORY

OF

MY SISTER ELLEN

Preface

The essays and addresses brought together in this book may thus be rescued for a while from the oblivion that is the speedy fate of writings, worthy or unworthy, unless durably embalmed.

Some have already been printed in journals, and one as part of a volume in company with the work of others. I offer thanks to the publishers for the privilege of reprinting in this form.

B. N. C.

New York, July, 1930.

— I —

*Law and Literature.**

First published by the Yale University Press in the *Yale Review* July 1925.

I AM told at times by friends that a judicial opinion has no business to be literature. The idol must be ugly, or he may be taken for a common man. The deliverance that is to be accepted without demur or hesitation must have a certain high austerity which frowns at winning graces. I fancy that not a little of this criticism is founded in misconception of the true significance of literature, or, more accurately perhaps, of literary style. To some a clearer insight has been given. There are those who have perceived that the highest measure of condensation, of short and sharp and imperative directness, a directness that speaks the voice of some external and supreme authority, is consistent, none the less, with supreme literary excellence. A dictum of Henri Beyle's, recalled not long ago by Mr. Strachey, will point my meaning. The French novelist used to say that "there was only one example of the perfect style, and that was the Code Napoléon; for there alone everything was subordinated to the exact and complete expression of what was to be said." The poor man succumbed to its charm to such an extent that he was in the habit of reading a few paragraphs every morning before breakfast. I do not seek to substitute this regimen for the daily exercise in calisthenics. Some of us prefer our literature like our food in less concentrated tablets. I do no more than suggest that the morsel hastily gulped down may have a savor all its own for the discriminating palate.

But I over-emphasize and exaggerate if I seem to paint the picture of any active opposition that is more than sporadic and exceptional to so amiable a weakness as a love of art and letters. A commoner attitude with lawyers is one, not of active opposition, but of amused or cynical indifference. We are merely wasting our time, so many will inform us, if we bother about form when only substance is important. I suppose this might be true if only one could tell us where substance ends and form begins. Philosophers have been trying for some thousands of years to draw the distinction between substance and mere appearance in the world of matter. I doubt whether they succeed better when they attempt a like distinction in the world of thought. Form is not something added to substance as a mere protuberant adornment. The two are fused into a unity. Not long ago I ran across a paragraph in the letters of Henry James in which he blurts out his impatience of these attempts to divide the indivisible. He is writing to Hugh Walpole, now a novelist of assured position, but then comparatively unknown. "Don't let any one persuade you—there are plenty of ignorant and fatuous duffers to try to do it—that strenuous selection and comparison are not the very essence of art, and that Form *is* not substance to that degree that there is absolutely no substance without it. Form alone *takes,* and holds and preserves substance, saves it from the welter of helpless verbiage that we swim in as in a sea of tasteless tepid pudding." This is my own faith. The argument strongly put is not the same as the argument put feebly any more than the "tasteless tepid pudding" is the same as the pudding served to us in triumph with all the glory of the lambent flame. The strength that is born of form and the feebleness that is born of the lack of form are in truth qualities of the substance. They are the tokens of the thing's identity. They make it what it is.

Up to this point at least, I have little fear of opposition. We shall, most of us, be agreed, I think, not merely that style is not an evil in the Sahara of a judicial opinion, but even that it is a positive good, if only it is the right style. *There* is the disquieting condition which checks the forward movement of triumphal demonstration. What is to be deemed the right style, or the right styles if there are more than one of them? Do the examples of the great masters reveal some uniformity of method for the instruction of the tyro? If uniformity is not discoverable, may there not at least be types or standards? If types or standards do not exist, shall we not find stimulus and interest in the coruscations of genius, however vagrant or irregular? If at times there is neither stimulus nor interest, may there not in lieu of these be the awful warning of example?

I suppose there can be little doubt that in matters of literary style the sovereign virtue for the judge is clearness. Judge Veeder in his interesting and scholarly essay, "A Century of Judicature," quotes the comment of Brougham upon the opinions of Lord Stowell: "If ever the praise of being luminous could be bestowed upon human compositions, it was upon his judgments." How shall his successors in the same or other courts attain that standard or approach it? There is an accuracy that defeats itself by the over-emphasis of details. I often say that one must permit one-self, and that quite advisedly and deliberately, a certain margin of misstatement. Of course, one must take heed that the margin is not exceeded, just as the physician must be cautious in administering the poisonous ingredient which magnified will kill, but in tiny quantities will cure. On the other hand, the sentence may be so overloaded with all its possible qualifications that it will tumble down of its own weight. "To philosophize," says Holmes in one of his opinions—I am quoting him from uncertain and perhaps inaccurate recollection—"to philosophize is to generalize, but to generalize is to omit." The picture cannot be painted if the significant and the insignificant are given equal prominence. One must know how to select. All these generalities are as easy as they are obvious, but, alas! the application is an ordeal to try the souls of men. Write an opinion, and read it a few years later when it is dissected in the briefs of counsel. You will learn for the first time the limitations of the power of speech, or, if not those of speech in general, at all events your own. All sorts of gaps and obstacles and impediments will obtrude themselves before your gaze, as pitilessly manifest as the hazards on a golf course. Sometimes you will know that the fault is truly yours, in which event you can only smite your breast, and pray for deliverance thereafter. Sometimes you will feel that the fault is with counsel who have stupidly misread the obvious, in which event, though you rail against the bar and the imperfect medium of speech, you will be solaced, even in your chagrin, by a sense of injured innocence. Sometimes, though rarely, you will believe that the misreading is less stupid than malicious, in which event you will be wise to keep your feelings to yourself. One marvels sometimes at the ingenuity with which texts the most remote are made to serve the ends of argument or parable. But clearness, though the sovereign quality, is not the only one to be pursued, and even if it were, may be gained through many avenues of approach. The opinion will need persuasive force, or the impressive virtue of sincerity and fire, or the mnemonic power of alliteration and antithesis, or the terseness and tang of the proverb and the maxim. Neglect the help of these allies, and it may never win its way. With traps and obstacles and hazards confronting us on every hand, only blindness or indifference will fail to turn in all humility, for guidance or for warning, to the study of examples.

Classification must be provisional, for forms run into one another. As I search the archives of my memory, I seem to discern six types or methods which divide themselves from one another with measurable distinctness. There is the type magisterial or imperative; the type laconic or sententious; the type conversational or homely; the type refined or artificial, smelling of the lamp, verging at times upon preciosity or euphuism; the type demonstrative or persuasive; and finally the type tonsorial or agglutinative, so called from the shears and the pastepot which are its implements and emblem.

I place first in order, for it is first in dignity and power, the type magisterial or imperative. It eschews ornament. It is meager in illustration and analogy. If it argues, it does so with the downward rush and overwhelming conviction of the syllogism, seldom with tentative gropings towards the inductive apprehension of a truth imperfectly discerned. We hear the voice of the law speaking by its consecrated ministers with the calmness and assurance that are born of a sense of mastery and power. Thus Marshall seemed to judge, and a hush falls upon us even now as we listen to his words. Those organ tones of his were meant to fill cathedrals or the most exalted of tribunals. The judicial department, he tells us, "has no will in any case. . . . Judicial power is never exercised for the purpose of giving effect to the will of the judge; always for the purpose of giving effect to the will of the legislature; or in other words, to the will of the law." The thrill is irresistible. We feel the mystery and the awe of inspired revelation. His greatest judgments are framed upon this plane of exaltation and aloofness. The movement from premise to conclusion is put before the observer as something more impersonal than the working of the individual mind. It is the inevitable progress of an inexorable force. Professor Corwin in an interesting volume, *John Marshall and the Constitution,* shows how even his contemporaries, the bitterest critics of his aggrandizement of federal power, were touched by this illusion. "All wrong, all wrong," lamented John Randolph of Roanoke, "but no man in the United States can tell why or wherein." I have reread a few of the most famous of his judgments: Marbury v. Madison; Gibbons v. Ogden; McCulloch v. Maryland; they are all in the grand style.

Listen to the voice of the magistrate in Marbury v. Madison: "The distinction between a government with limited and unlimited powers is abolished if those limits do not confine the persons on which they are imposed, and if acts prohibited and acts allowed are of equal obligation. It is a proposition too plain to be contested: that the Constitution controls any legislative act repugnant to it; or that the legislature may alter the Constitution by an ordinary act. Between these alternatives there is no middle ground. . . . If two laws conflict with each other, the courts must decide on the operation of each. So if a law be in opposition to the Constitution; if both the law and the Constitution apply to a particular case, so that the court must either decide that case conformably to the law, disregarding the Constitution, or conformably to the Constitution, disregarding the law, the court must determine which of these conflicting rules governs the case. This is of the very essence of judicial duty." Nothing is here of doubt; nothing of apology; no blurred edges or uncertain lines. "There is no middle ground." The choice that is made is "of the very essence of judicial duty." The voice has pealed forth. Let the wicked heed it and obey.

One will find this same suggestion of sure and calm conviction in some of the judgments of Lord Mansfield. The slave Somerset captured on the coast of Africa, is sold in bondage in Virginia, and brought to England by his master. The case comes before Mansfield on the return to the writ of habeas corpus: "The state of slavery is of such a nature that it is incapable of being introduced on any reasons, moral or political, but only positive law, which preserved its force long after the reasons, occasions, and time itself from whence it was created, are erased from memory. It is so odious that nothing can be suffered to support it, but positive law. . . . I care not for the supposed *dicta* of judges, however eminent, if they be contrary to all principle. The *dicta* cited were probably misunderstood, and at all events they are to be disregarded. Villainage, when it did exist in this country, differed in many particulars from West India slavery. The lord never could have thrown his villain, whether *regardant* or *in gross,* into chains, sent him to the West Indies, and sold him there to work in a mine or in a cane field. At any rate villainage has ceased in England, and it cannot be revived. The air of England has long been too pure for a slave, and every man is free who breathes it. Every man who comes into England is entitled to the protection of English law, whatever oppression he may heretofore have suffered, and whatever may be the color of his skin. '*Quamvis ille niger, quamvis tu candidus esses.*' Let the negro be discharged."

It is thus men speak when they are conscious of their power. One does not need to justify oneself if one is the mouthpiece of divinity. The style will fit the mood.

I have said that in dignity and power there is no method that can be matched with the method which I have characterized as magisterial or imperative. A changing philosophy of law has tended, none the less, to the use of other methods more conciliatory and modest. The development of law is conceived of, more and more, as a process of adaptation and adjustment. The pronouncements of its ministers are timid and tentative approximations, to be judged through their workings, by some pragmatic test of truth. I find in a dissenting opinion by Mr. Justice Brandeis a striking statement of this attitude of mind. Arguing for the restriction of a rule which had proved itself unworkable, he says: "Such limitations of principles previously announced and such express disapproval of *dicta* are often necessary. It is an unavoidable incident of the search by courts of last resort for the true rule. The process of inclusion and exclusion, so often applied in developing a rule, cannot end with its first enunciation. The rule as announced must be deemed tentative. For the many and varying facts to which it will be applied cannot be foreseen. Modification implies growth. It is the life of the law."

One cannot face the law in this spirit of cautious seeking without showing the changing point of view in a changing style and form. Universals will be handled more charily under the dominance of such a philosophy than in days when the law of nature supplied us with data that were supposed to be eternal and unyielding. Yet there are times even now when the magisterial method is utilized by men who know that they are masters of their calling. It is still utilized in fields where some established principle is to be applied to new facts or where the area of its extension or restriction is fairly obvious or narrow. But alas! even then it is the masters, and no others, who feel sure enough of themselves to omit the intermediate steps and stages, and leap to the conclusion. Most of us are so uncertain of our strength, so beset with doubts and difficulties, that we feel oppressed with the need of justifying every holding by analogies and precedents and an exposure of the reasons. The masters are content to say, "The elect will understand, there is no need to write for others." Perhaps there are opinions by Mr. Justice Holmes in which this mood can be discerned. The sluggard unable to keep pace with the swiftness of his thought will say that he is hard to follow. If that is so, it is only for the reason that he is walking with a giant's stride. But giants, after all, are not met at every turn, and for most of us, even if we are not pygmies, the gait of ordinary men is the safer manner of advance. We grope and feel our way. What we hand down in our judgments is an hypothesis. It is no longer a divine command.

I pass to other types which run into each other by imperceptible gradations, the laconic or sententious and the conversational or homely. There has been no stage of our legal history in which these methods have been neglected. The Year Books are full of wise saws and homely illustrations, the epigram, the quip, the jest. Perhaps this is but a phase of that use of the maxim or the proverb which is characteristic of legal systems in early stages of development. Dean Pound in a recent paper has traced the growth and function of the maxim with all the resources of his learning. If the maxim has declined in prevalence and importance, now that the truths of the law have become too complex to be forced within a sentence, there has been no abatement of recourse to the laconic or sententious phrase, to drive home and imbed what might otherwise be lost or scattered. Who will resist Lord Nottingham's adjuration: "Pray let us so resolve cases here, that they may stand with the reason of mankind when they are debated abroad"? Is there any armor proof against a thrust like the dictum of Lord Bowen's: "The state of a man's mind is as much a fact as the state of his digestion"? Next door to the epigram is the homely illustration which makes its way and sinks deep by its appeal to everyday experience. In the wielding of these weapons, the English judges have been masters. The precept may be doubtful in the beginning. How impossible to fight against it when the judge brings it down to earth and makes it walk the ground, the brother of some dictate of decency or of prudence which we have followed all our lives. Perhaps the kinship is not so close or apparent as it is figured. Who of us will have the hardihood to doubt the reality of the tie when it is so blandly assumed to be obvious to all? The common denominator silences and satisfies. The rule that is rooted in identities or analogies of customary belief and practice is felt and rightly felt to be rooted in reality. We glide into acquiescence when negation seems to question our kinship with the crowd. Something must be set down also to the sense of fellowship awakened when judges talk in ways that seem to make us partners in the deliberative process. "I entirely agree with my right honorable and learned friend upon the woolsack." We seem to be let into the mysteries of the conference, the sacrosanct "arcana," to quote Professor Powell's phrase, to which "the uninitiated are not admitted." Given such an atmosphere, with point and pungency thrown into it, the product makes its way into every crack and crevice of our being.

I limit my illustrations, though many are available. Take this by Lord Bramwell: "It does not follow that if a man dies in a fit in a railway carriage, there is a *prima facie* case for his widow and children, nor that if he has a glass in his pocket and sits on it and hurts himself, there is something which calls for an answer or explanation from the company." Take this by Lord Blackburn: "If with intent to lead the plaintiff to act upon it, they put forth a statement which they know may bear two meanings, one of which is false to their knowledge, and thereby the plaintiff, putting that meaning upon it, is misled, I do not think they can escape by saying he ought to have put the other. If they palter with him, in a double sense, it may be that they lie like truth, but I think they lie, and it is a fraud." One could cite other examples without number. What a cobweb of fine-spun casuistry is dissipated in a breath by the simple statement of Lord Esher in *Ex parte* Simonds, that the court will not suffer its own officer "to do a shabby thing." If the word shabby had been left out, and unworthy or dishonorable substituted, I suppose the sense would have been much the same. But what a drop in emotional value would have followed. As it is, we feel the tingle of the hot blood of resentment mounting to our cheeks. For quotable good things, for pregnant aphorisms, for touchstones of ready application, the opinions of the English judges are a mine of instruction and a treasury of joy.

Such qualities on the whole are rarer close at home, yet we have one judge even now who can vie with the best of his English brethren, past as well as present, in the art of packing within a sentence the phosphorescence of a page. If I begin to quote from the opinions of Mr. Justice Holmes, I hardly know where I shall end, yet fealty to a master makes me reluctant to hold back. The sheaf will be a tiny one, made up haphazard, the barest sample of the riches which the gleaner may gather where he will. Some hint of the epigrammatic quality of his style may be found in this: "The Fourteenth Amendment, itself a historical product, did not destroy history for the States and substitute mechanical compartments of law all exactly alike." In this: "We are in danger of forgetting that a strong public desire to improve the public condition is not enough to warrant achieving the desire by a shorter cut than the constitutional way of paying for the change." In this: "Legal obligations that exist but cannot be enforced are ghosts that are seen in the law but that are elusive to the grasp." And finally in this, words of solemn dissent, their impressiveness heightened by the knowledge that the cause has been already lost: "Persecution for the expression of opinions seems to me perfectly logical. If you have no doubt of your premises or your power and want a certain result with all your heart you naturally express your wishes in law and sweep away all opposition. To allow opposition by speech seems to indicate that you think the speech impotent, as when a man says that he has squared the circle, or that you do not care whole-heartedly for the result, or that you doubt either your power or your premises. But when men have realized that time has upset many fighting faiths, they may come to believe even more than they believe the very foundations of their own conduct that the ultimate good desired is better reached by free trade in ideas—that the best test of truth is the power of the thought to get itself accepted in the competition of the market, and that truth is the only ground upon which their wishes safely can be carried out. That at any rate is the theory of our Constitution. It is an experiment, as all life is an experiment. Every year if not every day we have to wager our salvation upon some prophecy based upon imperfect knowledge. While that experiment is part of our system I think that we should be eternally vigilant against attempts to check the expression of opinions that we loathe and believe to be fraught with death, unless they so imminently threaten immediate interference with the lawful and pressing purposes of the law that an immediate check is required to save the country."

There is another type or method which I have spoken of as the refined or artificial, smelling a little of the lamp. With its merits it has its dangers, for unless well kept in hand, it verges at times upon preciosity and euphuism. Held in due restraint, it lends itself admirably to cases where there is need of delicate precision. I find no better organon where the subject matter of discussion is the construction of a will with all the filigree of tentacles, the shades and nuances of differences, the slender and fragile tracery that must be preserved unmutilated and distinct. Judge Finch of the Court of Appeals of New York was an adept in the writing of opinions which carried with them this suggestion of precision and refinement. Occasionally, it shades into a faint and gentle sarcasm which is sometimes the refuge of the spokesman of a minority expressing his dissent. As an illustration, let me quote from the dissenting opinion in an election controversy which provoked in its day no little warmth of difference. The majority had held that despite the provision of the Constitution making each house of the legislature the judge of the elections, returns, and qualifications of its own members, the courts would refuse affirmative aid to a claimant for such an office if it found him ineligible in its own view of the law. Judge Finch protested against this holding. "And so," he said, "I deny the asserted doctrine of 'Invocation'; of a right to do evil that good may come; of excusable judicial usurpation; and if the doctrine has anywhere got its dangerous and destructive hold upon our law, which I do not believe, it should be resolutely shaken off. But let us not deceive ourselves. The excess of jurisdiction is not even excusable, for it has neither occasion nor necessity." A moment later, he has his fears that he has been betrayed into excessive warmth. His closing words are those of apology and deference: "If what I have said does not convince the majority of the court, nothing that I can say will do so. I have tried faithfully, and, I hope, with proper respect, for certainly I have not meant to be wanting in that, to point out the mistake which, it seems to me, they are about to make. Theirs, however, must be both the responsibility and its consequences."

Such a method has its charm and its attraction, though one feels at times the yearning for another more robust and virile. It is here that I pass into the type which I have characterized as demonstrative or persuasive. It is not unlike the magisterial or imperative, yet it differs in a certain amplitude of development, a freer use of the resources of illustration and analogy and history and precedent, in brief, a tone more suggestive of the scientific seeker for the truth and less reminiscent of the priestess on the tripod. One might cite many judges who have used this method with distinction. I think the work of Charles Andrews, for many years a judge and then the Chief Judge of the New York Court of Appeals, is a shining illustration. I can best describe the quality of his opinions in the words of a memorial written upon his death: "The majesty of his personal appearance," it was said, "is reflected in the majesty of his judicial style, the steady and stately march of his opinions from established premises to inevitable conclusions." Such a method, well pursued, has a sanity and a clarity that make it an admirable medium for the declaration of considered judgments. The form is no mere epidermis. It is the very bone and tissue.

My summary of styles may leave a cheerless impression of the solemn and the ponderous. Flashes of humor are not unknown, yet the form of opinion which aims at humor from beginning to end is a perilous adventure, which can be justified only by success, and even then is likely to find its critics almost as many as its eulogists. The story is told by Bernard Shaw of a man who wished to consult the writings of the great naturalist Buffon, and who startled the clerks in the bookstore by the pompous and solemn query, "Have you the books of the celebrated Buffoon?" One of the difficulties about the humorous opinion is exposure to the risk of passing from the class of Buffons where we all like to dwell and entering the class of celebrated Buffoons. The transition at times is distressingly swift, and when once one has entered the new class, it is difficult, if not indeed impossible, to climb over the fences and back into the old. None the less, there are subjects which only the most resolute have been able to discuss without yielding to the temptation of making profert of their sense of humor. A dog or a cat, or a horse if it is the occasion of a horse trade, has been the signal for unexpected outbursts of mirth and occasionally of pathos from the judges slowly stirred to emotion by the cinema of life.

Judge Allen's opinion on the "code duello" among dogs, was on the whole a fine success, but it has been responsible for the writing of some others that were not. There is an opinion by Baron Bramwell which deals with the propensities of pigs. A fence was defective, and the pigs straying did mischief to a trolley car. The decision was that the barrier should have been sufficient to protect the adjoining owner against the incursions, not of all pigs, but of pigs of "average vigour and obstinacy." "Nor do we lay down," said the learned Baron, "that there must be a fence so close and strong that no pig could push through it, or so high that no horse or bullock could leap it. One could scarcely tell the limits of such a requirement, for the strength of swine is such that they would break through almost any fence, if there were a sufficient inducement on the other side. But the company are bound to put up such a fence that a pig not of a peculiarly wandering disposition, nor under any excessive temptation, will not get through it." Perhaps the humor of this ruling was more unwitting than designed. Some may agree with Sir Frederick Pollock that the decision is "almost a caricature of the general idea of the 'reasonable man.'" In all this I would not convey the thought that an opinion is the worse for being lightened by a smile. I am merely preaching caution. Other flights and digressions I find yet more doubtful than the humorous. In days not far remote, judges were not unwilling to embellish their deliverances with quotations from the poets. I shall observe towards such a practice the tone of decent civility that is due to those departed.

I have had in mind in this excursus a humor that was conscious and intended. Perhaps I should have classed the opinion that is humorous or playful as an independent type, but I have preferred to treat it incidentally since I am not aware that any judge has employed it consistently or except on rare occasions. Humor also that is unconscious and unintended may be dug out of the reports if we take the trouble to extract it. I once gathered together for my own edification and amusement some gems that I had unearthed from the opinions of one of our local courts in days when it had an appellate branch of its own and handed down opinions which were faithfully reported. Unluckily, I have lost my memorandum, but a few of the items are still vivid in my mind. The question to be determined was the extent of the amendment of a pleading to be permitted upon the trial. The decisive principle was thus expounded: "The bed that litigants make and lie in up to the trial, should not be then vacated by them. They should continue to lie therein until the jury render their verdict." I understand that the modern Practice Acts have swept this principle away, and that the suitor, who seems to his adversary to be innocently somnolent, may now jump out of bed at the last moment and prove to be very much awake. This is the new doctrine, but where will you find a more vivid statement of the doctrine of an elder day which decried surprise and haste, and was satisfied that justice herself should have the privilege of a nap? I recall, too, a charge to a jury, never reported, but surely fit to be preserved. "In this case," said the trial judge, "I believe that Mr. A (the counsel for the plaintiff) knows as much law as Mr. B (the counsel for the defendant), and I believe that Mr. B knows as much law as Mr. A, but I believe that in my judicial capacity know as much law as both of them together." Whereupon he forgot to tell the jury anything else, but said they were to consider of their verdict and decide the case in accordance with the rules he had laid down. Well, his charge was sparse, but it enunciated an important truth. Our whole judicial system is built upon some such assumption as the learned judge put forward a trifle crassly and obscurely. This is the great convention, the great fiction, which makes trial in court a fair substitute for trial by battle or by casting lots. The philosopher will find philosophy if he has an eye for it even in a "crowner's" court.

I must not forget my final type of judicial style, the tonsorial or agglutinative. I will not expatiate upon its horrors. They are known but too well. The dreary succession of quotations closes with a brief paragraph expressing a firm conviction that judgment for plaintiff or for defendant, as the case may be, follows as an inevitable conclusion. The writer having delivered himself of this expression of a perfect faith, commits the product of his hand to the files of the court and the judgment of the ages with all the pride of authorship. I am happy to be able to report that this type is slowly but steadily disappearing. As contrasted with its arid wastes, I prefer the sunny, though rather cramped and narrow, pinnacle of a type once much in vogue: "We have carefully examined the record and find no error therein; *therefore* the judgment must be affirmed with costs." How nice a sense of proportion, of the relation between cause and effect, is involved in the use of the illative conjunction "therefore," with its suggestion that other minds less sensitively attuned might have drawn a different conclusion from the same indisputable premises.

I have touched lightly, almost not at all, upon something more important than mere felicities of turn or phrase. Above and beyond all these are what we may term the architectonics of opinions. The groupings of fact and argument and illustration so as to produce a cumulative and mass effect; these, after all, are the things that count above all others. I should despair, however, of any successful analysis of problems at once so large and so difficult within the limits of this paper. One needs a larger easel if one is to follow such a map. Often clarity is gained by a brief and almost sententious statement at the outset of the problem to be attacked. Then may come a fuller statement of the facts, rigidly pared down, however, in almost every case, to those that are truly essential as opposed to those that are decorative and adventitious. If these are presented with due proportion and selection, our conclusion ought to follow so naturally and inevitably as almost to prove itself. Whether it succeeds in doing this or not is something about which the readers of the opinion are not always in accord. To gain a proper breadth of view, one should consult counsel for the vanquished as well as counsel for the victor.

The thought of the vanquished brings me to the opinion that voices a dissent. The protests and the warnings of minorities overborne in the fight have their interest and significance for the student, not only of law itself, but of the literary forms through which law reaches its expression. Comparatively speaking at least, the dissenter is irresponsible. The spokesman of the court is cautious, timid, fearful of the vivid word, the heightened phrase. He dreams of an unworthy brood of scions, the spawn of careless *dicta,* disowned by the *ratio decidendi,* to which all legitimate offspring must be able to trace their lineage. The result is to cramp and paralyze. One fears to say anything when the peril of misunderstanding puts a warning finger to the lips. Not so, however, the dissenter. He has laid aside the role of the hierophant, which he will be only too glad to resume when the chances of war make him again the spokesman of the majority. For the moment, he is the gladiator making a last stand against the lions. The poor man must be forgiven a freedom of expression, tinged at rare moments with a touch of bitterness, which magnanimity as well as caution would reject for one triumphant.

A French judge, M. Ransson, a member of the Tribunal of the Seine, wrote some twenty years ago an essay on the art of judging, in which he depicts the feelings of a judge of the first instance when a judgment is reversed. I suppose the state of mind of one reversed is akin in quality to the state of mind of one dissenting, though perhaps differing in degree. "A true magistrate," says M. Ransson, "guided solely by his duty and his conscience his learning and his reason, hears philosophically and without bitterness that his judgment has not been sustained; he knows that the higher court is there to this end, and that better informed beyond doubt, it has believed itself bound to modify his decision.

Ought we even to condemn him, if having done his best, he maintains in his inmost soul the impression that perhaps and in spite of everything he was right? *Causa diis victrix placuit, sed victa Catoni.*" Cato had a fine soul, but history does not record that he feared to speak his mind, and judges when in the minority are tempted to imitate his candor. We need not be surprised, therefore, to find in dissent a certain looseness of texture and depth of color rarely found in the *per curiam.* Sometimes, as I have said, there is just a suspicion of acerbity, but this, after all, is rare. More truly characteristic of dissent is a dignity, an elevation, of mood and thought and phrase. Deep conviction and warm feeling are saying their last say with knowledge that the cause is lost. The voice of the majority may be that of force triumphant, content with the plaudits of the hour, and recking little of the morrow. The dissenter speaks to the future, and his voice is pitched to a key that will carry through the years. Read some of the great dissents, the opinion, for example, of Judge Curtis in Dred Scott v. Sandford, and feel after the cooling time of the better part of a century the glow and fire of a faith that was content to bide its hour. The prophet and the martyr do not see the hooting throng. Their eyes are fixed on the eternities.

I shall be traveling away from my subject if I leave the writing of opinions and turn to arguments at the bar. A word of digression may be pardoned, however, for the two subjects are allied. One is called upon often to make answer to the question, what sort of argument is most effective in an appellate court? Shall it be long or short, terse or discursive? Shall it assume that the judges know the rudiments of law, or shall it attempt in a brief hour to supply the defects in their early training? Shall it state the law or the facts? Shall it take up the authorities and analyze them, or shall it content itself with conclusions and leave analysis for the study? There is, of course, no formula that will fit all situations in appellate courts or elsewhere. If, however, I had to prepare a list of "Don'ts" for the guidance of the novice, I think I would say that only in the rarest instances is it wise to take up one decision after another for the purpose of dissection. Such autopsies have their value at times, but they are wearisome and gruesome scenes. In my list of "Don'ts," I would add, don't state the minutiae of the evidence. The judges won't follow you, and if they followed, would forget. Don't attempt to supplement the defects of early training. Your auditors are hardened sinners, not easily redeemed. Above all, don't be long-winded. I have in mind a lawyer, now lifted to the bench, who argued the appeals for one of the civil subdivisions of the State. His arguments lasted about a quarter of an hour. He told us his point and sat down. The audience in the rear of the court room might not applaud, but the audience in front did—at least in spirit—and since the latter audience has the votes, it is best to make your play for them. If you faithfully observe these cautions, let not your spirits droop too low when the decision is adverse, even though there be the added gall and wormwood of a failure of the court to crown your brilliant effort with the dignity of an opinion. Many a gallant argument has met the same unworthy fate.

Young men as they approach admission to the bar must sometimes say to themselves that the great problems have been solved, that the great battles of the forum have been fought, that the great opportunities are ended. There are moods in which for a moment I say the same thing to myself. If I do, the calendar of the following day is as likely as not to bring the exposure of the error. It is a false and cramping notion that cases are made great solely or chiefly by reason of something intrinsic in themselves. They are great by what we make of them. McCulloch v. Maryland—to choose almost at random—is one of the famous cases of our history. I wonder, would it not be forgotten, and even perhaps its doctrine overruled, if Marshall had not put upon it the imprint of his genius. "Not one of his great opinions," says Professor Corwin, speaking of Marshall's work, "but might easily have been decided on comparatively narrow grounds in precisely the same way in which he decided it on broad, general principles, but with the probable result that it would never again have been heard of outside the law courts." So, too, the smaller issues await the transfiguring touch. "To a genuine accountant," says Charles Lamb, "the difference of proceeds is as nothing. The fractional farthing is as dear to his heart as the thousands which stand before it. He is the true actor, who, whether his part be a prince or a peasant, must act it with like authority." That is the spirit in which judge or advocate is to look upon his task. He is expounding a science, or a body of truth which he seeks to assimilate to a science, but in the process of exposition he is practicing an art. The Muses look at him a bit impatiently and wearily at times. He has done a good deal to alienate them, and sometimes they refuse to listen, and are seen to stop their ears. They have a strange capacity, however, for the discernment of strains of harmony and beauty, no matter how diffused and scattered through the ether. So at times when work is finely done, one sees their faces change, and they take the worker by the hand. They know that by the lever of art the subject the most lowly can be lifted to the heights. Small, indeed, is the company dwelling in those upper spaces, but the few are also the elect.

— II —

*A Ministry of Justice.**

Printed in the *Harvard Law Review*, Vol. XXXV, p. 113 ff., and in *Lectures on Legal Topics 1921–22.*

THE courts are not helped as they could and ought to be in the adaptation of law to justice. The reason they are not helped is because there is no one whose business it is to give warning that help is needed. Time was when the remedial agencies, though inadequate, were at least in our own hands. Fiction and equity were tools which we could apply and fashion for ourselves. The artifice was clumsy, but the clumsiness was in some measure atoned for by the skill of the artificer. Legislation, supplanting fiction and equity, has multiplied a thousandfold the power and capacity of the tool, but has taken the use out of our own hands and put it in the hands of others. The means of rescue are near for the worker in the mine. Little will the means avail unless lines of communication are established between the miner and his rescuer. We must have a courier who will carry the tidings of distress to those who are there to save when signals reach their ears. Today courts and legislature work in separation and aloofness. The penalty is paid both in the wasted effort of production and in the lowered quality of the product. On the one side, the judges, left to fight against anachronism and injustice by the methods of judge-made law, are distracted by the conflicting promptings of justice and logic, of consistency and mercy, and the output of their labors bears the tokens of the strain. On the other side, the legislature, informed only casually and intermittently of the needs and problems of the courts, without expert or responsible or disinterested or systematic advice as to the workings of one rule or another, patches the fabric here and there, and mars often when it would mend. Legislature and courts move on in proud and silent isolation. Some agency must be found to mediate between them.

---

* *A Ministry of Justice.* Reprinted with the permission of the Harvard Law Review Association, publishers of the *Harvard Law Review*, Macmillan Company, publishers of *Lectures on Legal Topics*, the Association of the Bar of the City of New York, and Columbia University, the residuary legatee of the literary estate of Benjamin Nathan Cardozo.

This task of mediation is that of a ministry of justice. The duty must be cast on some man or group of men to watch the law in action, observe the manner of its functioning, and report the changes needed when function is deranged. The thought is not a new one. Among our own scholars, it has been developed by Dean Pound with fertility and power.[1] Others before him, as he reminds us, had seen the need, and urged it. Bentham made provision for such a ministry in his draft of a Constitutional Code.[2] Lord Westbury renewed the plea.[3] Only recently, Lord Haldane has brought it to the fore again.[4] "There is no functionary at present who can properly be called a minister responsible for the subject of Justice."[5] "We are impressed by the representations made by men of great experience, such as the President of the Incorporated Law Society, as to the difficulty of getting the attention of the government to legal reform, and as to the want of contact between those who are responsible for the administration of the work of the Commercial Courts and the mercantile community, and by the evidence adduced that the latter are, in consequence and progressively, withdrawing their disputes from the jurisdiction of the Courts."[6] In countries of continental Europe, the project has passed into the realm of settled practice. Apart from these precedents and without thought of them, the need of such a ministry, of some one to observe and classify and criticize and report, has been driven home to me with steadily growing force through my own work in an appellate court. I have seen a body of judges applying a system of case law, with powers of innovation cabined and confined. The main lines are fixed by precedents. New lines may, indeed, be run, new courses followed, when precedents are lacking. Even then, distance and direction are guided by mingled considerations of logic and analogy and history and tradition which moderate and temper the promptings of policy and justice. I say this, not to criticize, but merely to describe. I have seen another body, a legislature, free from these restraints, its powers of innovation adequate to any need, preoccupied, however, with many issues more clamorous than those of courts, viewing with hasty and partial glimpses the things that should be viewed both steadily and whole. I have contrasted the quick response whenever the interest affected by a ruling untoward in results had some accredited representative, especially some public officer, through whom its needs were rendered vocal. A case involving, let us say, the construction of the Workmen's Compensation Law exhibits a defect in the statutory scheme. We find the Attorney General at once before the legislature with the request for an amendment. We cannot make a decision construing the tax law or otherwise affecting the finances of the state without inviting like results. That is because in these departments of the law there is a public officer whose duty prompts him to criticism and action. Seeing these things, I have marveled and lamented that the great fields of private law, where justice is distributed between man and man, should be left without a caretaker. A word would bring relief. There is nobody to speak it.

For there are times when deliverance, if we are to have it—at least, if we are to have it with reasonable speed—must come to us, not from within, but from without. Those who know best the nature of the judicial process, know best how easy it is to arrive at an impasse. Some judge, a century or more ago, struck out upon a path. The course seemed to be directed by logic and analogy. No milestone of public policy or justice gave warning at the moment that the course was wrong, or that danger lay ahead. Logic and analogy beckoned another judge still farther. Even yet there was no hint of opposing or deflecting forces. Perhaps the forces were not in being. At all events, they were not felt. The path went deeper and deeper into the forest. Gradually there were rumblings and stirrings of hesitation and distrust, anxious glances were directed to the right and to the left, but the starting point was far behind, and there was no other path in sight.

Thus, again and again, the processes of judge-made law bring judges to a stand that they would be glad to abandon if an outlet could be gained. It is too late to retrace their steps. At all events, whether really too late or not, so many judges think it is that the result is the same as if it were. Distinctions may, indeed, supply for a brief distance an avenue of escape. The point is at length reached when their power is exhausted. All the usual devices of competitive analogies have finally been employed without avail. The ugly or antiquated or unjust rule is there. It will not budge unless uprooted. Execration is abundant, but execration, if followed by submission, is devoid of motive power. There is need of a fresh start; and nothing short of a statute, unless it be the erosive work of years, will supply the missing energy. But the evil of injustice and anachronism is not limited to cases where the judicial process, unaided, is incompetent to gain the mastery. Mastery, even when attained, is the outcome of a constant struggle in which logic and symmetry are sacrificed at times to equity and justice. The gain may justify the sacrifice; yet it is not gain without deduction. There is an attendant loss of that certainty which is itself a social asset. There is a loss too of simplicity and directness, an increasing aspect of unreality, of something artificial and fictitious, when judges mask a change of substance, or gloss over its importance, by the suggestion of a consistency that is merely verbal and scholastic. Even when these evils are surmounted, a struggle, of which the outcome is long doubtful, is still the price of triumph. The result is to subject the courts and the judicial process to a strain as needless as it is wearing. The machinery is driven to the breaking point; yet we permit ourselves to be surprised that at times there is a break. Is it not an extraordinary omission that no one is charged with the duty to watch machinery or output, and to notify the master of the works when there is need of replacement or repair?

In all this, I have no thought to paint the failings of our law in lurid colors of detraction. I have little doubt that its body is for the most part sound and pure. Not even its most zealous advocate, however, will assert that it is perfect. I do not seek to paralyze the inward forces, the "in-dwelling and creative" energies,[7] that make for its development and growth. My wish is rather to release them, to give them room and outlet for healthy and unhampered action. The statute that will do this, first in one field and then in others, is something different from a code, though, as statute follows statute, the material may be given from which in time a code will come. Codification is, in the main, restatement. What we need, when we have gone astray, is change. Codification is a slow and toilsome process, which, if hurried, is destructive. What we need is some relief that will not wait upon the lagging years. Indeed, a code, if completed, would not dispense with mediation between legislature and judges, for code is followed by commentary and commentary by revision, and thus the task is never done. "As in other sciences, so in politics, it is impossible that all things should be precisely set down in writing; for enactments must be universal, but actions are concerned with particulars." [8] Something less ambitious, in any event, is the requirement of the hour. Legislation is needed, not to repress the forces through which judge-made law develops, but to stimulate and free them. Often a dozen lines or less will be enough for our deliverance. The rule that is to emancipate is not to imprison in particulars. It is to speak the language of general principles, which, once declared, will be developed and expanded as analogy and custom and utility, and justice, when weighed by judges in the balance, may prescribe the mode of application and the limits of extension. The judicial process is to be set in motion again, but with a new point of departure, a new impetus and direction. In breaking one set of shackles, we are not to substitute another. We are to set the judges free.

I have spoken in generalities, but instances will leap to view. There are fields, known to us all, where the workers in the law are hampered by rules that are outworn and unjust. How many judges, if they felt free to change the ancient rule, would be ready to hold today that a contract under seal may not be modified or discharged by another and later agreement resting in parol? [9] How many would hold that a deed, if it is to be the subject of escrow, must be delivered to a third person, and not to the grantee? [10] How many would hold that a surety is released, irrespective of resulting damage, if by agreement between principal and creditor the time of payment of the debt is extended for a single day? [11] How many would hold that a release of one joint tortfeasor is a release also of the others? How many would not prefer, instead of drawing some unreal distinction between releases under seal and covenants not to sue,[12] to extirpate, root and branch, a rule which is today an incumbrance and a snare? How long would Pinnel's case [13] survive if its antiquity were not supposed to command the tribute of respect? How long would Dumpor's case [14] maintain a ghostly and disquieting existence in the ancient byways of the law?

I have chosen extreme illustrations as most likely to command assent. I do not say that judges are without competence to effect some changes of that kind themselves. The inquiry, if pursued, would bring us into a field of controversy which it is unnecessary to enter. Whatever the limit of power, the fact stares us in the face that changes are not made. But short of these extreme illustrations are others, less glaring and insistent, where speedy change is hopeless unless effected from without. Sometimes the inroads upon justice are subtle and insidious. A spirit or a tendency, revealing itself in a multitude of little things, is the evil to be remedied. No one of its manifestations is enough, when viewed alone, to spur the conscience to revolt. The mischief is the work of a long series of encroachments. Examples are many in the law of practice and procedure.[15] At other times, the rule, though wrong, has become the cornerstone of past transactions. Men have accepted it as law, and have acted on the faith of it. At least, the possibility that some have done so, makes change unjust, if it were practicable, without saving vested rights. Illustrations again may be found in many fields. A rule for the construction of wills established a presumption that a gift to issue is to be divided, not *per stirpes,* but *per capita.*[16] The courts denounced and distinguished, but were unwilling to abandon.[17] In New York, a statute has at last released us from our bonds,[18] and we face the future unashamed. Still more common are the cases where the evil is less obvious, where there is room for difference of opinion, where some of the judges believe that the existing rules are right, at all events where there is no such shock to conscience that precedents will be abandoned, and what was right declared as wrong. At such times there is need of the detached observer, the skillful and impartial critic, who will view the field in its entirety, and not, as judges view it, in isolated sections, who will watch the rule in its working, and not, as judges watch it, in its making, and who viewing and watching and classifying and comparing, will be ready, under the responsibility of office, with warning and suggestion.

I note at random, as they occur to me, some of the fields of law where the seeds of change, if sown, may be fruitful of results. Doubtless better instances can be chosen. My purpose is, not advocacy of one change or another, but the emphasis of illustration that is concrete and specific.

It is a rule in some jurisdictions that if A sends to B an order for goods, which C, as the successor to B's business, takes it on himself to fill, no action at the suit of C will lie either for the price or for the value, if A in accepting the goods and keeping them believed that they had been furnished to him by B, and this though C has acted without fraudulent intent.[19] I do not say that this is the rule everywhere. There are jurisdictions where the question is still an open one. Let me assume, however, a jurisdiction where the rule, as I have stated it, prevails, or even one where, because the question is unsettled, there is a chance that it may prevail. A field would seem to be open for the declaration by the lawmakers of a rule less in accord, perhaps, with the demands of a "jurisprudence of conceptions," [20] but more in accord with those of morality and justice. Many will prefer to turn to the principle laid down in the French Code Civil:

"L'erreur n'est une cause de nullité de la convention que lorsqu'elle tombe sur la substance même de la chose qui en est l'objet. Elle n'est point une cause de nullité, lorsqu'elle ne tombe que sur la personne avec laquelle on a intention de contracter, à moins que la considération de cette personne ne soit la cause principale de la convention." [21]

Much may be said for the view that in the absence of bad faith, there should be a remedy in quasi contract.[22]

It is a rule which has grown up in many jurisdictions and has become "a common ritual" [23] that municipal corporations are liable for the torts of employees if incidental to the performance or non-performance of corporate or proprietary duties, but not if incidental to the performance or non-performance of duties public or governmental. The dividing line is hard to draw.

"Building a drawbridge, maintaining a health department, or a charitable institution, confining and punishing criminals, assaults by policemen, operating an elevator in a city hall, driving an ambulance, sweeping and cleaning streets, have been held governmental acts. Sweeping and cleaning streets, street lighting, operating electric light plants or waterworks, maintaining prisons, have been held private functions." [24]

The line of demarcation, though it were plainer, has at best a dubious correspondence with any dividing line of justice. The distinction has been questioned by the Supreme Court of the United States.[25] It has been rejected recently in Ohio.[26] In many jurisdictions, however, as, for example in New York, it is supported by precedent so inveterate that the chance of abandonment is small. I do not know how it would fare at the hands of a ministry of justice. Perhaps such a ministry would go farther, and would wipe out, not merely the exemption of municipalities, but the broader exemption of the state.[27] At least there is a field for inquiry, if not for action.

It is a rule of law that the driver of an automobile or other vehicle who fails to look or listen for trains when about to cross a railroad, is guilty of contributory negligence, in default, at least, of special circumstances excusing the omission. I find no fault with that rule. It is reasonable and just. But the courts in some jurisdictions have gone farther. They have held that the same duty that rests upon the driver rests also upon the passenger.[28] The friend whom I invite to ride with me in my car, and who occupies the rear seat beside me, while the car is in the care of my chauffeur, is charged with active vigilance to watch for tracks and trains, and is without a remedy if in the exuberance of jest or anecdote or reminiscence, he relies upon the vigilance of the driver to carry him in safety. I find it hard to imagine a rule more completely unrelated to the realities of life. Men situated as the guest in the case I have supposed do not act in the way that this rule expects and requires them to act. In the first place, they would in almost every case make the situation worse if they did; they would add bewilderment and confusion by contributing multitude of counsel. In the second place, they rightly feel that, except in rare emergencies of danger known to them, but unknown to the driver, it is not their business to do anything. The law in charging them with such a duty has shaped its rules in disregard of the common standards of conduct, the everyday beliefs and practices, of the average man and woman whose behavior it assumes to regulate. We must take a fresh start. We must erect a standard of conduct that realists can accept as just. Other fields of law of negligence may be resurveyed with equal profit. The law that defines or seeks to define the distinction between general and special employers is beset with distinctions so delicate that chaos is the consequence. No lawyer can say with assurance in any given situation when one employment ends and the other begins. The wrong choice of defendants is often made, with instances, all too many, in which justice has miscarried.

Illustrations yet more obvious are at hand in the law of evidence. Some of its rules are so unwieldy that many of the simplest things of life, transactions so common as the sale and delivery of merchandise, are often the most difficult to prove. Witnesses speaking of their own knowledge must follow the subject-matter of the sale from its dispatch to its arrival. I have been told by members of the bar that claims of undoubted validity are often abandoned, if contested, because the withdrawal of the necessary witnesses from the activities of business involves an expense and disarrangement out of proportion to the gain. The difficulty would be lessened if entries in books of account were admissible as *prima facie* evidence upon proof that they were made in the usual course of business. Such a presumption would harmonize in the main with teachings of experience. Certainly it would in certain lines of business, as, *e.g.,* that of banking, where irregularity of accounts is unquestionably the rare exception. Even the books of a bank are not admissible at present without wearisome preliminaries.[29] In England, the subject has for many years been regulated by statute.[30] Something should be done in our own country to mitigate the hardship. "The dead hand of the common-law rule . . . should no longer be applied to such cases as we have here." [31]

We are sometimes slow, I fear, while absorbed in the practice of our profession, to find inequity and hardship in rules that laymen view with indignation and surprise. One can understand why this is so. We learned the rules in youth when we were students in the law schools. We have seen them reiterated and applied as truths that are fundamental and almost axiomatic. We have sometimes even won our cases by invoking them. We end by accepting them without question as part of the existing order. They no longer have the vividness and shock of revelation and discovery. There is need of conscious effort, of introspective moods and moments, before their moral quality addresses itself to us with the same force as it does to others. This is at least one reason why the bar has at times been backward in the task of furthering reform. A recent study of the Carnegie Foundation for the Advancement of Teaching deals with the subject of training for the public profession of the law.[32] Dr. Pritchett says in his preface: [33]

"There is a widespread impression in the public mind that the members of the legal profession have not, through their organizations, contributed either to the betterment of legal education or to the improvement of justice to that extent which society has the right to expect."

The Centennial Memorial Volume of Indiana University contains a paper by the Dean of the Harvard Law School on the Future of Legal Education.[34]

"So long as the leaders of the bar," he says,[35] "do nothing to make the materials of our legal tradition available for the needs of the twentieth century, and our legislative lawmakers, more zealous than well instructed in the work they have to do, continue to justify the words of the chronicler—'the more they spake of law the more they did unlaw'—so long the public will seek refuge in specious projects of reforming the outward machinery of our legal order in the vain hope of curing its inward spirit."

Such reproaches are not uncommon. We do not need to consider either their justification or their causes. Enough for us that they exist. Our duty is to devise the agencies and stimulate the forces that will make them impossible hereafter.

What, then, is the remedy? Surely not to leave to fitful chance the things that method and system and science should order and adjust. Responsibility must be centered somewhere. The only doubt, it seems to me, is where. The attorneys-general, the law officers of the states, are overwhelmed with other duties. They hold their places by a tenure that has little continuity or permanence. Many are able lawyers, but a task so delicate exacts the scholar and philosopher, and scholarship and philosophy find precarious and doubtful nurture in the contentions of the bar. Even those qualities, however, are inadequate unless reënforced by others. There must go with them experience of life and knowledge of affairs. No one man is likely to combine in himself attainments so diverse. We shall reach the best results if we lodge power in a group, where there may be interchange of views, and where different types of thought and training will have a chance to have their say. I do not forget, of course, the work that is done by Bar Associations, state and national, as well as local, and by other voluntary bodies. The work has not risen to the needs of the occasion. Much of it has been critical rather than constructive. Even when constructive, it has been desultory and sporadic. No attempt has been made to cover with systematic and comprehensive vision the entire field of law. Discharge of such a task requires an expenditure of time and energy, a single-hearted consecration, not reasonably to be expected of men in active practice. It exacts, too, a scholarship and a habit of research not often to be found in those immersed in varied duties. Even if these objections were inadequate, the task ought not to be left to a number of voluntary committees, working at cross purposes. Recommendations would come with much greater authority, would command more general acquiescence on the part of legislative bodies, if those who made them were charged with the responsibilities of office. A single committee should be organized as a ministry of justice. Certain at least it is that we must come to some official agency unless the agencies that are voluntary give proof of their capacity and will to watch and warn and purge—unless the bar awakes to its opportunity and power.

How the committee should be constituted is, of course, not of the essence of the project. My own notion is that the ministers should be not less than five in number. There should be representatives, not less than two, perhaps even as many as three, of the faculties of law or political science in institutes of learning. Hardly elsewhere shall we find the scholarship on which the ministry must be able to draw if its work is to stand the test. There should be, if possible, a representative of the bench; and there should be a representative or representatives of the bar.

Such a board would not only observe for itself the workings of the law as administered day by day. It would enlighten itself constantly through all available sources of guidance and instruction; through consultation with scholars; through study of the law reviews, the journals of social science, the publications of the learned generally; and through investigation of remedies and methods in other jurisdictions, foreign and domestic. A project was sketched not long ago by John Bassett Moore, then Professor at Columbia University and later judge of the International Court, for an Institute of Jurisprudence.[36] It was to do for law what the Rockefeller Institute is doing for medicine. Such an institute, if founded, would be at the service of the ministers. The Commonwealth Fund has established a Committee for Legal Research which is initiating studies in branches of jurisprudence where reform may be desirable. The results of its labors will be available for guidance. Professors in the universities are pointing the way daily to changes that will help. Professor Borchard of Yale by a series of articles on the Declaratory Judgment[37] gave the impetus to a movement which has brought us in many states a reform long waited for by the law.[38] Dean Stone of Columbia has disclosed inconsistencies and weaknesses in decisions that deal with the requirement of mutuality of remedy in cases of specific performance.[39] Professor Chafee in a recent article[40] has emphasized the need of reform in the remedy of interpleader. In the field of conflict of laws, Professor Lorenzen has shown disorder to the point of chaos in the rules that are supposed to regulate the validity and effect of contracts.[41] The archaic law of arbitration, amended not long ago in New York through the efforts of the Chamber of Commerce,[42] remains in its archaic state in many other jurisdictions, despite requests for change. A ministry of justice will be in a position to gather these and like recommendations together, and report where change is needed. Reforms that now get themselves made by chance or after long and vexatious agitation, will have the assurance of considerate and speedy hearing. Scattered and uncoördinated forces will have a rallying point and focus. System and method will be substituted for favor and caprice. Doubtless, there will be need to guard against the twin dangers of overzeal on the one hand and of inertia on the other—of the attempt to do too much and of the willingness to do too little. In the end, of course, the recommendations of the ministry will be recommendations and nothing more. The public will be informed of them. The bar and others interested will debate them. The legislature may reject them. But at least the lines of communication will be open. The long silence will be broken. The spaces between the planets will at last be bridged.

The time is ripe for betterment. "Le droit a ses époques," says Pascal in words which Professor Hazeltine has recently recalled to us. The law has "its epochs of ebb and flow."[43] One of the flood seasons is upon us. Men are insisting, as perhaps never before, that law shall be made true to its ideal of justice. Let us gather up the driftwood, and leave the waters pure.

REFERENCES

1. Pound, "Juristic Problems of National Progress," 22 *Am. J. of Sociology,* 721, 729, 731 (May, 1917); Pound, "Anachronisms in Law," 3 *J. Am. Judicature Soc.,* 142, 146 (February, 1920).
2. *Works,* IX, 597–612.
3. 1 Nash, *Life of Lord Westbury,* 191, quoted by Pound, *supra.*
4. Report of Lord Haldane's Committee on the Machinery of Government (1918).
5. *Ibid.,* p. 63.
6. *Ibid.,* p. 64.
7. 2 Bryce, *Studies in History and Jurisprudence,* 609.
8. Aristotle, *Politics,* Bk. II (Jowett's translation).
9. 3 Williston, *Contracts,* §§ 1834–1837; Harris v. Shorall, 230 N. Y. 343 (1921).
10. Blewitt v. Boorum, 142 N. Y. 357, 37 N. E. 119 (1894).
11. N. Y. Life Ins. Co. v. Casey, 178 N. Y. 381, 70 N. E. 916 (1904).
12. Gilbert v. Finch, 173 N. Y. 455, 66 N. E. 133 (1903); Walsh v. N. Y. Central R. R. Co., 204 N. Y. 58, 97 N. E. 408 (1912); *cf.* 21 *Columbia L. Rev.* 491.
13. 5 Coke, 117; *cf.* Jaffray v. Davis, 124 N. Y. 164, 167, 26 N. E. 351 (1891); Frye v. Hubbell, 74 N. H. 358, 68 Atl. 325 (1907); 1 Williston, *Contracts,* § 121; Anson, *Contracts,* Corbin's ed., p. 137; Ferson, "The Rule in Foakes v. Beer," 31 *Yale L. J.* 15.
14. 2 Coke, 119.
15. In jurisdictions where procedure is governed by rules of court, recommendations of the ministry affecting the subject-matter of the rules may be submitted to the judges.
16. I state the law in New York and in many other jurisdictions. There are jurisdictions where the rule is different.
17. Petry v. Petry, 186 App. Div. 738, 175 N. Y. Supp. 30 (1919), 227 N. Y. 621, 125 N. E. 924 (1919); Matter of Durant, 231 N. Y. 41, 131 N. E. 562 (1921).
18. N. Y. Decedent's Estate Law, § 47a; L. 1921, c. 379.
19. Boulton v. Jones, 2 H. & N. 564 (1857); 1 Williston, *Contracts,* § 80; *cf.* Boston Ice Co. v. Potter, 123 Mass. 28 (1877); Kelly Asphalt Co. v. Barber Asphalt Paving Co., 211 N. Y. 68, 71, 105 N. E. 88 (1914).
20. Pound, "Mechanical Jurisprudence," 8 *Columbia L. Rev.* 605, 608, 610; Hynes v. N. Y. Central R. R. Co., 231 N. Y. 229, 235, 131 N. E. 898 (1921).
21. Code Civil, Art. 1110.
22. Anson, *Contracts* (Corbin's edition), 31; Keener, *Quasi Contracts,* 358–360.
23. 34 *Harv. L. Rev.* 66.
24. 34 *Harv. L. Rev.* 67.
25. Workmen v. The Mayor, 179 U. S. 552, 574 (1900).
26. Fowler v. City of Cleveland, 100 Ohio St. 158, 126 N. E. 72 (1919).
27. Smith v. State, 227 N. Y. 405, 125 N. E. 841 (1920).
28. Read v. N. Y. C. & H. R. R. R. Co., 123 App. Div. 228, 107 N. Y. Supp. 1068 (1908); s.c., 165 App. Div. 910, 150 N. Y. Supp. 1108 (1914), affd., 219 N. Y. 660, 114 N. E. 1081 (1916); Noakes v. N. Y. C. & H. R.

R. R. Co., 121 App. Div. 716, 106 N. Y. Supp. 522 (1907), 195 N. Y. 543 88 N. E. 1126 (1909). For the just rule see Weidlich v. N. Y., N. H. & H. R. R., 93 Conn. 438, 106 Atl. 323 (1919); 31 *Yale L. J.* 101.

29. Ocean Bank v. Carll, 55 N. Y. 440 (1874); Bates v. Preble, 151 U. S. 149 (1894).

30. 42 & 43 Vict., c. 11; Stephen, *Digest of the Law of Evidence,* Art. 36.

31. Rosen v. United States, 245 U. S. 467 (1918). (The situation has been bettered in New York by a statute enacted since the writing of this paper. See Civil Practice Act sec. 374a, 1928.)

32. Bulletin No. 15, Carnegie Foundation.

33. *Ibid.,* p. xvii.

34. Pound, "The Future of Legal Education," 259.

35. *Ibid.,* 268.

36. Report of Dean of Columbia University Law School for 1916.

37. 28 *Yale L. J.* 1.

38. 34 *Harv. L. Rev.* 697.

39. The "Mutuality" Rule in New York, 16 *Columbia L. Rev.* 443.

40. "Modernizing Interpleader," 30 *Yale L. J.* 814.

41. 30 *Yale L. J.* 565, 655; 31 *id.,* 53.

42. Matter of Berkovitz, 230 N. Y. 261, 130 N. E. 288 (1921).

43. H. D. Hazeltine, 1 *Cambridge L. J.* 1.

— III —

*What Medicine Can Do for Law.**

Address before The New York Academy of Medicine, November 1, 1928.

THERE are those who say that the earliest physician was the priest, just as the earliest judge was the ruler who uttered the divine command and was king and priest combined. Modern scholarship warns us to swallow with a grain of salt these sweeping generalities, yet they have at least a core of truth. Our professions—yours and mine—medicine and law—have divided with the years, yet they were not far apart at the beginning. There hovered over each the nimbus of a tutelage that was supernatural, if not divine. To this day each retains for the other a trace of the thaumaturgic quality distinctive of its origin. The physician is still the wonder-worker, the soothsayer, to whose reading of the entrails we resort when hard beset. We may scoff at him in health, but we send for him in pain. The judge, if you fall into his clutches, is still the Themis of the Greeks, announcing mystic dooms. You may not understand his words, but their effects you can be made to feel. Each of us is thus a man of mystery to the other, a power to be propitiated in proportion to the element within it that is mystic or unknown. "Speak not ill of a great enemy," says Selden in his *Table-Talk*—and Selden, you must know, was one of the ancient sages of our law—"speak not ill of a great enemy, but rather give him good words that he may use you the better if you chance to fall into his hands. The Spaniard did this when he was dying; his confessor told him, to work him to repentance, how the Devil tormented the wicked that went to hell; the Spaniard replying called the Devil my Lord; I hope my Lord the Devil is not so cruel. His confessor reproved him; excuse me for calling him so, says the Don, I know not into what hands I may fall, and if I happen into his, I hope he will use me the better for giving him good words." So with judges and doctors and devils it is all one, at least in hours of extremity.

---

* *What Medicine Can Do for Law.* Reprinted with the permission of the New York Academy of Medicine and Columbia University, the residuary legatee of the literary estate of Benjamin Nathan Cardozo.

One of these hours of extremity is at hand, the hour for the delivery of an anniversary address. The president of your Academy, moved I know not by what impulse—perhaps by some such faint foreboding as shaped the words of the Don in addressing his confessor—has turned with fair and soft speech to one without the mystic guild and has called upon a judge to preach the lesson of the hour. This is extraordinary enough, yet still more extraordinary is the fact that the judge has responded to the summons. In thus responding he has not been beguiled into the vain belief that any message he has to offer is worthy of your patience. He disclaims even a faint foreboding that there is need to propitiate your favor as against some future hour when he may be driven to seek your ministrations in default of other aid. Nothing is there on his side except a gesture of mere friendliness, the friendliness that is due between groups united in a common quest, the quest for the rule of order, the rule of health and of disease, to which for individuals as for society we give the name of law.

Indeed, the more I think it over, the more I feel the closeness of the tie that binds our guilds together. In all this there is nothing strange. I was reading the other day a very interesting document, a report to the overseers of Harvard University by the president of the university, Dr. A. Lawrence Lowell. He speaks of a new educational concept, the concept, as he calls it, of the continuity of knowledge. The idea is taking root that the subdivisions of science, like those of time itself, have been treated too often as absolute and genuine—that there is need to recognize them more fully as mere figments of the brain, mere labor-saving devices, helps to thinking, but like other helps to thinking, misleading if their origin is neglected or forgotten. Thus it is that the physicist is learning from the chemist, the zoologist from the botanist, the economist from the statesman and the student of social science, the physician from the psychologist, and so on interchangeably and indefinitely. "The sharp severance," we are told, "is giving way, and we perceive that all subjects pass imperceptibly into others previously distinct." Something of this same concept of the continuity of knowledge is making its way into the law. In my own court at a recent session we had one case where a wise decision called for the wisdom of a chemist;

another for that of one skilled in the science of mechanics; another for that of the student of biology and medicine; and so on through the list. I do not say we were able to supply this fund of wisdom out of the resources of our knowledge, yet in theory, at least, the litigants before us were entitled to expect it, and our efficiency as judges would be so much the greater, the quality of the output so much the sounder and richer, in proportion to our ability to make the theory one with fact. More and more we lawyers are awaking to a perception of the truth that what divides and distracts us in the solution of a legal problem is not so much uncertainty about the law as uncertainty about the facts—the facts which generate the law. Let the facts be known as they are, and the law will sprout from the seed and turn its branches toward the light. We make our blunders from time to time as rumor has it that you make your own. The worst of them would have been escaped if the facts had been disclosed to us before the ruling was declared. A statute of New York, forbidding night work for women, was declared arbitrary and void by a decision of the Court of Appeals announced in 1907.[1] In 1915, with fuller knowledge of the investigations of scientists and social workers, a like statute was held by the same court to be reasonable and valid.[2] "Courts know today" (if I may borrow my own words) "that statutes are to be viewed, not in isolation or *in vacuo,* as pronouncements of abstract principles for the guidance of an ideal community, but in the setting and the framework of present-day conditions as revealed by the labors of economists and students of the social sciences in our own country and abroad." [3]

Examples to point the meaning come flocking at the call. Again and again we are asked to nullify legislation as an undue encroachment upon the sphere of individual liberty. Encroachment to some extent there is by every command or prohibition. Liberty in the literal sense is impossible for any one except the anarchist, and anarchy is not law, but its negation and destruction. What is undue in mandate or restrain cannot be known in advance of the event by a process of deduction from metaphysical principles of unvarying validity. It can be known only when there is knowledge of the mischief to be remedied, and knowledge of the mischief—to which, of course, must be added knowledge of the effectiveness of the remedy to counteract or cure the mischief—is knowledge of the facts. We do not turn to a body of esoteric legal doctrine, at least not invariably, to find the key to some novel problem of constitutional limitation, the bounds of permissible encroachment on liberty or property. We turn at times to physiology or embryology or chemistry or medicine—to a Jenner or a Pasteur or a Virchow or a Lister as freely and submissively as to a Blackstone or a Coke. Of course, even then we try to know our place and exhibit the humility that becomes the amateur. We do not assume to sit in judgment between conflicting schools of thought. Enough it is for us that the view embodied in a contested statute has at least respectable support—its sponsors, if perchance its critics—in the true abodes of science. Shall hours of labor be limited in one calling or another, for this group or for that? The physiologist as well as the sociologist must supply us with the body of knowledge appropriate to the problem to be solved. Such cases as People v. The Schweinler Press [4] decided by the Court of Appeals of New York in 1915, and Muller v. Oregon,[5] decided in 1908 by the Supreme Court of the United States, show the answer of the courts when the enlightening facts were put before them by workers in other fields. Shall compulsory vaccination be exacted of the children in the public schools? Read the answer of the courts in Matter of Viemeister,[6] decided in 1904, and Jacobson v. Massachusetts,[7] decided a year later. Only the other day my court had to deal with the propriety of the tuberculin test as applied to herds of cattle, the unfortunates who responded to the test being marked for quarantine or slaughter.[8] A question of scientific fact is at the core of other problems, juridical in form, and yet intense, or so I hear, in their emotional appeal. What is a beverage, and when is it intoxicating? Let me not open ancient wounds by a reminder of the answer.

We look then to you, to the students of mind and body, for the nutriment of fact, solid if not liquid, that in many a trying hour will give vitality and vigor to the tissues of our law. Conspicuously is this true today in the administration of the law of crime. The law of crime has dramatic features which make it bulk large in the public mind, though of all the cases in my court the criminal appeals make up a small proportion, say eight or ten per cent. None the less, from the viewpoint of its social consequences the criminal law has an importance that is imperfectly reflected in statistical averages or the tables of accountants. The field is one in which the physician is asserting himself year by year with steadily expanding power. Among students of criminology there are now many who maintain that the whole business of sentencing criminals should be taken away from the judges and given over to the doctors. Courts, with their judges and juries, are to find the fact of guilt or innocence. The fact being ascertained, the physician is to take the prisoner in hand and say what shall be done with him. Governor Smith in his message to the Legislature of 1928 recommended that this reform be studied by the Crime Commission. "Because," he said, "of my belief that justice sometimes miscarries because those charged with determining guilt are often affected by the thought of the sentence to be imposed for a given crime, I would suggest that the Crime Commission give careful study and consideration to a fundamental change in the method of sentencing criminals. After guilt has been determined by legal process, instead of sentence being fixed by judges according to statute, I should like to see offenders who have been adjudged guilty detained by the state. They should then be carefully studied by a board of expert mental and physical specialists, who after careful study of all the elements entering each case would decide and fix the penalty for the crime. I realize the complexity of such a fundamental change. It probably requires even constitutional amendment. Therefore I recommend that your honorable bodies request the Crime Commission to report to you, after due and careful study of the proposal, whether such a change is advisable and how it can be brought about. It appeals to me as a modern, humane, scientific way to deal with the criminal offender."

The reform thus proposed is no extemporized nostrum, no hasty innovation. It was recommended not many years ago by a committee of the Institute of Criminal Law and Criminology, of which the chairman was Victor P. Arnold, judge of the Juvenile Court of Chicago. This committee proposed *inter alia* "that in all cases of felony or misdemeanors punishable by a prison sentence the question of responsibility be not submitted to the jury, which will thus be called upon to determine only that the offense was committed by the defendant," and "that the disposition and treatment (including punishment) of all such misdemeanants and felons—*i.e.*, the sentence imposed, be based upon a study of the individual offender by properly qualified and impartial experts coöperating with the courts."[9] One of the most careful studies of the crime problem in recent years is that of Dr. S. Sheldon Glueck in his work on *Mental Disorder and the Criminal Law*. "If," he says,[10] "the socio-legal treatment of *all* criminals regardless of pathological condition were being considered, it would seem that the simplest device would be to permit the law to convict or acquit as is done today, but to provide for *an administrative* instrumentality (perhaps a commission composed of psychiatrists, psychologists, sociologists, and others) to begin to function in the case of convicted persons at the point where the law leaves off, to determine the appropriate socio-penal treatment adequate to the individual delinquent, as well as its duration." Developing this thought in an interesting essay, "A Rational Penal Code," published in the *Harvard Law Review*,[11] he puts forward the view that the minimum sentence should be fixed by law, but that the maximum in every instance should be left indefinite, to be determined for the individual prisoner by psychiatrists and physicians after a study of the individual case (*cf.* Gillin, *Criminology and Penology*, p. 153). Even now in some of the countries of continental Europe—in Switzerland, for example—a criminal whose mentality is low, though insanity is not suspected, is turned over for examination to psychiatrists in the service of the government, who make their recommendations to the court before sentence is pronounced.[12]

Not a little impetus has been given to these and like reforms by researches of bio-chemists into the operations of the ductless glands. If most of their conclusions are still in the stage of speculation or hypothesis, their writings have been useful, none the less, in awaking popular interest in the mentality of criminals, bringing home the need of study and the possibilities of a reformed penology to many who were blissfully unconscious of the existence of a problem. Our vices as well as our virtues have been imputed to bodily derangements till character has become identified with a chemical reaction. "The internal secretions," says an enthusiastic student of the endocrines,[13] "the internal secretions with their influence upon brain and nervous system, as well as every other part of the body-corporation, as essentially blood-circulating chemical substances, have been discovered the real governors and arbiters of instincts and dispositions, emotions and reactions, characters and temperaments, good and bad." A far cry is this from the voice of Socrates in the *Republic* of Plato: "My belief is, not that a good body will by its own excellence make the soul good; but, on the contrary, that a good soul will by *its* excellence render the body as perfect as it can be." The criminal of old was given copious draughts of exhortation and homily administered with solemn mien by reformers lay and cleric. The criminal of tomorrow will have fewer homilies and exhortations, but will have his doses of thyroxin or adrenalin till his being is transfigured. Good people sitting peacefully in their homes and reading fearsome tales of robbery and rapine, may take comfort in the thought that while the regeneration of character is in this process of "becoming," the body of the offender will be in the keeping of the law.

I have no thought in all this to express approval or disapproval of the project of withdrawing from the court the sentence-fixing power. One may see a wise reform there without acceptance of the creed that virtue and vice are not spiritual essences, but high-sounding synonyms for the hormones of the body. As to this last many of us, perhaps in our ignorance, will feel like echoing the words of Principal Jacks in his suggestive little book, *Constructive Citizenship*. "I think also," he says, "that while most of us are content to have our vices (but not our virtues) explained in this charitable manner by our neighbors, very few of us, and those the meanest, are in the habit of applying it to themselves. When we apply it to ourselves, a voice within seems to answer, 'It is false.'" He is speaking, as it happens, of another and earlier precept of criminology, the precept that virtue and vice are the products solely of environment; but his words are as apposite to the notion that they are the products chiefly of the glands, though in each case it is true that repugnance must not be taken as amounting to disproof. All this, however, is beside the mark, at least for present purposes. Like the neophytes of other faiths, the discoverers of the new theory that virtue and vice are synonyms for spontaneous secretions may have overshot the mark, may have loaded a useful notion with more than it can bear. To prove that genius is accompanied by certain bodily changes or reactions is not to prove that the bodily changes or reactions are identical with genius.* This does not detract from the fullness of my belief that at a day not far remote the teachings of bio-chemists and behaviorists, of psychiatrists and penologists, will transform our whole system of punishment for crime. Vain is the attempt to forecast here and now the lines of the transfigured structure. We must keep a sharp lookout, or you will supplant us altogether. Do they not tell the fable of Hippocrates that he burned the library of the Temple of Health at Cnidus in order to enjoy the monopoly of knowledge? How it will work out, whether we shall sit beside you or above you, or even perhaps below you, I am not wise enough to say. The physician may be merely the ally of the judge in the business of admeasuring the sentence, or, as to that branch of the work, may even drive the judge away. Detention of the offender may retain in respect of certain crimes the qualities, or some of them, belonging to our present system of imprisonment, and for other crimes may acquire a quality less punitive and rigorous. But transformation there will be.

For the present system is stern often when it should be mild, and mild often when it should be stern, or so, at least, its critics urge. It is a survival of the time when punishment for crime was thought of as a substitute for private vengeance, with its sequel private war. The familiar phrase, the King's Peace, means this and nothing more, that for the peace separately maintained by duke or count or bishop, each in his own domain, there was to be substituted one general or uniform peace, the king's, establishing a single rule throughout the kingdom far and wide. You will find it all set forth by Sir Frederick Pollock in one of his fascinating essays with the fullness of example that is dear to antiquarians.[14] We have put away the blood feud, the vendetta, the other forms of private war, but in the framing of our penal codes we have not forgotten the passions that had their outlet and release in pursuit and retribution. I do not say that it is wise to forget them altogether. The thirst for vengeance is a very real, even if it be a hideous, thing; and states may

---

* *Cf.* Bertrand Russell, *Philosophy,* p. 218.

not ignore it till humanity has been raised to greater heights than any that has yet been scaled in all the long ages of struggle and ascent. Disregard such passions altogether, and the alternative may be the recrudescence of the duel or the feud. The vigilance committee and Judge Lynch may shove aside police and courts. Even if vengeance be forgotten and the social consequences alone considered, there are inhibitions in the threat of punishment that society cannot afford to withdraw from any capable of feeling them. "The presence of mechanism," says Dr. Glueck,[15] "does not mean that human beings have not some spark of capacity for consciously and creatively guiding their conduct in conformity with legal sanctions." Punishment is necessary, indeed, not only to deter the man who is a criminal at heart, who has felt the criminal impulse, who is on the brink of indecision, but also to deter others who in our existing social organization have never felt the criminal impulse and shrink from crime in horror. Most of us have such a scorn and loathing of robbery or forgery that the temptation to rob or forge is never within the range of choice; it is never a real alternative. There can be little doubt, however, that some of this repugnance is due to the ignominy that has been attached to these and like offenses through the sanctions of the criminal law. If the ignominy were withdrawn, the horror might be dimmed.

All this I have in mind, yet even so, the present system, in the view of many, is as irrational in its mercies as in its rigors, and in its rigors as in its mercies. The casual offender expiates his offense in the company of defectives and recidivists, and after devastating years is given back an outcast to the society that made him. The defective or recidivist, whose redemption is hopeless, goes back after a like term, or one not greatly different, to renew his life of crime, unable to escape it without escaping from himself. Students of the mind and body are insisting, as never before, that in much of our criminology there is futility and waste. "It is foolish," says one of them, "to build institutions for detaining defectives for long periods as a punishment for a condition for which they are not responsible, and then discharge them without doing anything to remove the cause of their trouble." "For a large proportion of criminals," says another author, "—the percentage has yet to be determined—punishment for a period of time and then letting him go free is like imprisoning a diphtheria-carrier for a while and then permitting him to commingle with his fellows and spread the germ of diphtheria." [16] A beginning of a change has been made in this state by recent legislation, but with tests, in the thought of many, too mechanical and absolute. Not improbably the path of progress has been marked in an English statute which supplements the term of punishment in prison with another and elastic term of what is known as preventive detention in less rigorous surroundings, a camp in the Isle of Wight being set aside for that use.[17] Here or in some system not dissimilar may be found the needed adjustment between the penal and the remedial elements in our scheme of criminology.

Adjustment of some sort there must be if we are to fill the measure of our duty to our defective fellow beings. Run your eyes over the life history of a man sentenced to the chair. There, spread before you in all its inevitable sequence, is a story of the Rake's Progress more implacable than any that was ever painted by a Hogarth. The Correctional School, the Reformatory, Sing Sing or Dannemora, and then at last the chair. The heavy hand of doom was on his head from the beginning. The sin, in truth, is ours—the sin of a penal system that leaves the victim to his fate when the course that he is going is written down so plainly in the files of the courts and the stigmata of mind and body. I do not mean to say that any rule of thumb is to be adopted in dealing with these problems. My experience as a judge in other fields of law has made me distrustful of rules of thumb generally. They are a lazy man's expedient for ridding himself of the trouble of thinking and deciding. Try hard as we will, the problems of punishment, like the problems of law generally, are in their essence unique. "We must spread the gospel," writes Professor Powell, "we must spread the gospel that there is no gospel that will save us from the pain of choosing at every step." Human nature, like human life, has complexities and diversities too many and too intricate to be compressed within a formula. I would not shut the door of hope on any one, though classified in some statistical table as defective or recidivist, so long as scientific analysis and study of his mental and physical reactions after the state had taken him in hand held out the promise of redemption. Neither in punishment nor in any other form of judging shall we ever rid ourselves altogether of the heart-breaking burden of individual adjustment.

I do not say that either psychology or medicine or penology has yet arrived at such a stage as to make a revolution in our system of punishment advisable or possible. Here as in so many fields we shall have to feel our way, it may be, by slow advances, by almost insensible approaches. I have faith, none the less, that a century or less from now, our descendants will look back upon the penal system of today with the same surprise and horror that fill our own minds when we are told that only about a century ago one hundred and sixty crimes were visited under English law with the punishment of death, and that in 1801 a child of thirteen was hanged at Tyburn for the larceny of a spoon.[18] Dark chapters are these in the history of law. We think of them with a shudder, and say to ourselves that we have risen to heights of mercy and of reason far removed from such enormities. The future may judge us less leniently than we choose to judge ourselves.[19] Perhaps the whole business of the retention of the death penalty will seem to the next generation, as it seems to many even now, an anachronism too discordant to be suffered, mocking with grim reproach all our clamorous professions of the sanctity of life. Perhaps some new Howard will make us see in our whole prison system a reproach as great, a blot as dark, as the Howard of English history made visible to the eyes of all in the prisons and pest houses of a century and a half ago. I am not sure how this will be. Sure, however, I am that whatever enlightenment shall come will make its way, not through the unaided labors of the men of my profession, the judges and the advocates, but through the combined labors of men of many callings, and most of all your own. How quickly a great change can come about will be seen if we contrast the penal justice applied to children a quarter-century ago with the treatment in these days of the juvenile delinquent by the judges of the Children's Courts. You will find it all set forth in a recent study of Juvenile Courts in the United States by Dr. Herbert H. Lou in the Social Study Series of the University of North Carolina. The methods, the humane and scientific methods, that have thus prevailed will spread to other fields. This is your work, I am persuaded, as much as it is ours. Your hands must hold the torch that will explore the dark mystery of crime—the mystery, even darker, of the criminal himself, in all the deep recesses of thought and will and body. Here is a common ground, a borderland between your labors and our own, where hope and faith and love can do their deathless work.

One takes a large order when one offers to reshape from its foundations a scheme of penal justice. Those of us whose course has even now been largely run, may wish to have before us a prospect less Utopian. Let me call attention, therefore, to two features of the law of crimes where the coöperation of your profession will be helpful even now without wreaking our energies upon reforms that will flower at some distant day. I think the men of your Academy might well emphasize the need for a restatement of our law of homicide, and in particular of the distinction between murder in its two degrees. I think they might well emphasize another subject—one that has grown a trifle stale, but never to be abandoned till it had been settled right—the definition of insanity when viewed as an excuse for crime.

The law of homicide, and in particular the distinction between murder in the first and second degrees, may seem at first blush to be something that involves the mere technique of criminal law, and so a matter not for you, but one to be dealt with by the lawyers. The reason why I mention it to you is because the anomalies of the present distinction can be developed with special clearness and authority by the psychiatrist or the alienist or the student of psychology.

Homicide under our statute is classified as murder and as manslaughter, and murder itself has two degrees, a first and a second. "The killing of a human being, unless it is excusable or justifiable, is murder in the first degree when committed from a deliberate and premeditated design to effect the death of the person killed, or of another," as well as in certain other situations which, for the purpose of my present inquiry, it is not important to consider.[20] "Such killing of a human being is murder in the second degree, when committed with a design to effect the death of the person killed or of another, but without deliberation and premeditation."[21] There, you see, is the distinction, and it is at least verbally clear. Both first and second degree murder (laying aside the exceptions which I thought it unnecessary to state) require an intent to kill, but in the one instance it is deliberate and premeditated intent, and in the other it is not. If there is no intent to kill whatever, the grade (subject to exceptions) is reduced to manslaughter. I have said that on the face of the statute the distinction is clear enough. The difficulty arises when we try to discover what is meant by the words deliberate and premeditated. A long series of decisions, beginning many years ago, has given to these words a meaning that differs to some extent from the one revealed upon the surface. To deliberate and premeditate within the meaning of the statute, one does not have to plan the murder days or hours or even minutes in advance, as where one lies in wait for one's enemy or places poison in his food and drink. The law does not say that any particular length of time must intervent between the volition and the act. The human brain, we are reminded,[22] acts at times with extraordinary celerity. All that the statute requires is that the act must not be the result of immediate or spontaneous impulse. "If there is hesitation or doubt to be overcome, a choice made as the result of thought, however short the struggle between the intention and the act," there is such deliberation and premeditation as will expose the offender to the punishment of death.[23] Thus in a case decided in 1886,[24] the defendant ejected a trespasser; a fight ensued; the defendant stabbed the trespasser and flung him to the ground; having done this, he seized an ax and clove the victim's head. The interval between the knife blow and the falling ax was long enough to sustain the verdict that sent the murderer to his death. One may say indeed in a rough way that an intent to kill is always deliberate and premeditated within the meaning of the law unless the mind is so blinded by pain or rage as to make the act little more than an automatic or spontaneous reaction to the environment—not strictly automatic or spontaneous, for there could then be no intent, and yet a near approach thereto. The behaviorists would say, I suppose that what had happened was a conditioned reflex, a learned, as opposed to an unlearned, response.[25] Courts in other states (*e.g.,* Massachusetts) lay down the same rules or rules not greatly different.

I think the distinction is much too vague to be continued in our law. There can be no intent unless there is a choice, yet by the hypothesis, the choice without more is enough to justify the inference that the intent was deliberate and premeditated. The presence of a sudden impulse is said to mark the dividing line, but how can an impulse be anything but sudden when the time for its formation is measured by the lapse of seconds? Yet the decisions are to the effect that seconds may be enough. What is meant, as I understand it, is that the impulse must be the product of an emotion or passion so swift and overmastering as to sweep the mind from its moorings. A metaphor, however, is, to say the least, a shifting test whereby to measure degrees of guilt that mean the difference between life and death. I think the students of the mind should make it clear to the lawmakers that the statute is framed along the lines of a defective and unreal psychology. If intent is deliberate and premeditated whenever there is choice, then in truth it is always deliberate and premeditated, since choice is involved in the hypothesis of the intent. What we have is merely a privilege offered to the jury to find the lesser degree when the suddenness of the intent, the vehemence of the passion, seems to call irresistibly for the exercise of mercy. I have no objection to giving them this dispensing power, but it should be given to them directly and not in a mystifying cloud of words. The present distinction is so obscure that no jury hearing it for the first time can fairly be expected to assimilate and understand it. I am not at all sure that I understand it myself after trying to apply it for many years and after diligent study of what has been written in the books. Upon the basis of this fine distinction with its obscure and mystifying psychology, scores of men have gone to their death. I think it is time for you who speak with authority as to the life of the mind to say whether the distinction has such substance and soundness that it should be permitted to survive. Some appropriate committee there should be in the bar associations, on the one hand, and this Academy, on the other (if none exists already), whereby the resources of the two professions can be pooled in matters such as these where society has so much to gain from coöperative endeavor.

I have spoken of another branch of the law of homicide, the law defining and governing mental irresponsibility. In strictness, this is not a branch of the law of homicide alone, since the same definition applies to other crimes as well, yet it is in connection with homicide that the question commonly arises. In the early stages of our law, way back in medieval times, insanity was never a defense for crime. The insane killer, like the man who killed in self-defense, might seek a pardon from the king, and would often get one. He had no defense at law. Gradually there came in the law itself a mitigation of this rigor. A defense of insanity was allowed, but only within the narrowest limits. This was what has become known as the wild-beast stage of the defense. The killer was not excused unless he had so lost his mind as to be no more capable of understanding than if he were merely a wild beast. Then the limits of the defense were expanded, but still slowly and narrowly. The killer was excused if the disease of the mind was such that he was incapable of appreciating the difference between right and wrong. At first this meant, not the right and wrong of the particular case, but right and wrong generally or in the abstract, the difference, as it was sometimes said, between good and evil. Later the rule was modified in favor of the prisoner so that capacity to distinguish between right and wrong generally would not charge with responsibility if there was not capacity to understand the difference in relation to the particular act, the subject of the crime. The rule governing the subject was crystallized in England in 1843 by the answer made by the House of Lords to questions submitted by the judges in the famous case of McNaghten, who was tried for the murder of one Drummond, the secretary of Sir Robert Peel. The answer was in effect that "the jurors ought to be told in all cases that every man is to be presumed to be sane, and to possess a sufficient degree of reason to be responsible for his crimes, until the contrary be proved to their satisfaction; and that to establish a defense on the ground of insanity it must be clearly proved that, at the time of committing the act, the accused was laboring under such a defect of reason from disease of the mind, as not to know the nature and quality of the act he was doing, or, if he did know it, that he did not know he was doing what was wrong."[26]

The test established by McNaghten's Case has been incorporated into the law of New York by the mandate of the statute. Penal Law, § 34, provides: "A person is not excused from criminal liability as an idiot, imbecile, lunatic or insane person, except upon proof that at the time of the commission of the alleged criminal act he was laboring under such a defect of reason as either (1) not to know the nature and quality of the act he was doing; (2) not to know the act was wrong." It matters not that some uncontrollable impulse, the product of mental disease, may have driven the defendant to the commission of the murderous act. The law knows nothing of such excuses.[27] Again the statute is explicit: "A morbid propensity to commit prohibited acts, existing in the mind of a person who is not shown to have been incapable of knowing the wrongfulness of such acts, forms no defense to a prosecution therefor." [28] If the offender knew the nature and quality of the act and knew it to be wrong, he must answer for it with his life, if death is the penalty that would be paid by the sane. Of course, there is an ambiguity in all this which will not have escaped your quick discernment. What is meant by knowledge that the act is wrong? Is it enough that there was knowledge that the act was wrong in the sense that it was prohibited by law, or must there be knowledge also that it was morally wrong? Curiously enough, this question did not arise in New York till 1915. One Schmidt, a priest, was charged with the murder of a woman with whom he had been intimate. Upon the trial his defense was insanity. He said he had heard the voice of God calling upon him by day and night to sacrifice and slay. He yielded to the call in the belief that slaughter was a moral duty. The trial judge held that this belief was no defense if he knew the nature of the act and knew it to be wrong in the sense of being prohibited by law. On appeal this ruling was reversed.[29] We held that the word "wrong" in the statutory definition had reference in such circumstances to the moral quality of the act, and not merely to the legal prohibition. Any other reading would charge a mother with the crime of murder if she were to slay a dearly loved child in the belief that a divine command had summoned to the gruesome act. Let me say by way of parenthesis that Schmidt did not profit by the error in the charge, since he admitted under oath that the whole defense of insanity was an imposture and a sham.

Physicians time and again rail at the courts for applying a test of mental responsibility so narrow and inadequate.

There is no good in railing at us. You should rail at the legislature. The judges have no option in the matter. They are bound, hand and foot, by the shackles of a statute. Every one concedes that the present definition of insanity has little relation to the truths of mental life. There are times, of course, when a killing has occurred without knowledge by the killer of the nature of the act. A classic instance is the case of Mary Lamb, the sister of Charles Lamb, who killed her mother in delirium. There are times when there is no knowledge that the act is wrong, as when a mother offers up her child as a sacrifice to God. But after all, these are rare instances of the workings of a mind deranged. They exclude many instances of the commission of an act under the compulsion of disease, the countless instances, for example, of crimes by paranoiacs under the impulse of a fixed idea. I am not unmindful of the difficulty of framing a definition of insanity that will not be so broad as to open wide the door to evasion and imposture. Conceivably the law will have to say that the risk is too great, that the insane must answer with their lives, lest under cover of their privilege the impostor shall escape. Conceivably the twilight zone between sanity and insanity is so broad and so vague as to bid defiance to exact description. I do not know, though I am reluctant to concede that science is so impotent. Attempts at formulation of a governing principle or standard have been none too encouraging,[30] but betterment is attainable, though it be something less than perfection. Many states—Massachusetts, for example, and Alabama and Pennsylvania and Virginia and Vermont—recognize the fact that insanity may find expression in an irresistible impulse, yet I am not aware that the administration of their criminal law has suffered as a consequence.[31] Much of the danger might be obviated if the issue of insanity were triable by a specially constituted tribunal rather than the usual jury. Of this at least I am persuaded: the medical profession of the state, the students of the life of the mind in health and in disease, should combine with students of the law in a scientific and deliberate effort to frame a definition, and a system of administration, that will combine efficiency with truth. If insanity is not to be a defense, let us say so frankly and even brutally, but let us not mock ourselves with a definition that palters with reality. Such a method is neither good morals nor good science nor good law. I know it is often said, and very likely with technical correctness,[32] that the statute ought not to be viewed as defining insanity. What it does, and all that it does is to state the forms or phases of insanity that will bring immunity from punishment. All this may be true, yet it is hard to read the statute without feeling that by implication and suggestion it offers something more. It keeps the word of promise to the ear and breaks it to the hope. Let us try to improve its science and at the very least its candor. Here is another field for the coöperative endeavor of medicine and law.

Every now and then there crops up in popular journals a discussion of the problem of euthanasia. The query is propounded whether the privilege should be accorded to a physician of putting a patient painlessly out of the world when there is incurable disease, agonizing suffering, and a request by the sufferer for merciful release. No such privilege is known to our law, which shrinks from any abbreviation of the span of life, shaping its policy in that regard partly under the dominance of the precepts of religion and partly in the fear of error or abuse. Just as a life may not be shortened, so its value must be held as equal to that of any other, the mightiest or the lowliest. The mother will have the preference over an infant yet unborn, but from the moment of birth onward, humankind, as the law views it, is a society of equals. I am sure that thoughts of this order must rise sometimes to your minds when you move along the wards of hospitals and see the forms of men and women —the ugly and the beautiful, the wise and the foolish, the young and the old, the gay and the wretched—outstretched before you in the great democracy of suffering. You may find it of some interest to be told that the law has had to struggle with these problems and to know how it has resolved them. There are two classic cases—the case of the U. S. v. Holmes, reported in 1 Wallace, Jr., 1; Federal cases No. 15,383, a trial in the United States Circuit Court for the Eastern District of Pennsylvania, and the case of the Queen v. Dudley, reported in L. R. 14 Q. B. D. 273, a trial in the Court of Queens Bench of England. The Holmes case has recently been revived with a full statement of the testimony, the arguments of counsel, and the charge of the court in a book by Frederick C. Hicks, to which he has given the title *Human Jettison.* Any of you who care to read it will find a human document of absorbing interest. Holmes was a seaman on a ship, the *William Brown,* which set sail from Liverpool for Philadelphia in 1841 with eighty-two souls aboard, seventeen officers and crew, and sixty-five passengers. Thirty-seven days out the ship struck an iceberg and sank. Two boats were lowered. One, the Jolly, as it was called, bore the captain, two officers, six members of the crew, and one passenger. Six days later, just as the rations had given out, she was picked up and those aboard her saved. The other boat, styled the long one, in the charge of the first mate, had forty-two aboard, of whom thirty-three were passengers, the others crew. The long boat was long only by comparison with the other. She was overweighted with her human burden—men, women and children packed so close together in a boat already leaking that they could hardly move a limb. A squall came up the next day, and imminent was the danger that the boat would founder. The mate gave the order to jettison a portion of the human freight. Holmes and another carried out the mandate. Fourteen men were seized and, amid their protests and entreaties, were thrown over the side. Two women also were lost, but there is reason to believe that they jumped overboard of their own will, made desperate at the sight of the sacrifice of a brother. For the most part, however, the victims were the men. The boat, relieved of this burden, rode the waves in safety. The following morning a sail was sighted. Quilts and blankets were waved and hoisted. There was an answer to the signal. The ship came up and the remnant on the boat were saved.

When the story of the sacrifice of sixteen souls became known to the world, there were many who drew back revolted and said that it was murder. The mate and most of the seamen disappeared when there was talk of an arrest. Holmes came to Philadelphia and was charged with homicide on the high seas, a crime under the federal law. The grand jury refused to indict for murder, but did indict for manslaughter. For this he was tried and convicted. He was sentenced to imprisonment for six months, having already served nine months before his conviction, and also to a fine, which, however, was afterward remitted. I think there is little, if any, doubt that he had acted in good faith, believing all would be lost unless there was a sacrifice of some. His good faith did not purge him of the guilt of crime, though it called for mercy in the sentence. Where two or more are overtaken by a common disaster, there is no right on the part of one to save the lives of some by the killing of another. There is no rule of human jettison. Men there will often be who, when told that their going will be the salvation of the remnant, will choose the nobler part and make the plunge into the waters. In that supreme moment the darkness for them will be illumined by the thought that those behind will ride to safety. If none of such mold are found aboard the boat, or too few to save the others, the human freight must be left to meet the chances of the waters. Who shall choose in such an hour between the victims and the saved? Who shall know when masts and sails of rescue may emerge out of the fog?

A score of years later a case not dissimilar was brought before an English court. Three men and a boy were adrift in a small boat. Two of the men, Dudley and Stephens, made desperate by hunger, killed the boy and ate his flesh. Four days later they were picked up by a passing vessel, and, reaching England, were tried for murder. They were tried before an accomplished judge, Lord Coleridge, Chief Justice of the Queen's Bench. The jury returned a verdict of guilty, but the sentence of death was commuted to one of imprisonment for a term of months. The law falters and averts her face and sheathes her own sword when pronouncing judgment upon creatures of flesh and blood thus goaded by the Furies.

One thing medicine has already done for jurisprudence, and that a thing so important as to exact a word of mention in even the briefest statement of the relations between the two. For many years medicine has been laying stress upon the value of institutes of mere research. You will find a sketch of their history in Dr. Abraham Flexner's *Study of Medical Education*. The law has been a little slower in the acceptance of such methods and ideals, yet at last it has seen the light. I cannot doubt that your example has done much to open our eyes and sharpen our perceptions. Research is now the cry in the schools of law at Harvard, Yale, Columbia, Michigan, and elsewhere. They are seeking to train the practitioner who some day may develop, or shall I say descend, into a judge, but they are seeking to do more. They are seeking to train the scholars—the jurists in the true sense of that much-abused term—who will lead the vanguard of the march. Only the other day, Johns Hopkins University, which has done so much already to stimulate the growth of medicine, announced the formation of an Institute of Jurisprudence, devoted to research and nothing else. A group of scholars has been brought together, who at the beginning will have no pupils other than themselves. They have come together to meditate, to confer, to collate, to explore. They will study the law functionally, asking themselves not merely whether this or that rule has come down to us from medieval days, but whether this rule or that one is adapted to the present needs of life. So the spirit of disinterested inquiry, which has long inspired the students of the physical sciences, is spreading, we may justly believe, to the social sciences as well. I do not mean to convey the thought that the law which is mere innovation, a forced plant, so to speak, without roots in habit or custom or popular conviction, is to be looked to with great hopefulness as a curative or helpful force. What I fear and would avoid is the law that maintains a noxious life when the soil of habit and custom and conviction and utility has been washed away beneath it. I have no delusions as to the futility of mere extempore decretals. Even when changes are made, it is best at the beginning to mark out the general lines of tendency and direction, leaving details to be developed by the system of trial and error which is of the essence of the judicial process. "It is a peculiar virtue of our system of law"—the words are those of one of the great judges of our day—"that the process of inclusion and exclusion, so often employed in developing a rule, is not allowed to end with its enunciation, and that an expression in an opinion yields later to the impact of facts unforeseen." [33] We must not sacrifice this quality of resilient adaptability which persists while there is softness and suppleness in the bones of legal doctrine. I do not say that it is an easy matter to find a just mean between timidity and boldness, or, to put it from another aspect, between literature and dogma. In case of doubt I have a leaning, which is not always shared by others, toward the impressionism that suggests and illumines without defining and imprisoning. The prevailing tendency is perhaps the other way, and the majority may be right. They hold the mysticism of the impressionist to be incompatible with the dignity of science. I am satisfied that this is so when science has so experimented as to have the right to be certain of its ground. What I fear is a pseudo-science which has assurance without conviction. Very likely in this mental attitude I am exemplifying what has been described by a learned author as "the invertebrate habit of mind which thinks it is impartial merely because it is undecided, and regards the judicial attitude as that which refrains from judging." [34] When the seas are so boisterous and their perils so insidious, one creeps from cape to cape.

The law, like medicine, has its record of blunders and blindness and superstitions and even cruelties. Like medicine, however, it has never lacked the impulse of a great hope, the vision of a great ideal. Sometimes secreted in ancient forms and ceremonies one finds the inner life and meaning of an institution revealed in all its essence. I felt this not long ago while reading the form of oath administered even now in all its ancient beauty to the grand jurors of the county. You will find it in the Code of Criminal Procedure, but one not greatly different is in use by our English brethren in their home across the seas, and Sir Frederick Pollock has traced it back, in germ at least, to the days of the Saxon kings. In fitness and beauty and impressiveness it rivals the great oath that men associate even today with the name and genius of Hippocrates. Here is its form as it has endured through all the changing centuries: "You shall diligently inquire, and true presentment make, of all such matters and things as shall be given you in charge; the counsel of the people of this state, your fellows' and your own you shall keep secret; you shall present no person from envy, hatred and malice; nor shall you leave any one unpresented through fear, favor, affection or reward, or hope thereof; but you shall present all things truly as they come to your knowledge, according to the best of your understanding. So help you God!"

Like the tones of a mighty bell, these echoing notes of adjuration bring back our straying thoughts to sanctity and service. I cannot listen to them without a thrill. Here, I say to myself, here indeed, secreted in this solemn formula, is the true spirit of the law which knows no fear nor favor.

Not all her ministers have been true to the ideal which she has held aloft for them to follow. But here, imperishably preserved amid the grime and dust of centuries, the word has been proclaimed, to steady us when we seem to falter, to strengthen us when we seem to weaken, to tell us that with all the failings and backslidings, with all the fears and all the prejudice, the spirit is still pure.

And so it still is for the great profession that is mine, as still it is for yours, which year by year renews in conduct and in speech the pledge and promise of Hippocrates.

I thank you for the privilege that has been given me of bringing the two together in this hall of your Academy.

REFERENCES

1. People v. Williams, 189 N. Y. 131.
2. People v. Schweinler Press, 214 N. Y. 395.
3. Cardozo, *The Nature of the Judicial Process,* p. 81.
4. 214 N. Y. 395.
5. 208 U. S. 412.
6. 179 N. Y. 235.
7. 197 U. S. 11.
8. People v. Teuscher, July, 1928, 248 N. Y. 454.
9. 10 *Journal Criminal Law and Criminology,* p. 186; Glueck, *Mental Disorder and the Criminal Law,* p. 455.
10. Pp. 485, 486.
11. 41 *Harvard Law Review* 453.
12. *Cf.* the recent statute of Massachusetts, L. 1927, c. 59, which calls for an examination by psychiatrists of any person indicted for a capital offense or any person indicted for another offense after an earlier conviction for a felony. Such a statute will do much to remove the reproach that has attached so long and so persistently to the testimony of experts; sec. 13, *Mass. Law Quarterly,* 38, *et seq.*
13. Berman, *The Glands Regulating Personality,* p. 22.
14. Pollock, Oxford Lectures, *The King's Peace,* p. 64.
15. *Op. cit.,* p. 444.
16. S. W. Bandler, *The Endocrines,* p. 266; Berman, *The Glands Regulating Personality,* p. 310; Schlapp and Smith, *The New Criminology,* p. 270.
17. Gillin, *Criminology and Penology,* p. 412; Preventive of Crime Act, 8 Edw. 7 c. 59; Halsbury Laws of England, Title Crim. L. § 796.

On the same lines a recent amendment of the Prison Law of New York permits the detention of mental defectives at the State Institution at Napanoch after sentence has expired (Prison Law, §§ 467, 470; Laws of 1927, chap. 426), but the term mental defectives as used in statute (Mental Hygiene Law, § 136) embraces a narrower class than the same term is meant to embrace as it is used in this address. Very likely an extension of these provisions to prisoners of other types may be expected in the future.
18. 4 Blackstone, Comm. 18; *cf.* however, 1 Stephen *History of the Criminal Law of England,* 470.
19. *Cf.* Jung, *Das Problem des Natürlichen Rechts,* p. 74.
20. Penal Law, § 1044.
21. Penal Law, § 1046.
22. People v. Majone, 91 N. Y. 211.
23. People v. Leighton, 88 N. Y. 117
24. People v. Beckwith, 103 N. Y. 360.
25. Watson, *Behaviorism,* p. 103, and *cf.* B. Russell, *Philosophy,* p. 21.

26. McNaughton's Case, 10 Cl. & F. 200.

27. Flanagan v. People, 52 N. Y. 467; People v. Carpenter, 102 N. Y. 238; People v. Taylor, 138 N. Y. 398.

28. Penal Law, § 34.

29. People v. Schmidt, 216 N. Y. 324.

30. Glueck, *op. cit.*, pp. 452, 459.

31. See *e.g.*, Commonwealth v. Cooper, 219 Mass. 1; Parsons v. State, 81 Ala. 577; Commonwealth v. DeMarzo, 223 Pa. St. 573; State v. Dejarnette, 75 Va. 867; Doherty v. State, 73 Vt. 380.

32. See, *e.g.*, Oppenheimer, *Criminal Responsibility of Lunatics*, p. 247; Stephen, *Digest of Criminal Law*, Art. 29; Glueck, *op. cit.*, p. 43.

33. Brandeis, J., dissenting, in Jaybird Mining Co. v. Weir, 271 U. S. 609.

34. Dr. Figgis, Introduction to Lord Acton's *The History of Freedom and Other Essays.*

— IV —

*The American Law Institute.**

This address was made at the Third Annual Meeting, May 1, 1925, of the American Law Institute.

THE existence of this Institute is a declaration to the world that "laissez faire" in law is going or has gone the way of "laissez faire" in economics.

A gospel of effort takes the place of a gospel that has vacillated between inaction and despair. We will not sit by and refuse to do anything because the voice of pessimism may remind us with labored demonstration that try as hard as we may, we shall be unable to do everything. The changing mood reveals a changing outlook upon law, and the processes and methods that develop and perfect it. Throw yourself back, they used to tell us, upon the broad currents of history, and let the tide of the centuries sweep you to your goal. This was comforting doctrine, and doctrine that the inertia native to most of us made it pleasurable to follow, if only tide and current could be trusted to do their share. The wisdom of the precept was not doubted till we found ourselves sinking when the program required us to be floating, and doubt deepened into certainty upon the discovery that instead of moving to a haven, we were sprawling on the rocks. In one of these moments of discomfiture, this Institute was formed.

The year that has gone by since our last meeting has brought steady and substantial progress achieved by unremitting labor. I shall make no attempt to put before you in this address the details of our activities or to cover their entire range. You will find a fuller narrative in the report of our Director, to whose tact and wisdom and self-sacrificing industry the members of the Institute owe a debt, not easily computed, for whatever of bright promise attends their enterprise today. My concern at the moment is with the larger aspects of the problem. Again, as at our last meeting, a tribute is due to the spirit in which the Reporters, their advisers and assistants have approached the task before them.

---

* *The American Law Institute.* Reprinted with the permission of the American Law Institute and Columbia University, the residuary legatee of the literary estate of Benjamin Nathan Cardozo.

They have exhibited a patience and devotion that would be impossible were it not for the sustaining power of a belief that something monumental and enduring is taking shape under their hands. Draft after draft has been submitted and corrected, only to give way in the end to some new objection, entailing revision yet again, till minds less trained to scientific inquiry or less moved by its disinterested spirit, would have petulantly resigned the task, or challenged carping criticism to offer something better. One finds it hard to exaggerate the difficulties that have been met and overborne. They become manifest as soon as we attempt to reproduce in thought the steps and stages of the project. At the beginning there has been need to gather from the pronouncements of the courts the principle or the rule implicit in their judgments, to find the soul of the decision beneath its integument of clay. This in itself is a wearisome and poignant task, especially when the soul reveals itself in the end as a soul already lost, an erring and blighted spirit, unworthy to be released, lest, meeting its fellow spirits, it poison and corrupt them. But this is only part of the travail and the agony. You choose after long debate the principle or the rule that you are ready to espouse, and you think you understand it. There lies before you still the task of expressing it in words. At once new vistas of uncertainty are opened to your gaze. It is hard enough, shunning generalities, or putting them forward timidly as merely approximate hypotheses, to declare the rights and wrongs engendered by a concrete situation, definitely envisaged. It is harder still when, abandoning particulars, we must announce in magisterial tones the rationalizing principle in which particulars are enveloped, the coördinating rule under which they are subsumed.

This is the high emprise on which the scholars of the Institute have ventured. Not for them those provisional and tentative formulas, those reservations and conditions, those shadings and softenings, by which judges, made wary by many an ambush, have saved for hours of extremity an avenue of retreat. By the form and method chosen, the framers of the restatement have courted danger and defied it. In the fierce light that beats upon these categorical propositions, standing stark and unprotected in the open, there is room for truth and for error, but seldom for half truth or truth unwilling to declare itself. By all this the difficulty of the process is multiplied many fold, and multiplied the danger. I do not say that the authors of the restatement have triumphed over these obstacles altogether, that they have found it possible to handle universals as freely and securely as their brethren on the bench have been dealing with particulars. Only powers superhuman could compass that achievement. Indeed, I have ventured to believe that if the general scheme or spirit of their work was to be criticized at all, at least in some of the preliminary drafts, it was in a certain search and seeking now and again for definiteness and assurance and finality in fields where definiteness and assurance and finality must be left to the agency of time. Even that criticism is little applicable to the restatements now before you. It points, however, to a danger that we must be vigilant to avert. You will acquit me, I hope, of a merely selfish desire to exalt the prestige or the power of my guild if I say that in determining the tendencies and directions of legal development in the future, something will have to be left, even when the restatement is completed, to those tentative gropings, those cautious experiments, those provisional hypotheses, that are part of the judicial process. No group of men can be expected to be invariably at one in the location of the line of division between one method and the other, between impressionism and dogma. None the less, if we take it by and large, the outcome of the redactions is an admirable compromise and a memorable achievement. Many of the rules and principles to be extracted from the enormous body of our case law are there in the opinions, not as precepts explicitly avowed, but as assumptions, presuppositions, things felt rather than perceived. We may say the same thing of most of our legal treatises, for, in them as in judicial opinions, the discursive method of exposition does not lend itself readily to precision and completeness. Now, almost for the first time, at least on any scale so large, a multitude of these rules and principles, gathered from their setting and scientifically arranged, have been stated tersely, accurately, fully, with a definiteness of form approaching the pronouncements of a statute. We are now to see whether our law has found a medium of expression that will solve or help to solve the age-long problem of uniting flexibility to certainty, that will give us the virtues of a code without the blighting pretension to literal inerrancy, a code that instead of repressing the forces and tendencies of growth by the imposition upon the law of a form forever fixed, will stir them to new life by its revelation of a harmony and an order till then unthought of and unseen.

Today we lay before you the first fruits of the harvest. Much more has been done than these offerings might lead you to believe. Drafts of many other sections have been written and rewritten. We bring to you those sections only that have reached some measure of finality. The subject of Conflict of Laws is represented by forty-two sections, covering the law of domicile. If we were to put before you all the sections that have been covered by preliminary drafts, we could show you 156 sections of restatement and commentary covering jurisdiction in its general principles, and then, in greater detail, executive jurisdiction, legislative jurisdiction, and finally judicial jurisdiction, which has proved the most troublesome of all. To this there should be added seventy-nine sections dealing with the jurisdiction of a state to tax, which we have determined to discard as not falling within the scope of this restatement, though we hope to utilize it hereafter when the time arrives for a restatement of the law governing taxation. The subject of the law of Contracts is represented by seventy-two sections, dealing with fundamental definitions, the general principles governing the formation of contracts, and more particularly those governing the formation of the contracts classified as informal. Progress has been made, however, in the preparation of more than 100 other sections, dealing with such subjects as the formation of formal contracts, joint contractual rights and obligations, contractual rights of persons not parties to the contract, the assignment of rights and the delegation of duties. The subject of the law of torts is represented by seventy-seven sections dealing with some of the fundamental rights of personality. Progress has been made in the preparation of many more sections dealing in part with other rights of personality and in part with rights of property. The subject of Agency having been taken up later than the other subjects, is not before you at all, but the Reporter and his advisers are already well advanced in the preparation of 119 sections which deal with fundamental problems. Besides all this, we have a report by Dr. Lewis, covering the classification of Business Associations and indicating his own views as to the clearest and most fruitful treatment of the topic. If your appetites are not satisfied by what is set before you now, we can promise you a year hence a banquet so abundant that none of you will be permitted to go unsated from the feast. The dainties and tidbits of the law will be served in such profusion as to make the tables groan, to say nothing of the members. Sufficient, however, for the day are its labors and perplexities.

I warn you at the outset that they are neither few nor trivial. The subject the most innocent on the surface may turn out when it is probed to be charged with hidden fire. We begin with the Conflict of Laws, and surprise awaits us at the threshold. Domicile suggests the home, with the peace the freedom from contention, that is thought to reign about the fireside. If you had been present at our conferences, you would feel with me that strife, though it be excluded from the sanctuary, is hovering close at hand. I know my own home, and am prepared even after following the restatement, to maintain its identity against the competition of localities less favored. I am not so ready as once I might have been, to make unqualified assertions about the moorings of my friends. Perhaps you will think, since it is all a matter of definition, that the difference is not so very important after all, and that we are making a lot of fuss and pother about niceties of nomenclature. This is where I have an unfair advantage of you, for I have seen the later installments, and I know the dénouement of the story. I find as the plot thickens that the definition with which we start, far from being a matter of merely curious or speculative interest, makes all the difference in the world in determining the rule with which we end. Make no mistake. This narrow distinction between domicile and residence may start you in life as an heir or a pauper, and later, when you have grown up, may marry or divorce you. We must keep a close watch on its pretensions, and the time to watch is now. There is a lesson to be drawn from all this, for it is not for the mere humor of the thing that I have ventured to bring it to your notice. The lesson is, indeed, twofold, and the more our restatement progresses, the more we shall be conscious of its significance, and that in both its phases.

There is a lesson for legal science and a lesson for legal philosophy. The lesson for legal science is that the structure depends on the foundations; that the fundamental conceptions of the law breed others in their image, and that the progeny will be misshapen or distorted, unless the parent conceptions are sound and pure and clear, as only accurate analysis can make us certain that they are. But there is still another lesson, and this a lesson for legal philosophy or rather perhaps a warning. If fundamental conceptions are capable of this propagating power, at what point shall they be checked? Shall we follow their implications down the line as long as we can trace them to the limit of their logic? When, if at all, shall they yield to other and competing forces, the forces, let us say, of utility or convenience or usage or justice or mere luxuriant diversity? I shall not develop this inquiry by pointing out its practical application. I shall do no more than whet your appetite for the later numbers of the serial by promising you that such inquiries will be found to be very pertinent when you come to deal with some of the problems of judicial jurisdiction. I have felt so keenly about some of them that at one or two conferences I have had the temerity to break a lance in debate with Prof. Beale, knowing that it could be only honor and no disgrace to be unhorsed by such a foeman. Perhaps we are beginning to see that our differences will turn out in the end to be largely a war of words, and that by a few verbal emendations, logic and justice and convenience, which seemed to be far apart, may be brought together and reconciled and made to live in amity. I suspect that this is only typical of what has often happened before in other branches of the law, and that many a bizarre and harsh conclusion, supposed to be the legitimate offspring of a conception of a formula, will be shown forth as bastard when the formula or conception is recast in truer mold. So it is that the methods by which law develops, supply checks on one another, justice and utility putting us on the scent, so to speak, to discover and unearth what is spurious in logic. But the interesting thing, after all, is not the settlement of this little controversy or that, the adopion of one rule or another in some narrow and restricted field. The interesting thing is to find that the fabric which comes off the loom of the law, like the fabric of life itself, is all of a single piece;

that you can hardly mar or mend it at one point without marring or mending at others; and that seams and scars persist, and splendors and glories too, long after the moving shuttle has left them far behind.

I turn to the law of torts, and I find stuff for comment there. The installment before you deals with some of the rights of personality. If we were following the traditional arrangement, we should say that the subjects treated are battery, assault, and false imprisonment. Not the least of the merits of Prof. Bohlen's work is his departure from the traditional arrangement with its basis in the forms of actions, and his adoption of another dependent upon the nature of the interest invaded or the right infringed. The old arrangement did much, I think, to choke and stunt the law of torts in its natural and free development, its development in harmony with changing human needs. The tendency was for rights and duties to relate themselves to procedural restrictions instead of narrowing and broadening in correspondence with the human interests that are worthy of protection. I think the value of the new approach will be increasingly manifest when the later installments of the work shall introduce us to problems even more complex. For the moment, however, I am concerned with the present installment and no others. Here again, as in the Conflict of Laws, I gain a vivid sense of the vast accumulation of acquired and modifying characteristics that a legal conception, in its origin apparently the most simple, absorbs and gathers to itself in its march through the centuries with an expanding legal system. When I heard that the subjects to be covered at the beginning were battery, assault and false imprisonment, I thought there would be easy travel. I ask you to take my word for it, we have met with hard roads, and worse passes are ahead. A blow in the face seems a fairly palpable fact, but all sorts of mental reservations and concomitants have to be known and estimated before you can determine whether it is to be reckoned as an actionable wrong. The psychical is ever crowding upon the precincts of the physical. Was the blow an unprovoked affront? Was it in defense of life or property? Was it struck with leave and license? Can leave and license justify, or is there some public policy that overrides consent? Even our bodily persons may receive a fictitious extension, so to speak, by identification with the things that are closely attached to them, whether by physical bonds or by the invisible ligaments of thought and spirit. If these and like problems arise when we deal with acts and injuries that must have agitated the cavemen, we gain some notion of the troubles to come later when forgetting primitive man, we shall have to deal with wrongs that have their origin in a complex order of society—oppressive combinations, malicious interference with another's opportunities for betterment, the thousand and one devices of hatred, greed and envy.

I am not sure how to formulate the lesson that these difficulties teach, the warning that they give. Perhaps their precept is the same as the benison that has come to us from ancient days: Be bold. Be ever bold. Be not too bold. It is but a human impulse if the framers of a restatement are tempted to declare the law not only as the past has shaped it in judgments already rendered, but as the future ought to shape it in cases yet to come. Those of us whose lives have been spent on the bench or at the bar have learned caution and reticence, perhaps even in excess. We know the value of the veiled phrase, the blurred edge, the uncertain line. Well, I am strong for them even now, at least in their proper places, or rather I ought to say, for reservations and limitations which will preserve whatever of value there may be in impressionistic forms and phrases. Undoubtedly much may be done in the treatises supporting the restatements, with their more discursive methods, to mark the tendencies and directions that will determine growth hereafter. I am speaking of the magisterial pronouncements of the restatements themselves. In these, let us give definiteness and fixity of outline where there is definiteness and fixity in the law as it exists or where argument so preponderates that a choice is fairly safe. Let us not hesitate, however, in other situations to say in all frankness that the problem is yet unsolved, and while indicating competing considerations either way, to leave the answer to the years.

I have no time to remind you of the interesting problems in the law of Contracts that are latent in the preliminary chapters already in your hands. The choice between the objective and the subjective conception of a contract with all that this implies will have been made when these sections go forth with the *imprimatur* of the Institute. There is, however, one other problem that I am anxious to bring to your attention before the installments and the treatises accompanying them are made the subjects of discussion. So far as the restatements themselves are concerned, we have worked out during the two years of our existence a form and a method and a technique which, at least in their fundamental features, are not likely to be changed. It is otherwise, however, with the treatises. These have been put together with some haste, at least comparatively speaking, in order to give some understanding of the authorities and considerations supporting our conclusions. You will find, however, not only that they differ among themselves, but that still other forms are possible, and it is for the Council and the members to indicate their preference, if preference there be. Shall the treatise be encyclopedic in its scope, collating all the pertinent authorities, a complete exposition of the law in the present stage of its development? Shall it follow a method more selective, choosing typical cases, not meagerly, indeed, and yet not with indiscriminate profusion—so many as will illustrate and justify the principles and rules of the restatement, or exhibit the conflict of authorities—a balanced and orderly commentary, the distilled essence and elixir of study and reflection? Or finally discarding these forms, shall the treatise take the shape of notes upon doubtful or contentious passages, leaving others, neither uncertain nor disputed, to be verified by other means? I have my own notion as to the method that is preferable, though it is easier to express a preference than to draft the treatise that will give to an idea the reality of performance. Perhaps in the end we shall settle down to one method as the true one. Perhaps we shall find, on the other hand, that there must be a diversity of methods, as the nature of the subject emphasizes the need of expansion or compression. I am hopeful that your deliberations will yield suggestion and enlightenment that will clarify the choice.

My final word must be one of hope and grateful recognition. We may not accomplish all that we have planned. It is yet too soon to say. At least, there has been a brave beginning.

Swift in his *Tale of a Tub* made the father give to each of three sons a legacy of a new coat. "You are to understand," said the father, "that these coats have two virtues contained in them: one is that with good wearing they will last you fresh and sound as long as you live; the other is that they will grow in the same proportion as your bodies, lengthening and widening of themselves, so as to be always fit." The common law, it seems, is one of these coats, or so at least we have treated it. The body that it was meant to shield has grown; and we have been brought up in the faith that the coat would grow too. So, indeed, it seems to have done, for its stuff is as elastic as any that is made. Even now with all the wear and tear, it is still a good coat, far too good to be thrown away, though the stretching and the shrinking have not been uniform throughout, so that the sleeves are perhaps a little too short, and the tails, which are useless and old-fashioned anyhow, a trifle too long. Let us make it over as reverently as our fathers made it for us, and hand it down to our descendants.

— V —

*The Home of the Law.**

Address at the dedication of the new home of the New York County Lawyers' Association, May 26, 1930.,

Brethren of the Bench and Bar:

TO the cause to which our lives are dedicate, we now dedicate a home.

No temple this, with majesty of arch and pillar, with fretted vault and dim and awesome spaces. The genius of the spirit that will dwell within these walls is one too intimate, too friendly, too human, to be symbolized in forms designed for reverence and worship. And yet, no factory this, no mere coöperative office building, no bourse for sordid money getting, no mart of trade and commerce. The indwelling spirit will not be coaxed within these walls—will not irradiate their stones with the benediction of her presence—unless something finer than mere gain is here to beckon and beguile her. All this our architect has seen, and made visible to the eye of sense in forms of truth and beauty. He has chosen his symbol wisely. Not the symbol of the temple, still less the symbol of the market, but one gentler, simpler, friendlier, more intimate in its suggestions, more universal in its appeal, the symbol of the home.

So in this colonial dwelling, built in a style that Washington knew, facing the church in which Washington worshiped, this great family of the Bar of New York comes together today to renew the old greetings of brotherly devotion, to feel the uplift that is born of community of effort, and to make high resolve that never shall the indwelling spirit have cause to turn her face away for any stain of wrong to the honor of the family.

Why has this structure taken shape through the contributions of a few for the satisfaction of the many? What has kindled the generous ardor that has found expression in these forms? Not the mere desire to lay the foundations of a library to which students may repair. There are law insti-

* *The Home of the Law.* Reprinted with the permission of the New York County Lawyers' Association and Columbia University, the residuary legatee of the literary estate of Benjamin Nathan Cardozo.

tutes and reading rooms already, and new ones could be built at a fraction of this cost, if what was sought were nothing more. Not the will to create a clubhouse, a mere place of recreation. If play were the sole aim, there would be competitors too many and too strenuous on hill and dale and stream. If you would know the soul of our building, you must seek for something more than these. Library and club and meeting-house indeed are here, but neither singly nor collectively do they give the key to the structure, the secret of its life. I do not mean that its planners have been indifferent to mere convenience. Why, I am credibly informed that there is to be a pent-house on the roof where the pent-up emotions of the bar may find appropriate release when strained beyond endurance by the stupidity of judges. A worthy end again; yet even that, I am convinced, is not the key to the ardor that animates these stones. I go back to my Plato, as so many wiser than I have gone throughout the years, and in one of his eternal questions, I seem to see prefigured the answer to my own. "Can virtue then be taught?" The words are those of Dr. Woodbridge in a summary of Plato's thought. "Can virtue then be taught? Can education make a man good? The question is asked again and again in Plato's pages, but never receives a straight-forward unequivocal answer. It is left a question, the insistent human question as we make our way through the changes and chances of this mortal life."

Well, education means many things and a building like this is one of our modern answers to Plato's deathless query. There is education in books, but education in life also; education in solitude, but education also in the crowd; education in study, but education even greater in the contagion of example. Ask any youth who has gone through a university what part of his training has counted most in later life. Almost invariably, I am sure, the first place will be given, not to shreds of information, the book-learning of the schools, but to the transfigured sense of values that is born of companionship with lofty minds, the living and the dead. There is more to be bestowed by Alma Mater than the possession of a sheep-skin. There is more in membership in the bar than a license to sign a brief or intone a prosy argument.

This home has been built and is now opened in that

faith. It has been built and is now opened in the faith that this great conglomerate bar of ours, sodden and inert at times by reason of that very weight which might make it so irresistible a power for good, will yet be stirred in all its depths by the ferment of high thoughts and fine ideals, if once the leaven of fraternity shall vitalize the mass. Here in this home it will be given to us all to feel ourselves a part of an immemorial succession, to feel the pride and the poetry of keeping the succession true, and the shame and the taunt when it is ravished and disgraced. Who will forfeit the privilege of crossing the threshold of the dwelling house, an equal among equals? Who will deface and deflower the family inheritance when once he feels it to be *his* inheritance —when he counts as his own the memories and traditions that seem even as I speak, to be taking on a new form, to have become visible and incarnate in this hall resplendent with their presence?

There is in the making here a new and heightened sense of kinship that will bind us together with a tie of family solidarity, closer and more permanent than any that can be known without a common home, a common gathering place, a common focus and center of family activities. Here will develop the sense of corporate responsibility that will cause us all to tingle as at a personal affront when the honor of the guild is assailed in literature or in life with words of cynical disdain. Take this for illustration from the correspondence of Disraeli, his famous letter to Charles Austin, who had charged him with an attempt to bribe the voters at an election. "I am informed," he wrote, "that it is quite useless and even unreasonable in me to expect from Mr. Austin any satisfaction for those impertinent calumnies, because Mr. Austin is a member of an honorable profession, the first principle of whose practice appears to be that they may say anything provided they be paid for it. The principle of circulating falsehoods with impunity is delicately described as doing your duty towards your client, which appears to be a very different process from doing your duty towards your neighbor."

How the studied insolence of this thrust has kept its edge through all the years! How the flesh recoils and quivers even now as the words come hissing to the ear! One wonders how many of the men and women of our own day can hear in these reverberating taunts an echo of their own beliefs. One wonders how many have found fuel for such beliefs and worse in the scandals of the day and hour. One wonders how many are judging us, not by our best, but by our worst, and are visiting upon one and all the scorn and condemnation that should be the portion of a few. Here and now in the opening of the new building, the consecration of the home, let there be a rebirth of the resolve to smother such reproaches by lives that will render them impossible, and to prove ourselves worthy of our heritage of opportunity and power.

I have spoken of our heritage, and what a heritage it is! How many-sided in its interests! How rich in anecdote and story! Nothing in the whole realm of knowledge but is grist for our mill. The truth is brought home to one at times in unexpected turns and corners. I like to go through the old books and see how many of the ways of lawyers—habits and mannerisms to appearance the most modern—have their roots in distant centuries. We reproduce the ways of our predecessors as children and grandchildren recall the gait and manners of their ancestors. In the days of ancient Greece, the litigants recited speeches that were drafted for them by professional orators who were eloquent for a price. If you will turn to Dobson on *The Greek Orators,* you will find that a litigant hard beset would dwell with humility upon his own meager powers of eloquence or persuasion, and beseech the jurors to be on their guard against the eloquence and persuasion of his more experienced and gifted adversary. Why, you can go into the City Court of New York any day of the term, unless things have greatly changed since I used to practice law, and hear the same argument from men who would stare at you in wonderment if you were to tell them it was Attic Greek. Only the other day I was reading in convenient translation a speech by Cicero, extolled by rhetoricians, the oration in behalf of Archias, and the sly old advocate worked in page after page of wholly irrelevant digression in the belief that it would help if only he could create an atmosphere in favor of his client. He did it without being called to account and reminded of the issue, just as sometimes even now a perfervid orator will work in like digressions without being held to the point by the master of the revels, if so, without disrespect, I may characterize the judge presiding on the bench. There is nothing new in such frailties, the last infirmities of noble minds. Still less is there anything new in the ineradicable tendency of the guilty, or even of the innocent, to divert the issue from themselves and direct it to the conduct and motives and reputation of the complainant, the source of all the trouble. You can see the impulse exemplified in orations the most famous. Demosthenes in his oration on the Crown roundly vilified the prosecutor, who had all the evil qualities, it seems, that have been inherited by district attorneys in the view at least of counsel who practice in the court of sessions. Inveterate, too, has been the habit of inordinate prolixity. From time immemorial judges have struggled fruitlessly against it, offering rewards to brevity and laying burdens on garrulity, but all to small avail. Some one gave me only recently an order by the Court of Chancery made three centuries ago in which the draftsman of a verbose and impertinent replication was ordered to walk about the court with the pleading hanging about his neck and pay a fine to boot. Our methods of repression are less rigorous today, but the chancery replication was probably a *feuilleton,* an innocent brochure, when compared with briefs that I could offer as exhibits if the angry chancellor were here. In my own court, as you know, the time allowed for the argument of an appeal from a judgment used to be two hours on each side. Luckily comparatively few lawyers took advantage of the privilege, due, I think, to a pretty general notion that with us, as in the Appellate Division, the limit was an hour. Recently we have amended our rule to make it more in harmony with the current misconception. I understand that in other states, for example Pennsylvania, the time is even shorter, and that neither the court nor the cause of justice has suffered from the change, though I am not advised to what extent the clipping of the wings of flight has brought suffering to counsel. My heart smites me at times at the thought of curbing them at all. After all, there is something captivating in their zeal, something human and lovable, even if a little wearing. If they wander from the point, they never do so quite so blatantly as Demosthenes or Cicero.

When I meditate upon these things, the enthusiasms of forensic efforts, the fire that goes into them, the meaning of defeat or victory, not merely to the pocket of the advocate, but still more to his pride, his repute and his sense of duty done, I think with mounting wonder of the spirit of fraternal fellowship that animates the profession even now—the good temper, the humor, the acceptance of fortune fair or foul as all in the day's work. Especially I am impressed with the kindness and generosity of the bar in its relation to the bench. "We take our pleasures sadly," says an English essayist, writing of his countrymen, "but we take our troubles with a smile." Perhaps that is not as bad summary of the spirit of the bar. We judges are doing things all the time that must disappoint you sorely. We are handing down decisions in closely balanced cases where the patient and careful work, for months and even years, of conscientious members of the bar is shattered overnight. If one were to consider such a situation in the abstract, without knowledge of the facts, one might suppose that the results would be a chronic state of irritation and hostility between two contending camps. Nothing of the kind! If we do the day's work with a reasonable measure of intelligence and devotion, we are rewarded by a friendship which is really more than friendship—by a friendship so tinged with emotion that we can only describe it as affection. I can speak for one judge at least in saying that it evokes in his heart an affectionate response.

Popular the members of our profession have never been able to become through all the ages of its history. Perhaps that is one of the reasons why they have clung to one another with the solidarity that everywhere is born of persecution or resistance. It is a feature of nearly every Utopia, from Plato down to H. G. Wells, that there has been no place in it for lawyers. Here in the new world, the ancient hostility had certainly not vanished in colonial days and later. You will find it all commemorated very soon in that museum of our colonial legal history which was promised you today, the latest benefaction of the Maecenas of our bar. Hostility was not left to dubious or halting inference. I ran across the following a while ago, in rereading Lowell's letters. It is an extract from *The Letters of an American Farmer*, written in 1782. "Lawyers," he writes, "are plants that will grow in any soil that is cultivated by the hand of others, and when once they have taken root, they will extinguish every vegetable that grows around them. . . . The most ignorant, the most bungling member of that profession will, if placed in the most obscure part of the country, promote litigiousness, and amass more wealth without labor than the most opulent farmer with all his toils. . . . What a pity that our forefathers, who happily extinguished so many fatal customs, and expunged from their new government so many errors and abuses, both religious and civil, did not also prevent the introduction of a set of men so dangerous." Already, about a century before, Georgia had acted on this or like advice, and attempted to rid herself of the pest. She passed a single ordinance for the prohibition of rum and lawyers. She let up afterwards upon the less flagrant of these evils but she was inexorable about the lawyers. In New York, however, there were troubles of a different kind. Here, marvelous to relate, the lawyers were too few. In 1695 there were only forty-one lawyers in New York, and litigants with money used to retain the whole bar of the locality, leaving no one for their adversaries. Accordingly in the same year an act was adopted by the assembly of the Province to regulate the number of lawyers that any litigant might retain, just as laws were enacted to regulate the enjoyment of other luxuries of life. The number was fixed at two. "If they retain any more," said the statute, "it shall be lawful for the justices of the Bench where the suit is depending to order all such attorneys as shall be retained, more than two as aforesaid, to plead for the other side, without returning the fee received, anything contained in this or any other act to the contrary hereof in any wise notwithstanding." There was poetic justice for you! Lawyer number 3 or lawyer number 4, retained and paid by an enthusiastic plaintiff, might turn up on the day of the trial, the money in his pocket, espousing the cause of the defendant. What would our Grievance Committees have to say about such practices today? I must admit that in my judgment it would have been fairer, if every client was to be limited to two lawyers, to provide that every lawyer should be furnished with two clients. Very likely such a guaranty is a blessing too great to be attainable in any earthly commonwealth. At any rate the lawyers seem to have worried along without it. I wish the draftsmen of the act of 1695 could have a look at us today.

Evolutionists will have to tell us whether some vestigial survival of the spirit of these old colonial days when we were a little band of forty abides with us even now. The fashion is in these times to dwell upon the shortcomings of the bar and to touch lightly on its virtues. None the less, with all its faults and failings, it has exhibited in the main a comradeship, a spirit of good fellowship, which owes something of its persistence perhaps to the traditions of the inns of court, but which is seen to be something distinctive when we contrast it with the envies and suspicions in callings more or less allied. Shakespeare has told us in the lines so often quoted that we are to do "as adversaries do at law, strive mightily, but eat and drink as friends." The picture and the practice are so familiar that we have come to take for granted the spirit they exhibit. But it is not so commonplace as it seems. Asquith in his *Memories and Reflections* reminds us that among the leaders of the House of Commons there have been conflicting views as to the propriety of statesmen's holding friendly personal relations with their political opponents. So sturdy a figure as John Bright announced his opposition to the practice with constancy and vehemence. The seductions of a dinner were thought to have a tendency to mollify convictions and stimulate with the gastric juices a tendency to compromise. The tendency may be admitted, but, nowadays at least, men are seldom sure enough of their convictions to be willing to put inflexibility in the forefront of the virtues and compromise behind it. For lawyers, at all events, there has been a different tradition in England as with us. Perhaps the reason is that our rôles as champions for contending litigants are cut out for us in advance upon lines determinate and known. There is less of the dim penumbra, the borderland of vague approach, in which the views of the protagonists of the political arena shade off by insensible gradations from conformity into difference. For us, in any event, the tradition of fellowship and comradeship is something very fine and precious, to be stimulated and nourished with vivid recognition of its fructifying value. I can think of nothing more likely to foster it, to bring its seeds to maturity and reap the benefit of its fruits, than the building of a home wherein lawyers of all conditions, the old and the young, the great and the humble, may come together as co-workers and as equals in the spirit of the great democracy of justice in whose name they have enrolled.

We praise and celebrate today the symmetry of walls. Within those walls, in days now far away, when all our voices shall be hushed, an unnumbered multitude of our brethren will be busy with the endless quest for a symmetry still greater, the symmetry that men call justice, the adaptation of the rule of life to the symmetry they call divine.

May the work be worthy of the monument; the workers, of the home.

—VI—

*The Game of the Law and Its Prizes.**

Address at the seventy-fourth commencement of the Albany Law School, June 10, 1925.

Members of the Graduating Class, Ladies and Gentlemen:

SIR FREDERICK POLLOCK tells us in his new *Essays* in the Law that in medieval times there was a special patron saint to whom students used to pray that they might pass their examinations. The records do not inform us, he says, whether the intercession of the saint was supposed to strengthen the brain of the students, or soften the heart of the examiner. Enough that her power, whether exerted one way or the other, was never doubted by the faithful.

I remember the sense of relief, of an incubus cast aside, with which I took my last examination after the years that I had passed in college and in law school. There, I said to myself, was a chapter closed. I might make mistakes in the future, but I should no longer make them under the eye of examiners charged with the special duty of exposing my failings and giving them a quantitative value in comparison with my virtues. Exposure thereafter would be, so to speak, a matter of chance. A class of professional detectives would be no longer on my tracks.

I suppose some such dreams of felicity are stirring and elating you tonight. It gives me pain to dispel them, yet dreams they are, and nothing more. As long as you live, and surely as long as you practice law, an examiner will dog your foot-steps. When you enter some law office, an apprentice to some older lawyer, there will be some one looking over your shoulder, criticizing your work, pointing out its defects, cheering you, once in a while, by a concession of its merits, educating, examining, testing—the process repeated without end. When a little later you start for yourselves, there will be trial judges and juries and appellate courts, all examining, testing, approving or rejecting, just as in the days of adoles-

---

* *The Game of the Law and Its Prizes.* Reprinted with the permission of the Albany Law School and Columbia University, the residuary legatee of the literary estate of Benjamin Nathan Cardozo.

cence which you thought were left behind. Sometimes when these critics are compassionate or silent, you will have to meet a test still sterner, a scrutiny yet more rigid, the merciless test and scrutiny of a defeated and reproachful client. As years go by, some of you may cease to be advocates, and gain a seat upon the Bench. You may think then that you are safe, but alas! it is not so. Examiners still crowd about, and no longer are they to be propitiated by the invocation of a patron saint. If you happen to be a trial judge, there are the judges of the appellate courts. If you mount to one of those courts yourself, there are your colleagues, ever lying in ambush vigilant and keen, and perhaps some other court yet higher than your own. If you live through all these dangers with reason unimpaired there are other trials as searching. The Bar, with its associations and committees, and, worse than these, the law schools and the law reviews, are still waiting at the door. Let there be a joint in your armor, a flaw in your opinion, it will not be long before probe and scalpel will expose a gaping wound. The examiner is near at hand.

So, in very truth, gentlemen, this is not the end at all, but only the commencement. I was reading a few weeks ago a book by Abraham Flexner on *Medical Education* which has a lesson for lawyers too. "As a matter of fact," he says, "schools of engineering do not produce engineers or achitects; schools of law do not produce lawyers. The school's part is largely limited to training in method and technique, and to inspiration." Method is much, technique is much, but inspiration is even more. If you go out into the world thinking that the ordeal is over, or that it will be over when you have leapt one hurdle yet to come, the hurdle maintained by the State Board of Law Examiners, not very far away, if you go out into the world in this spirit, there will be the shock of many a disillusionment before the course is run. But if you bear in mind the truth that this is only the commencement, that troubles are only beginning, and if you act upon that faith behold, by some subtle necromancy, the pain that you foresee shall be transmuted into joy. The troubles will emerge as triumphs; the travail and the doubt will yield an unexpected peace; the great truth will have been learned that the quest is greater than what is sought, the effort finer than the prize, or, rather, that the effort *is* the prize—the victory cheap and hollow were it not for the rigor of the game.

I have spoken of it as a "game" and so indeed it is, though it will depend upon your notion of a game whether the metaphor shall elevate or cheapen. It is a game, but it is a game of skill, and that is why there has been need of this elaborate preparation to give you a working knowledge of its rules, of its method and technique. When I contrast the training that is given to the law student of today with the training that was given to me in the prehistoric days before my admission to the bar, I am filled with a spirit of envy that makes me anxious to step down and take my place in your ranks, forgetting, for the moment, that your examiners would probably refuse to pass me. In the days of my study at the law school, we had courses in the law of contracts, real estate, torts, equity, evidence, and practice. That was about all, and this little was taught out of some old-fashioned text-book, with slight reference to the cases and little or no discussion of them by students or professors. Take such a subject as the law of corporations; we had no instruction in it at all. Perhaps the notion was that no corporation would be foolish enough to retain us at the beginning, and that by the time such retainers came to us we could pick up the knowledge for ourselves. Whatever may have been the reason, I do no more than report the fact. If some one had asked us to state the difference between a bond and a share of stock, I fear that most of us, for all that we had learned to the contrary at law school, would have been in the position of a woman of my acquaintance, who, when a similar question was propounded to her, eyed her questioner quizzically for a moment, and then exclaimed triumphantly, "I know. They are the same." So it is that in an envious spirit I contrast my own meager preparation with the copious and varied courses that it has been your privilege to follow.

You have gained something, however, which is more than mere knowledge of principles and rules and precedents. These are so many and so diverse that with all the facilities of the modern law school and with all the industry and zeal that you could exhibit in the endeavor to become masters of them, you would find in the end that you had only scratched the surface. The thing even more important that you have learned is the ability to think legally, an understanding of the method, the technique, by which the judicial process works. It is in truth a fascinating process, baffling, elusive, infinite in the variety of its aspects, and yet infinite also in its appeal to the heart and mind and spirit of generous and ambitious youth. The new generations bring with them their new problems which call for new rules, to be patterned, indeed, after the rules of the past, and yet adapted to the needs and the justice of another day and hour. Yours will be the task of formulating these rules when we, who have done our little as best we could, shall have laid the burden down. One must be historian and prophet all in one—the qualities of each united in a perfect blend—who would fulfill that task completely. Rights and duties are to be defined in such terms as to fit them to the complexities of modern life, yet all the time, in defining them, we speak the words and perpetuate the thought of the judges of long ago who penned some ancient writ of emperor or king. "The last of the Caesars has fallen," I quote the words of Roscoe Pound, "but the thought of the jurisconsults of the days of the first Caesar is still law in half of the world." Here is a game, a puzzle, a conundrum, to mystify and pique. Here is a task, a summons, a vocation, to rouse and stir and quicken. Give what you have, whether what you have be much or little. You will be sharers in a process that is greater than the greatest of its ministers.

Yes, indeed, it is a wonderful and inspiring opportunity that confronts you in this year of grace as you turn your backs upon the law school to take your places at the bar. The process of justice is never finished, but reproduces itself, generation after generation, in ever-changing forms, and today, as in the past, it calls for the bravest and the best. Pretty soon we old fellows shall be leaving the scene, and you will be coming forward to fill the broken ranks. I should like to come back a generation or so from now, just to get a peep at the state of the law, make my bow, and retire. I suppose I should find big changes. Many of the opinions that I have written would probably by that time have been overruled, or charitably distinguished. The chief effort of my successors would be, very likely, to find some respectful and respectable way of avoiding or forgetting them. These things might destress me a little, but I have small doubt they would be right. I should feel, doubtless, when I thought it all over, that the movement was in the right direction, that we were getting closer to the goal. Very possibly I should wish to know the names of those who were doing the work of the day, who were carrying the standard forward, who were keeping alive the great tradition. They would show me the roll of honor, and there I should read the names of some who look into my face tonight. It will be your fault if it is not so.

I come back to my metaphor of a game, a game which exacts skill but which, like every game worth playing, exacts something more important, and that something is the sportsman's spirit, which is only another word for character. This is the chief thing, more important far than skill, for skill without this will be palsied and perverted. Play the game like sportsmen, or give it up at the beginning, and choose some other calling, which, if its aims are less exalted, will at least spare you the reproach of insincerity, since its members will not have pledged themselves to be votaries of justice. I do not ask the impossible. I know that for most of you, the law, though a profession, must also be a means of livelihood. I know that worldly success is pleasant in itself, and that it is also for many who live in the world the badge of all success. I do not ask you to turn yourselves into hypocrites by pretending that you are indifferent to it, or that you would not gain it and gain it in the fullest measure if you could have it on terms consistent with dignity and honor. But you would not cheat at football or at tennis or at cards, though the game were thereby assured to you and detection a remote possibility, or even impossible altogether. You would know that your honor had been pledged, and the zest of the sport would be more precious than success. So it is with the life-game upon which you are to enter. You know its ideals. You have said that they are yours. You will be as good as your word, and as proud as your heritage.

Some of you may have read the charming and stirring address that was given by Mr. Barrie not long ago as Rector of St. Andrews. He called it "Courage": and the courage that he praised and the courage that he invoked was the courage of the sportsman, of the young sportsman, the courage of adventurous youth. You will need it now and again in the years that are ahead of you. The tests of character come to us silently, unawares, by slow and inaudible approaches. We hardly know that they are there, till lo! the hour has struck, and the choice has been made, well or ill, but whether well or ill, a choice. The heroic hours of life do not announce their presence by drum and trumpet, challenging us to be true to ourselves by appeals to the martial spirit that keeps the blood at heat. Some little, unassuming, unobtrusive choice presents itself before us slyly and craftily, glib and insinuating, in the modest garb of innocence. To yield to its blandishments is so easy. The wrong, it seems, is venial. Only hyper-sensitiveness, we assure ourselves, would call it a wrong at all. These are the moments when you will need to remember the game that you are playing. Then it is that you will be summoned to show the courage of adventurous youth. There are some unquenchable spirits who never lose it, though the calendar may say that they have left youth behind and reached manhood or old age. "Be inspired with the belief," said Gladstone, "that life is a great and noble calling; not a mean and grovelling thing that we are to shuffle through as we can, but an elevated and lofty destiny."

You think I ask too much of you. I ask of you nothing that you are not competent to give. More than that, I ask of you nothing that will not mean success and honor if only you have the will and the strength to give it. I take as my text two utterances that have consoled and inspired me in many a doubting hour. The one is that of William James; the other is that of Emerson. The one shall stimulate your minds. The other shall cheer your souls. The one shall teach that intellectual effort is not wasted and never can be. The other shall teach that spiritual effort, the force of fine and noble character, is destined to a kindred triumph.

Skill is not won by chance. Growth is not the sport of circumstance. Skill comes by training; and training, persistent and unceasing, is transmuted into habit. The reaction is adjusted ever to the action. What goes out of us as effort comes back to us as character. The alchemy never fails. "Let no youth," says James, "have any anxiety about the upshot of his education whatever the line of it may be. If he keep faithfully busy each hour of the working day, he may safely leave the final result to itself. He can with perfect certainty count on waking up some fine morning to find himself one of the competent ones of his generation, in whatever pursuit he may have singled out. Silently, between all the details of his business, the power of judging in all that class of matter will have built itself up with him as a possession that will never pass away. Young people should know this truth in advance. The ignorance of it has probably engendered more discouragement and faint-heartedness in youths embarking on arduous careers than all other causes put together."

I know not where you will find a more heartening or tonic gospel. Our fates are in our own hands. We make and remake our own selves. We are "the captains of our souls." Nature pants with the desire to make us what we wish to be. The wish is the reality. What we think, that we are.

So much for the triumph of mind and spirit in the shaping of our own lives. There is something even stranger. It is the power of mind and spirit to shape the lives of others. Here I hold fast to Emerson. Again Nature is inflexible, inflexible in beneficence for those who serve as she is inflexible in indifference for those who stand aloof. The words in which Emerson to the very end gave utterance to this faith are as fine, a wise critic has said, as anything in literature.

"If you love and serve men," he writes, "you cannot by any hiding or stratagen escape the remuneration. Secret retributions are always restoring the level, when disturbed, of the Divine justice. It is impossible to tilt the beam. All the tyrants and proprietors and monopolists of the world in vain set their shoulders to heave the bar. Settles forevermore the ponderous equator to its line, and man and mote, the star and sun, must range to it, or be pulverized by the recoil."

A robust doctrine this, and one for stout hearts and placid and unruffled souls. Not the less for that are its validity and power. There may be hours of discouragement and rebuff. When the course is run, we shall see them in their true perspective. We shall know in the end that the game was worth the effort.

"Most of the troubles of life," says the French philosopher, "would be avoided if men would only be content to sit still in their parlors." Ah! but they will not, even those of them who have the parlors, and that is their glory, if it is also their undoing. The ceaseless drive is there; the lure that prods and teases; the shining, if shifting, goal, which, like the lighthouses of today, may summon with a revolving light, but ever swings full circle, a beacon to the wandering traveler.

This is no life of cloistered ease to which you dedicate your powers. This is a life that touches your fellow men at every angle of their being, a life that you must live in the crowd, and yet apart from it, man of the world and philosopher by turns.

You will study the wisdom of the past, for in a wilderness of conflicting counsels, a trail has there been blazed.

You will study the life of mankind, for this is the life you must order, and, to order with wisdom, must know.

You will study the precepts of justice, for these are the truths that through you shall come to their hour of triumph.

Here is the high emprise, the fine endeavor the splendid possibility of achievement, to which I summon you and bid you welcome.

— VII —

*The Comradeship of the Bar.**

Address at a luncheon of the New York University Law School Alumni Association, December 20, 1927. Printed in the *New York University Law Review,* vol. V, p. 1 ff.

Mr. Chairman, Brethren and Friends of New York University:

I HAVE no message for you today that is worthy of your greeting. I have come here as a friend to bear witness to my friendship. Your University has honored me with the guerdon of a degree. Your association, gracefully and graciously, has said that there shall be no distinction between sons of the whole blood and sons adopted of other parents, and in that spirit of fraternal fellowship has made me one of its vice-presidents. I have been brought within the family circle, and so I am going to talk things over with you in the desultory and intimate way appropriate for relatives and friends.

Perhaps I may say a word at the beginning to those of you who are very young, the tyros of the bar who have the future all before you, and then another word that the tyros will share with those who are a little older, for as I look over this assembly I discover no one who is really old.

The fledglings of the profession are very close to my heart. In my days of practice at the bar, I used to act as counsel for a good many of the younger men, though, as I look back at it now, I can see that I was pretty young myself, and so I came in contact with my brethren, and with the most ingenuous, the warmest, the friendliest of my brethren, to a greater extent than many a lawyer whose experience in other ways was more extensive than my own. I was impressed in those days by the high quality of the work that could be done by youths of ability after a year or two of practice. The impression has been confirmed and deepened by my experience on the bench. I think the quality is due to the efficiency of the modern law school, which gives to

---

the young men of the present a training that for breadth and intensiveness was utterly unknown to the law school of my day. The years bring their changes. In Lord Mansfield's day, a special box in the courtroom was set apart for students who picked their learning up by gathering such crumbs of knowledge as fell from their elders during the progress of the trial. There is a note by the reporter in one case that Mansfield requested one of the counsel to state the case for the benefit of the students in the box before the court delivered a reserved judgment. The noble lord believed, beyond a doubt, that he had been graciously condescending, and that his dutiful audience, advised of the dispute by this statement of the facts, would receive the considered judgment of the court with the meek and reverent acquiescence that was due to holy writ. Those were the good old days before law reviews existed, with the picked men of the law school as courts of ultimate appeal. The Mansfields of the present, if there are any, will know that they can get from students as good as they can give, at least if the goodness of the counsel can be measured by its vigor. I may seem to jest, but I am more in earnest than you think. I sometimes feel I might escape some of the mistakes that I am sure I often make, if I had the training that is given in the law schools of today. I went to Columbia Law School in the transition days when it was passing from the old method of instruction by textbook—itself a long advance over the method of Mansfield's time—to the case method now in vogue. I had been there more than a year under Dwight and Chase and their associates when Prof. Keener, fresh from Harvard, descended on a bewildered class. The course was so nearly over that he had little time to do more than endeavor to convince us that we had learned nothing in the past, were learning nothing in the present, and were not likely, unless we improved a good deal, to learn anything in the future, which truth he proceeded to expound with great variety of illustration, with much satisfaction to himself, and with effects upon the class varying from rage to incredulity, and from incredulity to despair. You have fallen upon happier days, the fledglings who have gone forth of recent years from the shelter of the law school nest. Whole fields of the law that have been traversed and explored by you were never opened to my gaze at all until I learned to know of them in practice. There was no course in corporations—none in constitutional law, unless one took an optional course in an allied school—none in international law, public or private—none in criminal law, except some optional lectures: and many other subjects that are now dealt with separately, such as bailments, carriers, bankruptcy—had only the incidental treatment that was given in a summary paragraph or section in Parsons' book on Contracts. You will wonder how we managed to worry along as passably as we did. They tell us of Lord Bacon that at the beginning of his career he determined not to practice. Lord Birkenhead commenting upon this choice, remarks that "a man of commanding and acknowledged intellect may well have shrunk from submitting with deference to the views of mental inferiors on the bench." I fear my self-revelation may have carried me too far, and may have filled you with disdain for at least one of the incumbents of high judicial office.

I had occasion some months ago to consider the statistics of application for admission to the bar. Until I read them, I sometimes thought that the popularity of the profession would wane with the waning importance of mere forensic skill. The throng of would-be lawyers is evidence that there was no substance to my fear. Yet a change there has been, a change even since my own time, and still more a change since the time of others who came before me. More and more the work of the lawyer is done in the office. The specialists in litigation are comparatively few. Many of my friends in the profession never go into court at all, and many more go there at infrequent intervals and with sounds of lamentation. Lord Bryce observed in his book on the American Commonwealth that the best intellect of the country was attracted to the bar. I feel quite certain that it is the court, and not the office, that is the attraction for ambitious youth. The struggle for justice would lose its zest if law could be turned, as I believe medicine is turning in some degree, into a prophylactic science ordered with such nicety that litigation would become as catastrophic as the plague. I feel sure that even now the dream of ambitious youth knocking at the door of the profession, is the dream of successful effort in the courts. New land-marks (they say to themselves) are to be raised along the ancient highways; new courses are to be marked where the lines of growth and development are still uncharted and uncertain; justice is to be made to prevail when threatened with defeat by its foes, the forces of deceit and darkness. Better still, the court is to be made to eat its own words or the words of its predecessors, avow itself in error, and right an ancient wrong. I do not mean to suggest that courts thrive upon such a diet, or partake of it when there is a fair excuse for choosing a dish less indigestible. All the greater is the thrill that comes to the implacable pursuer when the judge, driven at last to cover, reaches out for the cup of medicine, and drains it as befits a man. These are dreams of youth, not always realized in life, but coloring, none the less, and irradiating the vision that lies ahead. If numbers tell the tale, the vision is still seen.

I have been talking to the fledglings. It is time to keep my promise and reserve some portion of my discourse for them and for their elders.

I was reading not long ago a series of addresses by Stanley Baldwin, Prime Minister of England. Delightful they are in their urbanity, their quiet humor, their mellow culture, their modesty and wisdom. In one of these addresses, he is talking to the members of his own party in the House of Commons. "Don't ever lose touch," he says, "with your constituency; don't ever mistake the voice of the clubman and the voice of the press man in London for the voice of the country. It is the country that has returned you; it is the country that will judge you." One would not give precisely that advice to a judge, and yet, in essence perhaps, the advice would not be greatly different. Let him not trouble himself overmuch about the voice of clubman or of press. Honest enough and well-meaning it will be, yet the artist, if he is to be judged with understanding, will throw himself upon his peers, upon those who are practiced in the art. So the judge, if he is to steer his course wisely, will never lose touch with the one constituency that is competent to judge him, the constituency of the bar. I count it a happy thing that the bar today has so many organs of expression by which it can make vocal thoughts and sentiments that might otherwise be uncommunicated and hidden. There are the law journals, increasing year by year alike in number and in power; there are the bar associations with their committees, their reports, their multiform activities;

and now, with developing importance, there are the banquets and luncheons and receptions of these same associations, and of the graduates of law schools, where asperities of criticism will be steeped perhaps and mollified in the mellower and gentler medium of fellowship and friendship. All these organs of expression have a message for the judge who has the ear and will to listen. The law reviews will give him some hint of the unplumbed abysses of his ignorance. The bar associations by their committees will sum up his defects and merits with coldly critical judgment, and inform him whether the balance is plus or minus. At reunions of this kind he will learn something else which has an importance almost equal. By these intimate contacts, he will be the better able to learn whether in the judgment of this high constituency he has permitted the official in him to swallow up the man.

There have been judges in the past who suffered that disaster. I am happy to report that the type is rapidly disappearing, if it be not quite extinct. I have something more in mind than the egotism that displays itself in harsh and overbearing manners, in explosive vigor of voice, or in a suspicious familiarity with the sections of the Civil Practice Act under the title of "Contempt." Exuberances such as these are at times the result of infirmities of temper not unknown altogether to the bench though happily uncommon; more often they are the defensive appliances of weakness or incapacity, conscious of its failings, and hopeful to divert attention by what seems to be a manifestation of its strength. I think there is another way, however, in which the official may submerge the man, more subtle, more insidious, if less odious and brutal. One can have an outlook on the law itself which will be the outlook of the drill-master rather than the genuine strategist, the official rather than the man. Take such a thing as the call of the calendar and the administration of calendar rules. There is a way of doing such things as a drill-master and a way of doing them as a man. I had little or no experience with such problems as a judge, so perhaps I have no right to talk of them—I have sometimes feared that I should make a mess of them myself—but, after all, I watched the doings of others while I was a member of the bar: so I am entitled to an opinion, whether it is worth much or little. Then when you pass from practice to higher problems, you get the same antithesis. Some of the worst decisions the courts have ever made have come from just this opposition. They thought they were not derogating from the soundness of a judgment when they admitted its brutality. I concede that there are times when the two will stand together—chiefly, I think, when the rule to be applied is one declared by statute. Yet the concurrence is rare, is to be viewed with deep distrust, and is to be deplored as much as it is distrusted. The common law, unless bound and riveted by statute, has instruments at hand of many varieties and shapes for the molding of that justice which is the end of her endeavor. The truth seems obvious enough, yet at times judges have been blind to it. Dean Pound in one of his papers tells us about judges who preferred a "strong" decision. By this they meant a decision that worked out some harsh result by the undeviating application of the method of strict logic to the development of a precedent or a rule. They thought that in so doing they were vindicating the power and majesty of law. So, in a delightful article by Mr. Buckland, a sketch of Frederick W. Maitland, we are told of an English judge who was said to exult in a harsh judgment, and seemed to be friendly to injustice when the choice was nicely balanced. Perhaps to these illustrations I should add the western judge whose strictness was a subject of one of Lincoln's anecdotes. "He would hang a man for blowing his nose in the street, but he would quash the indictment if it failed to specify what hand he blew it with."

I am not saying that examples so horrible as these can be found among the many judges I have known in years of practice too long to be stated at a festive meeting. None the less, the slumbering beast is in us, and may be waked to life and fury if we feed him overmuch. The ravening official will seek to swallow up the man. I interpret the invitation to be with you today as an expression of your judgment that whatever mistakes I may have made—and I know that they have been more than I like to figure or remember—I have at least avoided this one, I have not allowed the official to swallow up the man. I don't mean that I am entitled to a great deal of credit for so modest an achievement. In a court where the tradition of courtesy and equity is so ingrained and inveterate as it is in the Court of Appeals, one would have to be a pretty hardened sort of sinner to be guilty of the particular form of wrongdoing that has its origin in the pride of office. But then, when you come to think of it, virtues are important in the inverse order to the credit that is due to those who cultivate and practice them. No one of us struts about with satisfaction for the self-restraint involved in refraining from the crime of homicide, yet if the importance of the virtue were the measure of the credit we should all be crowing and cawing with the pride of moral excellence. So I don't assume to pride myself on the very modest virtue of being merely a human being. Charles Francis Adams says in his autobiography that as he looked back through the mists of the years the predominant feeling was one of satisfaction that at least he had gone through life without making a conspicuous ass of himself. That, I may say in passing, is my own paean of jubilation at the end of each judicial year. I am thinking that I ought to add another verse, a verse of thanksgiving that I have been able to be a human being. That is a modest achievement, as I have said. Perhaps it is not wholly negligible. I think we are coming more and more to a knowledge of the truth which I have been emphasizing today, that officialdom, however it displays itself, is the husk and that what is precious is the man within.

So I thank you for the privilege of meeting you as your comrade in this intimate and delightful way. It has helped and stimulated me. Your kindness is so great that I shall never know if the experience was impressed with a different quality for you. In the luncheons that will follow during the years that are to come, there will be brought together, with the tie of this Association to bind them, judges and lawyers of all qualities and degrees, good ones and, perhaps by some rare fortuity, poor ones, high and low, the men who have been successful, and the men who are waiting for success, but to whom success will surely come if only they are firm and strong. May the spirit of comradeship that has been ours today, abide with them too, and with the profession that we love.

BIBLIOGRAPHY

WRITINGS BY MR. JUSTICE CARDOZO

Address delivered at luncheon of the New York University Alumni Association, December 20, 1927. New York University Law Review 5:1–6, January 1928.

———. Law and Literature. New York, Harcourt, 1931. (Comradeship of the Bar, pp. 176–90.)

Address delivered at the New York State Bar Association meeting at Hotel Astor, New York City, January 22, 1932. New York State Bar Association Report, 55:263–307, 1932.

Address delivered at the annual bar dinner of the New York County lawyers, December 17, 1931, at which Judge Cardozo was guest of honor. New York County Lawyers Association Yearbook, 1932, pp. 369–378.

Address delivered at the seventy-fourth commencement of the Albany Law School, June 10, 1925. (Albany Law School, Albany, N. Y. Lectures and addresses delivered in the Hubbard course on legal ethics), 11 p.

———. In Law and Literature. New York, Harcourt, 1931. (The Game of the Law and Its Prizes, pp. 160–75.)

Growth of the Law. New Haven, Yale University Press, 1927, 145 p.

Hiscock, Frank, Appreciation. New York County Lawyers Association Yearbook, 1927, pp. 257–261.

Identity and Survivorship (in Hamilton, Allen McLane and Lawrence Godkin. System of Legal Medicine. New York, E. B. Treat, 1909, v. 1:213–42).

Jurisdiction of the Court of Appeals of the State of New York. 2d ed., covering all important adjudications to January 1, 1909. Albany, Banks, 1909, 331 p.

Law and Literature. Address. Connecticut State Bar Association, annual meeting, January 16, 1926. Connecticut State Bar Association, 1925, pp. 90–107.

Law and Literature and Other Essays and Addresses. New York, Harcourt, 1931, 190 p.

Law Is Justice: Notable Opinions of Mr. Justice Cardozo. With a foreword by Hon. Robert F. Wagner. Edited by Abraham Lawrence Sainer. New York, The Ad. Press, 1938, 441 p.

Mr. Justice Holmes. 44 Harvard Law Review 682–92, March 1931.

———. Appeared as introduction in: Mr. Justice Holmes. Ed. by Felix Frankfurter. New York, Coward-McCann, 1931, pp. 1–20.

Ministry of Justice. Harvard Law Review 35:113–26. D 21.

———. Law and Literature. New York, Harcourt, 1931, pp. 41–69.

———. Lectures on Legal Topics, 1921–22. New York, Macmillan, 1926.

Nature of the Judicial Process. New Haven, Yale University Press, 1928, 180 p.

Our Lady of the Common Law. St. John's Law Review, 13:231–241, April 1939.

Paradoxes of Legal Science. New York, Columbia University Press, 1928, 142 p.

Pound, Roscoe, Introduction of Legal History. Review by B. N. Cardozo. Harvard Law Review, 37:279–83, D 23.

To Rescue: "Our Lady of the Common Law." American Bar Association Journal, 10:347–9, May 1924. See also errata note, page 443.

Selected Readings on the Law of Contracts. Comp. and ed. by the Association of American Law Schools. Introduction by Benjamin N. Cardozo; vii–xi. New York, Macmillan, 1931.

Values: a commencement address (sometimes called "The Choice of Tycho Brahe") delivered at exercises of the Jewish Institute of Religion on May 24, 1931. News Bulletin of the Jewish Institute of Religion, 2:6–13, January 1931.

———. Christian Century, 49:253, February 24, 1932.

———. National Education Association Journal, 21:278, December 1932.

ABOUT MR. JUSTICE CARDOZO

Books

Hellman, George Sidney. Benjamin N. Cardozo, American Judge. New York, Whittlesley House, McGraw-Hill Book Company, 1940, 339 p.

Lehman, Irving. Benjamin Nathan Cardozo: a memorial, read at a meeting of the American Bar Association on the twenty-fifth of July, 1938. Stamford, Conn., printed at the Overbrook Press, 1938, 18 p.

———. American Bar Association Journal, 24:728–730, September 1938.

Lehman, Irving. Influence of Judge Cardozo on the Common Law. Garden City, Doubleday, Doran & Company, 1942, 33 p. (Association of the Bar of the City of New York. Committee on post-admission legal education. Benjamin N. Cardozo Lectures, No. 1.)

———. Law Library Journal, 35:2–10, January 1942.

Levy, Beryl Harold. Cardozo and Frontiers of Legal Thinking, with Selected Opinions. New York, Oxford University Press, 1938, 315 p.

Pollard, Joseph Percival. Mr. Justice Cardozo: A Liberal Mind in Action, with a foreword by Roscoe Pound. New York, Yorktown Press, 1935, 327 p.

Articles

Acheson, Dean G. Mr. Justice Cardozo and the Problems of Government. *Michigan Law Review,* 37:513–539, February 1939.

America Judges Her New Judge. *Literary Digest,* 112:9, February 27, 1932.

Aronson, Moses Judah. Cardozo's Doctrine of Sociological Jurisprudence. *Journal of Social Philosophy,* 4:5–44, October 1938.

Backstage in Washington (Portrait). *Outlook,* 160:171, March 1932.

Bar Presents Resolutions in Memory of Justice Cardozo to the Supreme Court. *American Bar Association Journal,* 25:33–7, January 1939.

Beer, H. W. Late Justice Benjamin Nathan Cardozo. *New Jersey Law Journal,* 62:437, 439, December 28, 1939.

Benjamin N. Cardozo: A Great Judge. *Law Times,* 186:171–2, September 3, 1938.

Benjamin Nathan Cardozo, 1870–1938. *Law Quarterly Review,* 54:491–3, October 1938.

Benjamin Nathan Cardozo and His Legal Decisions. *New York University Law Review,* 4:97–103, April 1927.

Cardozo on the Third Degree. *Outlook,* 156:450, November 19, 1930.

Carswell, William B. Benjamin Nathan Cardozo. *Brooklyn Law Review,* 8:1–3, October 1938.

Chafee, Zechariah, Jr. Mr. Justice Cardozo. *Harpers,* 165:34–44, June 1932.

Cohen, Morris R. Benjamin Nathan Cardozo. *National Lawyers' Guild Quarterly,* 1:283–286, September 1938.

Duffus, R. L. Judge Cardozo's Philosophy of the Law. *New York Times,* February 21, 1932.

Fairman, Charles. The Late Mr. Justice Cardozo. *State Bar Journal of the State Bar of California,* 13:19–23, December 1938.

Farnum, George R. Justice Benjamin N. Cardozo, Philosopher. *Boston University Law Review,* 12:587–99, 1932.

Frankfurter, Felix. Mr. Justice Cardozo. *American Bar Association Journal,* 24:638–639, August 1938.

Gordon, Franklin. Judge Cardozo Honored. Holder of highest judicial Office in the State of New York tendered post on Permanent Court of International Justice. *American Hebrew,* September 9, 1927.

Green, Leon. Benjamin Nathan Cardozo. *Illinois Law Review,* 33:123–5, June 1938.

Hamilton, Walton H. Cardozo the Craftsman. *University of Chicago Law Review,* 6:1–22, December 1938.

Hamilton, Walton H. Justice Cardozo: The Great Tradition. *New Republic,* 95:328–329, July 27, 1938.

Hand, Learned. Judge Cardozo's Work as a Judge. *United States Law Review,* 72:496–8, September 1938.

Hand, Learned. Tribute to Benjamin Nathan Cardozo. *Contemporary Jewish Record,* 1:29–31, 1938.

Hardman, Thomas P. Mr. Justice Cardozo. *West Virginia Law Quarterly,* 38:187–194, April 1932.

Hyman, Jerome I. Benjamin N. Cardozo, a Preface to His Career at the Bar. *Brooklyn Law Review,* 10:1–28, October 1940.

Jackson, Samuel. Cardozo and the Supreme Court. *Indiana Law Journal,* 7:513–535, June 1932.

Jurist and Humanist. *Nation,* 147:60, July 16, 1938.

Jurist and Prelate. *Scribners,* 104:74, November 1938.

Justice Holmes' Successor. *Outlook,* 160:105, January 27, 1932.

Lehman, Irving. Memorial to Justice Cardozo—Read by Hon. Edward R. Finch. *American Bar Association Journal,* 24:728–30, September 1938.

Lerner, Max. Mr. Justice Cardozo: A Man of Good Will. *New Republic,* 83:283–4, July 17, 1935.

Light, Charles P., Jr. The Future Constitutional Opinions of Mr. Justice Cardozo. *Cornell Law Quarterly,* 17:541–567, 1932.

MacDonald, W. A. A Day in Court with Cardozo. *Boston Evening Transcript,* February 17, 1932.

Massa, Edward C. Cardozo Succeeds Holmes. *Notre Dame Lawyer,* 7:387–89, March 1932.

Mr. Justice Cardozo (Portrait). *Fortune,* 13:80–82, May 1936.

Nussbaum, Aaron. Appraisal of Cardozo's Style. *Law Student,* 10:23–24, May 1933.

Oppenheim, Leonard. Civil Liberties Doctrines of Mr. Justice Holmes and Mr. Justice Cardozo. *Tulane Law Review,* 20:177–219, December 1945.

Otis, Merrill E. Benjamin N. Cardozo; a Sketch. *Brief,* 31:149–152, 1932.

Patterson, Edwin Wilhite. Cardozo's Philosophy of Law. *University of Pennsylvania Law Review,* 88:71–91, 156–176, November–December 1939.

Pollard, Joseph Percival. Cardozo (Portrait). *World's Work,* 61:27–28, 66, April 1932.

Pollard, Joseph Percival. Mr. Justice Cardozo. *American Mercury,* 31:183–93, February 1934.

Pollard, Joseph Percival. Mr. Justice Cardozo. *Docket,* 4:3676–80, 1934.

Pollard, Joseph Percival. Philosopher-at-Law, the Career of Judge Benjamin Nathan Cardozo. *Forum,* 87:32–38, January 1938.

Rittenberg, Louis. Cardozo Bends Law to Benefit Humanity. *American Hebrew,* December 25, 1931.

Rooney, Miriam Theresa. Mr. Justice Cardozo's Relativism. *New Scholasticism,* 19:1–47, January 1945.

Shientag, Barnard L. Opinions and Writings of Judge Benjamin N. Cardozo. *Columbia Law Review,* 30:597–650, May 1930.

———. Reprinted in Moulders of Legal Thought. New York, Viking Press, 1943, p. 1–98.

Taft, Henry W. One Aspect of Judge Cardozo's Noteworthy Career. Address of the New York County Lawyers Association: December 17, 1931. *American Bar Association Journal,* 18:172–173, March 1932.

Tullis, Robert Lee. Benjamin Nathan Cardozo—Jurist, Philosopher, Humanitarian. *Louisiana Law Review,* 1:147–156, November 1938.

U. S. Supreme Court. Proceedings in Memoriam. 305 U. S. v–xxviii, October 3, 1938.

Villard, Oswald Garrison. Issues and Men. *Nation,* 147:69. July 16, 1938.

Wilson, Arthur Jess. Guide to the Genius of Cardozo, a close investigation into the distinguishing literary and philosophic characteristics of the opinions, written works, and addresses of Justice Cardozo. *Law Student,* 16:8–20, March 1939.

Columbia Law Review, Harvard Law Review and *Yale Law Journal* jointly dedicated their January 1939 issue to Mr. Justice Cardozo, publishing simultaneously the following articles: Mr. Justice Cardozo, by Harlan F. Stone, by Rt. Hon. Lord Maugham, by H. V. Evatt, and by Learned Hand; Judge Cardozo in the Court of Appeals, by Irving Lehman; Mr. Justice Cardozo and the Law of Torts, by Warren A. Seavey; Mr. Justice Cardozo and the Law of Contracts, by Arthur L. Corbin; Mr. Justice Cardozo and Public Law, by Felix Frankfurter; and Law and Literature, by Benjamin N. Cardozo (with a foreword by J. M. Landis).

BOOK REVIEWS

The Growth of the Law. 1924

Friese, Philip C. *New York University Law Review,* 4:181–2, April 1927.
Hart, James. *Political Science Quarterly,* 40:479–80, September 1925.
Husik, Isaac. *University of Pennsylvania Law Review,* 73:327–8, March 1925.
Jacobs, Avrom M. *Columbia Law Review,* 25:121–23, January 1925.
Kidd, A. M. *California Law Review,* 13:188–91, January 1925.
Roberts, Lewis W. *Kentucky Law Journal,* 14:87–88, November 1925.
Rundell, Oliver S. *American Bar Association Journal,* 11:319–20, May 1925.
———. *Illinois Law Review,* 20:112–113, May 1925.
Waite, John B. *Michigan Law Review,* 23:682–85, April 1925.
Wickersham, George W. *Yale Law Journal,* 34:917–19, June 1925.
Cambridge Law Journal, 2:263–64, 1925.
Justice of the Peace, 88:737, December 6, 1924.
Notre Dame Lawyer, 1:162–64, March 1926.

Law and Literature and Other Essays and Addresses. 1931

Clark, Charles E. *Yale Law Journal,* 40:1011–12, April 1931.
Cox, Oscar. *Cornell Law Quarterly,* 17:189–92, December 1931.
Dennis, Charles H. *American Bar Association Journal,* 17:401–2, June 1931.
Fraenkel, Osmond K. *St. John's Law Review,* 5:315–18, May 1931.
Gorfinkel, John A. *California Law Review,* 19:653–54, September 1931.
James, Daniel. *Indiana Law Journal,* 6:579–80, June 1931.
Jenkins, John B., Jr. *Virginia Law Review,* 18:920–21, June 1932.
Klaus, Samuel. *Columbia Law Review,* 31:906–8, May 1931.
McCormick, J. Byron. *Southern California Law Review,* 6:82–85, November 1932.
McWilliams, J. Wesley. *University of Pennsylvania Law Review,* 80:933–936, April 1932.
Martin, James W. *Kentucky Law Journal,* 20:106, November 1931.
Powell, Thomas Reed. Law and Literature—Both Meat and Grace. *Herald Tribune Book Review,* March 15, 1931.
Russell, Isaac Franklin. *New York University Law Quarterly Review,* 8:703–4, June 1931.
Woodruff, E. H. *Harvard Law Review,* 44:1154–56, May 1931.
Yntema, Hessel E. *American Political Science Review,* 25:749–50, August 1931.
Law Quarterly Review, 47:593–94, October 1931.
United States Law Review, 65:347, June 1931.

Nature of the Judicial Process. 1921

Burch, Rousseau A. *Yale Law Journal,* 31:677–81, April 1922.
Dodd, W. F. *American Political Science Review,* 16:710–11, November 1922.
Hand, Learned. *Harvard Law Review,* 35:479–81, February 1922.
Hardman, Thomas P. *West Virginia Law Quarterly,* 29:145–48, January 1923.
Hough, C. M. *Cornell Law Quarterly,* 7:287–90, April 1922.
Isaacs, Nathan. *Michigan Law Review,* 20:688–90, April 1922.
Johnston, Frank, Jr. *Illinois Law Review,* 17:152–71, June 1922.

Martin Willis J. *University of Pennsylvania Law Review,* 70:345–48, June 1922.
Radin, Max. *California Law Review,* 10:367–69, May 1922.
Stone, Harlan F. *Columbia Law Review,* 22:382–85, April 1922.
Juridical Review, 34:358, December 1922.
Justice of the Peace, 86:393, August 19, 1922.

Paradoxes of Legal Science. 1928

Burch, Rousseau A. *Michigan Law Review,* 27:637–49, April 1929.
Cook, Walter Wheeler. *Yale Law Journal,* 38:405–7, January 1929.
Dickinson, John. *American Political Science Review,* 23:200–2, February 1929.
Frankfurter, Felix. *University of Pennsylvania Law Review,* 77:436–38, January 1929.
Harper, Fowler Vincent. *Oregon Law Review,* 8:212–14, February 1929.
Levinthal, Louis E. *Temple Law Quarterly,* 3:222–23, February 1929.
Radni, Max. *California Law Review,* 17:74–76, November 1928.
Rountree, George. *North Carolina Law Review,* 7:223–25, February 1929.
Smith, Bryant. *Texas Law Review,* 7:333–34, February 1929.
Thilly, Frank. *Cornell Law Quarterly,* 14:116–20, December 1928.
Juridical Review, 40:288–90, September 1928.
Law Quarterly Review, 45:248–49, April 1929.
United States Law Review, 63:555, October 1929.

TABLE OF CASES

To Mr. Justice Cardozo's Opinions in the United States Supreme Court

Adams, Receiver v. Champion, Trustee in Bankruptcy. 294 U. S. 231 (1935).

Aero Mayflower Transit Co. v. Georgia Public Service Commission *et al.* 295 U. S. 285 (1935).

American Life Insurance Co. v. Reese Smith Stewart *et al.* 300 U. S. 203 (1937).

American Surety Co. v. Westinghouse Electric Manufacturing Co. *et al.* 296 U. S. 133 (1935).

American Telephone & Telegraph Co. *et al.* v. United States *et al.* 299 U. S. 232 (1936).

Anderson, Collector of Internal Revenue, v. Wilson *et al.*, executors. 289 U. S. 20 (1933).

Atlantic Coast Line Railroad Co. v. Florida *et al.* 295 U. S. 301 (1935).

Baldwin, Commissioner of Agriculture & Markets, *et al.* v. G. A. F. Seelig, Inc. 294 U. S. 511 (1935).

Baltimore National Bank v. State Tax Commission of Maryland. 297 U. S. 209 (1936).

Bemis Bro. Bag Co. v. United States. 289 U. S. 28 (1933).

Brooklyn Eastern District Terminal v. United States. 287 U. S. 170 (1932).

Brown v. O'Keefe, Receiver. 300 U. S. 598 (1937).

Buffum, Trustee in Bankruptcy v. Peter Barceloux Co. 289 U. S. 227 (1933).

Burnet, Commissioner of Internal Revenue, v. Guggenheim. 288 U. S. 280 (1933).

Burnet, Commissioner of Internal Revenue, v. Wells. 289 U. S. 670 (1933).

Chisholm *et al.* v. Gilmer, Receiver. 299 U. S. 99 (1936).

Clark v. United States. 289 U. S. 1 (1933).

Clark, Commissioner of Insurance, Receiver, v. Williard *et al.*, Trustees, *et al.* 294 U. S. 211 (1935).

Clark, Receiver, v. Williard *et al,* Trustees, *et al.* 292 U. S. 112 (1934).

Columbus Gas & Fuel Co. v. Public Utilities Commissioner of Ohio *et al.* 292 U. S. 398 (1934).

Cooper, Trustee in Bankruptcy, v. Dasher. 290 U. S. 106 (1933).

Cortes, Administrator, v. Baltimore Insular Line, Inc. 287 U. S. 367 (1932).

Daube v. United States. 289 U. S. 367 (1933).

Davis v. Aetna Acceptance Co. 293 U. S. 328 (1934).

Dayton Power & Light Co. v. Public Utilities Commission of Ohio. 292 U. S. 290 (1934).

Doty *et al.* v. Love, Superintendent of Banks. 295 U. S. 64 (1935).

Duparquet Huot & Moneuse Co. *et al.* v. Evans *et al.* 297 U. S. 216 (1936).

Duplate Corporation *et al.* v. Triplex Safety Glass Co. 298 U. S. 448 (1936).

Dupont v. Commissioner of Internal Revenue. 289 U. S. 685 (1933).

Escoe v. Zerbst, Warden. 295 U. S. 490 (1935).

Federal Trade Commission v. Algoma Lumber Co. *et al.* 291 U. S. 67 (1934).

First National Bank & Trust Co., Trustee, v. Beach. 301 U. S. 435 (1937).

Fox v. Capital Company. 299 U. S. 105 (1936).

Fox v. Standard Oil Company of New Jersey. 294 U. S. 87 (1935).

General Import & Export Co., Inc. v. U. S. 286 U. S. 70 (1932).

General Motors Acceptance Corp. v. United States. 286 U. S. 49 (1932).

George Moore Ice Cream Co., Inc. v. Rose, Collector of Internal Revenue. 289 U. S. 373 (1933).

Great Northern Railway Co. v. Sunburst Oil & Refining Co. 287 U. S. 358 (1932).

Gully, State Tax Collector for Mississippi, v. First National Bank in Meridian. 299 U. S. 109 (1936).

Hale *et al.* v. State Board of Assessment and Review. 302 U. S. 95 (1937).

Hartford Accident & Indemnity Co. *et al.* v. N. O. Nelson Manufacturing Co. 291 U. S. 352 (1934).

Hawks *et al.* v. Hamill *et al.* 288 U. S. 52 (1933).

Hegeman Farms Corp. v. Baldwin *et al.* 293 U. S. 163 (1934).

Helvering, Commissioner of Internal Revenue, *et al.* v. Davis. 301 U. S. 619 (1937).

Henneford *et al.* v. Silas Mason Co. Inc. *et al.* 300 U. S. 577 (1937).

Highland Farms Dairy, Inc., *et al.* v. Agnew *et al.* 300 U. S. 608 (1937).

Hill, Warden, v. United States ex rel. Wampler. 298 U. S. 460 (1936).

Holyoke Water Power Co. v. American Writing Paper Co. 300 U. S. 324 (1937).

Hopkins Federal Savings & Loan Ass'n *et al.* v. Cleary *et al.* 296 U. S. 315 (1935).

Hulburd v. Commissioner of Internal Revenue. 296 U. S. 300 (1935).

International Milling Co. v. Columbia Transportation Co. 292 U. S. 511 (1934).

Interstate Commerce Commission v. New York, New Haven & Hartford Railroad Co. *et al.* 287 U. S. 178 (1932).

Interstate Commerce Commission v. United States ex rel. Campbell *et al.* 289 U. S. 385 (1933).

Jennings, Receiver, *et al.* v. United States Fidelity & Guaranty Co. 294 U. S. 216 (1935).

Knox National Farm Loan Ass'n *et al. v. Phillips.* 300 U. S. 194 (1937).

Landis *et al.* v. North American Co. 299 U. S. 248 (1936).

Lee, Comptroller, v. Bickell *et al.* 292 U. S. 415 (1934).

Life & Casualty Insurance Co. of Tennessee v. McCray. 291 U. S. 566 (1934).

Life & Casualty Insurance Co. of Tennessee v. Barefield. 291 U. S. 575 (1934).

Lowden *et al.*, Trustees, v. Northwestern National Bank & Trust Co. 298 U. S. 160 (1936).

McCandless, Receiver, v. Furlaud *et al.* 296 U. S. 140 (1935).

Marine National Exchange Bank of Milwaukee *et al.* v. Kalt-Zimmer Manufacturing Co. *et al.* 293 U. S. 357 (1934).

Martin v. National Surety Co. *et al.* 300 U. S. 588 (1937).

May *et al.* v. Hamburg-Amerikanische Packetfahrt Aktiengesellschaft. 290 U. S. 333 (1933).

Michigan v. Michigan Trust Co., Receiver. 286 U. S. 334 (1932).

Mississippi Valley Barge Line Co. v. United States *et al.* 292 U. S. 282 (1934).

Morley Construction Co. *et al.* v. Maryland Casualty Co. 300 U. S. 185 (1937).

Morrison *et al.* v. California. 291 U. S. 82 (1934).

Mutual Life Insurance Company of New York v. Johnson, Administrator. 293 U. S. 335 (1934).

New Jersey v. Delaware. 291 U. S. 361 (1934).

National Paper Products Co. v. Helvering, Commissioner of Internal Revenue. 293 U. S. 183 (1934).

New York v. Maclay *et al.*, Receivers, *et al.* 288 U. S. 290 (1933).

New York Life Insurance Co. v. Viglas. 297 U. S. 672 (1936).

Nixon v. Condon *et al.* 286 U. S. 73 (1932).

Norfolk & Western Railway Co. v. North Carolina ex rel. Maxwell, Commissioner of Revenue. 297 U. S. 682 (1936).

Norwegian Nitrogen Products Co. v. United States. 288 U. S. 294 (1933).

Ohio Bell Telephone Co. v. Public Utilities Commission of Ohio. 301 U. S. 292 (1937).

Old Company's Lehigh, Inc. v. Meeker, Receiver, *et al.* 294 U. S. 227 (1935).

Palko v. Connecticut. 302 U. S. 319 (1937).

Pennsylvania Railroad Co. *et al.* v. Public Utilities Commission of Ohio *et al.* 298 U. S. 170 (1936).

Planters Cotton Oil Co., Inc., *et al.* v. Hopkins, Collector of Internal Revenue. 286 U. S. 332 (1932).

Pokora v. Wabash Railway Co. 292 U. S. 98 (1934).

The Prudence Co. Inc. v. Fidelity & Deposit Company of Maryland *et al.* 297 U. S. 198 (1936).

Puget Sound Stevedoring Co. v. State Tax Commission. 302 U. S. 90 (1937).

Radio Corporation of America *et al.* v. Radio Engineering Laboratories, Inc. 293 U. S. 1 (1934).

Radio Corporation of America v. Raytheon Manufacturing Co. 296 U. S. 459 (1935).

Realty Associates Securities Corp. *et al.* v. O'Connor *et al.* 295 U. S. 295 (1935).

R. H. Stearns Co. v. United States. 291 U. S. 54 (1934).

Roberts, Receiver, *et al.* v. New York City *et al.* 295 U. S. 264 (1935).

St. Louis Southwestern Railway Co. v. Simpson, Administratrix. 286 U. S. 346 (1932).

Shapiro v. Wilgus *et al.*, Receivers. 287 U. S. 348 (1932).

Shapleigh *et al.* v. Mier. 299 U. S. 468 (1937).

Shepard v. United States. 290 U. S. 96 (1933).

Shoshone Tribe of Indians v. United States. 299 U. S. 476 (1937).

Sinclair Refining Co. v. Jenkins Petroleum Process Co. 289 U. S. 689 (1933).

Smyth, Executor, v. United States. 302 U. S. 329 (1937).

Snyder v. Massachusetts. 291 U. S. 97 (1934).

Steelman, Trustee in Bankruptcy, v. All Continent Corp. 301 U. S. 278 (1937).

Steward Machine Co. v. Davis, Collector of Internal Revenue. 301 U. S. 548 (1937).

Stockholders of the Peoples Banking Co. v. Sterling, Receiver. 300 U. S. 175 (1937).

Terminal Warehouse Co. v. Pennsylvania Rairoad Co. *et al.* 297 U. S. 500 (1936).

Travelers Protective Association of America v. Prinsen. 291 U. S. 576 (1934).

Tuttle *et al.* v. Harris *et al.* 297 U. S. 225 (1936).

United States *et al.* v. Chicago, Milwaukee, St. Paul & Pacific R. Co. *et al.* 294 U. S. 499 (1935).

United States v. Commercial Credit Co. Inc. 286 U. S. 63 (1932).

United States v. Darby. 289 U. S. 224 (1933).

United States v. Factors & Finance Co. 288 U. S. 89 (1933).

United States v. The Great Northern Railway Co. 287 U. S. 144 (1932).

United States v. Henry Prentiss & Co. Inc. 288 U. S. 73 (1933).

United States v. Mack *et al.* 295 U. S. 480 (1935).

United States v. Memphis Oil Co. 288 U. S. 62 (1933).

U. S. v. The Ruth Mildred. 286 U. S. 67 (1932).

United States v. Safety Car Heating & Lighting Co. 297 U. S. 88 (1936).

United States v. Swift & Co. *et al.* 286 U. S. 106 (1932).

Utley *et al* v. St. Petersburg. 292 U. S. 106 (1934).

Van Beeck, Administrator, v. Sabine Towing Co. Inc. *et al.* 300 U. S. 342 (1937).

Warner, Administratrix, v. Goltra. 293 U. S. 155 (1934).

Washington v. Oregon. 297 U. S. 517 (1936).

Welch v. Helvering, Commissioner of Internal Revenue. 290 U. S. 111 (1933).

West Ohio Gas Co. v. Public Utilities Commission of Ohio (No. 1). 294 U. S. 63 (1935).

West Ohio Gas Co. v. Public Utilities Commission of Ohio (No. 2). 294 U. S. 79 (1935).

Williams, Receiver of the Washington, Baltimore & Annapolis Railroad Co. v. Mayor and City Council of Baltimore. 289 U. S. 36 (1933).

Woolford Realty Co., Inc. v. Rose, Collector of Internal Revenue. 286 U. S. 318 (1932).

W. B. Worthen Co., Trustee, *et al.* v. Kavanaugh, Trustee. 295 U. S. 56 (1935).

Zellerbach Paper Co. v. Helvering, Commissioner of Internal Revenue. 293 U. S. 172 (1934).

Zimmern *et al.* v. United States. 298 U. S. 167 (1936).

Concurring Opinion

A. L. A. Schecter Poultry Corp. *et al.* v. United States. 295 U. S. 495 (1935).

Dissenting Opinions

Anglo-Chilean Nitrate Sales Corp. v. Alabama. 288 U. S. 218 (1933).

Ashton *et al.* v. Cameron County Water Improvement District No. One. 298 U. S. 513 (1936).

Binney *et al.* v. Long, Commissioner of Corporations and Taxation. 299 U. S. 280 (1936).

Carter v. Carter Coal Co. *et al.;* Helvering, Commissioner of Internal Revenue, v. Carter *et al.* 298 U. S. 238 (1936).

Chicago Title and Trust Co. v. Forty-One Thirty-Six Wilcox Bldg. Corp. 302 U. S. 120 (1937).

Concordia Fire Insurance Co. v. Illinois. 292 U. S. 535 (1934).

Coombes v. Getz. 285 U. S. 434 (1932).

Fairmont Glass Works v. Cub Fork Coal Co. *et al.* 287 U. S. 474 (1933).

Freuler, Administrator, v. Helvering, Commissioner of Internal Revenue. 291 U. S. 35 (1934).

Graves, Governor of Alabama, *et al.* v. Texas Company. 298 U. S. 393 (1936).

Great Northern Railway Co. v. Washington. 300 U. S. 154 (1937).

Herndon v. Georgia. 295 U. S. 441 (1935).

Interstate Commerce Commission *et al.* v. Oregon-Washington Railroad & Navigation Co. *et al.* 288 U. S. 14 (1933).

Jones v. Securities & Exchange Commission. 298 U. S. 1 (1936).

Landress v. Phoenix Mutual Life Insurance Co. *et al.* 291 U. S. 491 (1934).

Louis K. Leggett Co. v. Lee, Comptroller, *et al.* 288 U. S. 517 (1933).

Mayflower Farms, Inc. v. Ten Eyck, Commissioner of the Department of Agriculture & Markets of New York, *et al.* 297 U. S. 266 (1936).

O'Donoghue v. United States. 289 U. S. 516 (1933).

Panama Refining Co. *et al.* v. Ryan *et al.* 293 U. S. 388 (1935).

Reed *et al.* v. Allen. 286 U. S. 191 (1932).

Rogers v. Guaranty Trust Company of New York *et al.* 288 U. S. 123 (1933).

Sanders v. Armour Fertilizer Works *et al.* 292 U. S. 190 (1934).

Schuylkill Trust Co. v. Pennsylvania. 296 U. S. 113 (1935).

Stewart Dry Goods Co. v. Lewis *et al.* 294 U. S. 550 (1935).

Texas *et al.* v. Donoghue, Trustee. 302 U. S. 284 (1937).

Thomas, Collector, v. Perkins *et al.* 301 U. S. 655 (1937).

United States v. Constantine. 296 U. S. 287 (1935).

INDEX